THE PLAYS OF
WILLIAM
DOUGLAS HOME

THE PLAYS OF
WILLIAM
DOUGLAS HOME

HEINEMANN

MELBOURNE LONDON TORONTO

William Heinemann Ltd

MELBOURNE LONDON TORONTO

CAPE TOWN AUCKLAND

THE HAGUE

Published in 1958

ALL rights whatsoever in these five plays are strictly reserved. Applications for professional performances must be made to Curtis Brown Ltd., 13 King Street, Covent Garden, London, W.C.2. Applications for amateur performances should be made as follows:

'*Now Barabbas . . .*' and *The Chiltern Hundreds* to Samuel French Ltd., 26 Southampton Street, London, W.C.2.

The Thistle and the Rose to Curtis Brown Ltd.

The Bad Samaritan and *The Reluctant Debutante* to Evans Bros., Ltd., Montague House, Russell Square, London, W.C.1.

Performances may not be given unless a licence has been obtained.

ISBN 9999032584

Printed in Great Britain by
W. & J. Mackay & Co Ltd, Chatham

CONTENTS

INTRODUCTION   7

'NOW BARABBAS . . .'   23

THE CHILTERN HUNDREDS   111

THE THISTLE AND THE ROSE   191

THE BAD SAMARITAN   279

THE RELUCTANT DEBUTANTE   353

INTRODUCTION

'*NOW BARABBAS* . . .', the first play in this volume, is a natural. There was no conception, no pregnancy, no labour at its birth. Had it been written in a garden it would no doubt have appeared under a gooseberry bush. For the record, since I chose a wood as my study, it was found under a spruce.

On a Monday morning in June, 1945, I sat down beneath this magic tree, with a new note-book and a couple of pencils. By Saturday, working from 10 a.m. until 7 p.m. with hourly intervals for lunch and tea, the play had written itself.

I then typed it, read it through, wrote in the Visiting Scene in the last act, and typed that. By the following Wednesday, exactly ten days from the date on which the first word had been written down, the play was finished. Thereafter, save for the cutting of one short scene for length, no line was ever altered in the script.

I cannot attempt to explain this. To say that the play was already in my head when I began is no answer, besides being untrue. Admittedly, at that date, I had prisons on my mind, but neither the theme, nor the plot, nor the characters were with me on that Monday morning when I wandered down the ride and chose my tree. Maybe the wood was enchanted. One morning on my way to work I found a roebuck lying dead beside the ride. Perhaps the little people, suffering from brain fatigue, had called for extra meat. No doubt if I were Barrie-minded, I would seize upon this theory, and clap my tiny hands. Half English as I am, however, I content myself with stating that if inspiration ever came to any man it came to me that week. Since then, though on occasion dropping in for a short call, or even for a night or two, it has not stayed that long.

'*Now Barabbas* . . .' is a good play. As its author I make no apology for that assessment. Detached as I am, in some strange way, from its inception, I feel at liberty to discuss it with that same proprietary impartiality assumed by an author's secretary when she discusses her employers' manuscript. It may even be a great play. It has the necessary qualifications for great drama—integrity, simplicity and inevita-

7

bility. In addition, it was produced by a director of genius, and acted by a company so exquisitely balanced and superbly interwoven that instead of flickering from moonlight to obscurity and back again, as leads were disconnected and connected up again (as in so many plays), the stage was lit throughout by twenty separate stars.

The second play, *The Chiltern Hundreds*, was my first commercial success. The greater part of it was written in the weeks immediately succeeding the lightning completion of '*Now Barabbas* . . .'. It was inspired by my father's reaction to his butler's announcement that my eldest brother had lost his seat in Parliament. In 1945, it will be remembered that the voting in the General Election took place at the beginning of July, and in order to allow for the collection of votes from the Forces overseas, the result was deferred until the 25th. On that day, after lunch, my father was doing his crossword puzzle; my mother and sister were knitting and I, myself, was having a nap on the sofa. Mr Collingwood entered the room with downcast eyes. 'He's lost, my Lord', he said. The family looked up, bewildered. 'Who's lost what?' my father asked. It occurred to me then that there was something inherently comic in the fact that a family butler should display concern at the heir's defeat in an election, while the family remained indifferent, if indeed they remembered that he had been standing for Parliament at all.

I sent this play to H. M. Tennent Ltd. In due course Hugh Beaumont forwarded to me a report he had received from one of his readers, Archibald Batty, suggesting that I go and meet him with a view to doing some revision on the script. After the interview I returned to Scotland, under orders to write a new scene as the second scene in Act I, and to make some further revision to Act III. This I completed to the satisfaction of both Archie Batty and the management in three days. H. M. Tennent, however, with their vast production schedule, were too slow for me, and on the expiry of the option period, I gave the play to Linnit & Dunfee. Once again, Colin Chandler, my favourite producer of '*Now Barabbas* . . .' and the initial production of *The Thistle and the Rose*, was put in charge. The beloved and fabulous figure of A. E. Matthews, complete in deerstalker hat, gum-boots, and riding breeches, first came into my life. The remainder of the cast, including Marjorie Fielding, and Michael Shepley, immortalizing Mr Collingwood, assembled at the first rehearsal on the stage. After seeing the first night in London my father, referring to Mr Matthews, said, innocently, 'Dear old fellow, he couldn't be bothered with the unimportant things.' He never said a truer word.

The third play, *The Thistle and the Rose*, represents my first attempt at historical drama. I am not ashamed of it. It was a commissioned work in the sense that I commissioned it myself for the Edinburgh Festival. What more natural than that a young playwright, recently eulogized for '*Now Barabbas* . . .', and having acquired a temporary financial independence with *The Chiltern Hundreds*, should wish for recognition in his country's capital? Born in Edinburgh, brought up on the banks of the Tweed, within two or three miles of Flodden, where the young King lost his life stepping 'three feet on to English ground' at the behest of Anne of Brittany, my choice of theme was easy.

Since all my plays are written in a kind of rhythm, I will not confuse the issue by stating that I wrote *The Thistle and the Rose* in verse. Rather did I emphasize the normal rhythm and endeavour to stylize and date the dialogue. It is not for me to say if I succeeded. All I can assert with confidence is that when my mother came in to tea, after reading the first draft, and said 'Methinks I'll have some jam', it became clear to me that I had exceeded my brief. That evening I removed a regiment of 'Methinks' from the script, leaving only a few scattered at strong points through the scenes, like cloves within an apple pie.

The Thistle and the Rose has yet to reach its goal. It has been acted in London and in Glasgow, but never yet in Edinburgh. An ancestor of mine, called John Home, once wrote a tragedy called *Douglas*, and on its first appearance a voice from the gallery shouted, 'Whaur's your Willie Shakespeare noo?' I have a feeling that if ever *The Thistle and the Rose* is produced at the Edinburgh Festival, another voice up in the gallery may be heard shouting, 'Whaur's your John Home noo?' That voice, for want of any other, might well be my own.

The Bad Samaritan was first produced at Bromley in the form in which the play is printed here. It was a great success. When it was transferred to London, it had been emasculated beyond all reason, and it only limped along for six or seven months. It is tempting, but unnecessary, to enter into the details of this operation. Suffice it to say that the Prologue and the Epilogue, the pivot on which I had first constructed the play, were cut. I know now that I should not have permitted this. It is always a difficult decision for a playwright to decide whether he should take advice before production or stick to his guns. Usually, except with minor alterations or additions, such as we have recently discussed in *The Chiltern Hundreds*, the latter course turns out to be the wisest in the end. At that time, however, I was a newly married man with a wife and a small son, and a still smaller income. *The Bad Samaritan* appeared to be my only means of a potential livelihood. I therefore allowed myself to be persuaded, against my better judgement, to remove the Prologue and the Epilogue, and to rewrite the third act. I hated every moment of my task. The Prologue, in my view, introduced my theme in such a way that the main part of the play when seen thereafter became just that much more interesting. The Epilogue provided for forgiveness and hope, as well as an intensely dramatic scene, which I found profoundly moving when I saw it in the theatre at Bromley. What is more, it held the audience. Now here was I removing my twin loves, and substituting a lot of weighty and ponderous matter between the Dean and his least interesting son in order to fill in the final act. The result was disastrous. The critics, with total justification, assailed me for failing to conclude my theme, and for ending on a hopeless and unhappy note. I am grateful to my publisher for agreeing to print the original script as it was acted at Bromley. I hope for a revival in due course.

The idea for the fifth and last play, *The Reluctant Debutante*, came to me one evening in my father-in-law's flat in London in the year when my sister-in-law was a debutante. He was sitting, on his return from the City, reading, when the telephone bell rang. My sister-in-law rose to answer it. From the conversation it became clear that a young man was waiting for her downstairs. 'Why don't you bring your young men up here?' asked my father-in-law. 'You can't want to meet them, Daddy, do you?' she replied. 'No', said he, 'but I'd just like to know whether they are black or white.' 'They vary, Daddy,' came the answer, as she left the room. It might be rewarding, I thought, to write a play about a father who, feigning nonchalance, was in reality concerned about his daughter's happiness. It was.

The first three scenes, written with a slight temperature and a mild attack of 'flu, took three mornings in bed. The last scene took a year. Finally acting on a brilliant suggestion of my wife's, I finished it. Archibald Batty, to whom I sent the play, suggested some scene shifting in Act I, Scene 1, and a lengthening of Act I, Scene 2, both of which I carried out. Apart from a few minor changes for Celia Johnson, and putting the play into two acts instead of three, on the advice of Jack Minster, the inspired director, I left it as it was. The name, suggested by George Bishop of the *Daily Telegraph* one afternoon on Ashridge Golf Course, was the last thing to be written in! In the hands of Celia Johnson, that most beloved of all actresses, Wilfred Hyde White, the most imperturbable of fathers, the untrained expert, Anna Massey, and a flawless cast, we went into rehearsal. The result could scarcely have been happier.

That, then, is the background of the five plays in this volume. I hope you will enjoy reading them as much as I have enjoyed writing them. It is not for me to assess my status as a playwright. I leave that to the dramatic critics. I can only do my best. Once, in my salad days, I was introduced to Harley Granville Barker as a potential playwright. 'How interesting', he said. 'Tell me, are you trying anything new?' 'No,' I answered, shyly, 'I am just trying to write a play.' I am still doing just that. The task is not an easy one.

W.D.H.
1958

To
my wife
with love

'NOW BARABBAS...'

CAST OF FIRST PRODUCTION

'NOW BARABBAS . . .' *was first produced at the Boltons Theatre, Kensington, on 11 February 1947, with the following cast:*

Officer King	STANLEY BEARD
4288 Smith	OWEN HOLDER
3762 Brown	STANLEY ROSE
1091 O'Brien (Paddy) . .	JULIAN SOMERS
2746 Anderson	HARRY QUASHIE
6145 Spencer . . .	BARRY PHELPS
6146 Roberts	JOHN MACKWOOD
3804 Medworth . . .	BASIL GORDON
6147 Richards	PETER DOUGHTY
Officer Jackson	DAVID DUNCAN
Tufnell	RICHARD LONGMAN
Officer Jones	PERCY WALSH
Officer Gale . . .	RICHARD FOAT
The Governor	TRISTAN RAWSON
The Chaplain	ANTHONY MARLOWE
Chief Officer Webb . . .	JOSS CLEWES
Kitty	JILL BENNETT
Mrs Brown	ELSA PALMER
Winnie	BARBARA BIRKENSHAW
8146 Robinson	RAYMOND DUVEEN
'Erb	JACQUELINE BOITEAUX

The Play directed by
COLIN CHANDLER

subsequently presented by Tom Arnold and Linnit and Dunfee Ltd. at the Vaudeville Theatre on 7 March 1947, with the following changes in the cast:

The Chaplain	DENIS WEBB
'Erb	JOHN BARON
Robinson	JOHN LAWSON
Mrs Brown	VIOLET GOULD
A Warder	RICHARD WIGHTMAN

Denis Webb replaced Anthony Marlowe, who was under previous contract to appear elsewhere. The part of 'Winnie' was deleted from the play.

W.D.H.—B

CHARACTERS

OFFICER KING

4288 SMITH

3762 BROWN

1091 O'BRIEN (PADDY)

2746 ANDERSON

6145 SPENCER

6146 ROBERTS

3804 MEDWORTH

6147 RICHARDS

OFFICER JACKSON

TUFNELL

OFFICER JONES

OFFICER GALE

THE GOVERNOR

THE CHAPLAIN

CHIEF OFFICER WEBB

KITTY

MRS BROWN

WINNIE

8146 ROBINSON

'ERB

STAGE DIRECTIONS

The scene throughout has a steel-railed balcony running across the front of the stage some 15 feet above ground level. On each side the balcony is connected with the ground by a narrow spiral staircase. It is in the cells along this balcony and on other balconies rising to three or four levels that the convicts live and sleep. A desk for the Officer-in-Charge stands at the bottom of the staircase leading from the balcony.

The central portion of the stage is:

1. *Ten Mess. A room formed out of two cells knocked into one – a barred window, a long deal table, highly scrubbed, benches, and a couple of stools; magazine colour features pinned on whitewashed walls; a small pot of geraniums on the window-sill. There are also shelves for the crockery used at meals and a small deal table for the draught-board where the convicts play at recreation time.*

2. *The Condemned Cell. This is better furnished, with a carpet, chair, a recess for the visitor's grille, a bed, a table, magazines and draughts.*

3. *The Governor's Office is a normal cell with a flat oak desk, a swivel chair, a safe, a cupboard in which he keeps his whisky, and a linoleum floor.*

4. *The Visiting-room is a small recreation room with a long table on either side of which the visitors and convicts sit.*

SYNOPSIS OF SCENES

SCENE: An English Prison

TIME: The Present

ACT ONE   A Monday
- Scene 1.   Ten Mess
- Scene 2.   The Condemned Cell
- Scene 3.   The Governor's Office
- Scene 4.   Ten Mess

ACT TWO   A Monday — One week later
- Scene 1.   The Condemned Cell. Morning
- Scene 2.   Ten Mess. Midday. After dinner
- Scene 3.   The Governor's Office
- Scene 4.   The Condemned Cell. Evening
- Scene 5.   Ten Mess. Evening recreation time.

ACT THREE   One week later
- Scene 1.   Ten Mess. Visitor's Hour. Afternoon, Monday
- Scene 2.   The Condemned Cell. Evening. Monday
- Scene 3.   The Governor's Office. 7.50. Morning. Tuesday the 21st
- Scene 4.   Ten Mess. Just after 8.

'Then cried they all again, saying, Not this man, but Barabbas. Now Barabbas was a robber.'

ST JOHN *xviii*, 40

'NOW BARABBAS...'

ACT ONE

ENTRE-SCENE. THE LANDING

Scene outside back-cloth. Prison clock striking seven. Officer King is standing beside the desk, looking up to the balcony.

KING (*he is cheerful, tubby*): All messmen there?

VOICES (*off*): Ten Mess missing, sir.

KING (*shouting upwards*): Messmen. Ten Mess. Messmen. Ten Mess. Get a move on.

SMITH (*upstairs*): Comin', sir. Just comin', sir.

KING: No hurry, lads. No hurry. We like waiting. Will I bring your breakfast up?

SMITH (*appears over balcony*): Wot. 'Am an' eggs? O.K.

KING: You a messman?

SMITH: Yessir. Overslept. I dreamt you was me mum. I lay there waiting for me cup o' tea.

KING: Come on.

SMITH: Sir.

KING: Get movin'.

SMITH: Sir. Morning', sir. (*Falling in*) Mornin', boys.

Smith falls in beside the other messmen.

KING: Fall in before I put you on the peg for being late.

Brown, elderly, wizened, slithers down the other staircase and falls in round the corner.

VOICES (*off*): Come on, yer lazy – –

KING: O.K. I'll do the talking. Smith, where's yer mate?

BROWN: Ten Mess, sir. 'Ere, sir.

KING: 'Ow did you get 'ere. On wings?

BROWN: I been 'ere all the time. (*Bell rings.*)

KING (*shouting*): Fall in. Stand to yer doors, A Wing. Put yer lights out. Messmen. Right turn. To the kitchen. Lead on. A44. A51. Put yer flaming lights out, or I'll put yer both inside. (*Runs upstairs and looks along balcony.*) A Wing – one pace forward – March. Right turn. Lead on. Come on. Get a move on.

SCENE 1. TEN MESS

Paddy, aged 33, tall, thick-set, rough-featured Irishman, comes in singing. In distinction from the other prisoners he wears a yellow armband.

PADDY (*singing*):
> 'Some day maybe I'll go to Ireland
> If it's only at the closing of my day,
> To see again the moon rise over Claddagh
> And to watch the sun go down on Galway Bay.'

Anderson comes in.

ANDERSON (*big, black, lugubrious negro*): Mornin', Paddy. Mornin', Paddy. Lovely mornin'. Lovely mornin'. Got a fag-end for your old pal Arthur?

PADDY (*ignoring him and setting the table*):
> 'For the winds that blow across the sea from Ireland
> Bring the perfume of the heather as they blow,
> And the women in the uplands, picking tatties,
> Speak a language that the English do not know.'

Spencer comes in.

SPENCER (*neat, dapper, 40 to 50*): Oh, I say, is this Ten Mess?

PADDY: Sure it has been for the last three bleedin' years.

SPENCER: Oh, thanks. (*Puts head out and calls.*) This is us.

Roberts, young, fresh, good-looking, Scotch, comes in. Both stand near door.

PADDY (*sings*):
>'The English came and tried to teach us their way
>And blamed us for being what we are.
>Well, they might as well go try and catch a moonbeam
>Or to hitch a penny candle to a star.'

Enter Medworth, 60, thin hair, horn-rimmed glasses, small, pointed beard, well-spoken.

ANDERSON: Mornin', Mr Medworth. Morning', Mr Medworth, sir.

MEDWORTH: Good morning. Morning, Paddy.

Paddy nods.

ANDERSON: Got a tab-end for your old pal Arthur? Come on, Mr Medworth. Be a pal.

MEDWORTH (*throwing a cigarette-end, which he has just stubbed out, to Anderson*): You receptions in last night?

SPENCER: Yes. My name's Spencer. Squadron Leader. R.A.F.

MEDWORTH: Mine's Medworth. How are you? (*He turns his attention to Roberts.*) And you?

ROBERTS: Jock Roberts. Pleased to meet you.

ANDERSON: Mr Roberts, have a cigarette.

ROBERTS: Oh thanks.

Anderson holds out empty box and laughs.

ANDERSON: Oh, Mr Roberts, I can see you've not been in before. No, sir, you not been in before. Tobacco here is just like gold. It's just like gold. You never heard a man say, 'Have a bar of gold.' No, sir, you never did.

Roberts is bewildered, rather than hurt, by Anderson's good humour.

MEDWORTH: You doing long?

SPENCER: Six months. I flew a fighter down the Strand – at zero feet. The high-up boys got scared. They made me an example.

MEDWORTH: Rotten luck.

SPENCER: Oh, well, I'll get a rest.

PADDY (*who has been looking at Roberts*): You get a 'Lifer,' lad?

ROBERTS: Who, me?

MEDWORTH: Oh, this is Paddy. Runs our mess.

PADDY: Oh, cut the gag. The mess runs me. Well, how much?

ROBERTS: Two years.

PADDY: Oh, just a hair-cut.

ANDERSON: Not even a hair-cut. Just a shave. Yes. Mr Roberts, you're in for a shave with just a rusty razor-blade. (*He laughs alone.*)

MEDWORTH (*to Roberts*): You stage?

ROBERTS: No. Merchant Navy. Drunk too much one night in Rio. Lost me balance and upset the till. What's your trouble?

Medworth turns, without replying, and walks to his place at the table.

PADDY (*quickly*): Sure, we're not a lot of daft Jehovah Witnesses. We don't ask questions here, me lad.

ROBERTS: Oh, sorry.

Enter Brown and Smith with porridge and tea in buckets.

PADDY: Come on in, yer lousy crooks.

SMITH: Me mother always calls me that. Don't make me 'omesick, Paddy boy.

PADDY: Here, give us that.

Paddy takes porridge from Smith. Brown pours the tea. Smith turns with cockney cheerfulness to the newcomers.

SMITH: 'Ow-de-do all. Welcome to College. I'm Smithy. Artfullest dodger on the race-course – bar the bloomin 'dogs. I done it for me mother. Judge was cryin' when I left 'im in the court. (*Enter Mr King.*) 'E liked the look o' me, yer know. 'E saw as 'ow I had a 'eart of gold. These judges gets ter know a thing or two.

Mr King comes in to check the number present and overhears this comment.

KING: I'll say they do.

SMITH (*bowing ceremoniously*): Good mornin', Mr King.

KING (*counting*): One-two-three-four-five-six-seven – O.K., Paddy. Seven.

PADDY: Yes, sir. Two receptions, sir.

KING: O.K. (*Jots it down on pad.*) 'Ere, Smithy, mum's the word at breakfast if yer wants a wife.

SMITH: Me mother likes it, sir.

KING: Yer father dead?

SMITH: Yessir. 'Ere – take that coat off!

King pushes him down into his seat, grinning.

RICHARDS (*enters, and speaks with a precious accent*): I'm trying to find Ten Mess, sir.

SMITH (*imitation*): Oh my. You've found it, dear.

KING: Come on. Sit down. Are you reception?

RICHARDS (*tall, very long hair elaborately arranged, theatrical gestures*) Of course I am, you don't think I've been in before, I hope. (*Sits.*) Good morning, boys.

KING: Well, don't be late again, me lad. O.K. then, that makes eight. (*Exit King.*)

BROWN: Seven an' a arf, if yer ask me.

RICHARDS (*outraged*): Well, I never did. In all my life. (*To Paddy.*) Are you going to let him be so rude to me?

PADDY: I'm thinking that it won't upset you over-much.

RICHARDS: You are a beast. (*Looks round and sees Medworth.*) Oh well, you look nice. I love your beard. It's sweet. I'm sure that you aren't in for stealing or beastly things like that.

PADDY: You eat your breakfast, lad. Pipe down.

RICHARDS: The way you talk!

PADDY: *Shut up.*

There is silence for a while as they eat, until it is broken by Brown.

BROWN: I'm going to see old Smithy this morning.

SMITH: 'E don't mean me, 'e means me dad! The governor.

BROWN: Two ruddy years I been here, an' I seen old Smithy every ruddy week. I've asked 'im the same question every ruddy time. Each time I've had the same reply. It's always ruddy, ruddy, ruddy NO.

MEDWORTH: I wonder you don't give it up.

BROWN (*aggressively*): Why should I give it up? She's my unmarried wife – not 'is. If 'e wants to write to 'is unmarried bit, I don't say 'No, no, Mr Smith. Yer mustn't, Mr Smith.'

MEDWORTH: Yes, Brownie, but he's not inside.

BROWN: 'E would be if I 'ad me ruddy way. 'E would an' all.

Having verbally disposed of the Governor to his own satisfaction, Brown resumes his interrupted breakfast.

RICHARDS: Please, can I have a mug?

PADDY: One missin'. Anybody seen it?

MEDWORTH: They were here last night.

SMITH: 'Ere, don't tell me that there's thieves around these parts. Come on, 'ave mine.

RICHARDS: Oh. Thanks.

ANDERSON (*pushing away his plate*): The job is finished. Now I'll have a smoke.

> *He takes out the tab-end which Medworth gave him, and wanders to the door.*

MEDWORTH: Is it true that Tufnell's coming in today?

SMITH: 'E come last night. I seen the Screw what brought 'im.

PADDY: Poor young sod.

SMITH: 'Ere, steady on. 'E shot a copper down in Marylebone.

PADDY: Good luck to him.

MEDWORTH: He won't get off.

PADDY: He would in Eire.

SMITH: Out there the copper would 'ave shot 'im first.

PADDY: You shut your mouth.

SMITH: It's dragging Paddy, eh?

PADDY: Oh, shut your mouth.

SPENCER: He's very young, as far as I remember from the Press.

BROWN: They say that copper 'ad five kids. Five ruddy little flatties – think of that.

PADDY: He should have shot him sooner.

SMITH: Up the I.R.A.

> *Paddy gets up to go. Stops as Richards speaks.*

RICHARDS: I think hanging's *simply* terrible. The thought of it just turns my tummy up. (*Laughs.*) No – honestly.

PADDY: They ought to hang the likes of you.

> *Paddy goes out angrily, and Smith looks after him.*

SMITH: It's draggin' for old Paddy. Something cruel. (*To Brown.*) Come on yer bum-faced bigamist. Get washin' up!

ROBERTS: What happens now?

MEDWORTH: Oh, smoke – then exercise. And then you'll see the Chaplain and the Governor. He's quite a decent chap. Here, have a cigarette.

ROBERTS (*after hesitating*): Oh, thanks a lot.

MEDWORTH (*smiling*): It's nice to see new faces now and then. (*To Spencer.*) Come and see the Colonel fellow in Nine Mess. He'd like to meet you.

> *Medworth and Spencer go out. Others drift out. Brown, seeing the chance of a financial deal, turns to Roberts.*

BROWN: Like me bread?

ROBERTS: Thanks. (*Takes it.*)

BROWN: I ain't a ruddy vicar at a charity bazaar.

> *Roberts is bewildered.*

SMITH (*to help him out*): 'E wants the doings – or a fag.

ROBERTS: Oh, sorry. Yes, of course. Well, here you are. Afraid I haven't got a fag. (*Gives him a penny.*)

BROWN: 'Ere, give it back. The price is twopence.

ROBERTS: Oh, I'm sorry. (*Gives him another.*)

SMITH: You double-crossin' convict – cut it art. Come on. (*He is fiddling tie-wards.*) Come on now, Bluebeard. You just looks as though yer wants a shave. Come on. Come on. (*Takes out razor-blade.*)

BROWN (*horror-struck, with his back to the wall*): 'Ere, put that ruddy blade away.

SMITH: Yer wives won't like yer if I spoils yer looks. O.K. (*Brown gives back penny. Goes out.*) Catch it, lad. 'Ere, wot's yer name?

ROBERTS: It's Roberts – Jock.

SMITH: O.K. then, Jock. Shake 'ands. (*They do.*) Mine's Clarence. (*Nodding over his shoulder.*) It don't do to tell them bastards that. You married?

ROBERTS: No.

SMITH: A girl?

ROBERTS: Oh, yes, of course.

SMITH: 'Ow many kids?

ROBERTS: Why, none. We're just engaged.

SMITH: Yer never know wot anybody's got round 'ere. Old Brownie's got nine kids and two wives. I'd rather tuck up with a 'ipperpotamus meself.

ROBERTS: How long's he got?

SMITH: 'Oo? Brownie, two more weeks. So's Medworth.

ROBERTS: Is that all? And you?

SMITH: Another blinking year.

ROBERTS: Bad luck. Are you engaged or anything?

SMITH: Nah. I'm looking after Mum.

ROBERTS: And does she mind?

SMITH: I dunno. I suppose she does. Still, I done it for 'er.

ROBERTS: Done what? Oh Lor'. I mustn't ask.

SMITH: You didn't ask. I'm tellin' yer. I forged the winnin' ticket on the dawgs. I sent 'er fifteen 'undred quid in eighteen months. Not bad. She ain't been well since father died – you know, bad 'eart. And then the war – but still she doesn't 'ave ter work; not now – least not so much. You like to 'ave a squint at 'er?

Takes out photograph. Brown comes back.

ROBERTS: I would.

SMITH: That's 'er. And that's my grey'ound pup. She's lovely, isn't she?

BROWN: 'Oo's the tart?

SMITH: Yer want a clip across the ear, me lad?

Bell rings.

JACKSON (*voice off*): Messmen. Messmen.

SMITH: Come on, me old cock-sparrer. Off we go. (*Ruffling Roberts's hair as he goes.*) Be seein' yer. (*As he passes Anderson, outside the door.*) I'se a-comin', boss. Yessir.

Smith and Brown depart with buckets. Roberts takes out photograph of his own and looks at it.

ANDERSON (*coming in, laughing*): Ay – Smithy! Got a tab-end, Mr Roberts? Got a tab-end, please?

ROBERTS: No, sorry, no.

ANDERSON: O.K. That's quite all right. That's quite all right. Mr Roberts hasn't got a tab-end. (*He steals a look at the photograph.*) He's just got a girl. He's got a girl instead.

JACKSON (*shouting above*): Exercise inside. Exercise inside. Exercise on the Fours. All up on the Fours. Get moving.

ANDERSON: It always rains in England. Yes. It wouldn't be old England if it didn't always rain. (*He goes out.*)

> *Enter Medworth to get his bread which he had rolled in his handkerchief and left on the table.*

MEDWORTH: That your wife?

ROBERTS (*shyly, putting it away*): No. Just my girl.

MEDWORTH: You look too young to have a girl. May I? (*He takes the photograph.*) She's beautiful. You love her very much?

ROBERTS: Well, just a bit.

MEDWORTH: I'm sure that it's returned.

ROBERTS: Oh. Why?

MEDWORTH: Why not? I'll tell you some time. After all, we're strangers still.

JACKSON (*comes in. He is lame, bad-tempered, cruel*): Come on. Is this a Mothers' Meeting?

MEDWORTH: Sorry, sir. (*Goes out quickly.*)

JACKSON: Are you reception?

ROBERTS (*going out more slowly*): Yes.

JACKSON: Come here. Yes what?

ROBERTS: Yes, sir.

JACKSON: Well, fall in on the Ones. And do your tie up straight. Come *here*. (*Roberts is slow.*) I said, You do your tie up straight. (*Roberts sulkily adjusts his tie.*) I'm Mr Jackson. You'll get to know me. Everybody knows me in this place.

ROBERTS (*sulkily*): Yes, sir.

JACKSON: Now, get a move on. On the Ones. And watch your step, my lad. (*Roberts goes out. Jackson follows and shouts upwards.*) Now, get a move on. Receptions on the Ones. Exercise on the Fours. Receptions on the Ones for the Governor. Applications for Governor on the Ones. Get moving on the Fours. Get moving, lads.

END OF SCENE 1

ENTRE-SCENE. THE LANDING

Enter Chief Officer Webb.

JACKSON (*saluting*): A Wing. Eighty-four on the Fours, sir. Exercise. Two on Governor's receptions. One for interview.

CHIEF: Thank you, Mr Jackson.

JACKSON: Come on. Get moving there. Anderson, get a move on. Touch up on the pair in front. Get on.

Enter Richards.

CHIEF: What do you want, lad?

RICHARDS: Are you the Governor, please, sir?

CHIEF: No, lad. I'm just the Chief.

RICHARDS: Oh, sorry sir. With all that lovely gold, I thought – (*Chief goes off.*)

JACKSON: Stop thinkin'. What is it you want?

RICHARDS: They said I had to see the Governor.

JACKSON: Who said?

RICHARDS: The boys downstairs.

JACKSON: You do.

RICHARDS: Oh, how exciting. Where?

JACKSON: I'll fix that for you, lad. You stay right where you bloomin' are. You want to get your hair out of your eyes. You see the barber, lad, at six tonight.

RICHARDS: Oh, sir, it isn't long.

JACKSON: It's long and it'll be lousy in a week. We'll ask the Old Man for a transfer down to Holloway. Fall in on the Ones. (*Looks up.*) Who's that smoking in the recess? Here, come out. Mr King, there's someone smoking in the recess.

KING: No, there ain't. (*Mr King is on the balcony.*)

JACKSON (*running up flight*): There is, I see him. . . . Fetch him out.

KING (*depressed voice*): O.K. I've got him 'ere.

JACKSON: He's on the peg.

KING: O.K., sir.

JACKSON : What's his name?
KING : 2746 Anderson, sir.
JACKSON : O.K. Thank you, Mr King.

SCENE 2. THE CONDEMNED CELL

*Tufnell, young, pale, tired-looking, sitting at table playing draughts with
Mr Jones, typical retired Army N.C.O. Mr Gale, young, neat, rakish, sits
reading the paper with his cap on back of head. The Governor enters followed
by the Chief.*

GOVERNOR : Good morning, Tufnell. Doctor seen you?
TUFNELL : Yes, sir.
GOVERNOR : Sleep all right?
TUFNELL : Yes, sir.
GOVERNOR : Food all right?
TUFNELL : Yes, sir.
GOVERNOR : Any troubles?
TUFNELL : No, sir.
GOVERNOR : Everything all right, Jones?
JONES : Yessir. All correct, sir.
GOVERNOR : Good morning, Gale.

Exit, followed by Chief. They go on playing.

JONES : Your move, lad. (*He moves.*) Oh, that's a nasty one,
'Ere, 'ave a fag.
TUFNELL : Oh, thanks. Was that the Governor or Dep.?
GALE : His nibs himself.
TUFNELL : Is he O.K.?
GALE : He's tough.
JONES : 'E's just the straightest boy I ever knew. A D.S.O. and bar.
TUFNELL : This war?
JONES : Last war.
TUFNELL : He doesn't look that old.
JONES : 'Ere, take it easy, lad. You'll 'ave me reachin' for me
shroud.
TUFNELL : I see you got the D.C.M. What rank?
W.D.H.—C

JONES: A C.S.M. A C.S.-bloody-M.

TUFNELL: I bet they liked you though.

GALE: They had to. He was armed.

JONES: They never said as much. Still, most of 'em was decent lads. I've met a few of 'em inside from time to time.

GALE: The heroes who came back.

JONES: That's it.

TUFNELL (*looking at the door at the back of the condemned cell, which leads to the execution shed*): What's through that door?

JONES (*ignoring Tufnell's question*): The Army's all right, though.

TUFNELL: What's through – –?

GALE: 'Ere. Stop this Forces programme. I'll finish that.

JONES (*winking at Tufnell and moving away from the table*): 'E's just a screw.

TUFNELL (*to Mr Gale, who is setting out the pieces*): You always been an officer?

GALE: Yes, sir.

JONES: 'Is mother found 'im in a little uniform among the gooseberries. Poor lad, 'e's never 'ad a chance.

GALE: O.K. – Old Bill. (*To Tufnell.*) I'll play you for a brace of fags.

JONES: I'll witness that. You watch, m' lad. Remember 'e's a screw.

> *They play. Occasionally Tufnell looks up and seems to forget the game. Jones reads the paper, a very paternal figure with steel-rimmed spectacles. The Chaplain, a Welshman, in macintosh and grey homburg hat, comes in.*

CHAPLAIN: Good morning, Jones. Good morning, Gale. (*Both officers stand up, salute him, say 'Good morning, sir,' go out.*) It's very wet. A nasty day. You winning? (*He is left alone with Tufnell.*)

TUFNELL (*shyly*): I don't know.

CHAPLAIN (*to break the ice*): Well, come along. Whose move?

TUFNELL: Your move.

> *They play for a moment or two, the Chaplain watching him.*

CHAPLAIN: Oh, dear. I've let Gale down. Your game.

TUFNELL: Yes. Thanks.

CHAPLAIN: Like reading?

TUFNELL: Sometimes. Yes.

CHAPLAIN: I'll bring you in some books. I'll feed you with them. What sort do you like?

TUFNELL: Oh. Anything.

CHAPLAIN: Adventures? Novels? Poetry? All sorts?

TUFNELL: Yes. Anything'll do.

CHAPLAIN: I'll bring them in. *Alice*?

TUFNELL: What's that?

CHAPLAIN: *Alice in Wonderland*. What isn't it! My favourite book, I know it's that. I'll try and find a copy. You can tell me what it is. (*He laughs.*) It's pretty wet. . . . Afraid you won't get exercise to-day. (*Pause.*) Feeling all right?

TUFNELL: Oh yes.

CHAPLAIN: Good boy. You're C. of E., of course?

TUFNELL: That's right.

CHAPLAIN: Confirmed?

TUFNELL: I was.

CHAPLAIN: Communicant?

TUFNELL: At home, I was.

CHAPLAIN (*casually*): Believe in God?

TUFNELL: I did.

CHAPLAIN: You did?

TUFNELL: Before – –

CHAPLAIN: I understand.

TUFNELL: Before the war.

CHAPLAIN: Oh yes. I see. Before the war. (*Pause.*) Your parents living?

TUFNELL: No, thank God.

CHAPLAIN (*gently*): You do believe in God. Both dead?

TUFNELL: That's it. In 1944. A doodle-bug. On June the 21st. At eight o'clock at night. In Sevenoaks. (*Silence.*) And I was sitting somewhere outside Caen.

CHAPLAIN: And what about the family?

TUFNELL: No family. The only child.

CHAPLAIN: What age?

TUFNELL: Just twenty-three.

CHAPLAIN: War service? Yes, of course.

TUFNELL: Commando, yes. Dieppe and Sicily and Normandy.

CHAPLAIN: What rank?

TUFNELL (*smiling*): A drunken private of the Buffs.

CHAPLAIN (*smiling back at him*): I see you read.

TUFNELL: My old man gave me that when I joined up.

CHAPLAIN: A volunteer?

TUFNELL: I was.

CHAPLAIN: I heard you did quite well. A mention, wasn't it?

TUFNELL: I did have one.

CHAPLAIN: Old Jones'll be your pal for life. He's Army mad.

TUFNELL: Don't tell him, please.

CHAPLAIN: You tell him.

TUFNELL: No. He hates this job enough.

CHAPLAIN: We all do that.

Tufnell looks at him half-aggressively.

TUFNELL: Does Mr Gale?

CHAPLAIN: Gestapo, eh? (*Tufnell lowers his eyes and turns away.*) Don't lose your sense of humour, boy.

TUFNELL: I'll try.

CHAPLAIN: What is your Christian name?

TUFNELL: Richard. They call me Dick.

CHAPLAIN: Well, I shall call you Dick. Is that all right?

TUFNELL: Yes, quite all right. Were you an Army padre?

CHAPLAIN: Yes, I was. At Narvik.

TUFNELL: Yes?

CHAPLAIN: Those Stukas. Phew! They scared my pants clean off!

TUFNELL: When they were dropping them – did you believe in God?

CHAPLAIN: I think I called Him up. Yes. Yes, I did.

TUFNELL: You found it hard?

CHAPLAIN: Sometimes.

TUFNELL: Like now?

CHAPLAIN (*looking him straight in the eyes*): Like now.

TUFNELL (*speaking impetuously*): I like you, Padre – you're straight. Come in and see me often. Will you, please?

CHAPLAIN: Yes. Every day.

TUFNELL: You have to, don't you?

CHAPLAIN: Yes. (*Rising and going for his coat and hat.*) But still – it's nice when duty's pleasure too. You sent in a petition?

TUFNELL: Yes, I have.

CHAPLAIN: Well, don't lose heart.

TUFNELL: I won't.

CHAPLAIN: Good boy. You having any visitors?

TUFNELL: My girl.

CHAPLAIN: Is she still true?

TUFNELL: She's Catholic.

CHAPLAIN: Is that an answer?

TUFNELL: Yes, I think so.

CHAPLAIN: Why?

TUFNELL: They seem to know – how to forgive.

CHAPLAIN: Don't we?

TUFNELL: Perhaps – unwillingly.

The Chaplain smiles and moves across to him.

CHAPLAIN: You said that you were twenty-three. You talk like seventy. The only child. I'm one myself. We're very introspective, aren't we? Friends would call us that. And enemies? – well – exhibitionists.

The Chaplain pats his shoulder and turns for the door.

Well, Dick, I'll send you in the books.

TUFNELL: Oh, thanks.

CHAPLAIN: And then another day we'll talk of other things.

TUFNELL: All right. Please tell me, Padre. Is there any hope?

CHAPLAIN: There's always hope. Would you like to say a prayer?

TUFNELL (*angrily*): No. (*Recovering himself.*) Not today.

CHAPLAIN: We'll talk of that another day – as well.

TUFNELL: Perhaps.

The Chaplain turns, then as an afterthought.

CHAPLAIN: I wonder. Would you like it if I saw your girl some time?

TUFNELL: Oh, would you? Yes.

CHAPLAIN: I'll write her. What's her name?

TUFNELL: Miss Sullivan. Miss Rosie Sullivan.

CHAPLAIN (*writing in his note-book*): Address?

TUFNELL: 6 Holmwood Mansions, Paddington.

CHAPLAIN: Miss Rosie Sullivan, 6 Holmwood Mansions, Paddington. O.K. (*At door.*) She won't refuse to see a heretic?

TUFNELL: Oh, no.

CHAPLAIN (*smiling*): Well, nor will I. (*The cell door opens and Jones and Gale return.*) I lost your money, Gale. I think you would have lost it anyway.

GALE: That's all right, sir.

CHAPLAIN: Well, I'll be off to interview my Taffy friends. We're all Welshmen in here.

JONES (*coming in*): The best place for 'em, sir.

All laugh but Tufnell.

END OF SCENE 2

ENTRE-SCENE. THE LANDING

Anderson, Roberts and Spencer come on to the landing, followed by Mr Jackson. He calls their names. Richards arrives a little later, and Brown only when Mr Jackson has shouted his name twice. This does not improve Mr Jackson's temper.

JACKSON: Now, come along. Governor's applications. Get in line. Pay attention. 2746 Anderson – 6146 Roberts – 6147 Richards – 6145 Spencer – 3762 Brown. (*No Brown.*) 3762 Brown! (*Enter Brown.*) Where you been, eh?

BROWN: Mailbag shop, sir.

JACKSON: O.K. (*He walks away.*)

ANDERSON: O.K. O.K. It's all O.K. in England. Everything's O.K.

BROWN: You'll be on 'chokey.'

ANDERSON: Yes? Well, that's O.K. Yes, that's O.K.

JACKSON (*coming back*): You shut your mouth.

BROWN: I wasn't talking, sir.

JACKSON: Just shut your mouth, I said. (*He goes off again.*)

BROWN (*through his teeth*): O.K.

ANDERSON: It's all O.K. You shut your mouth and still it's all O.K.

JACKSON (*up on the balcony*): Who's talking there?

BROWN: Not me, sir.

JACKSON: Who was it? Richards, you?

RICHARDS: I never said a word. Across my heart.

JACKSON: You – Roberts?

ROBERTS: No, sir.

JACKSON: Spencer?

SPENCER: No, sir.

JACKSON: Anderson then. You talking?

ANDERSON: Well, sir, p'raps I was and p'raps I wasn't.

JACKSON: Were you bloody talking – Yes or No?

ANDERSON: Well, sir, p'raps in my mind. Yes, p'raps my mind was talking through my lips. I couldn't help it, sir.

JACKSON: You tell the Governor. (*Enter King.*) O.K. Will you look after 'em? I'm witnessing. Five. (*Goes off.*)

KING: Five. (*He checks the number.*)

ANDERSON: He can't be happy in himself. He can't be happy in himself. I don't think he can be a happy man.

KING: Who can't?

ANDERSON: Why, Mr Jackson, Mr King. He never smiles. He nearly never smiles.

KING: You think there's much to smile at around here?

ANDERSON: Oh, I don't know. The British always smile. (*At this point the Chief walks across the landing, on his way to the Governor's Office. Anderson suspends his lecture on the British until he has passed.*) The British always smile. The British go on smiling until they're dead. Why me on a report? I only had a tiny little draw. A tiny draw.

KING: I saw yer 'avin' 'arf a bloomin' cigar.

ANDERSON: Oh no, sir. Mr King, look here. (*He takes out his cigarette-box.*) It wasn't more than just a draw. That's all I've got. That's all old Arthur's got.

KING: Let's 'ave a look. (*Puts in tab-ends.*) Shove it away. (*He goes back to the desk.*)

ANDERSON: Now, Mr King, yes, you're a happy man. Yes, you're a happy warder, Mr King.

KING: And so are you – you leathery old heathen – now.

ANDERSON: Yes, sir. I am.

JACKSON (*off*): (*shouting*) Governor's applications, right turn. Lead on.

SCENE 3. THE GOVERNOR'S OFFICE

The Governor is seated at his desk. The Chief shouts 'Anderson' at the door, then stands on his right. Warder outside shouts 'Anderson' again. Anderson comes in fast followed by Jackson.

CHIEF: Name and number to the Governor.

ANDERSON: 2746 Anderson, sir.

GOVERNOR: Well, Mr Jackson.

JACKSON: This man was smoking in the recess during exercise this morning, sir.

GOVERNOR: Anything to say?

ANDERSON: I didn't mean no harm. No, sir. I didn't mean no harm.

GOVERNOR: The law is not concerned with what you mean – but what you do. You know the prison rules.

ANDERSON: Yes, sir. I'm sorry, sir. (*He has an idea, and decides to try it out.*) The scrubbing party gets me down. It's getting on my nerves. My nerves is bad. That's right. I has to smoke to keep them quiet. Yes, sir. That's right.

GOVERNOR: Mr Jackson, what's his general behaviour like?

JACKSON: It's bad, sir. Talking on parade as well. I warned him twice.

GOVERNOR: Today, as well?

JACKSON: Yes, sir.

GOVERNOR: Three – three – and one.

ANDERSON: Three – three and one!

CHIEF: Three days solitary confinement. Three days lost remission. One day bread and water. Now get out. (*Exit Anderson and Jackson, Anderson casting a reproachful look at the Governor.*) Roberts. (*Enter Roberts.*) Name and number to the Governor.

ROBERTS: 6146 John Roberts, sir.

GOVERNOR: Two years?

ROBERTS: Yes, sir.

GOVERNOR: The Merchant Navy?

ROBERTS: That's right, sir.

GOVERNOR: You'd drunk too much, I take it?

Smiles at him.

ROBERTS: Well, maybe I had had one or two.

GOVERNOR: All right. Keep smiling, lad.

CHIEF: Get out. (*Roberts goes.*) Richards. (*Enter Richards.*) Name and number to the Governor.

RICHARDS: 6147 Evelyn Richards, sir.

GOVERNOR: Your job?

RICHARDS: Well, choruses. I've done a bit of ballet-dancing too.

GOVERNOR: Six months. (*Richards nods.*) You get your hair cut right away.

RICHARDS: Oh, sir.

He starts forward towards the Governor's desk in protest, but is checked by the Chief.

CHIEF: Don't answer back.

GOVERNOR: Now, Richards, just a warning. You behave yourself here. You understand?

RICHARDS: Yes, sir.

GOVERNOR: One false step and you're out. Just one. Straight back to a local. No messes, no smokes, no recreation there. You understand?

RICHARDS: Yes, sir.

GOVERNOR: I don't want to see or hear of you until you come up here in four months' time to say good-bye. You understand?

RICHARDS: Yes, sir.

GOVERNOR: All right.

CHIEF: Get out. (*Richards, tossing his head defiantly at the Chief, departs. Spencer comes in.*) Name and number to the Governor.

SPENCER: 6145 Spencer, sir.

This is a very different Spencer from the Ten Mess brand. His bluff avails him nothing now.

GOVERNOR: Well, Spencer, slipped again?

SPENCER: Yes, sir.

GOVERNOR: The same old story.

SPENCER: Yes, sir – much the same.

GOVERNOR: Where – this time?

SPENCER: Marks and Spencer, sir.

GOVERNOR: He keeps it in the family at any rate. Get off with much?

SPENCER: Two handbags and a lady's camisole.

GOVERNOR: And how'd they catch you?

SPENCER: House-detective, sir.

GOVERNOR: How much? (*The Governor consults his case-book.*) Six months. You think it's worth it, eh?

SPENCER: No, sir. I just can't help it, sir.

GOVERNOR: What rot. Of course you can.

SPENCER: No, sir; I can't.

GOVERNOR: Let's see. You were an admiral last time. What are you now?

SPENCER (*shyly*): I'm nothing, sir.

CHIEF: He's Air Force this time – Squadron Leader, sir.

GOVERNOR: I say, that's dashing. Flying upside-down?

SPENCER: No, sir. Too low.

GOVERNOR: I see. That's quite appropriate. Well, all right, Spencer. Try and gain a bit of height. All right.

CHIEF: Get out. (*Exit Spencer.*) Brown. (*Enter Brown.*) Your name and number to the Governor.

BROWN: 3762 Brown, sir.

GOVERNOR: Yes?

BROWN: I put an application in to see you, sir.

GOVERNOR: I know.

BROWN: I want a special letter, sir.

GOVERNOR: Who to?

BROWN: Me wife, sir, please.

GOVERNOR: Which one?

BROWN: Please – me unmarried one, sir, please.

GOVERNOR: Refused. (*Brown looks aggrieved.*) Now listen, Brown. You've been to see me every week for the last twenty-three and a quarter months – each time you've asked exactly the same question and each time you've got exactly the same answer – that occurred to you at all?

BROWN: Yus, sir. I'll say it 'as.

GOVERNOR (*smiling*): Well, what's the game?

BROWN: I want to tell 'er that I loves 'er, sir.

GOVERNOR: But do you really think you do?

BROWN: Yes, sir. I do. When I can't tell 'er that I do.

GOVERNOR: Now Brown, you've got a wife already and nine children, haven't you?

BROWN: Yes, sir. I 'ave an' all.

GOVERNOR: Well, what about that little lot?

BROWN (*aggressively*): Well, what about them, sir?

GOVERNOR (*patiently*): When you go out in two weeks' time, what are you going to do?

BROWN: I'm goin' back to 'er.

GOVERNOR: Back to your legal wife?

BROWN: That's right. That's why I want the letter, sir – to tell me second wife I'm doin' that.

GOVERNOR: Now, Brown, the Chaplain wrote and told her that, you know he did.

BROWN: Yes, sir.

GOVERNOR: Well, what's this letter I won't give you for?

BROWN: I've told yer, sir. To tell 'er that I loves 'er – once for all – and get it off my chest.

GOVERNOR: I see.

BROWN (*snatching at this straw of understanding*): Yer do, sir? Can I have it then?

GOVERNOR: No, Brown, you can't. I'm sorry, Brown, you can't. Now run along.

CHIEF: Get out. (*Brown exits as Chaplain enters.*)

GOVERNOR: Our weekly chat with Casanova Brown. Any more?

CHIEF: No, sir.

GOVERNOR: Come in, Tom. All right, Mr. Webb. (*Chief exits.*) You seen that boy?

CHAPLAIN: I have.

GOVERNOR: You like him? (*Chaplain nods.*) Yes, so do I. You talked about his incident at all?

CHAPLAIN: No, not today.

GOVERNOR (*lighting his pipe*): Why do they do these things?

CHAPLAIN: The war?

GOVERNOR: Perhaps. You saw his hands? Of course you did. Long, thin, artistic fingers. If the Devil hadn't snaffled him, he might have been a useful citizen. And did he talk?

CHAPLAIN: A bit.

GOVERNOR: I doubt if he'd talk to me.

CHAPLAIN: I shouldn't think so. No.

GOVERNOR: Why not? Am I so stern?

CHAPLAIN: Inside these walls, a bit. You're all right when I get you in a pub.

GOVERNOR (*smiling*): I pass outside. I'm glad.

CHAPLAIN: You pass inside as far as I'm concerned.

GOVERNOR: What did he say?

CHAPLAIN: Oh, nothing much. He talked about the war.

GOVERNOR: He did quite well.

CHAPLAIN: I know. He also gave me the address of his young lady.

GOVERNOR: Oh. Respectable?

CHAPLAIN: What? Her address? It's Paddington.

GOVERNOR: My aunt lives there.

CHAPLAIN (*smiling*): Her name's not Rose, by any chance?

GOVERNOR: No . . . Agatha.

CHAPLAIN: Good God!

GOVERNOR: Victorian, you know. Long skirts. Lorgnettes. Black ribbons round the throat.

CHAPLAIN: Please don't.

GOVERNOR: I'm sorry. I forgot your leftish leanings. Have a drink?

CHAPLAIN: If you will. Yes.

GOVERNOR: I will.

Goes to chest to get whisky and glasses.

CHAPLAIN: The date been fixed?

GOVERNOR: Tuesday, the 21st.

CHAPLAIN: Will he get off?

GOVERNOR: He might.

CHAPLAIN: Petition in?

GOVERNOR: It is. The old man's got it now.

CHAPLAIN: What grounds?

GOVERNOR: The war – his youth – the girl – his family. The usual stuff.

CHAPLAIN: He won't get off.

GOVERNOR: I said he might.

CHAPLAIN: What do you really think?

GOVERNOR: I daren't think till Tuesday fortnight, Tom. Here's luck. (*They raise their glasses.*)

GOVERNOR: What about old Brown?

CHAPLAIN (*still thinking of condemned cell*): I'm writing to the girl-friend. That all right?

GOVERNOR: What girl-friend?

CHAPLAIN: Tufnell's.

GOVERNOR: Yes, of course it is.

CHAPLAIN: Who's Brown?

GOVERNOR: Old Bluebeard. Casanova Brown.

CHAPLAIN: Oh, him. He wants a letter, doesn't he?

GOVERNOR: He does.

CHAPLAIN: You gave it to him?

GOVERNOR: No.

CHAPLAIN: Aunt Agatha!

GOVERNOR: You evil man. What will he do when he goes out?

CHAPLAIN: What all the others do.

GOVERNOR: What's that? Go back?

CHAPLAIN: Perhaps.

GOVERNOR: To whom?

CHAPLAIN: To Mrs. Brown and family.

GOVERNOR: And then?

CHAPLAIN: That all depends on Mrs Brown.

GOVERNOR: Is she a steady girl?

CHAPLAIN: She's fifty-five.

GOVERNOR: A dear old apple-cheeked affair?

CHAPLAIN: A charlady. She looks like hell.

GOVERNOR: Oh, dear. A bucket and a scrubbing-brush and horny hands. And Mrs. B. the second?

CHAPLAIN: Twenty-four – and blonde.

GOVERNOR: Unfixed abode?

CHAPLAIN: Lyons' Corner House.

GOVERNOR: What *can* she see in him?

CHAPLAIN: A background for herself, perhaps.

GOVERNOR: A rose-bush on a dunghill. What a world!

The Chief returns. The Chaplain finishes his drink and gets up.

CHAPLAIN: Well, I must go and churn a sermon out. It's aimed at you. The theme is Pontius Pilate. (*Exit.*)

GOVERNOR (*to Chief*): Come on, Webb. Let's see the kitchen first. Your half-day off?

CHIEF: Yes, sir.

GOVERNOR: Get moving then. I'm backing Arsenal.

CHIEF: Yes, sir.

GOVERNOR: You fancy Chelsea, eh?

He goes out of the door. Richards is scrubbing, in the way.

CHIEF (*shouting*): Get that bucket out of the road. Stand up when the Governor goes past. You'll have to learn to use your eyes in here, me lad.

He passes on after Governor. Richards makes rude face and resumes scrubbing. King enters and stands by while Richards scrubs.

END OF SCENE 3

ENTRE-SCENE. THE LANDING

Evening. The prison clock strikes seven. Bell rings.

KING (*shouting*): Stand to yer doors. Stand to yer doors, A Wing. Come on, get inside yer step. Get back. Yer should 'ave done yer slopping hours ago. Get movin'. It's yer recreation time – not mine. 'Ere. Hi! I said, 'No sloppin' out no more.' Yer 'oldin' up the wing. 'Ere you, get back inside and stand outside yer door. 'Oo is it, Paddy? 'Oo's that boy?

PADDY (*upstairs*): Can't see, sir.

KING: Who is it, Medworth?

MEDWORTH (*voice off*): It's Richards, sir.

KING: Well, kick 'is backside for 'im. Get inside. Hi! You!

RICHARDS: Yes, sir.

KING: What's eatin' yer? You've got all night to use yer Pond's Cold Cream.

RICHARDS: I've just been washing out my hair.

KING: I thought they 'ad it off.

RICHARDS: Not all of it. I thought the scissors might be dirty – so I washed it out.

Voices shouting 'Go on, Polly.'

KING: Lor' bless my ruddy soul. Hey, Polly. Get yer curling papers in.

RICHARDS: Oh, Mr King!

KING: An' let us know when you're ready, lad. And we'll all go down and 'ave a smoke.

RICHARDS: I'm ready now.

KING: No 'urry, I assure yer. Take yer time. I'm paid for this. (*Shouting.*) Switch off yer lights. Down for recreation – A Wing. One pace forward. March. Right turn. Lead on. All applications. Come along to me. Come on. Get movin'. Get out all yer ruddy old cigars. O.K. boy. Yes?

He goes off round the corner with the Application Book.

SCENE 4. TEN MESS

Richards is sitting combing out his hair. It is not much shorter. Paddy slops in, singing gloomily.

PADDY:
　　'And if there's going to be a life hereafter
　　And sometimes I think there's going to be –
　　Well, I'm going to ask my God to make my heaven
　　In that little place beyond the Irish sea.

RICHARDS: You're home-sick, aren't you?

PADDY: You a fortune-teller?

RICHARDS (*ignoring sarcasm*): What sentence have you got?

PADDY: Seven.

RICHARDS: Poor Paddy. How much have you done?

PADDY: Three bleedin', flamin', stinkin', lousy years.

RICHARDS: Poor Paddy. I'm so sorry.

PADDY: Don't you waste your tears on me. It's not meself that worries me.

RICHARDS: What is it, then?

PADDY: It's Jean.

RICHARDS: Oh, dear. A woman in the case. Who's Jean?

PADDY: My wife. That's all. (*Turning round full of feeling.*) The sweetest, beautifullest, softest lass you ever saw. We married. Just six months before I came in here.

RICHARDS: Why did you come in here?

PADDY: I got fed-up. A railwayman. I didn't want to stay in England, so I tried to blow the line one night at Crewe.

RICHARDS (*still combing*): Whatever for?

PADDY: They called it sabotage. I don't know why I did it really. P'raps I thought the seat of the Empire wanted shaking up a bit.

RICHARDS: What? All the little children and their mothers in the train?

PADDY: It was a goods – an ammunition train. And anyway be damned to that. The bleedin' Government's to blame.

RICHARDS: Well, Paddy, even if they are, why should the Government be outside Crewe?

PADDY (*sitting down near him*): Now listen here. For nigh on three hundred years the Irish nation – –

RICHARDS (*interrupting*): Paddy, please. It's just a waste of time. I'm just a die-hard old Conservative. I always was.

PADDY: I'll tell you something, boy. Old England's never given us – –

RICHARDS (*putting his hand over his mouth*): Shut up. It's dragging for you, Paddy, isn't it?

PADDY (*turning away*): I guess it is.

RICHARDS: Well, tell me about Jean.

PADDY: You want to hear?

RICHARDS: Of course I do.

PADDY (*after making sure he does*): I met her at the races – down in Cork. She's waiting for me. (*Pause.*) Five and a half years. She was nineteen the day we married. She'll be twenty-five when I get out. She's waiting for me now. (*Intensely.*) You think she can?

RICHARDS: Can what?

PADDY: Wait. All that time?

RICHARDS (*sympathetic*): Well, the war-time women did.

PADDY: Some of them did. (*Longer pause.*) She's writin' regular.

We haven't got a kid. She's beautiful. She's lovely dark brown eyes about a foot apart. And sort of silky auburn hair. Something like yours.

RICHARDS: Poor Paddy. I'm so sorry for you.

PADDY: I believe you are.

Walks over and looks down at him.

RICHARDS: Of course I am. You see, I understand.

PADDY: Are you an Englishman?

RICHARDS: My mother's Scots.

PADDY: Ah, that explains it – why I told you. Do you know, I've never told another soul in all these years. In three whole years. We've got a thing or two, we Celts, the Anglo-Saxons haven't got.

RICHARDS: Such as?

PADDY: Oh, sympathy and tenderness and – things.

RICHARDS: This lousy comb. It hurts.

Paddy takes it from him and pulls it through his hair, then turns away again.

PADDY: Why don't you break it up – and find a girl?

RICHARDS: I don't like women. They're cruel.

PADDY: Not all of them.

RICHARDS: The ones I've met.

PADDY: In Leicester Square?

RICHARDS: No – everywhere. My mother got divorced.

PADDY: I see.

RICHARDS: She ran away with a rich Jew, when father was abroad. She left me with a friend. I've never seen her since.

PADDY: And your old man?

RICHARDS: He lives in Birmingham.

PADDY: What does he do?

RICHARDS: He opens bottles. Then he empties them.

PADDY: Poor kid.

RICHARDS (*synthetic cheerfulness*): Oh, I can take it.

PADDY: Here, have a cigarette. Have two. (*Enter Medworth.*) I get 'em off old Brownie.

RICHARDS (*smiling up at him*): Oh, thanks.

Enter Brown and Spencer rolling cigarettes.

W.D.H.—D

BROWN : And I says to Smithy – I says, 'If yer don't ruddy well give me that letter, I'll write to the Commissioners, I will.'

SPENCER : I say. By Jove.

RICHARDS : Good evening, Squadron Leader.

SPENCER : Evenin'. How are you?

RICHARDS : Oh, top hole, thanks.

BROWN (*seizing Spencer by the arm*) : And then old Smithy looks at me a bit, taken aback like – see? – and then 'e turns to Webbie like – for comfort, see? I could see what was goin' on be'ind 'is mind-like. 'This guy means business,' 'e was kinda saying – foller me? 'I can't get rid of Brownie with a lot o' bull.' An' then 'e leans across 'is desk, like – confidential-like, like this. (*Sits and demonstrates.*) 'Now Brown,' 'e says – like man to man, yer see? 'I'd let yer 'ave yer letter if I could. But I just can't.' And then 'e tells me, like, as 'ow 'is 'ands is tied. 'It's the 'Ome Secretary,' 'e says, 'don't understand like you an' me does, Brown,' 'e says. 'I'd give it to yer, Brown, honest I would, but then I dursn't do it, 'cos I'd get the sack. These ruddy politicians got me there.' (*Appropriate gesture.*)

PADDY : You ruddy liar.

BROWN : 'Oo's a liar? Strike me dead if that ain't true. Cor strike me bloomin' dead.

PADDY : And sure He would if he was doin' time. And had to listen to you every night for years and years and ruddy years.

BROWN : It's draggin' for yer, Paddy. Take it easy, boy. (*Turns back to Spencer, and re-engages his attention with a whistle.*) An' then 'e says, 'Well, Brown, it breaks me 'eart to 'ave ter do it – ' 'cos I knows yer loves this girl an' she loves you. Cor blime, 'ow I wish that I could 'elp,' he says. Then reaches out 'is 'and – to get the letter like – (*Dramatic.*) Then I says, 'No, I wouldn't take it, Smithy boy,' I says. 'I'll make a sacrifice,' I says. And then I leaves 'im – sudden, case I changed my ruddy mind.

Enter Smith.

SMITH : Where's Arthur?

BROWN : 'E's on bread-and-water. Chokey – three and one – –

SMITH : So 'e is. Well – you'll do. 'Ere, Brownie, come an' 'ave a game against two blokes in Nine.

Exit Brown and Smith.

SPENCER: You know, I like the Governor.

RICHARDS: Don't tell us that he held your hand as well.

SPENCER: He's understanding. He quite sympathized. He said, 'A Squadron Leader's only human – like the other boys – but if he shows it! Well, he takes a harder knock.'

RICHARDS: Did you fly much?

SPENCER: I got the M.B.E.

RICHARDS: I love the boys in blue. They're so – young. (*To Spencer.*) I bet you pinched the rations.

SPENCER: As a matter of fact, I was stunting over Charing Cross.

RICHARDS: I say!

SPENCER: At zero feet.

PADDY (*quietly*): We're not all crackers here.

Spencer turns nervously.

SPENCER: I beg your pardon.

PADDY: I'm not biting. Get me? No one ever got six months for flying low.

SPENCER: Not always. No, that's true. But I was flying upside-down.

PADDY: Get out. (*Pause.*) I said, *Get out.*

SPENCER: But – I'm a member of this mess.

PADDY: *Get out,* I said. Before I throw you out. (*Advancing on him.*) Go on. And take your bloody aeroplane and fly away before I clip you one. Go on. (*With a lightning movement he throws Spencer out.*) I'll give you upside-down, you little rat. The runway's yours. Take off again, and mind your ruddy wings. (*Comes back into mess.*) He makes me sick.

MEDWORTH (*to Richards*): Like a game of draughts?

PADDY (*quickly*): Richards! Come on, let's take a walk among the boys.

Richards, after a momentary hesitation, goes out, followed by Paddy, who gives Medworth a contemptuous glance. Medworth sits down. Roberts appears in the doorway, and seeing Medworth turns to go, but Medworth stops him.

MEDWORTH: Like a game of draughts?

ROBERTS (*perhaps pitying him a little*): All right.

Medworth fetches board.

MEDWORTH: You know, I can't help thinking of that boy.

ROBERTS: Who? Tufnell?

MEDWORTH: Did you see his picture in the paper? He looked nice. So young. Such lovely eyes.

ROBERTS: Maybe the bobby's eyes were lovely too.

MEDWORTH: Oh no. He was quite old. (*They play.*) You read the Bible much?

ROBERTS: Can't say I do.

MEDWORTH: You should. I do. I've read it twice since I came in. I'll get you one tomorrow. I work in the Library.

ROBERTS (*no enthusiasm*): Thanks.

MEDWORTH: And will you read it if I do?

ROBERTS: I might.

MEDWORTH: I'll tell you what to read. You ought to start with Kings. It's beautiful. David and Jonathan. You've heard of them.

ROBERTS: At school I did.

MEDWORTH: They loved each other very much.

ROBERTS: Your move.

MEDWORTH: And Jonathan was much, much older than his friend.

ROBERTS: What? A dirty old man!

MEDWORTH: Oh, no. Don't talk like that. Oh, please don't talk like that.

ROBERTS (*laughing*): I'm sorry. It was just a crack.

MEDWORTH: The Bible's all I've got. I've lost the rest. I have no friends. That's all I've got. Don't spoil it, please.

ROBERTS (*becoming irritated and a little nervous*): I've said I'm sorry, haven't I?

MEDWORTH: You've said it – yes. But are you?

ROBERTS: Oh, shut up. (*Medworth looks deeply hurt.*) Here. Why are you in here?

MEDWORTH: Domestic troubles.

ROBERTS: Married?

MEDWORTH: No.

ROBERTS: Why not?

MEDWORTH (*recovering himself*): Well, everybody isn't married, after all. I was a schoolmaster. I had no time for anything but work. I loved it. Teaching.

ROBERTS: Going back to that?

MEDWORTH: Oh, no. I've finished now.

ROBERTS (*after a pause, suddenly*): What makes you talk to me?

MEDWORTH: Why not?

ROBERTS: You talk to no one else.

MEDWORTH: Perhaps I'm shy. With schoolmasters – one's friends are often younger than oneself. (*He smiles.*) Like Jonathan's. I made an awful mess of things. I wasn't strong enough. (*Appealingly.*) You understand?

ROBERTS: You mean you swiped the fees?

MEDWORTH: Oh, no. How cynical you are – and hard. Why are you hard?

ROBERTS: I guess one has to be.

MEDWORTH: You're not a bit like David. Not a bit. Except to look at. Then you make me think of him.

ROBERTS: A pretty tough old bastard, wasn't he?

MEDWORTH: Not when he was a boy. He was ruddy and withal of a beautiful countenance.

ROBERTS: Like Polly Richards, eh?

Roberts laughs heartily at his own joke.

MEDWORTH: No. No. No, not a bit like him. Much more like you.

Mr King appears at the door. Medworth looks at board again.

KING (*coming in*): Both cheatin', eh? (*Looks over board.*) 'Ere, wot's the matter, lad? Take that – and that – and that – and there's a ruddy king. (*Does so.*)

Enter Smith.

SMITH (*bowing elaborately*): A ruddy king. Good evening, Mr King. I trust I find you well?

KING: You do, me lad, you do. I'll 'ave a pint inside me inside 'arf an hour.

SMITH: You lucky swine.

KING: 'Ere, 'ere, we can't 'ave that. Remember I'm a screw.

SMITH (*round table*): You look more like a midwife, Mr King.

KING (*taking out truncheon*): You want a clip with this?

SMITH: You want the sack? (*Sitting down.*) Why don't you get a decent job instead of 'anging round these lousy crooks?

KING: You get me one when you go out.

SMITH: O.K. We'll do the race-tracks. Wotcher say?

KING: You 'ave a go at goin' straight.

SMITH: That's wot me mother always says.

KING: Yer mother's right – poor woman – bless 'er 'eart.

SMITH: And wot may your old mother think of you?

KING: She thinks I'm tops.

SMITH: She ever seen yer in that uniform?

KING: She 'as. So what?

SMITH: So nothin', Mr King.

KING: Well, good night, boys. I'll drink a pint for yer tonight.

SMITH: Drink two.

KING: I'll maybe manage three.

SMITH: And mother too?

KING: Yes. She'll be there. She likes 'er drop o' gin.

SMITH: She married?

KING: 'Course she was.

SMITH (*shouting after him*): A widder, eh? 'Ere, Mr King, would she 'ave me?

KING (*popping his head back round the door*): Gaw blime. Good night, father. Oh, my Lord. (*Exit King.*)

Smith sits at the table, reading the paper.

MEDWORTH (*to Roberts, the game now over*): May I read your hand?

ROBERTS: Oh, hell.

MEDWORTH: No, would you mind? It looks so interesting.

SMITH (*coming over*): Lor' bless us. Madame Petulengro. 'Ere, read mine.

MEDWORTH: Another time.

SMITH (*resumes reading*): O.K. I'll join the queue.

ROBERTS: They're rather sticky, I'm afraid.

MEDWORTH: You're very emotional. Very sentimental.

SMITH: Pr'aps that's why 'is 'ands is 'ot.

MEDWORTH (*trying to ignore these flippant interruptions*): You don't know what to make of life. Not yet. Your character's just forming now.

SMITH: Lord 'elp 'im if it forms in 'ere.

MEDWORTH: You're going through a difficult time.

SMITH: 'Ere, I could tell 'im that.

MEDWORTH: You're terribly in love – a pretty girl.

ROBERTS: Come on, you saw her photograph.

MEDWORTH: I know, but I can see her here as well. You've given her your heart. You give completely – and unselfishly. You ask for nothing back. Perhaps that's just as well.

ROBERTS: What do you mean?

MEDWORTH: You won't be quite so disappointed if you get let down, you'll soon replace her with some other love. You have to have it all the time.

> *Paddy enters and stands hands stuffed into belt, smoking, looking angry. He leans against the wall. He has heard the remarks about the girl letting Roberts down.*

You'll need affection, understanding, and a lot of love and friendship then. And as I say – you have to have these things – like sunshine to a flower.

PADDY: You cut that out.

MEDWORTH: I'm only looking at his hand.

PADDY: Well, cut it out.

> *Medworth sheepishly drops his hand.*

MEDWORTH: Oh well, all right. (*Silence as he gets up.*) I'll go up to my cell.

PADDY: The best place for you.

MEDWORTH (*ignoring him*): Good night, Roberts. Good night, Smithy.

SMITH: Toodle-oo.

MEDWORTH (*as he passes*): Good night, Paddy. (*No reply.*) (*Exit.*)

> *Paddy still leans against the door. Smith goes on reading the paper. Roberts, at whom Paddy is looking hard, gets up and slowly puts the draughts away. Paddy sings, mournfully.*

PADDY:

'For the winds that blow across the seas from Ireland
Bring the perfume of the heather – as they blow –
And the women . . .!'

*He stops, throws his cigarette on the floor, stamps on it angrily,
looks at Roberts again, then mutters with intense emotion:*

Mother of God. Holy Mother of God.

CURTAIN

ACT TWO

SCENE 1. THE CONDEMNED CELL. MORNING

OFFICER JONES (*smoking his pipe*) : An' then old Jerry started landin' 'em on our H.Q. The Captain says, 'Now 'op it, Jonah boy – you go an' see the boys is all O.K.' 'Not bloody likely, sir,' I says. 'Now Sergeant-Major Jones,' says 'e, 'an order is an order. Get along.' So off I goes. 'E saved me ruddy life. I never seen old Bob again. The bravest, finest gentleman I ever 'opes to see. And them there Reds – like Windy 'ere – says 'Officers be damned.' Be damned to them, I says. There's something more in these 'ere public schools nor dukes and lords and ruddy racin' cars. They may not be so bloomin' clever like the laddies at the Marble Arch on Sunday afternoons – but then they turns 'em out with guts. (*Relights his pipe.*) And guts is something that I likes to see. And plenty of 'em – like in dear old Bob. A lord 'e was. I found 'is guts all over our H.Q. when I got back. God rest 'is soul.

GALE : You're a blinkin' spoon-fed old reactionary, Jonah.

JONES : So what, me lad ? So bloody what, me lad ?

GALE : You're out of date.

JONES : I'm out of date. O.K., I'm out of date. Let's shake on it. (*He shakes Gale's hand.*) I'm glad I'm out of date.

TUFNELL (*coming over to the table from his bed*) : You any war experience ?

JONES : No. I've told yer once. 'E's just a screw.

TUFNELL : You do the death watch quite a lot.

GALE : Three times a year, perhaps.

TUFNELL : You like it, don't you ?

GALE : No. It bores me stiff.

TUFNELL : It bores you, does it ? Is that all it does ?

GALE : I get a bit of sitting down as well. Old Jonah does it just as often anyway.

JONES : I does it for the cash.

TUFNELL : I'm glad you do.

JONES: Come on, let's 'ave a game of draughts.

Enter the Governor and Chief.

GOVERNOR: Morning, Jones; morning, Gale. Everything all right?

JONES: Yessir. All correct, sir.

GOVERNOR: All right, Tufnell?

TUFNELL: Yes, sir.

GOVERNOR: Anything you want?

TUFNELL: No, sir.

GOVERNOR (*smiling*): You've got a visitor tonight, I think.

TUFNELL: Yes, sir – my girl. (*Governor is going out.*) Oh, sir, is my petition . . .?

GOVERNOR: Still out, lad.

TUFNELL: Oh, thank you, sir.

GOVERNOR: Don't pin your hopes on it too much.

TUFNELL: No, sir. I won't.

GOVERNOR: But keep your chin up just the same. (*Friendly smile.*) That all?

TUFNELL: Yes, thank you, sir.

GOVERNOR: All right. Good day.

Goes out, followed by the Chief.

JONES: Come on, lad. Set the pieces out.

TUFNELL: No, I don't want to play just now. (*He turns away, back to his bed, then feels ashamed of himself.*) I'm sorry.

JONES: All right, lad, all right. Come on, you lousy Red, let's 'ave a game. 'Ere, 'ave yer ever done salutin' drill? Hup 1–2–Away. You never 'ave. Now watch me, lad. Or else yer'll never be a Chief. Now. HUP 1–2–AWAY. (*Tufnell is smiling.*)

GALE: Sit down. You ought to be in Chelsea Barracks – you. (*They play.*) You ever studied politics at all?

JONES: Politics! I've studied 'uman nature, lad, a bit.

GALE: That's not enough. You want to study economics.

JONES: No, I don't.

GALE: You'll never understand financial problems till you do.

JONES: Now look 'ere, lad. As long as I've me weekly envelope, the missis and a pint o' beer, I'm 'appy, see? (*Takes a piece with emphasis.*)

GALE: Of course it's not your fault. Your generation never had no education.

JONES: Didn't we? Me father taught me 'ow ter keep me place and keep me 'ands off other people's business and other people's cash.

GALE: Conservative!

JONES: Well, what are you? Karl Ruddy Marx?

GALE: It's economic servitude you like.

JONES (*getting down to it now*): 'Ere, Windy boy, why don't yer give it up? Go up to the old man and say, 'Look 'ere. I'm Jackie Gale, the future Preemier. I don't want yer little envelope each week – thank yer. I don't like the ruddy Civil Service – thank yer. I don't like the 'Ome Secetry, or the Commissioners – or the Governor – or the screws – or the prisoners. There's only one thing in this bloomin' world I likes and that is – Mr Ruddy Windy Gale.'

GALE: Go on. You're talkin' silly now.

JONES: Why don't yer, eh? I'm askin' yer.

GALE: Well, if I did, I'd get the sack.

JONES: So what? Ain't that the freedom that yer wants?

GALE: You think I want to starve?

JONES: I don't, me lad, I don't. But if yer 'ad the guts, yer would. Yer'd take that blinkin' coat off – an' that perky little 'at an' yer'd be 'oppin' on yer little biscuit box – an' shootin' off yer mouth around 'Yde Park. That's if yer 'ad the guts.

GALE: And what about my girl?

JONES (*winking at Tufnell*): Yer wot?

GALE: My girl, I said.

JONES: I'll bet she likes ice-cream.

GALE: Just what does that mean, Jonah?

JONES: Listen 'ere. You 'aven't got a 'eart as big as that there bit o' stoppin' in me tooth – yer see? (*Shows it to him.*) Not 'arf as big as that. And yet yer tells us there's a woman in yer life. Well, I'll be blowed. Well, I'll be bloomin', blinkin', blasted blowed. (*He gets up to refill pipe, winking at Tufnell.*)

GALE: Go on, old timer.

JONES: O.K. Wot's 'er age?

GALE: Eighteen.

JONES: It's cradle-snatchin' – yes it is – I get it now. That uniform – that crooked 'at – that little perishin' moustache – (*pause*) – them pearly teeth yer puts beside yer bed at night. (*Walks about chuckling.*) Well, I dunno. It takes all sorts to make a world. That's wot they say. Come on, lad, 'ave a smoke.

TUFNELL (*to Gale*): Have you a photograph?

GALE (*suspicious*): I think I have.

JONES: O' course 'e 'as. 'E kisses it at night. I've seen 'im, boy. An' then 'e puts it in the tooth-glass with 'is teeth.

TUFNELL: Please. May I see?

GALE (*throwing it on table*): There it is.

TUFNELL: She looks most awfully nice.

GALE: I think so too.

TUFNELL: And awfully kind.

JONES: Let's 'ave a dek. (*Takes it.*) She must be kind. She's goin' ter be a bloomin' martyr. Just like Joan of Arc. (*Looks up with change of tone.*) She's O.K., boy – yer lucky swine.

GALE: Oh thanks. (*Taking it back.*)

TUFNELL: Please. May I look at it again?

GALE: You have an eyeful. I don't blame you, lad.

   Enter Chaplain.

CHAPLAIN: Morning all. (*Jones and Gale go out. Chaplain sits.*) Well, how are things?

TUFNELL: All right, sir, thanks.

   The Chaplain sees the photograph.

CHAPLAIN: Miss Sullivan?

TUFNELL: No. Mr Gale's girl. She's sweet.

CHAPLAIN: The honey and the lion. No, he's all right. Just sensitive and shy, that's all. He steels himself against the world – and looks for sharp, unpleasant things to rub against and try his temper. Right?

TUFNELL: I wouldn't know.

CHAPLAIN (*casually*): What made you do it, Dick?

TUFNELL (*after a pause*): I lost my temper. That was all.

CHAPLAIN: Your temper bad?

TUFNELL: Yes, very bad – at times.

CHAPLAIN: Dieppe? And Normandy?

TUFNELL: No – long before. When I was very small, I shut my best friend in the back door by his hair. When I was six.

CHAPLAIN: That's nothing, Dick. We've all done that. I sometimes think we've all done almost everything – or would, in certain circumstances. Like the books?

TUFNELL: Yes, thanks.

CHAPLAIN: I haven't found an *Alice* yet. I'm trying still. The Crown said that it wasn't in a fit of temper – didn't they?

TUFNELL: I know.

CHAPLAIN: They said premeditated. Why was that?

TUFNELL: Because I followed him right back towards the station. And I – shot him when he came and told me I was drunk.

CHAPLAIN: And were you, Dick?

TUFNELL: By Army standards – no.

CHAPLAIN: What made you pick on him?

TUFNELL: I'd seen him earlier that night. He told my girl to move along. As though she was a tart.

CHAPLAIN (*slowly*): Don't mind me saying this but – wasn't she?

TUFNELL: Before I met her – yes, she was.

CHAPLAIN (*after a pause*): I got a letter from her yesterday.

TUFNELL: Yes. So did I. She told me you had written. Thanks a lot. She's going to come and visit me tonight. And then again next week the night – the night before – –

CHAPLAIN (*interrupting quickly*): That's good. I'm glad.

TUFNELL: And will she see you first?

CHAPLAIN: Or afterwards. I hope so, Dick.

TUFNELL: Please like her, won't you? Please.

CHAPLAIN: I hope that she'll like me. Can I do anything to help? In any way at all?

TUFNELL: You're doing lots. (*With almost pathetic eagerness.*) Will I get off?

CHAPLAIN: Your record's good.

TUFNELL: Is that the only thing?

CHAPLAIN: It's something, Dick.

TUFNELL: I've got a feeling that I will.

CHAPLAIN: Good man, hang on to that.

TUFNELL (*speaking rapidly*): I've been so sorry for the thing I did. I'll tell you something, Padre, I – I prayed last night – for hours. I asked God to forgive me for the awful thing I did – and to be nice to 'him' – and to forgive me for it all. I think He did. I felt so much, much – clearer, afterwards. Oh, Padre, I'm quite sure He did. (*Looks up.*)

Could He have done? Could He have done? Please tell me, could He really have forgiven me?

CHAPLAIN: Of course He could. (*Goes over to shelf of books, talking as he looks for a place in the Bible.*) If you repented – really. Well, that's what He wanted, isn't it? Of course it is. Read that.

TUFNELL (*after reading verses marked by Chaplain's pencil*): That's wonderful!

CHAPLAIN: You see – He doesn't want your death.

TUFNELL: Well then, who does?

CHAPLAIN: Society. The law. No, not the law. The Devil and his angels want a sacrifice of blood to purge them of the crime they made you do. Keep on like this. It's much the best thing you can do.

TUFNELL: Oh, Padre, I don't want to die. There's so much good –

CHAPLAIN: Don't think like that. Not for yourself. Just keep on as you did last night. Well, s'long, Dick.

TUFNELL: Don't go. Oh, please don't go. I feel so happy suddenly. And, if you go, perhaps I won't.

CHAPLAIN (*smiling*): Of course you will. You've done it all – not me.

TUFNELL: Oh, Padre, I'm so full of grand ideas. I'm going to write. I'll write a lot of lovely simple children's books. Of all the lovely clean forgiving things. The flowers and birds and – men and women with straight eyes. Like you.

CHAPLAIN: Not me. That's Rupert Brooke.

TUFNELL: I know. My officer had that. In Sicily – before – we read it on the landing-craft. (*Gets up and paces about.*) If I'm reprieved – and when I've done my fifteen years I'm going to have a little cottage. P'raps in Kent or Sussex. No, they make me think of war. Say Oxfordshire – or Gloucestershire, with all the fields – and trees – and roses on the wall. And Rosie too. Yes, Rosie must be there. We'll sit and write. At least I will. And, in the evening, I'll read what I have written, and she'll tell me if it's good – she'd better say it's good! Then we'll wander through the village to the pub – and have a pint or two – then back and lean against a stile – and kiss and watch the moon. Then home, and up to bed – and then tomorrow – just the same again.

Sits down with rapt expression on his face. Chaplain lays a hand on his shoulder.

CHAPLAIN: Yes, that's all right. But don't forget tomorrow, Dick, the real one. Just the same again – in here – and the next day. You must remember that. But please remember all the other things as well. The writing and – your visits. And keep praying all the time. (*Turns as he nears the door.*) Why don't you write it down? Write something now. You got a note-book?

TUFNELL: Yes. You think I could?

CHAPLAIN: Of course you could. Why, man alive, you never know what you can do until you try. You read it me tomorrow when I come.

TUFNELL: I bet it stinks. (*He picks up pencil.*)

CHAPLAIN (*laughing*): I'll bet it's good. Well, Dick, I must be off. You've stopped me handing out my daily dope to men who want to join the choir because the seats are soft. I'm glad you've joined me without that. S'long.

Goes out. Tufnell sits writing. Jones and Gale return.

JONES: 'Ullo. 'Ullo. Bill Shakespeare? Wot's the play?

TUFNELL: It hasn't started yet.

JONES: Well, let us 'ear it when it's done.

TUFNELL: O.K. I will.

GALE: You see, Jonah. It's all very well to say the Tories is honest and above board, but you don't know they are.

JONES: Well, you don't know they ain't. Yer got my fags? That's it. I thought yer 'ad. Mark you, I didn't know fer certain, 'cos I couldn't 'elp but think the Padre might 'a' snaffled them. They're very absent-minded – some o' them, about them worldly things like fags, yer know.

GALE: Now listen, Jonah. The Tory Party or the Unionists or the National or the Conservative Party – or whatever they call themselves – have always been – –

JONES: Shut up. Shut up. Here, 'ave a smoke. 'E's writin', can't yer see. (*Gale starts to put Jones's cigarettes in his pocket again.*) Nah, give 'em back. Thanks, Mr Gale. Is that wot's known as State Control? Come on, let's 'ave a game. I'll show yer 'oo's on top. I'll show yer, lad. (*He lays out pieces.*)

GALE (*looking at Bible*): Hullo. Defacing prison property?

TUFNELL: The Padre marked that bit.

GALE (*reading*): Here, Jonah, here's a bit for you – 'Turn from your wickedness, and live.'

JONES: Come off it. (*Snatches it away and shuts it up.*) That ain't tub-thumpin'. That's right above yer mark, me lad. 'Ere, come on. White to play.

CURTAIN. END OF SCENE 1

ENTRE-SCENE. THE LANDING

Chief Officer Webb at the desk. The Chaplain passes.

CHIEF: Excuse me, sir.

CHAPLAIN: Good morning, Chief.

CHIEF: Good morning, sir. I think you ought to see this letter, sir.

CHAPLAIN: What's this? (*Takes it.*)

CHIEF: Young Smith, sir.

CHAPLAIN: Yes. His mother, eh? (*He reads the letter through, slowly.*) Poor lad. To lose a mother when one's doing time. What's he like, Chief?

CHIEF: A cockney, sir. A cheeky little blighter. When he says 'Good morning' to me, makes me think he's saying something else.

CHAPLAIN: How will he take it? Did he know she had a heart?

CHIEF: I don't know, sir. But pretty rough, I'd say. Meant quite a lot to him, if you ask me. King's always ragging him about her. Both their mothers' darling. That's the form.

CHAPLAIN: All right. I wish that you could see him for me, Chief.

CHIEF: I know, sir; but better not a screw.

CHAPLAIN: All right. I'll keep it till tonight. He'll find it easier to take it then. All right. I'll send for him at recreation time.

CHIEF: I'll have him waiting for you, sir.

CHAPLAIN: No. Don't do that. I may be late. I might be with young Tufnell. I'll find him in the mess.

CHIEF: All right, sir. Thanks.

He salutes. Exit Chaplain.

SCENE 2. TEN MESS. MIDDAY (AFTER DINNER)

Spencer and Richards washing up. All in but Smith, who is smoking outside.

ANDERSON: Exactly like an Englishman. That's right, 'cos I'm a black. He gives me three and one, 'cos I'm a black. Three – three – and one 'cos I'm a black man. If I'd been white, he would have given me six – six – and two. That's right. He would have given me six – six – and two, if I'd been a Great White Chief. (*Laughs.*) Now come on, Admiral, just one tab-end.

SPENCER: I haven't got one, Anderson. And what's all this stuff about an admiral? If you must talk to me at all please call me – –

ANDERSON: I know. There's lots of things I want to call you. But I'll call you Squadron Leader just the same. A tab-end, Squadron Leader, please. Oh well, I'll have to go some other place. (*Strolls to door.*) Just like an Air Vice Marshal, no tab-ends.

> *Sees Smith outside. Goes out and can be seen making his usual request. The bell rings.*

PADDY: Come on, Spencer, get a move on. You're always late. You must have missed a lot of raids through being late.

> *Richards goes, with one bucket.*

KING'S VOICE: Messmen. Messmen. Ten Mess. Ten Mess.
SMITH (*outside*): Comin', sir. Just comin', sir.
KING'S VOICE: Come on. I bet I know who's late.
SMITH: Don't tell a soul. Let's keep it to ourselves.
KING'S VOICE: Come on.
SMITH: 'Tain't me, sir. Not this time.

> *Spencer runs out with the other bucket.*

BROWN: I'm goin' up to see the Governor this afternoon. Yer know wot for? I'm goin' ter ask 'im for a bloomin' letter ter me second wife. I nearly 'ad it last time, when 'e says – –

MEDWORTH: Please, Brown. We've had all this before. I don't feel up to it. I'm feeling tired.

W.D.H.—E

Brown: All right. All right. But – (*shaking his finger in Medworth's face.*) – You bet yer ruddy boots – I'll 'ave that letter from 'im. If I bust.

Medworth: Let's hope you bust.

Brown: Betcher I gets it – and yer don't get yours.

Medworth: I won't be asking for a letter anyway. I'm seeing him on private business.

Roberts: How much?

Brown: I'll bet yer eightpence. Betcher all me pay.

Roberts: I'll take it, Brownie.

Brown: Yus. O.K.

Paddy: That's betting on a certainty.

Roberts: That's right. Why not? It means another fag or two.

Paddy: It isn't fair.

Roberts: Go on – what is? (*To Medworth.*) It's all right, isn't it?

Medworth: Of course it is.

Roberts: You see, I've got the masters on my side. (*Gets up.*) I'm going up to see if there's a letter for me on the board. I haven't had one from my girl this month. (*He goes to the door.*)

Medworth: I'll come along.

Roberts (*going out*): O.K.

Paddy (*as Medworth is half-way to the door*): Medworth, you put an application in?

Medworth: I have. (*Going out.*)

Paddy: (*sharply*): What for?

Medworth: I want to see the dentist. Satisfied?

Paddy: Sit down and shut the door.

Medworth: I'm going up with Roberts.

Paddy: You're sitting down, me lad, or else I'll put you down. (*To Brown.*) Buzz off. (*Brown goes.*) Now shut the door.

Medworth (*shuts it. Sits down*): Now look here, O'Brien.

Paddy: Isn't Paddy good enough? It's good enough for me.

Medworth: All right, then, Paddy. What's the matter with you?

Paddy: Lots.

Medworth: You haven't spoken to me since last week and now – –

Paddy: You missed it much?

Medworth: I've noticed it.

PADDY: I've noticed quite a lot as well.

MEDWORTH: Such as?

PADDY: That you and I are going to quarrel good and soon.

MEDWORTH: It won't be my fault if we do.

PADDY: Oh no. I'll be to blame. We just don't hit it off together, you and I. I'm just a tough, bone-headed Irishman. You're soft as butter, with your education and your intellectual baloney – and your beard.

MEDWORTH: I'm also almost twice your age.

PADDY: Exactly. Well, behave as if you were.

MEDWORTH: I'm sure I don't know what you mean.

PADDY: You must be thick as well as daft.

MEDWORTH: I've lived too long with schoolboys to be much put out by insults.

PADDY: You're telling me.

MEDWORTH: Exactly what's all this in aid of?

PADDY: I'm just warning you. That's all. I never liked your sort. You make me sick. The sight of you. The soft and smarmy way you talk – just makes me sick. You're like a stoat.

MEDWORTH (*trying to rise*): Must I sit here and listen to you?

PADDY (*pushing him back*): Yes.

MEDWORTH: I'm old enough to be your father. I've had – by and large – a fairly useful life. I've slipped, admittedly. Like every other man who comes in here. I've paid the penalty. I should have thought that was enough.

PADDY: It would be. If you had some self-control.

MEDWORTH: I'm using up a lot of it just now. I'm taking insults, (*his temper is rising*) quite unfounded insults – from an Irish saboteur. That's what you are. An Irish saboteur. And I'm an educated patriotic Englishman.

PADDY: That doesn't count in here.

MEDWORTH: If there were people here who didn't get above themselves – it would.

PADDY: There's nothing counts in here. Except yourself. No educated soft-voiced schoolmasters – no tough-necked members of the I.R.A. – no little Merchant Navy cabin-boys. It's Medworth, Roberts and O'Brien here. On equal terms. Three convicts with a level chance of coming through.

MEDWORTH: I don't see why you have to bring young Roberts into this.

PADDY: Well, take a pull and try and see. And take a warning, pal. Three years ago you wouldn't have required a visit to the dentist, just because you wouldn't have had a sound tooth to speak of in your head – –

> *Paddy turns away to curb his temper. Medworth foolishly pursues the argument.*

MEDWORTH. You've been like this since Richards came.

PADDY (*almost a hiss*): What's that?

MEDWORTH: I said, 'You've been like this since Richards came.'

PADDY: So what?

MEDWORTH: It's rather funny, isn't it?

PADDY: What's funny? Eh?

MEDWORTH: Well – giving cigarettes away and – –

PADDY (*springing towards him as Medworth rises to protect himself*): Shut your mouth. You low down, lousy, spying skunk. Shut up.

MEDWORTH: I'm sorry, Paddy. But I'm very much against such things.

PADDY: You little – –

> *Enter Smith and Richards.*

SMITH: 'Ere, steady, Paddy. Wot's the ruddy game?

PADDY: You shut yer mouth.

SMITH: Now Meddy. Don't start a-gettin' tough. There's quite enough jui-jitzer boys round 'ere – without you joinin' in. (*He has calmed the atmosphere.*) There's not a ruddy screw in 'ere wot 'asn't won the golden belt. They must spend all their ruddy evenin's swinging one another round like cats. (*Sits down.*) Well, I dunno. I 'ad me name up on the letter board an' now they've scratched it off. Old Webbie said they'd give it me tonight.

RICHARDS: P'raps there was something dirty in it.

SMITH: P'raps there was. I'll go and ask old Kingie wot 'e knows. (*Exit.*)

RICHARDS: What's the trouble? Lovers' tiff?

MEDWORTH: I hope I haven't got to waste time arguing with you as well. (*Gets up and goes out.*)

RICHARDS: Oh dear. I'm snubbed. I say, old Beaver's given me the bird. (*He takes out his cigarette-box.*) Oh dear, I haven't even got a draw.

PADDY (*holding out box*): Have one of mine.

RICHARDS: Oh thanks. What's up with you and Meddy?

PADDY: Nothing much.

RICHARDS: Don't bully him. He just can't help himself.

PADDY: He ought to be put down.

RICHARDS: My. Aren't you tough!

PADDY: Yes. Any reason why I shouldn't be?

RICHARDS: No, not that I can see. I like tough men. (*Walks to door.*) Here, Meddy, Meddy. Paddy wants to say he's sorry. Come in here.

Medworth, to Paddy's disgust, comes in.

ROBERTS (*bounding in with a letter*): Whoopee. She's comin', boys. My Kitty's comin' on a visit – Monday next. Coo. Ain't that grand!

MEDWORTH: Yes, marvellous. (*Smiles at him.*) You must be very pleased.

RICHARDS: He wants to say he's sorry, Med. I said you couldn't help it. And he wants to say he's sorry now.

MEDWORTH (*embarrassed, as is Paddy. Roberts watches them*): Oh, well. That's quite all right. (*To Paddy.*) Well. Thanks.

PADDY (*mellow now*): Oh, get away with you – before I pull your beard.

END OF SCENE 2

ENTRE-SCENE. THE LANDING

Officer King is standing at desk. Anderson scrubbing floor, with bucket and scrubber.

ANDERSON: Ah well. Ah well. (*Stretching his back.*)

KING: You crackin' up, old man?

ANDERSON: That's right. I'm cracking up. I'm dying with a smile. I'm dying with a smile. (*Starts scrubbing again.*) Are you on all the morning, Mr King?

King: No, sir.

Anderson: Is Mr Jackson coming on at all?

King: He is. I'm on the old man's applications, lad.

Anderson: Old Arthur never has a break. Old Arthur never has a break. You haven't got a tab-end, Mr King?

King: You haven't got much shyness, 'ave yer, lad?

Anderson: Ask and ye shall receive. Ask and ye shall receive. (*King gives him handful of cigarette-ends out of the depth of his pocket.*) Thanks, Mr King. Keep smilin', Mr King. Don't change at all. Just keep on as you are. Just as you are. (*Continues scrubbing.*) That fellow going to swing?

King: I couldn't say.

Anderson: You don't know if they'll top him, Mr King? You don't know, eh?

King: I wouldn't tell you, Mr Nosey, if I did.

Anderson: I see, you wouldn't tell me 'cos I'm black. The white man's secret, Mr King. The white man's secret. (*He resumes scrubbing.*) Any matches, Mr King? You any matches, Mr King?

King: Shut up. I've got some bloody work to do.

Anderson: Oh, sorry, Mr King. The white man's burden. Sorry, Mr King. (*He goes on scrubbing.*) Will you be on the death watch, Mr King?

King: Not bloody likely, son.

Anderson: Will Mr Jackson, Mr King? Will Mr Jackson go and drink his blood? Will Mr Jackson cook him in a pot?

King: Shut up, yer heathen. Pack it in.

Anderson (*warming to his theory*): That's what they'll say. That's what the Sheriff say. 'Now, Mr Jackson, there's the body. Young and fresh and tender. Have it fried.'

King (*suspicious*): 'Ere. You a cannibal?

Anderson: Not me. No, sir. But Mr Jackson is. Yes, sir. Yes, Mr Jackson, he's a man-eater. Not me. I'm Anderson of the British Empire dyin' with a smile.

King (*work finished; walking over to him, with a friendly smile*): How long yer got?

Anderson: Five years. Just five short years. They go like wind. The days fly by like wind. The nights I just lie dreamin' of my son.

King: Cor love a duck – you 'aven't bred?

ANDERSON: Yes, sir. My wife she died when he was born. Yes, sir, she died. She passed out with a smile. He's in the Indies now. He's with his grannie there. His grannie doesn't know I'm here. She thinks I'm with the British Navy. Sinkin' with a smile.

KING: The Navy never 'as the likes o' you.

ANDERSON: No, sir. The Merchant Navy. (*He rises, stretching.*) Still she doesn't know no better. I was cook along with P. & O. Yes, sir, with P. & O.

KING: And then yer bought a bawdy-'ouse in Liverpool.

ANDERSON: That's right. I bought a house of rest for sailors down on Merseyside.

KING: It serves you right. It damn well serves you right.

ANDERSON: Ah, yes. It serves me right. I shouldn't not have bought it – not in Liverpool. Should have bought it down in London where they doesn't mind a sailors' home. Yes, sir. I would have been a millionaire. Old Arthur would have been a millionaire by now. (*Drops to his knees again and resumes scrubbing. Then, after a pause, he begs again.*) Oh, Mr King, you haven't got a piece of soap?

KING: Yer don't want soap. Yer surely don't want *soap*!

ANDERSON: All right. All right. I only thought you might have had a bit of soap. I didn't want to see you walkin' round with soap you didn't want. That's quite all right. (*Bell.*)

KING (*shouting*): Fall in, Governor's applications. Fall in, Governor's applications.

JACKSON (*enters*): O.K., Kingie.

KING: O.K., Jacko. I'll be off and round them up. (*Goes.*) Fall in, applications.

JACKSON (*watching Anderson*): Don't   scrub the ruddy floor away.

ANDERSON: No, I'll be careful. I'll be careful, yes.

JACKSON: Don't answer back and call me 'sir.'

ANDERSON (*puzzled*): Don't answer back and call me 'sir.' Yes, sir. No, sir. Don't answer back and call me 'sir.' (*Pause.*) Mr Jackson, did you ever hear of Mr Wilberforce?

JACKSON: Just shut your mouth and scrub the floor. (*Going off with application book.*) Scrub it, I said – not stroke it.

ANDERSON (*sadly to himself*): No, Mr Jackson never heard of Wilberforce. He never heard of Mr Wilberforce. No, sir.

Looks up to see Chief smiling at him as he passes and hurriedly resumes scrubbing.

CHIEF: Buzz off.

Anderson exits with bucket.

SCENE 3. THE GOVERNOR'S OFFICE

Governor seated. Chief Officer standing at his side.

GOVERNOR: Well, who've we got? Good Lord, not Brown again?

CHIEF: Yes, sir. There's Brown and Medworth. Both Ten Mess.

GOVERNOR: All right. (*Webb to door.*) I say. If something comes from the Home Office, have it brought right in.

CHIEF: Yes, sir. (*Goes out. Talks to King.*) Medworth. (*Enter Medworth.*) Name and number to the Governor.

MEDWORTH: 3804 Medworth, sir.

GOVERNOR: Yes, Medworth. What can I do for you?

MEDWORTH: I want to see the dentist, sir.

GOVERNOR: What's the trouble?

MEDWORTH: Filling, sir.

GOVERNOR: He comes on Thursdays. Is that right?

CHIEF: Yes, sir.

GOVERNOR: You wait till then?

MEDWORTH: I hope so, sir.

GOVERNOR: You're going out next week.

MEDWORTH: Yes, sir.

GOVERNOR: You couldn't wait till then?

MEDWORTH: No, sir. I'd rather get it done.

GOVERNOR (*smiling*): What, on the cheap? (*Medworth looks hurt.*) Got money here?

MEDWORTH: A bit, sir.

CHIEF: Half a crown – extraction. Five bob – stopping, sir.

GOVERNOR: You cover that?

MEDWORTH: I hope so, sir. I'm not quite sure how much I've got. Sir, could I have a special letter to get some in? I'll need some anyway for going out.

GOVERNOR: Yes. Yes, of course. Who to?

MEDWORTH: The manager of Barclay's Bank in Leicester, sir.

GOVERNOR: Won't that need a cheque? Why don't you write a friend to slip you in a pound or two?

MEDWORTH: I have no – well – I'd rather write the bank.

GOVERNOR: I see. The dentist and a special letter. (*Writes it in book.*) Good.

CHIEF: Get out.

> *Medworth half-turns towards the door, then faces the Governor again.*

MEDWORTH: Excuse me, sir. There's something else.

GOVERNOR: Well, carry on.

MEDWORTH: A man called Richards, sir – in Number Ten.

GOVERNOR: Yes. What of him?

MEDWORTH: Well, sir. It's difficult to say.

GOVERNOR: Well, Medworth, I'm not pressing you at all.

MEDWORTH: I know, sir. But I think I ought to speak.

CHIEF: Well, get a move on. Get a move on, man.

MEDWORTH: Well, sir, I've – tried very hard to start again since I've been here. You know that, sir. I've done my best. I want to – forget the past. I want to start afresh. And help others to – as well.

GOVERNOR: Yes. Yes.

MEDWORTH: Well, Richards has an evil influence.

GOVERNOR: On you?

MEDWORTH: No, sir. No, not on me.

GOVERNOR: On whom?

MEDWORTH: I'd rather not say, sir.

GOVERNOR: Now look here, Medworth. Try and see this from my point of view. You come in here and squeal about a fellow-prisoner. Without the trimmings, that's it, isn't it? I don't approve of squealers – never did. Still, in this unpleasant job one has to take one's tips without too nice a conscience. Understand? Now, if you've got to squeal, let's have it straight. I can't take action till I have it straight. If not, get out.

MEDWORTH: May I suggest you ask the leader of the mess?

GOVERNOR: Who is it, Webb?

CHIEF: O'Brien, sir.

GOVERNOR: An Irishman, my Lord. You jib yourself and then – refer me to an Irishman – and you an educated man.

MEDWORTH: That's all I can do, sir.

GOVERNOR: All right. Now, take my tip, and keep your mouth shut. If you want to keep that tooth. (*Exit Medworth.*) Send for Richards and O'Brien, Webb.

CHIEF: Sir. (*Goes to door and talks to King. Off, shouting.*) O'Brien. Richards. (*Chief returns.*)

GOVERNOR: Well, Webb? (*The Chief shrugs his shoulders. Clearly he has little time for Medworth and his type.*) Has Richards any friends?

CHIEF: O'Brien's always exercising with him, sir.

GOVERNOR: O'Brien, eh? (*Pause.*) Anybody there?

CHIEF: There's Brown, sir.

GOVERNOR: Brown can wait. No, come on, Webb. Don't weaken. We're not afraid of Mr Brown. Show the blighter in.

CHIEF (*at door*): O'Brien's here now, sir. Come on in, lad. (*Enter Paddy.*) O'Brien, sir.

GOVERNOR: O'Brien, I want some advice.

PADDY: I'm glad to give it, sir, I'm sure.

GOVERNOR: That's friendly, thanks. This fellow Richards in your mess?

PADDY: Yes, sir – he is.

GOVERNOR: You know him?

PADDY: Sir.

GOVERNOR: A friend of yours?

PADDY: Well, yes, sir. In a way.

GOVERNOR: What sort of way?

PADDY: He's just a friend.

GOVERNOR: I see. I've always looked on you as one of those who – walked alone. I didn't think you liked your English colleagues very much.

PADDY: Maybe that's true.

GOVERNOR: But now – you've taken to yourself a friend.

PADDY: Yes, sir.

GOVERNOR: Why so?

PADDY: Perhaps it's dragging, sir.

GOVERNOR: I'm sure it's dragging for you, lad. It even drags for me sometimes. But when I choose a friend, I choose a good one. Not a rotten little – –

PADDY (*interrupting*): Perhaps you have a wider choice.

GOVERNOR: I'll grant you that.

PADDY: He's not so bad. He's quite a decent chap.

GOVERNOR: You know his case?

PADDY: He's told me quite a bit. I guessed the rest.

GOVERNOR: And still you want to be his friend?

PADDY: Well, sir, I think it takes all sorts to make a world.

GOVERNOR: Perhaps it does, but why encourage him?

PADDY: I think he's lonely, sir.

GOVERNOR: O'Brien, don't be soft. Forget for once that you're a sentimental Irishman.

PADDY: No, sir, I can't do that. I can't forget I'm Irish, sir.

GOVERNOR: Perhaps I've asked too much. But, please, cut out this lad. (*Paddy is looking obstinate.*) Now look, O'Brien. I put you in charge of this mess because I thought that you deserved a break. You've taken what you got with guts and courage and a sense of humour. You've got character and a strength of mind – –

PADDY (*interrupting again*): Excuse me, sir – why worry then?

GOVERNOR: Because prison's not a normal place to be. (*Paddy laughs.*) Why do you laugh?

PADDY: I've heard that said before – a lot of times. But not by you. It sounded funny, sir.

GOVERNOR: Perhaps, but still it's true.

PADDY (*with great feeling*): It's true all right.

GOVERNOR: Well, give him up.

PADDY: No, sir. I won't. I like the kid.

GOVERNOR: You must.

PADDY: No, sir. I won't.

GOVERNOR (*after a momentary pause, during which he contemplates the line he means to take*): You bloody Irishman. (*Smiles.*) Get out.

PADDY (*smiling back*): Good morning, sir.

Goes out. Richards enters.

CHIEF: Richards, sir.

GOVERNOR: I've been thinking quite a lot about you lately, Richards.

RICHARDS: Have you, sir?

GOVERNOR: I don't think that you quite – fit in. The work's too rough. The men are not your type. I think you need a change.

RICHARDS: I'm very happy, sir.

GOVERNOR: I don't agree. I'm going to send you to a local prison. You'll have lots of leisure there and – lots of time to read – and make yourself a better chap. (*Richards has tears in his eyes.*) You've done well here. I'm sure you've tried. But everybody doesn't fit in here. You'll go tomorrow morning. (*Stands up and holds out his hand.*) So I'll say 'Good-bye', and wish you luck. (*Richards bursts into tears.*) Get him out, Webb.

CHIEF: Come on. Come on. You big cry-baby. I've a little boy at home who'd sooner die than let me see him cry. Come on. Come on. (*Takes him out. Shouts.*) Brown.

> *Mr King comes in with sealed letter and salutes. The Chief takes it from him, hands it to the Governor, with a whispered 'For you, sir,' then returns to the door and shouts 'Brown' again. Brown comes in.*

CHIEF: Name and number to the Governor.

BROWN: 3762 Brown, sir.

GOVERNOR (*who is just slitting the envelope*): Yes, Brown?

BROWN: I've a request to make, sir.

GOVERNOR (*starting to read*): Yes.

BROWN: Please, sir. I'd like to 'ave a letter to me second wife.

GOVERNOR (*looking up, with unseeing eyes and mind far away*): Yes.

CHIEF: Get out. (*Brown goes out, amazed.*)

GOVERNOR (*pushing letter across the desk to Chief*): That wretched little beggar's got to swing.

END OF SCENE 3

ENTRE-SCENE. THE LANDING

King and Jackson at the desk.

JACKSON: You got that Richards's kit-card, Kingie?

KING: Yep. (*Passes it over.*) Looks like the old man's got a down on 'im.

JACKSON: Here, what's the time?

KING: 'Bout arf-past two.

JACKSON: I got a tip last night. The three o'clock.

KING: Wot sort o' tip?

JACKSON: From One *Who* Knows. C Wing. A bookie guy.

KING: 'Oo gives yer tips? I thought they loathed yer guts.

JACKSON: I have my contacts, boy, Herodotus. They pulled it down at Newmarket last week.

KING: 'Oo did?

JACKSON: The jockey had too kind a heart. He wouldn't use his spurs.

KING: O.K. A tanner on fer me.

JACKSON: O.K.

KING: Young Tufnell's goin' ter swing.

JACKSON: Well, what'd you think? You can't go liquidating policemen, lad.

KING: You helping on the job?

JACKSON: I am.

KING: Well, you can have it, chum.

JACKSON: Go on, boy. If they did you up, you'd like to see them topped.

KING: I don't suppose I'd mind – a-sittin' up in them there clouds – a-doin' football pools be'ind me 'arp.

JACKSON (*shouting*): Richards. Come down here.

KING: I never seen no good in 'angin'. Never 'ave an' never will.

JACKSON: It's worth a quid or two to me. I take the kids to Richmond Park and have a bit of boating with the wife. And then what's left – I shove it on a horse. That's why I'm doing this Herodotus. It's sort of ante-post. (*Enter Richards.*)

RICHARDS: Did you want me, sir?

JACKSON: Me want you, lad? I don't suppose yer mother even wanted you. Sign there. Here, read it first. All there?

RICHARDS: Is that all, sir?

JACKSON: You're going out tomorrow morning. Eight o'clock. Be on the centre – seven-forty-five – with all your kit.

RICHARDS: Where am I going to, sir, please?

JACKSON: You'll know that when you get there, lad.

RICHARDS: Which officer is taking me, sir, please?

JACKSON: Your grannie's coming down from heaven on a broom-stick – made for two. Is that O.K.?

RICHARDS (*cowed*): Yes, sir.

JACKSON: Well, hop it then.

As Richards turns to go, King stops him.

KING: Oh, Richards, I'll say 'Good-bye.' I won't be on tomorrow. Well. So long. (*Shakes hands.*)

RICHARDS: Good-bye, sir.

KING: Keep your chin up. Don't be bullied. Tell 'em all to go to hell.

Pats him on the shoulder and sends him off.

JACKSON (*who had been watching this interlude, with a sardonic smile*): You ought to chuck this job and be a nursemaid.

KING: I never 'ad no children, Jacko boy.

JACKSON: You never had no bloody common sense. (*Clock strikes three-quarters.*) Here, where's that tanner? (*Takes it.*) See you later, boy.

SCENE 4. THE CONDEMNED CELL. EVENING

Jones sits reading the paper. Tufnell is talking to his visitor, whose shadow can be seen through the visitor's grille.

TUFNELL (*voice off*): Well, so long. I'll be seeing you. Here's hoping. Cheerio. See you next week. So long.

Comes in cheerfully, followed by Gale, as the door through which she came is locked.

JONES: Well, lad, how's tricks?

TUFNELL: O.K. How grand she is.

JONES: Cor blime, look at that. Herodotus, 100 to 6. (*He turns over the pages of the evening paper.*) Hullo, that fellow Robinson 'as got a 'lifer' – serve 'im right.

TUFNELL: What did he do?

JONES: 'E run a fellar down when 'e was takin' off the doings in a car.

GALE: The chap who stole the furs from that big store?

JONES: That's 'im. The dirty bastard. Never tried to stop. Still, 'e'll 'ave time ter wish 'e'd pressed the brake.

TUFNELL: Yes. All his life.

GALE: Not him. Just fifteen years. Or maybe ten – if he behaves himself.

TUFNELL: I hope if I'm reprieved – I don't get more than ten.

JONES (*putting down paper and walking across*): Well, 'ow's the book?

TUFNELL: All right.

GALE: What is it? (*Looking over it.*) Poetry?

TUFNELL: Sort of.

GALE: Let's hear it, lad. I used to read a bit of poetry at school.

TUFNELL: You did?

GALE: Some sloppy tripe about a garden and a girl, and some daft coot who hung around the place at night.

TUFNELL: What? Tennyson?

GALE: It wasn't bad. I'll say it wasn't bad. You know. You want to be right in the mood. (*To Jones.*) You know, you can't just read those big-pots anywhere. It's no use reading Shakespeare and those boys inside the Tube. You want to read them in the country somewhere – sittin' on a stile. Or with a girl. That right?

TUFNELL: I think so, too.

JONES: Well, there's only one bit o' poetry – as yer might say – that I ever learnt. I learnt it 'cos old Bob – yer know, the Captain wot got 'is – 'e made me, like.

TUFNELL: What was it, Mr Jones?

JONES: Lor' love us, lad. You've got me there. I can't remember it. Let's see. It's comin' back. Let's see.

> I strove with none 'cos none was worth me strife
> Nature I loved, and – next ter nature – Art.
> I warmed both 'ands beside the fire o' life.
> (*Finishing quickly and triumphantly.*)
> It sinks an' I'm a-ready to depart.

Not bad, old-timer, after thirty years. And that's all the poetry I knows.

GALE: Thank God for that.

TUFNELL: Please, will you write it down for me?

JONES: Why, did you like it?

TUFNELL: Yes. It's fine.

JONES: I allus liked it too. But Gawd knows what it means! Still, poetry, yer know.

TUFNELL: Please. (*Pushing note-book over.*)

GALE: Let's hear yours first. Don't write it, Jonah, till he gives us his.

TUFNELL (*smiling shyly*): All right. (*Reads it slowly.*)
When I shall take you in my arms tomorrow
And brush away your tears and hold you fast
Your love will kill the wickedness and sorrow,
    And drive away the past.
And down the moonlit country lanes we'll wander,
Watched by the rabbits peeping from their holes,
And – darling – you and I will never squander
    The beauty in our souls.

JONES: That's not poetry. I can understand that.

GALE: I'm no great shakes at verses. Still, I liked it, lad.

TUFNELL: I felt like that – that's all. I know it isn't very good.

JONES: Yer'll have ter change that bit about the bunnies. Rabbits don't come out at night.

GALE: Who said? They do. They ruddy do. You drive along a lane at night and see them in the headlights. Thousands of them. Course they do.

JONES: O.K. Well, p'raps it's 'ares I mean. Still, keep on trying, lad. Yer've got it in yer.

TUFNELL: Yes, I will. I'm full of things to – –

Enter Governor and Chief. Both Warders stand and salute, as always.

GOVERNOR: Tufnell, I have been instructed by the Home Secretary to inform you that in view of the fact that your petition has failed, the law must take its normal course, and that the execution will be carried out on Tuesday, the 21st (*Tufnell leans forward against the table, silent.*) I am very sorry.

The Governor and the Chief go out. Tufnell sinks down at the table, head in hands. Gale moves towards him with his cigarette-case.

JONES: For Gawd's sake let 'im be.

Gale takes a cigarette himself. The Chaplain, hatless, enters. Gale and Jones go out.

CHAPLAIN: Dick. (*No answer.*) Dick. (*He moves his head.*) Just think of all the boys who fell beside you in the war. You must be brave. What would they say? You mustn't let them laugh at you. You want to look them in the face and say, 'Well, I could take it, too.' (*Long pause.*) You won't be lonely – after – this. With all your friends you thought that you had lost. They'll all be waiting for you – over there. The same as ever – all their little jokes. Your parents, too. With all their love you've missed so much.

TUFNELL (*dazed, dead voice*): You said He had forgiven me. You said He didn't want my death.

CHAPLAIN: I know. I know. He *has* forgiven you. He's watching now. He wants you to be brave – like Him. (*Tufnell stares in front of him.*) I've brought you this. Here's *Alice* that I talked to you about. (*He lays it on the table.*) I couldn't get a copy – but I've got one now. My mother lent it to me – and it's very precious. She was glad to – when she knew it was for you.

Tufnell looks at him with wild hopeless eyes, then loses all control.

TUFNELL: You take your bloody books away. (*He snatches it from the table and throws it at the Chaplain.*) It's you – you hypocrite. It's you – you lied! You lied! You know you lied. You crawling priests. Your stinking wars! (*He advances on him.*) You've no more right to wear that collar than the Devil has. You've less. You've less. You've bloody less. Because you lied! (*Screaming.*) You lied! You lied!

Gale and Jones rush in as Tufnell seizes the Chaplain by the coat.

GALE: Shut up. You shut your mouth.

JONES: You'd better go, sir.

TUFNELL: You lying hypocrite!

CHAPLAIN: Yes, I'll come back later when he's quietened down. (*Exit.*)

TUFNELL (*shouting after him, hysterical*): If you come back, I'll slit

W.D.H.—F

your throat. You hypocrite. You preaching, canting liar. Hypocrite. (*They are holding his arms.*) Let go. Let go. Let bloody go.

> *Tufnell wrenches away from Gale and hits Jones on the jaw. Gale returns to the assault and floors him. As he falls Tufnell hits his head on the bed.*

JONES (*holding his jaw*): You didn't 'ave ter do that, boy.

GALE: 'E'd 'ave murdered you if I 'adn't. Here, put him on the bed. (*They lay him there. He is unconscious.*) Face all right?

JONES (*holding his jaw*): Yes, it's all right. Call the 'ospital. Some stitches for 'is 'ead. (*Gale rings alarm-bell. Jones picks up the chair and sits down, writing the poem into Tufnell's note-book, while Gale bandages Tufnell's head.*)

                                                    – worth me strife
(*Turns to Gale.*) 'Ow do yer spell 'Nature'?

> *Gale does not reply.*

END OF SCENE 4

ENTRE-SCENE. THE LANDING

JACKSON: Come on now. Get inside. The bell's not gone yet. Get inside. Four-twenty-four. Come on. I'm telling you. I don't just shout for fun. I'm not a crooner. Get inside. (*Enter Anderson.*)

ANDERSON: Excuse me, sir.

JACKSON: Who told you to come down?

ANDERSON: I want to see the doctor, sir.

JACKSON: Well, go sick in the morning. I'm no bloomin' specialist.

ANDERSON: Please, sir, I want to see the doctor now.

JACKSON: You can't. Unless it's urgent. What's the matter, strained yourself?

ANDERSON: My hand, please, sir. A pain inside my hand. Whenever I hold something tight, it hurts my hand.

JACKSON: Oh, yes.

ANDERSON: Yes, sir. It hurts me something terrible.

JACKSON: What, scrubbers' cramp?

ANDERSON: It may be, sir. It may be, yes.

JACKSON: All right. I'll put you sick. (*Casually.*) A pity, you were going on the Gardening Party in the morning. Outside work. Still, if you've a pain, I'll put you sick.

ANDERSON: Oh, that's all right. You've healed it, Mr. Jackson. It feels better now.

JACKSON: And if you try that on again with me, I'll run you in.

ANDERSON: I'm sorry, sir. Faith-healing, sir. I'm sorry, sir. (*Bell rings.*)

JACKSON (*shouting*): Stand to your doors. A Wing. Stand to your doors. (*To Anderson.*) And, incidentally, I've heard of Mr Wilberforce. I went to school.

ANDERSON: You did, sir. Oh, you did. Well, Mr Wilberforce was grand.

JACKSON: You ask me, Mr Wilberforce was nuts. (*Shouting.*) A Wing, one pace forward, march. Right turn. Lead on.

SCENE 5. TEN MESS

BROWN: Just as I'm goin' in, old Webbie brings 'im in a letter. Then I puts the query to 'im good an' strong.

SMITH: What query, Brownie?

BROWN: I says to 'im, 'I 'ave a request ter make, sir.' Judgin' me time like. 'E says, 'Wot's that, Brownie?' I says – quick as lightnin' – 'I wish to 'ave a letter to me second wife.'

SMITH: Cor. What a teaser. It ain't fair ter take a feller by surprise like that!

BROWN: An' then 'e reads the letter, like. I tip-ters forward, cautious-like an' reads it upside-down.

SPENCER (*scornfully and disbelieving*): How could you read it upside-down?

SMITH: The same way as yer flies yer blinkin' Fortress upside-down. Sheer force of 'abit, like. Wot did it say?

BROWN: 'Dear Governor, I understand – from houtside hinformation – that a prisoner called Brown requires a letter to 'is second wife.'

SMITH: Go on, yer killin' me.

BROWN: 'I writes ter say if yer don't give the man the letter double-quick, yer'll maybe 'ave ter look around an' find yerself another job.' That's straight.

SMITH: An' so's a bloomin' corkscrew. 'Ere, 'oo signed it, boy?

BROWN: Couldn't see. I just sees 'Yours' an' then a scrawl an' then ' 'Ome Secretary' like.

SMITH: No kisses, Brownie?

BROWN: Not as I could see. Then 'e looks up – as though 'e were afraid o' me. 'All right,' 'e says, 'that's granted, Brown,' 'e says. Yer could've knocked me down with 'arf a pint.

Anderson enters.

SPENCER: And did you get the letter? No, of course, you didn't.

BROWN: Didn't I! I told yer. Didn't I – an' all! (*Waves it at him.*) So what, me old sky-pilot? (*To Roberts.*) Come on. Eightpence, boy.

ROBERTS: I've only seven, I'm afraid.

SMITH: 'Ere you are. I've 'ad me bits o' fun.

ROBERTS: Till pay-day?

SMITH: That's O.K. I'll get it off me mum when I goes out.

BROWN: O.K. (*Counts it and puts it carefully away.*) That's all right. Now listen 'ere. (*Reads letter.*) 'My lovely one, I'm comin' out next Tuesday and I wants ter see yer prompt. I'll be at Nottin' 'Ill Gate station, ten, on Tuesday, sharp. So don't be late – or else I'll swipe yer, Jim.'

SMITH: That's nice. That's very nice. That girl's a lucky girl ter get a 'billy-doo' like that.

BROWN: It's orlright, ain't it? Tells 'er 'ow things go.

SMITH: It's lovely, Brownie. Don't yer change a word. It's somethin' like me mother writes ter me.

BROWN: I'll 'op upstairs an' put it in the box.

SMITH: That's right. Don't keep it till the mornin'. Or you might not feel so sentimental. (*Exit Brown.*)

ANDERSON: You got a tab-end, Smithy? Have you got a tab-end, please?

SMITH: Sorry, Arthur. 'Ad the lot.

ANDERSON: That's quite all right. That's quite all right.

RICHARDS: I've got one. It's a farewell gift. I'm leaving in the morning.

SMITH: 'Oo said so?

RICHARDS: The Governor.

SMITH: I'll 'ave ter see me dad.

SPENCER: Why? Did he say?

RICHARDS: Perhaps he thinks it's bad for Squadron Leaders to associate with me.

ROBERTS: Does Paddy know?

RICHARDS (*nervously*): No. Paddy's at the lecture, isn't he?

SMITH: Come on, let's 'ave a game. I'm sorry, Polly. When yer came I thought yer stank. But now I think yer quite a decent kid.

RICHARDS: Oh, thanks.

SMITH (*pushing Spencer as he sets board out*): 'Ere, Wing Commander, move yerself. I'm comin' in ter land.

ANDERSON: I'll be on the Garden Party in the morning. 'Stead of scrubbing, I'll be tending English roses. Lovely English roses. Roses with an English smile.

Re-enter Brown.

MEDWORTH: Well, sent it off?

BROWN: I've posted it.

MEDWORTH: Your wife won't like this much.

BROWN: Blime, 'er? I've got 'er there, me lad. I've got 'er there. When I'm around it's mum's the (*makes gesture.*) word – or else.

MEDWORTH: And will you be – around?

BROWN: Ruddy wives – they ain't no good.

SMITH (*looking up from his game*): You tell that to me mum. She'd split yer blinkin' ear-ole.

BROWN: Well, they ain't. I've 'ad a bit – an' all. She's come ter see me every ruddy month since I've bin 'ere. Ho yus, she thinks 'er Brownie's goin' back.

SMITH: 'Ere come orf that, yer come orf that! There's a fellar over there not a 'undred yards away. 'E won't 'ave no more chance next week of comin' back ter nobody. Yer thank yer bloomin' stars it isn't you.

BROWN: You've never seen my missus, 'ave yer, kid?

SMITH: Can't say I 'ave. But she's a plucked-un. 'Owd I know? 'Cos I seen you.

BROWN: All right. All right. Yer mother's baby boy?

Brown ruffles his hair, and Smith springs up and takes out his razor-blade, then quietens down.

SMITH: Yer frightened of 'er – that's yer trouble, boy. 'Ere, listen, son, go back, take off yer 'at an' wave yer oily curls an' force a tear – – you 'ave a drop o' gin before yer goes – an' say, 'Me darling, save me from meself.' It works, me old cock-sparrer, every time. (*Paddy comes in. Smith finishes the game.*) You've lost, me lad. Yer've lost yer final game.

Paddy looks round but does not register his remark.

RICHARDS: Well, thanks a lot.
MEDWORTH (*to Roberts*). You like a game?
ROBERTS: O.K.

Medworth and Roberts take the places at the draughts-table.

SMITH (*to Richards*): And no more cigarettes from Paddy boy.
RICHARDS: I know. I want to cry.
PADDY: What's that?

Medworth is setting out the board.

SMITH: 'E's goin' to a local. Aint' yer 'eard?
PADDY: Who said so?
RICHARDS: Just the Governor – that's all. He thinks I don't quite fit.
PADDY: Where to?
RICHARDS: I dunno. Jacko wouldn't tell me that.

Paddy kicks the board, which Medworth had just set out, off the table with his foot.

MEDWORTH: Here, what's the game?
PADDY: It isn't draughts. (*Ugly Silence.*) You saw the Governor this morning, didn't you?
MEDWORTH: I did – about my teeth.
PADDY: What else?
MEDWORTH: Some personal affairs.
PADDY: What sort?
MEDWORTH: Quite private – if you want to know.

PADDY: I do.

MEDWORTH (*turning away*): Well, I should ask the Governor.

PADDY: I'm asking you.

MEDWORTH: Well, I'm not telling you.

PADDY (*seizing him by the shoulder*): You damn well are.

MEDWORTH: Please don't forget my age.

He takes off spectacles and hands them to Roberts.

PADDY: Don't mind your age. You've lived too long. You told the Governor some dirty stuff about this lad.

MEDWORTH: Which lad?

PADDY: Richards – or me.

MEDWORTH: You seem concerned about it, anyway.

PADDY: Admit it, do you, eh?

MEDWORTH (*frightened*): All right. I did my best to put things right.

PADDY: You double-crossing bastard. Squealing skunk.

Hits him hard across the face.

SMITH (*standing up*): He's an old man, Paddy. Let 'im be. (*Paddy hits him again. Medworth falls to the floor.*) 'Ere, let 'im be. 'E's old.

PADDY: Keep out of this. (*Kicks Medworth on the floor.*)

SMITH: I won't. You let 'im be.

He draws the razor-blade from his tie. Paddy turns from Medworth, hits at Smith, cuts his wrist, whips it to his lips.

PADDY: You little rattle-snake.

SMITH (*standing his ground*): You let 'im be.

JACKSON (*off*): Smith.

PADDY (*turning away*): O.K. He's had enough. Here, you two. (*Points at Anderson and Spencer.*) Take him up and dump him in his cell. (*They go over to him.*) And watch the screw.

Jackson comes in. Smith and others stand between him and Medworth so that he cannot see him.

JACKSON (*to Smith*): Smith, think I'm going to bust me throat shouting for you? The Chaplain wants you. On the Ones. And make less noise, in here. You understand?

SMITH: The Chaplain? Cor! What for?

PADDY: Yes, sir.

JACKSON: Come on, lad. He's up there waiting for you now. You deaf?

SMITH (*deliberately*): Me mother boxed me ears too much when I was small. That's 'er. (*He points at a magazine cut-out of a sparsely dressed film-star. Jackson looks round, and Brown replaces Smith in front of the prostrate Medworth.*) O.K. (*Smith departs.*)

JACKSON: And cut the talking down a bit.

PADDY: Yes, sir. (*Jackson goes.*) Dump him in his cell, when Jacko's clear.

SPENCER: He's coming to.

ROBERTS: Is that the way they train you in the I.R.A.?

SPENCER: You're all right, Meddy. You're quite all right.

ROBERTS: Is that the way the Irish fight? Against old men with boots?

PADDY (*recovered now*): Hullo. Hullo. Another turkey-cock.

ROBERTS: You've been in here too long.

PADDY: You're telling me.

ROBERTS: There's nothing wrong with him. He's old – that's all.

PADDY: There's nothing wrong with Richards – 'cept he's young.

ANDERSON: Come on. Come on. (*Medworth is getting up.*) He's bleeding with a smile. Yes, sir. He's bleeding with a smile.

MEDWORTH (*nose bleeding*): Oh, thanks. I'm quite all right.

He sits down, handkerchief to nose. Roberts hands him his spectacles. There is silence.

ANDERSON: I'm going to cry. Yes, sir, I'm going to cry. (*Pause.*) Will someone sing a song? Will someone sing? The British always sing before they cry.

Smith comes in slowly, carrying an open letter.

RICHARDS: Please, Paddy. My last night. Hullo! What's the matter with Smithy?

All look round at him, and he tries to force a brave smile.

SMITH: Me Aunt Jemima's died and left me all 'er debts.

He sits down.

PADDY (*to Roberts*): You mind? I don't sing with my boots. (*Roberts shrugs and turns away.*)

> *Sings.*

'Many years have rolled over since the Irish rebellion
When Britannia came with her guns roaring loud,
And the bold I.R.A. men stood shoulder to shoulder
And the blood from their bodies ran down Sackville Street.'

> *During the ensuing verse, Anderson goes over to Smith and offers him a tab-end from his cigarette-box. Smith is too shattered to accept the offering, so Anderson removes a tab-end from the box, and places it with infinite gentleness on the table at which Smith is sitting, with his letter crumpled in his hand.*

'The Four Courts of Dublin the English bombarded,
The spirit of freedom they came for to quell,
When from out those grim buildings – a voice – "no surrender."
'Twas the voice of Jim Connelly, the Irish reb-el.

'Outside Mountjoy Prison, the great crowd assembled,
Their heads were uncovered, they knelt in the rain.
While inside that grim building, a young Irish hero,
Gave his life for the country he loved so well.

'The black flag was hoisted, the cruel deed was over,
The English departed – amidst all the rain.
There was hardly a dry eye in Dublin that morning,
When they murdered Jim Connelly, the Irish reb-el.'

> *On the word 'murdered' Jackson comes in.*

JACKSON: Break it up. I've warned you once. (*Paddy finishes the song triumphantly, with all his hatred of the English in his voice. The bell rings.*) Get upstairs. Get along. (*As Paddy passes him.*) O'Brien, watch your step.

PADDY: Yes, sir.

> *All have gone save Anderson, still watching the unhappy Smith.*

JACKSON (*to Anderson*): Get along. (*He still lingers.*) Go on. (*Smith rises. Jackson turns on him.*) Sit down! (*Smith sits again.*

Anderson goes, followed to the door by Jackson. Shouting upwards.) Get in. I'll have you if you're out there a second more. Get in. (*Door slams. He returns to Smith.*) O.K. O.K., boy. Cut along. The coast's clear now. (*Smith gets up and makes for the door.*) Come 'ere. (*Smith stops and comes back. Jackson hands him a packet of cigarettes. Smith goes in tears.*) You on the Threes. You get inside yer bleedin' cell and shut yer door. Get in, I said. Get in.

CURTAIN. END OF ACT II

ACT THREE

SCENE 1. TEN MESS. VISITORS' HOUR.
AFTERNOON

Mr Jackson sits at one end of the table, swinging his keys on their chain.

KING (*coming in, escorting Kitty, young and pretty. Jackson doesn't get up*): Will yer sit 'ere, missie? Make yerself at 'ome. 'E won't be long. I'll fetch 'im right away. (*Goes out.*)

KITTY: Thank you. (*Long pause.*) Isn't it a lovely day?

JACKSON: I've not been out. All days is much the same in here.

KITTY: Yes, I suppose they are. (*Long pause.*) Do you know Jock?

JACKSON: There's lots of Jocks in here. They come and go.

KITTY: Jock – Roberts.

JACKSON: Sometimes there's a brood of Robertses too. I know him, yes.

KITTY: Is he – all right?

JACKSON: Well, if he was all right he wouldn't be in here. Well, would he now?

KITTY (*she does not like Jackson*): I don't know, I'm a-sure. I mean, is he – well – cheerful? Does he mope a lot?

JACKSON: Lor' love us, lass. I'm not a bloomin' nurse.

KITTY: I'm sorry. I suppose I – well, I suppose I mustn't ask you things like that.

JACKSON: Oh, ask away. It's not the questions that are rationed – it's the answers. See my meaning? (*He points at the Prison Notices on the wall.*) Roberts is all right.

KITTY: Oh, thanks.

JACKSON (*warming*): He's not a bad young kid at all. Are you his girl?

KITTY: Well, I – –

Pauses in confusion. Roberts, looking radiant for the first time since we met him, is shown in by King, who goes again.

ROBERTS: Kitty, darling. This is swell. My darling Kit.

He starts towards other side of table. Jackson pulls him back.

JACKSON: Here, none of that. Embraces at the end.

ROBERTS (*the prisoner again*): Oh, sorry, sir. (*He sits opposite her.*) Oh, Kit, it's grand to see you.

KITTY: Is it, Jock? How are you, Jock?

ROBERTS: I'm tops. At least, I am – since seeing you. How's everybody?

KITTY: Everybody's fine.

ROBERTS: That's grand. Your Mum and Dad?

KITTY: Yes, they're well.

ROBERTS: They send me any messages?

KITTY (*after a pause*): I think so, Jock. I – I forget the things that people say.

ROBERTS: I know. Don't worry, love. Just give 'em mine.

KITTY: Yes, Jock. I will.

ROBERTS: Still working up the road? Still same old job?

KITTY: Yes. Still the same.

ROBERTS: You had a rise?

KITTY: No, Jock – not yet.

ROBERTS: Still showing off the evening gowns?

KITTY: No, I'm the 'sports' department, now.

ROBERTS: You must look swell. What sort of things?

KITTY: Oh – riding-clothes. And ski-ing-pants – and swimming-suits.

ROBERTS: Oh, gee, I envy those old trouts. I bet they bring their boy-friends with them, eh? (*Kitty giggles shyly.*) I bet they do! And I'm not blaming them. Is this your afternoon?

KITTY: It's Monday, no. Mine's Saturday.

ROBERTS: I thought it was.

KITTY: I asked for this instead of Saturday.

ROBERTS: You've not lost Saturday for me, I hope.

KITTY: Well, no. I've got a holiday.

ROBERTS: Oh, boy. You've got a week?

KITTY: I've got a fortnight, Jock.

ROBERTS: I say! The old firm's done you proud. Come up and see me often, will you, Kit? I've got some visits up my sleeve – –

KITTY: I won't be here. I'm going to the sea.

ROBERTS: The sea? Who with? I know – a gang of screaming mannekins. Be careful, Kit. Don't let them lead you wrong.

KITTY: That's silly, Jock. (*To Jackson.*) Excuse me, do you sit here all the time?

JACKSON: I do. I'm sorry if I'm in the way.

KITTY: No, you can't help it. It – it's not your fault.

JACKSON: That's right. It's only orders, lass.

KITTY: I know. I should have known.

ROBERTS: Feels funny, eh? A bit shy-making, ducks?

KITTY: It is a bit.

ROBERTS: The next time you'll be used to it. You haven't changed a bit. You look as swell as ever.

KITTY: Thank you, Jock. That's very sweet.

ROBERTS: I changed at all?

KITTY: I think I see a grey hair – don't I? – there!

ROBERTS: You pick them up in here.

KITTY: Poor Jock.

ROBERTS: I bought it, love. I'll see it through. I like your hat. The firm's?

KITTY: No, it's a present.

ROBERTS (*kidding*): Eh? Who from?

KITTY: Oh, just a friend. (*Casually.*) Tom gave it me.

ROBERTS: Who's Tom?

KITTY: You know. Tom Jewkes – the boy who works next door.

ROBERTS: Next door? He's out in Haifa, isn't he?

KITTY: He was. He's back. He got back just a month ago.

ROBERTS: Oh, hell, I'd like to see old Tom again. Remember how he used to shin up lamp-posts and turn somersaults. Remember?

KITTY: Yes. He doesn't do that any more. He's only got one arm.

ROBERTS: I say, that's bad.

KITTY: I'll tell him, Jock.

ROBERTS: Yes, tell him. Tom still keen on you?

KITTY: Oh, what a question, Jock!

ROBERTS (*smiling*): Of course he is – that blooming hat. Here, tell old Tom to come and see me, love. (*Kitty laughs.*) No, honest, Kit. He's just the grandest guy. You make him take you to the pictures. Lots. I'll pay him back when I come out. (*He laughs.*) Don't think I'm cooling off. I've only got to keep you happy till I'm home again. Two ruddy years.

KITTY: It's like a lifetime, isn't it?

ROBERTS: No. Not as bad as that.

KITTY: Jock, do you think you'll be the same when you come out?

ROBERTS: I hope I will.

KITTY: No, serious. Inside your mind, I mean.

ROBERTS: What, me go crackers. Think so, love?

KITTY: People change so – fast. The things you liked when you came in – perhaps you won't feel – well – the same. In two years' time.

ROBERTS: That's silly, ducks. This place has got you down. (*Attempt to relieve her intensity.*) The only thing that's bound to alter is me stomach. That'll shrink a bit.

KITTY: Why, is the food so bad?

ROBERTS: No, it's all right – for slimming pigs.

JACKSON: Here, take it easy, lad.

ROBERTS: I'm sorry, sir.

KITTY: What will you do when you go out?

ROBERTS: I'll get a nice fat job and settle down.

KITTY: Oh, won't you go to sea again?

ROBERTS: You want to come?

KITTY: You ought to, Jock.

ROBERTS: Come on. Don't kid. I think it's time I settled down and had a home.

KITTY: But, will you get a job – all right?

ROBERTS: Of course, why not?

KITTY: Now that you've been in here.

ROBERTS: That doesn't matter, love. It isn't only me that's been in jug. There's decent, educated chaps in here. They'll help me out. Oh, anyway – it doesn't make a bit of difference nowadays.

KITTY: Jock, I believe it does.

ROBERTS: Well, anyway, there's lots of jobs. I might try choruses. (*Smiling.*)

KITTY (*she won't smile*): It isn't only jobs I'm thinking of. All sorts of things. All sorts of ways. It sort of stamps you, Jock. Your family, your friends, your home – –

ROBERTS: My wife?

KITTY: Well, yes. Your wife.

ROBERTS (*beginning to sense something*): Well, lovie, what about my wife?

KITTY: Your wife would have to be – well – I don't know.

ROBERTS: Come on, let's have it, kid.

KITTY: Oh, I don't know. So faithful, so unselfish, so – so brave.

ROBERTS (*very quietly*): Well, isn't she?

KITTY: Oh, Jock, I – (*Looks at Jackson.*) Jock, I – –

ROBERTS: 'Course you are, you lovely kid.

KITTY (*suddenly desperate*): Jock, listen, please. I've got to tell you this. I'm not unselfish. I'm not brave. I know you think I am, but you're wrong. Jock, listen, dear. I've got to tell you this – –

ROBERTS (*rising and going to her*): Poor kid.

JACKSON: Get back.

ROBERTS (*to Jackson*): This place has got her down.

JACKSON: Sit down.

> *He sits again. She is almost crying, looks up, about to try again, when Mrs Brown and 'Erb come in, shepherded by Mr King. Mrs Brown is very ugly and untidy and scrawny. 'Erb is seven and inquisitive.*

KING: I'll go and fetch 'im. 'E won't be a moment, mum. (*Goes out.*)

JACKSON (*impatiently. Hits table with hand*): Sit there.

MRS BROWN: Yer ain't got lots o' sauce nor nothin', 'ave yer?

JACKSON: There. Please, mum.

MRS BROWN: That's better. (*Settles herself.*) I'm old enough ter be yer mother. I've got boys as big as you. Bert's as big as you – an' 'e don't speak ter me like that. Yer'd better come along and meet our Bert. 'E'd give yer somethin' from 'is mum, would Bert. Yer gets a bit too cocky in this dump.

JACKSON (*keeping his temper*): Just sit still for a moment, madam. Then your husband will be here.

> *Enter Brown, escorted by Mr King.*

MRS BROWN: It's not me man wot's cocky, boy. It's you I'm talking to.

'ERB: Hey, Mum, there's Dad.

MRS BROWN: Yer 'ave a bit too much yer own way inside 'ere.

'ERB: Hey, Mum. There's Dad!

Mrs Brown: Well, what's so funny about that? (*Brown sits opposite his wife.*) Wot's bitin' yer? We come ter see 'im, didn't we? We come ter see yer dad.

'Erb: 'Ere. Let me 'ave another sweetie, Mum.

Mrs Brown: Yer've 'ad enough. Yer've 'ad a dozen since yer left the Toobe.

'Erb: Jest one more, Mum.

Mrs. Brown: All right. But that's yer last. (*Gives him one and turns to Kitty.*) 'Ave a sweetie, dear.

Kitty: No, thanks.

Mrs Brown: Go on. (*Gives her one. To Roberts.*) You like one, love?

Jackson: Here!

Mrs Brown: Oh, come orf it. (*Gives Roberts one.*)

Roberts: Oh, thanks. (*Takes it.*)

Mrs Brown (*to King*): Come on, you 'ave one. You look 'ungry, like. (*King takes it, grinning. She nods towards Jackson.*) We give 'im one? (*To 'Erb.*) All right, yer give yer boy-friend one. (*'Erb takes it to Jackson, drops it on the floor. As Jackson stoops to pick it up, Mrs Brown flips a packet of Players across the table to Brown, who takes them like a trout. To Kitty.*) Yer come by Toobe?

Kitty: No, bus.

Mrs Brown: I couldn't do. 'E always ups 'is dinner in a bus. 'E's like 'is dad. Me ninth 'e is.

Pointing at 'Erb.

Kitty: How nice.

Mrs Brown: Me eldest's out in Palestine. There's two still in Germany. An' one in Pentonville. Three married girls. They're like their mum. They likes a man around. 'Ave you got any yet?

Kitty: No. I'm not married.

Mrs Brown: Careful 'oo yer marries, love.

'Erb: Yer comin' 'ome termorrow, Dad? I wants a cycle bell.

Mrs Brown: Dad won't 'ave money with 'im, 'Erb. Don't talk so daft.

'Erb (*to Jackson*): Say, you a screw?

Jackson: That's right.

'Erb: Dad says screws stink. (*Brown looks awkwardly at King, who laughs aloud. Returning to the attack against Jackson.*) You 'anging anybody soon? Mum said you was.

JACKSON: I might hang you.

'ERB (*recoiling*): 'Ere, Mum. 'E says 'e's going to 'ang me, Mum.

MRS BROWN (*offhand*): It serves you right. (*She turns to Kitty.*) I 'ates these visits. Never think of nought to say.

KITTY (*jumping up suddenly*): Jock, I've got to go.

ROBERTS: Our time's not up.

KITTY (*to Jackson*): There's nowhere else where we could go?

JACKSON: I'm sorry, miss. This here's the place. There ain't no other.

MRS BROWN: 'Ope we ain't upset yer, love.

KITTY: No, no, you've been most kind. Well, Jock, I'm going now. There's something I must say before I go. I came to tell you, Jock, but everything – well. Jock, I'm going to marry Tom. I am. I'm sorry, Jock.

ROBERTS (*half-rising*): Here, take it easy, ducks.

KITTY: It's true. Tomorrow afternoon. It's all arranged. I want to get it over. Better, too, for you. I thought – like that. To get it done with. Jock, I couldn't – couldn't wait. Besides, he loves me lots. Forgive me, Jock. You'll find a much, much nicer girl. I know you will. A braver one than me.

ROBERTS: But, Kitty – –

KITTY: Please. Don't argue, Jock. (*To King.*) Please take me out. There's nothing more to say.

KING: O.K. 'Ere, lad, you goin' ter say good-bye?

ROBERTS: Kitty, can I kiss you once?

KITTY: Yes, Jock.

Jackson nods permission and he goes to her and takes her in his arms.

ROBERTS: Good-bye, my darling one.

KITTY: Good-bye. (*She goes out quickly, crying.*)

ROBERTS: Kit! (*He tries to follow, Jackson stops him.*)

'ERB: 'Ere, she was cryin'. Did yer see the lady, Mum?

MRS BROWN: Yer shut yer trap.

JACKSON: (*watching Roberts*) Wait on the Ones.

He walks to the door, and turns again in despair.

W.D.H.—G

MRS BROWN (*to Roberts*): I'm sorry, love. Yer better off. Yer are and all. Jest look at me – (*her voice breaks*) – and Dad.

> *Brown shrugs his shoulder in disgust and irritation. Roberts slumps out dejectedly.*

END OF SCENE 1

ENTRE-SCENE. THE LANDING

Medworth crosses stage with books on his way to the Library as Roberts enters from the Visiting-room.

MEDWORTH: What's the matter, Jock?

ROBERTS: I've had it, Med.

MEDWORTH: What's happened?

ROBERTS: I've had it. I've had it good and hard. The sloppy bitch, she's chucked me up. She's marrying a blue-eyed boy tomorrow afternoon.

MEDWORTH: I'm sorry, Jock.

ROBERTS: Remember when you read my hand? I'll need those bloody, soupy, sloppy, stinking, soulful friends – like hell I will. Like hell I bloody will.

JACKSON (*entering, with Brown*): Fall in – next to him. (*To Medworth.*) Buzz off. . . (*Medworth exits.*) You got anything?

ROBERTS: No, sir.

JACKSON: You got anything, Brown?

BROWN: No, sir. Cross me 'eart I ain't.

JACKSON: Come on, we'll have to look you over. Open up your shirt, me lad. No fags, no bluebacks, nothing, lad? (*Searches Roberts.*)

ROBERTS: No, sir.

JACKSON: Here, Brown. No fags, no jemmies, nothing, eh?

BROWN: No, sir.

JACKSON: Let's have a look.

KING (*entering*): Yer wanted, Jacko; wanted at the lodge. That Mrs. Brown, she wants yer blood.

JACKSON: Oh drat 'er. (*Starts to go off.*) O.K., you finish this.

KING: 'Ere, give 'em 'ere. I'll give 'em back.

Brown passes over fags.

JACKSON (*re-enters*): There's no one there.

KING: Oh, sorry – thought there was.

JACKSON: Here, open up. (*Searches Brown.*) O.K. Now hop it, lads. Right turn, lead on.

Turns to desk. King flips back Brown his cigarettes and goes out whistling.

SCENE 2. THE CONDEMNED CELL. EVENING, MONDAY

Jones and Gale are playing draughts. Tufnell writing – on his bed – a plaster on his head.

GALE: Here, you know Fox and Geese?

JONES: No. I don't like no fancy games.

GALE: Come, now, see if you can get through.

JONES: 'Ere. You've got four and I've got one.

GALE: Come on. You weak-kneed old contemptible!

TUFNELL: Oh, please, be quiet.

JONES: Oh, sorry, kid.

TUFNELL: No, go on talking. I've just reached the end.

JONES: That's all right, lad. You please yourself. This crook's just trying one on me.

TUFNELL: Poor Jonah. (*Comes over.*) Look. Move there. You see. You're through.

JONES (*moving triumphantly*): There, Mr Clever-fingers. There, take that.

GALE: The younger generation had to help you out.

JONES: The older generation saw the move – but didn't take it – 'cos it 'as an 'eart.

GALE: O.K., Grandpa. (*To Tufnell.*) Another poem, eh?

TUFNELL: No. Just a letter to my girl. I know she's coming in a minute, but that's all the things I want to say and won't be able to.

JONES: Yer say just wot yer wants, me lad – and don't mind us.

TUFNELL: Oh, no, it isn't that. It's just – well, when one sees someone one loves and – hasn't got much time, the things one really means to say aren't said.

JONES: 'Ere, let me work that out. (*Chief enters.*)

CHIEF (*to Tufnell*): Your visitor, she's on the way.

TUFNELL: Oh, thanks. How long is it?

CHIEF: One hour.

> *He goes out. Simultaneously the door leading to the visitors' grille can be heard opening.*

JONES: Don't worry, lad – you carry on an' never 'eed the time.

GALE: Come on. (*He takes him to recess.*)

TUFNELL (*voice off*): Hullo, Rosie. How's yourself? (*Silence.*) Now, Rosie, don't. (*Sobs.*) Now, Rosie, don't be silly. I'm O.K. I'm laughing. Look. (*More sobs.*) Here, Rosie, Rosie, cut it out. (*Louder sobs.*) Oh, Rosie, for God's sake. (*Crying hysterical.*) Oh, Christ above! I can't take this. (*He comes back white and shaking, followed by Gale. The cries grow less and less – a door clangs shut – there is silence. Pacing up and down the cell.*) Poor kid. I never should have made her come. How bloody selfish people are. One never thinks. One never thinks. Until it's too damn late – and then it's done.

JONES: Sit down, an' do a bit more writin', lad. She won't be long. They'll quiet 'er down an' she'll be back in 'arf a jiff. (*Tufnell gets up and walks wildly about the cell. The prison clock strikes eight. He stops and listens.*) Sit down, lad. Take it easy. She'll not be long.

TUFNELL: Will you be here at eight o'clock tomorrow, Jonah? Mr Gale?

GALE: No, lad.

JONES: No, we goes off at ten tonight. Sit down.

TUFNELL: Thank God. I couldn't bear to think that you – –

JONES: Sit down. Come on, an' 'ave a game.

TUFNELL: Who's on tomorrow?

GALE: Mr Jackson's one.

TUFNELL: What's he like? Will I hate him? Will I hate him, Mr Gale?

GALE: There's some in 'ere as wouldn't 'old 'is 'and.

TUFNELL: Who else?

GALE: A lad from Liverpool.

TUFNELL: You know him?

GALE: No. He's not been here before.

TUFNELL: And does the – other fellow – come tonight?

GALE: He has to sleep here. Yes.

TUFNELL: What's he look like?

JONES: Here, cut it out. Sit down. You make me tired. (*Tufnell sits.*) Old Jacko, 'e was down at Dartmoor in the mutiny. I guess it soured him up a bit. They put the old man in the boiler. Sorry, lad. It wasn't lit. (*He chuckles.*)

GALE (*playing up*): What, Smithy?

JONES: No – another fellar. But old Jacko – 'e was just a newish screw, like Windy 'ere. 'E wanders down the Wing, yer know – old 'ands in pockets – whistlin' a tune. And, blime, some great 'airy tough, 'e's 'iding in a recess – an' 'e grabs 'im as 'e passes – runs 'im up the stairs on to the Fours – and swings 'im up – old Jacko kicking like a frog and thinkin' it was kingdom-come – and drops 'im. Course they 'ad the wire across. It caught 'im, but 'e broke 'is leg an' 'urt 'is back. It served 'im right, the cocky pup.

GALE: It's pretty dumb. Falling for that.

JONES: Don't you be too sure – me young cock-sparrer. You watch out for yerself. Yer won't get me a-catchin' yer. I ain't played cricket now for twenty years.

CHIEF (*entering*): Your visitor. She's coming back.

> *He goes. Gale and Tufnell go to recess again. The Chaplain comes in and sits with Jones.*

TUFNELL (*voice off*): Hullo, Rosie. (*Sobs again. Quickly.*) There's only time to say good-bye. There's nothing else to say. I love you, Rosie. That's all. Don't forget. You've been a pal. Bye-bye, my love. I love you always – all my life. (*His voice breaks.*) Keep your chin up, kid. Good-bye. (*He comes in again. Sits staring in front of him. Gale and Jones go out.*) You know the time?

CHAPLAIN: It's ten past eight.

TUFNELL: I'm rather like the White Rabbit. I'm always taking out my watch.

CHAPLAIN: You liked it, didn't you?

TUFNELL: I loved it, yes. It made me feel a kid again. Please give her this.

CHAPLAIN: Yes, certainly. (*He takes letter.*)

TUFNELL: Well, thanks a lot. I think I'll go to bed. I'm feeling tired.

CHAPLAIN: Yes, that's the stuff.

TUFNELL: Will I see you in the morning?

CHAPLAIN: Yes. I'll be there.

Tufnell looks at the Chaplain and then crosses to him.

TUFNELL: Well, Padre, (*holds out his hand*) thanks a lot. I'm sorry for last week. And thanks for *Alice*. Am I still forgiven?

CHAPLAIN: Yes, of course you are. There's nothing more?

TUFNELL (*smiling at him*): You want to pray? I know. Poor Padre, always on the job.

CHAPLAIN: You like to?

TUFNELL: Yes, I think I would.

He sits and buries his face in his hands. The Chaplain takes off his hat and stands over him.

CHAPLAIN: Almighty and most merciful Father, we have erred and strayed from Thy ways, like lost sheep. We have followed too much the devices and desires of our own hearts.

TUFNELL (*looking up*): Can Gale and Jonah come along?

CHAPLAIN: Of course. (*To door.*) Come in. (*Gale and Jones stand awkwardly, caps off.*) We have offended against Thy holy laws. We have left undone those things which we ought to have done, and we have done those things that we ought not to have done. And there is no health in us.

The Chief comes in and whispers something to Gale and goes out. As the door bangs, the Chaplain looks up almost irritably. Gale explains the message.

GALE (*to Chaplain*): The young lady wants to see you in the lodge before she goes, sir.

CHAPLAIN: Yes, of course. (*He continues with the interrupted prayer.*) But Thou, O Lord, have mercy upon us, miserable offenders.

Spare Thou them, O God, that confess their faults. Restore Thou them that are penitent, according to Thy promises declared unto mankind, through – –

END OF SCENE 2

ENTRE-SCENE. THE LANDING. 7.45 A.M., TUESDAY

Enter Mr King, to desk. Enter Chief Officer Webb.

KING : Good morning, sir.

CHIEF : Good morning. Everything O.K.

KING : Yes, sir.

CHIEF : Get all of 'em locked up when the bell goes. We want no trouble. Understand?

KING : Yes, sir.

CHIEF : Discharges for the Governor at ten to eight. You see to that. Then when they've seen him, lock 'em up as well. You understand?

KING : Yes, sir.

CHIEF : Then, when the bell goes, let 'em out, just after eight. Five minutes' smoke. Then exercise inside. O.K.?

KING : O.K., sir – yes. (*The Chief goes off. Bell rings. Mr King starts shouting.*) Come on. Get up the stairs and shut yer doors. Discharges 'ere. Just leave yer kit. Yer goin' back upstairs. Get movin'. (*Angrily.*) Anderson, put that bloody fag-end out or else I'll run yer in. Now, shut yer doors. (*Losing his temper.*) 'Ere, Anderson, come down 'ere. Now Brown and Medworth. (*Brown and Medworth enter.*) When yer've seen the old man, straight upstairs and shut yer doors. An' when the bell rings, bring yer kit down 'ere. (*Enter Anderson.*) You fall in. You're on the peg. I may be easy-going but that doesn't mean I'm soft.

ANDERSON : But, sir – –

KING (*furious*) : Shut up, yer bleedin' black.

Anderson goes off with a terribly hurt expression on his face.

SCENE 3. THE GOVERNOR'S OFFICE. JUST BEFORE EIGHT

King comes in and stands behind the Governor.

KING (*saluting*): Good morning, sir. I'm deputizing for the Chief.

GOVERNOR: I know.

KING (*shouting*): Anderson! (*As Anderson enters.*) Name and number to the Governor.

ANDERSON: 2746 Anderson, sir.

KING: I warned 'im twice, sir, not to smoke – just now, sir.

GOVERNOR: Well? (*He has noted King's unusual emotion.*)

ANDERSON: I didn't hear him, sir. I didn't hear.

GOVERNOR: The next time you don't hear, I won't hear you. You understand?

ANDERSON: Yes, sir.

KING: Get out.

Exit Anderson. Enter Medworth.

GOVERNOR: Well, Medworth, feel all right?

MEDWORTH: Yes, sir.

GOVERNOR: Got friends to go to?

MEDWORTH: Well, I'm going on a holiday to Southend, sir.

GOVERNOR: To friends?

MEDWORTH: No, lodgings, sir.

GOVERNOR: I see. Well, thanks for what you've done. I'm glad you told me about Richards. Nipped some trouble in the bud. It makes me think you mean to take a pull.

MEDWORTH: I do, sir, yes.

GOVERNOR: Good man. Well, don't forget us, will you? I'm always here, the Chaplain's always here. If we can help you, we'll do our best.

MEDWORTH: Yes. Thank you, sir.

GOVERNOR: That all?

MEDWORTH: Please may I write a letter to a prisoner?

GOVERNOR: No, sorry, Medworth, no. Against the rules.

MEDWORTH: I see, sir.

GOVERNOR (*stands up and holds out his hand*): Good-bye. Good luck. (*Exit Medworth. Enter Brown.*) Well, Brown, you want to go?

BROWN: Last night I cried me eyes out, sir.

GOVERNOR: Thought you would. Still, all good things must end – some time.

BROWN: That's right.

GOVERNOR: Going back to your wife?

BROWN: Yes, sir. I've turned over a new leaf, sir.

GOVERNOR (*looking at him quizzically*): She's meeting you at Notting Hill Gate station, isn't she?

BROWN: Wot! Is she, sir?

GOVERNOR: I'm asking you.

BROWN: Cor stone the crows, I 'ope not, sir.

GOVERNOR: Go easy, Brown. The police are very busy men. You mind if I shake hands?

BROWN: A pleasure, sir. (*Shakes it mightily.*) Good-bye, sir. (*At door.*) So long, Kingie boy. (*Exit.*)

GOVERNOR (*laughing*): A pal of yours? (*The Governor turns to King, laughing, sees how highly strung-up he is, then pats his shoulder understandingly.*) How's the time?

KING: Almost time, sir.

GOVERNOR: Go round and see that every man's inside his cell – behind a lock.

KING (*salutes, goes out. Shouting outside*): Get moving, Brown. Yer shut that door. (*Door slams.*)

> There is dead silence in the prison, for the first time. The Governor walks to the cupboard, gets out a strong drink, stands looking out of the window. He drinks all his drink. He stands motionless, head lowered slightly. Then, squaring his shoulders, he walks off through the door towards the execution shed.

END OF SCENE 3

ENTRE-SCENE. THE LANDING

Mr King comes slowly on towards his desk. As he crosses the landing the prison clock starts striking. He stops, and then, towards the eighth chime, he removes his cap. After a few moments he replaces it and goes and leans against the desk, gripping it hard, under great emotional stress. Then the bell rings. Signs of life are heard in the prison again. Mr King pulls himself together and resumes his routine job.

KING (*shouting*): Open up. (*Sound of locks.*) All downstairs. Five minutes' smoke. Then exercise. Discharges 'ere – with kit.

> *Footsteps come down the stairs, but – for the first time there is no talk. Brown and Medworth appear.*

BROWN (*to Medworth*): 'Tain't natural. . . . That's what I say, 'tain't natural.

KING (*at desk*): Shut up. (*Angrily.*) Yer ain't out yet.

BROWN (*after a pause*): And wot ain't natural, ain't right.

KING: Come 'ere. Wot's that yer said?

> *Chief comes in, looking drawn, unseen by King.*

BROWN: Oi said, "'Tain't natural, an' wot ain't natural – ain't right.'

KING: Well, shut yer ruddy mouth.

> *He looks over Medworth's kit.*

CHIEF: Brown, come over here. (*Brown does.*) Here, buy yourself a drink (*slips him a florin.*) – and – take my tip – and steer off Notting Hill Gate.

> *Roberts appears, looking very subdued.*

KING: Wot you want, lad?

ROBERTS: Please, may I say good-bye to Medworth, sir?

KING: Buzz off.

CHIEF: No, Mr King. Yes, all right, lad.

ROBERTS: Well, so long, Med.

> *Chief moves away. King still at the desk.*

MEDWORTH (*shaking hands*): So long.

BROWN: So long, kid.

Roberts does not answer, stands by Medworth.

KING: Come on, now. We'll chuck yer out. (*To Roberts.*) Yer comin' too?

ROBERTS: No, sir.

KING: Well, 'op it. Don't stand dreamin' 'ere.

SCENE 4. TEN MESS. A MOMENT LATER

All subdued, Paddy, Spencer, Smith, Anderson, Robinson, new, unattractive nonentity.

ANDERSON: He's pushin' up the roses now. He's pushin' up the roses now. (*Silence.*) Yes, sir, he's pushin' up the roses – or the spuds.

PADDY: Oh, shut yer mouth.

ANDERSON: The English always smile when they're dead. They always smile when they're dead. (*Silence.*) Now, Mr Robinson, you just come in last night?

ROBINSON: That's right.

ANDERSON: I want to ask you somethin'. You a tab-end? Don't give all you've got. Don't overdo it, Mr Robinson. Just one's enough.

ROBINSON: I'm sorry. 'Aven't got a thing.

ANDERSON: That's quite all right. That's quite all right. I'll ask again. I'm almost sure to ask again. (*Enter Roberts.*) Ah, Mr Roberts. Got a tab-end, Jock? (*He does not answer.*) It's draggin', Mr Roberts. Yes, it's draggin'. Well, I'll have to light one of my own.

He strolls to the door.

SMITH (*to Robinson*): Wot you in for?

ROBINSON: Lifer.

SMITH: Coo, wot for?

ROBINSON: Oh, just a job. I run a bastard down when I was taking off the stuff.

SMITH: Wot stuff?

ROBINSON: Fur coats. Ten thousand quid.

SMITH: You got it still?

ROBINSON : Sure thing.

SMITH : Yer need a partner, eh?

ROBINSON : I guess I might.

ANDERSON (*who has wandered to the door, returns*) : Here, Smithy, Brownie's going for his papers. Quick.

SMITH (*rushing out and shouting up*) : So long, Brownie. Give my love ter Mrs B. the second. So long, Romeo, so long.

ROBINSON : You in for screwing, eh?

SPENCER : No, I'm a Squadron Leader, R.A.F. I buzzed my kite down Oxford Street a bit too low.

ANDERSON : An' upside-down. (*Smith comes in again.*)

ROBINSON (*admiringly*) : Tough guy. (*Bell rings.*)

KING'S VOICE : Exercise on the Fours. Exercise on the Fours.

ROBINSON : Wot's that?

SPENCER : Exercise. You coming?

SMITH : Nah, come off it. Robinson's my pal. We're goin' inter partnership. Come on.

Exit Robinson and Smith.

ANDERSON (*to the disappointed Spencer*) : Come on, Admiral. Old Arthur wants to hear about your plane. Old Arthur wants to hear about your kite. It always rains in England. Yes, it isn't England if it's fine.

Exit Anderson and Spencer.

KING (*upstairs*) : Come on. Get movin'. Up on exercise. All on the Fours.

Roberts stands, tearing up Kitty's photograph.

PADDY (*still sitting there*) : It draggin', Jock?

ROBERTS : I wish that I was Tufnell. It's not dragging. It's just bloody stopped.

He throws himself down at the table.

PADDY : Feel funny down in here – 'bout Tufnell? So do I – –

ROBERTS : You do?

PADDY (*coming over to him*) : Oh, cheer up, lad. It won't be long.

ROBERTS : Two bloody years.

PADDY : I've got that too. Let's take it – arm-in-arm.

Pause. He stands behind Roberts, looking down at his hair. His hand steals out towards it, but he checks himself.

Here, have a fag?

ROBERTS: Oh, thanks.

PADDY: Have two.

ROBERTS: Can you spare two?

PADDY: There's lots more where those came from. Just you say the word.

ROBERTS: You're awfully decent, Paddy boy.

KING (*voice off*): All up on the Fours, for exercise. Come on. Come on.

PADDY: Let's walk around together. Eh?

ROBERTS: Why not?

PADDY: Come on. Let's go.

He puts his arm through Roberts's and they wander out. A second later Mr King puts his head through the door, goes out, and shouts from the open door.

KING (*shouting upwards*): All on the Fours. Come on. Get movin'. Break it up, this ain't 'Yde Park on Sunday night. Get movin'. (*Shouting louder and angrily.*) O'Brien! Roberts! If yer likes it arm-in-arm, I've got a pair of bracelets here. (*He swings his handcuffs in his hand.*) Come on. Get movin'. Get a move on, lads.

He moves off. Footsteps are heard shuffling round the top landings, and subdued voices, as the curtain falls.

THE
CHILTERN HUNDREDS

THE CHILTERN HUNDREDS *was first produced in London at the Vaudeville Theatre on 26 August 1947. It was presented by Linnit & Dunfee Ltd., with the following cast:*

The Earl of Lister	A. E. MATTHEWS
The Countess of Lister . . .	MARJORIE FIELDING
June Farrell	LEORA DANA
Bessie	DIANE HART
Beecham	MICHAEL SHEPLEY
Lord Pym	PETER COKE
Lady Caroline Smith	EDITH SAVILE
Mr Cleghorn	TOM MACAULAY

The Play directed by
COLIN CHANDLER

CHARACTERS

THE EARL OF LISTER, Lord Lieutenant
THE COUNTESS OF LISTER, his wife
JUNE FARRELL of the American Embassy
BESSIE
BEECHAM
LORD PYM, Lord Lister's son
LADY CAROLINE SMITH, Lord Lister's sister
MR CLEGHORN

W.D.H.—H

SYNOPSIS OF SCENES

The action of the play takes place in the sitting-room of Lister Castle in the summer of 1945.

ACT ONE

Scene 1.   General Election Result Day. Lunch-time.
Scene 2.   The next morning. Breakfast time.

ACT TWO

Scene 1.   Saturday evening, the following week-end. After Dinner.
Scene 2.   The By-Election. Nomination Day. Breakfast time.

ACT THREE

Scene 1.   The By-Election Result Day. A fortnight later. Lunch.
Scene 2.   The same evening. After Dinner.

THE
CHILTERN HUNDREDS

ACT ONE

SCENE 1

SCENE. – *The sitting-room of Lister Castle.*
TIME. – *Summer, 1945.*
It is lunch-time on the day of the General Election result. Lady Lister is seated at her desk finishing a letter. June Farrell, wearing shorts and sandals, lies full length on the sofa, fast asleep. Lord Lister is in the armchair, reading a book on sport and absent-mindedly filling his pipe. From time to time he surveys the garden, which is somewhat overgrown with grass and weeds. A small rook rifle stands against the arm of his chair.

LADY LISTER (*about to read from the letter*): What do you think of this, Joe?

LORD LISTER: Excellent, my dear. First class.

LADY LISTER: Joe! Just look at June. June, dear, I really think you might have gone with Tony. After all, you are engaged.

LORD LISTER: This fellow says 'rabbits are most fond of those shrubs which grow within their reach.' Dashed interesting.

LADY LISTER: I don't suppose the poor things know how nice the others taste. (*She sees the mess on the floor.*) I wish you'd keep your tobacco inside your pipe, Joe. I saw a fox down by the stables after breakfast, dear.

LORD LISTER: Why the devil didn't you tell me before?

LADY LISTER: We've had so much to think about – and anyway it ran away when June went down to bathe.

LORD LISTER: Don't blame it. I'd run away if I saw a dashed Red Indian popping out of the water right under my nose, when I expected a duck.

LADY LISTER: Joe, you mustn't talk like that. It's so rude – even in fun. After all, America wasn't all Indians. Surely after the War of Independence there must have been some white people settled there. You ought to know – you went to Eton, Joe.

JUNE: Say, is it really true they won old Waterloo around the campus there?

LADY LISTER: I meant it, June. I think you should have gone with Tony, June.

JUNE: I know. I heard you.

LADY LISTER: It would have given him moral support.

JUNE: Oh, hell. I couldn't go and watch a walk-over like this. I want to see a fight.

LADY LISTER: I always used to go with Joe and hear the 'count.'

LORD LISTER: As far as I remember, dear – you used to wear a skirt.

LADY LISTER: But still, the spirit's just the same. Besides, she's got such very pretty legs.

LORD LISTER: You wouldn't have dressed like that if my father had been alive – pretty legs or no pretty legs. Would have tickled you up with a riding crop, and the prettier your legs the more he would have tickled you up.

JUNE: I read about a guy like him at college once.

LADY LISTER (*who has moved down and picked up the rifle*): If your father had been alive, Joe, I don't suppose you'd have kept a rifle in the sitting-room.

LORD LISTER: Got to, my dear girl. In self-defence. (*To Lady Lister, who is dusting his rifle.*) Be careful, Molly, or you'll knock the sight. (*To June.*) My dear girl, my father had eighteen gardeners, ten footmen, and six keepers here. Forked out a thousand a year to keep the rabbits off the borders. Now, after three damn wars, I've got no gardener – one gamekeeper who is an ex-conscientious objector and faints when he sees a rabbit in a snare – –

LADY LISTER: You've still got Beecham, dear. (*She replaces the rifle and dusts the table beside him.*)

LORD LISTER: That damn fellow!

JUNE: I love Beecham, he's just swell. He's England, Joe.

LORD LISTER: He may be England, but he's damned expensive.

LADY LISTER: You're most unfair to Beecham, Joe. When he came here in nineteen twenty, we engaged him as a footman. There was nothing to suggest he would have to guard the herbaceous border in his spare time – as a sort of scarecrow and retriever mixed. (*She is on her knees, dusting the legs of the table.*)

LORD LISTER: Moll, I wish you'd stop fiddling about.

LADY LISTER: Well, someone's got to do the dusting, dear.

JUNE: I did it before breakfast, Moll.

LADY LISTER: You might have told me, June.

LORD LISTER: It's dashed well time we got a maid.

LADY LISTER: We've got one, Joe. At last. I do hope Tony's won.
(*She crosses to the radio table, puts on her glasses and picks up the 'Radio Times'.*) It should be through by lunch-time, shouldn't it?

LORD LISTER: It isn't only rabbits in the garden now. Dashed foxes too.

JUNE: Say, you can't wait! You just can't wait to hear the news!

LORD LISTER: I take no part in Party Politics. I haven't done for twenty years.

JUNE: But, Joe, he's your son!

LORD LISTER: The Labour fellow's someone's son as well. He's very sound I'd say.

LADY LISTER: I hope so – I voted for him.

JUNE: Say! Say, what is this? Joe, YOU didn't vote against your only son?

LORD LISTER: I haven't got a vote. In England we disfranchise lunatics and peers.

JUNE: Not peeresses?

LORD LISTER: Not under the second heading, anyway. It's up to the Medical Authorities to decide whether some of 'em come under the first.

JUNE: What makes Tony stand Conservative if you're both like this?

LADY LISTER: Oh, Tony's very young. He's got lots of time to learn.

JUNE: Say, don't you realize what's happening today? Tony, your son and heir, is fighting an Election that's been won since Cromwell's time by the eldest son of the family.

LADY LISTER: That's right, dear. I explained that to you when you came here first.

JUNE: Well, gee, it's NEWS. It gets right back behind your skin. It's like the Coronation.

LORD LISTER: Better weather – far. I had to walk from West-minster to Dover Street in all my robes. Couldn't get a taxi anywhere.

LADY LISTER: You should have gone by Underground.

LORD LISTER: I didn't dare. Afraid I'd catch my ermine in the moving stairs.

LADY LISTER: What will Tony do if he gets beaten, Joe?

LORD LISTER: He won't get beaten, Moll. This Seat's been Tory ever since Queen Anne.

LADY LISTER: Joe, Queen Anne's dead (*She turns on the radio.*)

LORD LISTER: The Tories aren't, round here. They never die.

LADY LISTER: But Tory doesn't mean a thing. (*The voice of the Announcer begins to come through.*) They vote for something just because they like its face. That's exactly why I wanted June to go today.

LORD LISTER: It's too late now, my dear. They voted weeks ago.

RADIO ANNOUNCER: . . . and the Opposition parties hold a hundred seats. Here is the state of parties up to twelve o'clock this morning. Conservatives twenty-two, Nationals one, Liberal Nationals one, Labour ninety-nine, Independent one. The party gains and losses are as follows:—Conservative gains one, losses forty-five; Labour gains forty-eight, losses none; Liberal gains none, losses two.

LADY LISTER: You see! There's going to be a change. I knew it, Joe. How horrid people are. (*She switches off the radio.*) I can't listen any more. Poor Mrs Churchill! He's ringing up in any case.

JUNE: P'raps Mrs Churchill voted Labour, Moll.

LADY LISTER: She couldn't have.

JUNE: Well, you did, dear.

LADY LISTER: I know, but I've been Labour all along. (*She crosses to the desk and sits.*) Now listen, Joe – are these all right? This is if Tony wins. (*Reading from a letter.*) 'Dear Mr Cleghorn, As you know, my husband, being Lord Lieutenant of the County, takes no part in Party Politics.'

JUNE: Say, what's a Lord Lieutenant?

LORD LISTER: Oh, a Gauleiter, my dear. Yes, yes – go on.

LADY LISTER: 'We therefore feel able to write and say how much we appreciate the spirit in which you fought the Election. And we hope that you will come and see us any time you care to call.' And this is if HE wins. 'Dear Mr Cleghorn, As you know, my husband, etc., etc., etc. We feel able to write and congratulate you on your victory over our son, and we hope that you will come and spend a week-end with us so that we can get to know each other better. Yours sincerely, Molly Lister.'

LORD LISTER: Asking him to stay!

LADY LISTER: We must, Joe. You're Lord Lieutenant.

LORD LISTER: But – dash it all – he called me a parasite!

LADY LISTER: What nonsense, dear.

LORD LISTER: He did, my dear. It's in the *Advertiser*. (*He rises to get it from the table.*) Here. Listen to this, by Jove. (*He reads from it.*) 'In a speech at Lister Market, Mr James Cleghorn, the Labour Candidate, said: "I ask you, the Electors of East Milton, to vote for me, Jackie Cleghorn, the workers' candidate, the man who has slaved for thirty years beneath the heel of the plutocrat – –" '

LADY LISTER: That's not 'parasite', dear. That's 'plutocrat.' It's rather flattering – I wish that it was true.

LORD LISTER: Listen, woman. (*He continues reading.*) – 'and NOT to vote for Viscount Pym, the young aristocrat from Lister Castle, the boy who went from Eton and Oxford into the Household Cavalry – the son of a million Listers – the heir to a thousand capitalists – the last of a long, and alas, uninterrupted line of plutocrats and peers and parasites.' There you are.

LADY LISTER: Yes, but he doesn't say, actually, you – Joe.

LORD LISTER: Maybe. (*He puts down the paper.*) But he leaves it open. Dashed open, I'd say.

LADY LISTER: Besides, these politicians never say the things they mean. They put them straight in prison if they do. And so they never do.

LORD LISTER (*looking out of the window*): It's there, Molly. It's there, by Jove.

LADY LISTER: What, dear? That naughty fox?

LORD LISTER: Don't move. Don't move an inch. (*He moves down for his rifle.*) A huge buck rabbit! (*He loads the rifle.*) I've got to get this infernal window open.

LADY LISTER: Joe, you must NOT fire that gun in here.

LORD LISTER: Be quiet, my dear.

LADY LISTER: I'm going out. I cannot bear that noise.

LORD LISTER: You can't go out. It'll see you through the passage window. Get inside the cupboard if it frightens you. Go on. It won't sit feeding there all day.

> *The telephone rings. Lady Lister makes a move towards the desk.*

LADY LISTER: It's Tony, Joe. It's sure to be.

LORD LISTER: Get back, Molly! Get back!

LADY LISTER: I should have thought the result of the election's more important than a silly rabbit.

LORD LISTER: Balderdash. There'll be another one in five years' time. ·

LADY LISTER: All right – well, answer it yourself.

LORD LISTER: I can't.

> *Bessie enters. The telephone rings again – an intermittent country ring.*

Get out. Send Beecham here at once.

> *Bessie hurries out.*

What am I to do, Molly? If I open the window, the telephone'll frighten it. Can I shoot it through the glass?

LADY LISTER: Certainly not. There's quite enough bomb-damage unrepaired without you adding to it.

> *Beecham enters.*

BEECHAM: You sent for me, my lord?

> *The telephone rings again.*

LORD LISTER: I did. That telephone. It's ringing. Hear it, eh?

BEECHAM: I do, my lord.

LORD LISTER: Well, answer it.

BEECHAM: Very good, my lord. (*He shuts the door and starts to walk across.*)

LORD LISTER: Hi. Beecham, halt! You cross that sky-line by the sofa and I'll sack you on the spot. Stoop, man, stoop.

The telephone rings again as Beecham crosses to the desk, stooping.

And sit down when you get there.

Beecham sits on the chair at the desk and answers the telephone.

BEECHAM: Hullo . . . Yes – this is Lister Castle – yes.

LORD LISTER: And keep down, man.

BEECHAM (*bobbing*): His Lordship's Agent. Yes, Mr Brown . . . No. His lordship and her ladyship are both – are both out shooting in the grounds.

LORD LISTER: Don't chatter, Beecham. Cut it short.

BEECHAM: I'll take a message, certainly . . . I see. Two thousand. Thank you, sir . . . He started back some time ago? I thank you, sir. (*He hangs up.*) His lordship's Agent on the line, my lord.

LORD LISTER: I gathered that. Now pack it in.

LADY LISTER: What happened, Beecham? Did he win?

BEECHAM: Master Tony lost, my lady. By two thousand votes.

JUNE (*jumping up*): He couldn't have. The little sap!

LORD LISTER (*at boiling point*): JUNE!

JUNE (*subsiding on to the sofa again*): O.K., Joe. Sorry. Let it have the works.

BEECHAM (*as Lord Lister is at last about to open the window*): It's terrible, my lord.

LORD LISTER: What's terrible? The people like a change. Relax.

BEECHAM: This seat's been won from Lister Castle by the Tories for two hundred years, my lord.

LORD LISTER (*losing patience*): Beecham! You come in here and sit about discussing politics as though you owned the place. Shut up. Will you – SHUT UP! (*Dangerously calm.*) I'm opening the window now. (*To Beecham.*) If anybody talks again – take their name.

Lady Lister disappears into the cupboard. For the first time there is silence. He opens the window, raises his rifle, takes aim. The loud fluctuating note of a motor horn is heard; tyres swish over the gravel; brakes squeal; a door slams.

Damnation! Hell and blast! He's frightened it. (*He slams the window shut.*)

JUNE: Joe – take the shell out, Joe.

LORD LISTER: I'll never get another chance like that. (*He unloads, and stands the rifle up by the window.*)

BEECHAM: May I get up, my lord?

LORD LISTER: That's up to you. Depends on how you feel.

BEECHAM: I thought perhaps the creature might be contemplating further nourishment, my lord.

LORD LISTER: What! Nourishment! My foot! Would you be keen on feeding if a screaming Yankee horn like that went off when you were having lunch?

BEECHAM: It often has, my lord. On occasions I have suffered indigestion – but invariably I return to finish what is left upon my plate.

Tony enters.

TONY: I say, what's happened? Beecham feeling faint?

LORD LISTER: Dash it, Tony, can't you drive a car more like a gentleman?

JUNE: Hell, Tony, how'd you lose?

TONY: Because the other fellow got more votes.

JUNE: I guess he must have done.

TONY: Where's mother?

LORD LISTER (*crossing to the cupboard*): Oh, my God! Molly, you can come out now.

LADY LISTER (*appearing*): Is it all over? It's very hot in there – like a Turkish Bath. (*She sees Tony.*) Poor Tony. I'm so sorry.

JUNE: Well! You voted Labour, what do you expect?

LADY LISTER: Yes, yes. I know I did. I backed the losing side. I always do. But now they've won, they've lost my sympathy.

TONY: A bit late then. I say, I'm hoarse. Hey, Beecham, what about a drink?

BEECHAM: I'll fetch the sherry in, my lord.

TONY: I had to make a speech and tell old Cleghorn what a decent chap he was. And so he is.

LADY LISTER (*to Beecham, who is standing at the door*): What's the matter, Beecham?

BEECHAM (*to Tony*): May I say how mortified I am to hear of your defeat, my lord.

TONY: Oh, thanks. Oh, thanks a lot.

BEECHAM: I dare not contemplate what the Tenth Earl, your grandfather, would have remarked on this unhappy day, my lord.

LORD LISTER: I'll tell you what he would have remarked, Beecham.; Just what I'm remarking now. 'Get out and fetch those something something drinks.'

BEECHAM: Er – very good, my lord.

> *He goes out.*

LORD LISTER: Damned ninny! Crying over spilt milk. I'm going to wash. (*He goes out.*)

LADY LISTER: Yes, come along. I'm sorry, Tony dear. And if it wasn't for the rabbit, your father would be sorry too. (*She exits.*)

JUNE: Oh, hell, I think you stink. Old Beecham could have won this dump.

TONY: If he'd had you to help him, eh?

JUNE: I guess so. Yeah.

TONY: Of course, you know so much about our politics.

JUNE: Well, tell me some.

TONY: It isn't me that stinks. The Tory party stinks.

JUNE: It's a bad workman who complains of his tools.

TONY: It's a silly fool who tries to win a seat from Lister Castle in a modern world. Of course, you wouldn't understand. Americans are snobs. They bite a fellow's ear off if he has a coronet. That doesn't happen here.

JUNE: I guess it might. (*She bites his ear, playfully.*) I guess they twist his tail instead. Poor little man. (*She kisses him.*) Just go on trying.

TONY: I'm damned if I'll try again. I've had the Tories.

JUNE: What's the next move, then?

TONY: Oh, chivvy rabbits round for Dad. Or nip around the house for Mother, dusting things and sweeping up the crumbs.

JUNE: Say, aren't you just ambitious! What's our Bessie for?

TONY: I dunno. I was wondering last night. In bed, you know. I couldn't sleep before the Count. Old Bessie kind of crossed my mind, that's all.

> *Beecham enters with the sherry.*

(*To Beecham.*) I say, what's Bessie do?

BEECHAM: In what respect, my lord?

TONY: About the house.

BEECHAM (*relieved*): She does the rooms, my lord. The usual routine housemaid's work – assisted by her ladyship, of course. (*He places the sherry on the table.*)

JUNE: She's parlourmaid and kitchenmaid and housemaid all rolled into one?

BEECHAM: Precisely, miss.

TONY: Oh, damn. That's closed an avenue.

BEECHAM (*pouring out two glasses of sherry*): Have you found Bessie wanting then, my lord, in some respect?

TONY: Oh, no. Oh, rather not. What should she want?

BEECHAM: I find it difficult to say, my lord.

JUNE (*watching him closely*): She's pretty, Beecham, isn't she?

BEECHAM: Yes, miss. I will concede she has a certain rustic charm. (*He moves towards her, with two glasses of sherry on a tray.*)

JUNE: Say, Beecham, do you ever bounce her on your knee?

BEECHAM: Some sherry, miss? (*She takes it.*) For you, my lord.

TONY (*taking it*): Oh, thanks. Did Bessie vote for me?

BEECHAM: I couldn't say, my lord. I doubt it, though. She's Commonwealth. (*He returns and replaces the tray on the table.*)

JUNE: What's that?

BEECHAM (*considering*): Well, miss – a nervous spinster's version of a Communist might meet the case.

TONY: Good show. I'll drink her health. To Bessie – What's her name?

BEECHAM (*disapproving strongly*): Miss Sykes, my lord.

TONY: To Bessie Sykes! Escaped from Toryism and the shackles of Conservative Decay. (*He lifts his glass and drinks.*)

BEECHAM: You seem to take defeat with fortitude, my lord.

TONY: I do. Why not?

BEECHAM: Provided your reaction's prompted by your native grit – and not by irresponsibility – I have no axe to grind, my lord.

He exits.

TONY: I suppose he thinks I ought to cry a bit?

JUNE: I'm glad there's someone here who understands what's happened to the family.

TONY: June, dash it! Not you too! Come and kiss me, please.

Lord Lister enters.

Lord Lister: Dashed close thing, Tony, eh?

Tony: Two thousand odd.

Lord Lister: I had my finger on the trigger as you blew the horn.

Enter Lady Lister.

June: I'm telling Tony he's got to find a job.

Lady Lister: I've got a job for Tony. I want a run made of wire netting for my ducks.

Lord Lister: Well, that's all right. There's always something to be done if one can only find it and someone hasn't done it first. (*He pours himself a glass of sherry.*)

Lady Lister: I've asked the Labour man to stay this week-end, dear.

Tony: Oh, jolly decent of you.

Lady Lister: Oh, and, Joe – your sister Caroline.

Lord Lister: What for? She bores me blue.

Lady Lister: Well, you won't have to talk to Mr Cleghorn all the time.

June (*in Lord Lister's ear*): There's a bunny eating your begonias.

Lord Lister: What? What?

June: A bunny – eating – your – –

Lord Lister: What! Dash the thing, Beecham was right. (*He puts his glass on the table and picks up the rifle.*) Stand still.

Beecham enters.

Beecham: Luncheon is – –

Lord Lister: Shut up.

Lady Lister: I think his lordship is preparing dinner, Beecham.

Lord Lister has opened the window and is taking aim. He fires.

Lord Lister: After it, Beecham. Quick!

Beecham goes out of the window at the double.

Don't worry about the Election, Tony. It's just the swing of the pendulum. Take Charles the First and Cromwell. Different types – that's all. (*Shouting through the window.*) Hey! Not there, you fool. By the box bush. That's it. Pick it up. It's not a tiger, man.

Lady Lister: Joe, what are you going to do with Tony?

Lord Lister (*with an eye on operations outside*). Oh, go back to the Army. Go into the Church. (*The rabbit has been retrieved; he turns back to the room.*) All sorts of things to do. I knew a fellow once, became a bookie. He lost thirty thousand quid in seven weeks. Oh, lots of things to do.

Beecham enters through the window, carrying a dead rabbit.

BEECHAM: Luncheon is served, my lady.

LADY LISTER: Thank you, Beecham. Come along, June.

She crosses with two letters from the desk, followed by June. Beecham is holding the door open for them.

(*To Beecham.*) Oh, will you post these, please? No, just the one with M.P. on the end. (*She tears the other up.*)

Lady Lister and June go out. Tony and Lord Lister move to follow them.

TONY (*as he passes the rabbit*): Not a very big one, is it, Dad?

LORD LISTER: Too many of 'em here. We'll never get 'em down if we don't fight 'em back. We must fight back.

Tony and Lord Lister have disappeared. Beecham starts to clear the tray at the table above the sofa. The telephone rings. He goes to answer it, rabbit in hand.

BEECHAM: Hullo? Lister Castle . . . Yes, the *Advertiser*? . . . His lordship's reaction. Lord Pym's do you mean? . . . No, quite, you heard his speech . . . The Earl himself? Lord Lister is at lunch just now, but I can let you have his views. As Lord Lieutenant, Lord Lister is neutral, taking no part in Party Politics. As a man, and a Pym, his lordship feels the situation most acutely. The effect on the human organism of two hundred years' tradition overthrown since one o'clock is hard to gauge at first. All we can say is that the mind is numbed, while kindly nature breathes her healing balm around her stricken child . . . A statement? No, I cannot possibly disturb the Earl at lunch. One moment. (*He thinks for a moment and remembers.*) You may quote his lordship as saying – shortly after the result was declared – 'We must fight back.' Yes, that is it. (*He repeats it, in a voice vibrant with emotion.*) WE MUST FIGHT BACK.

He hangs up the receiver and crosses to collect the sherry tray. Then, tray in one hand and rabbit in the other – leaves the room.

CURTAIN

SCENE 2

The following morning.

There is a round table laid ready for breakfast.

Bessie, obviously behindhand, is laying the last two places. As she finishes she picks up the silver basket and makes for the door, meeting Beecham bringing in the coffee. She goes out.

Beecham crosses to the table and puts down the coffee. He crosses to the trolley, takes the morning papers from the middle shelf and places them on the radio table. Retaining 'The Times' for himself, he comes down and, with varying expressions on his face, starts to look through it for the articles devoted to the Election results.

Lord Lister enters through the French windows, carrying a rabbit snare.

LORD LISTER: Is breakfast ready yet?

BEECHAM: It is, my lord.

LORD LISTER: About time too. (*Holding up the snare.*) I found this in the potting shed. A rabbit snare. Dashed useful things. (*He puts it beside his plate.*) The bath water was cold today.

BEECHAM: I'm sorry to hear that, my lord.

LORD LISTER: It's not your sympathy I want. (*He takes the paper from Beecham.*) However sorry you may be, that doesn't heat the bath water. The fire must be kept in – at night. That's all one asks. It isn't much to ask. Who's job is it?

BEECHAM: It should be the odd-man's, my lord – but as we don't employ one – the responsibility devolves on me, my lord.

LORD LISTER: Well, why the devil was the water cold?

BEECHAM: I'm afraid the boiler slipped my mind last night, my lord. The day's events had served to drive domestic details of that nature from my head.

LORD LISTER: What day's events? What happened yesterday?

BEECHAM: According to the papers, the Electorate conspired to bring the Socialists to power, my lord.

LORD LISTER: Oh, that! Well – what the devil's that to do with you?

W.D.H.—I

BEECHAM: I feel the matter very strongly, as I told your lordship yesterday.

LORD LISTER: Daresay you do. That's no excuse for going round and sabotaging everything. That's anarchy, by Jove.

BEECHAM: I did it unintentionally, my lord. I felt so low last night, I took a sleeping draught and went to bed at nine.

LORD LISTER: What sort of sleeping draught?

BEECHAM: Three Veganin, washed down with port, my lord.

LORD LISTER: Now look here, Beecham. Pull yourself together – and get this in your head. The Labour Party's IN, and nothing you can do or say can get 'em out again.

BEECHAM: A counsel of despair, my lord.

LORD LISTER: It's common sense. So stop sulking. Why – damn it – anyone would think you were Winston from the shindy you're kicking up.

BEECHAM: I can't help taking Master Tony's failure as a personal affront, my lord. After all your lordship has done for the County, I regard it as the height of ingratitude to spurn your son in favour of a man without tradition – or refinement – or one single link with those who made this country what it is. I mean, of course, the British aristocracy, my lord.

LORD LISTER: Oh, poppycock! We've been found out, that's all.

BEECHAM: I can't agree, my lord. I regard yesterday's poll as a direct result of the sinister influence emanating from those countries now in the grip of social revolution. I refer, of course, to – –

LORD LISTER: Anyway, I bet old Stalin's bath water is hot.

BEECHAM: That may be so, my lord. But – if it is – the reason is not far to seek. The servants in the Kremlin doubtless fear the axe.

LORD LISTER: Exactly. There's a lot of good in Communism – if one takes a thoroughly unbiased view.

BEECHAM: I cannot agree, my lord.

LORD LISTER: I don't expect you to.

BEECHAM: Whatever your lordship may say, I regard the future with profound distrust. If I may crave – –

LORD LISTER (*who has been trying to read the paper for some time*): Beecham! How the devil can I read the cricket scores if you keep chattering? One more word about politics – just ONE more, mark you – and I'll send you off to Blackpool for a month.

Beecham, discouraged and silenced, fiddles round the table and picks up the snare.

BEECHAM : Will I place this in the gun-room, then, my lord?

LORD LISTER : No. You will not. You'll place it in the border – by the box bush – where I shot the rabbit yesterday.

BEECHAM : Yes – very good, my lord.

LORD LISTER : It works like this. You stick the wooden peg straight into the ground. Like this. (*He stuffs it through the loaf.*) You bend the wire like this. And then the noose hangs down – just right – and pretty near the ground. You see?

BEECHAM : I do, my lord.

LORD LISTER : And then the rabbit comes along like this. On it's run, you see? It doesn't see the wire, and pops its head right through – like this.

The final graphic gesture ensnares his wrist. Beecham is in the act of releasing him when Lady Lister enters.

LADY LISTER : Joe! What are you doing, Joe?

BEECHAM : Excuse me, my lord.

LORD LISTER : It's all right, Moll, don't fuss. I'm getting Beecham's mind off politics. (*To Beecham.*) Now take it out and set it. Keep your feet out of the bed – and let it clear the ground by just an inch.

BEECHAM : Yes – very good, my lord.

Beecham goes out into the garden.

LORD LISTER : Poor devil'll go crackers if he doesn't get a hobby. Goes on harping on the General Election. If we don't watch it, he'll get to be as big a bore as Gladstone was. The bath water was cold, my dear.

LADY LISTER : I know. Perhaps that's why you haven't made your bed this morning, dear.

LORD LISTER : Oh, sorry – I forgot.

LADY LISTER : It doesn't matter actually. (*She has been looking through her letters.*) The Laundry's coming, so we must change the sheets. Still, you mustn't let things slide.

LORD LISTER : What's that?

LADY LISTER : I said you mustn't let things slide. Dear Joe, I know exactly how you feel. But, dear, the Labour Party's IN and nothing you can do or say can get 'em out again.

LORD LISTER: Well, I'll be damned!

> *Beecham enters through the french window, wiping soil off his hands.*

BEECHAM: The gin is in position now, my lord.

LORD LISTER: Oh, right.

LADY LISTER: So stop worrying about the Election, or else I'll have to send you off to stay with Caroline.

> *Lord Lister looks awkward. Beecham goes out.*

LORD LISTER: I'd rather shoot myself than stay with Caroline.

LADY LISTER: What nonsense, dear. She's your own flesh and blood.

LORD LISTER: In spite of that, she looks exactly like a horse.

LADY LISTER: Now, don't be catty, dear.

LORD LISTER: I'm talking about horses, Moll.

LADY LISTER: I've got a letter from her here. (*Reading.*) 'Dearest Molly, – How too, too terrible! You poor dears! My heart goes out to you and Joe in your unhappiness – –'

LORD LISTER: What the devil is she nattering about now?

LADY LISTER: The Election, dear. (*Reading on.*) 'I've just heard the wireless. How hateful people are. After all poor dear Mr Churchill has done for them – –'

LORD LISTER: I like that! She loathed old Churchill's guts before the war.

LADY LISTER: Please don't keep interrupting, dear. It's very difficult to read. (*She reads on.*) 'They turn against him now, and spurn him like a stranger cur – –' (*puzzled*) then in brackets – 'Julius Caesar.' What does she mean, dear?

LORD LISTER: Dashed if I know.

> *Tony comes in, he is in battle dress – M.C. ribbon and Africa Star – looking very smart and rather hurried.*

TONY: Morning, Mother. Morning, Father.

LADY LISTER: Tony dear – what's a stranger cur?

TONY: Dashed if I know. I suppose – a cur that's stranger than another cur.

LADY LISTER (*to Tony*): This is from Aunt Caroline. (*She reads on.*) 'Thanks for asking me for next week-end. I don't want to come – –'

LORD LISTER: Good.

LADY LISTER: ' – – but I will – –'

LORD LISTER: Damn.

LADY LISTER: ' – – to help you, you poor darling – –'

LORD LISTER: I shall go to Blackpool.

LADY LISTER: Why Blackpool, dear?

LORD LISTER: Well, Brighton – Bognor Regis – anywhere.

LADY LISTER: You won't, my dear; you asked her here.

LORD LISTER: Me? Never in a thousand years.

LADY LISTER (*reading on*). 'I suppose that dreadful, vulgar – –' (*As Tony kisses her.*) Good morning, dear. ' – – self-made Mr Cleghorn will be there. Why MUST Joe ask a mountebank like that to stay at Lister? If poor dear father were alive I'm sure he would turn in his grave – –'

LORD LISTER: He couldn't, dear – he was cremated!

LADY LISTER (*reading on*): 'Give poor dear gallant Anthony my love and kisses – –'

TONY: UGH!

LADY LISTER (*ignoring him*): 'Tell him I am grateful to him for saving me from Hitler, even if East Milton is not – –'

LORD LISTER: What on earth would Hitler want with Caroline?

LADY LISTER (*sailing on*): 'Oh, noble Anthony!' (*Puzzled again.*) 'J. Caesar' – in brackets again.

LORD LISTER: Why the devil does she keep harping on that fellow Caesar?

LADY LISTER: I don't know, dear.

LORD LISTER: What the blazes has Caesar got to do with East Milton?

LADY LISTER: I still don't know, dear. It's almost finished now. (*She reads on.*) 'Your ever loving Caroline. P.S. – And what's poor Tony going to *do*?' Twice underlined. Tony dear – what *are* you going to do?

TONY: I'm going to the Depot to report.

LADY LISTER: And then?

TONY: I'm going to ask the Adjutant for week-end leave.

LORD LISTER: What? Why walk into it?

June enters.

LADY LISTER: He wants to see Aunt Caroline again.

TONY: I don't. I want to talk to Cleghorn about politics.

JUNE: Why talk to him?

TONY: Oh, I dunno. I always like to learn the other fellow's point of view.

LADY LISTER: Good morning, June.

JUNE: Good morning, Moll. Good morning, Joe.

LORD LISTER: What's that?

JUNE: I said, 'Good morning, Joe.'

LORD LISTER: Ah, yes. I've set a snare.

JUNE: You have? What for?

LORD LISTER: Oh – rabbits chiefly. It's a rabbit snare, you know.

LADY LISTER: Joe, do stop talking about rabbits!

LORD LISTER: Why? They interest me.

LADY LISTER: Yes, dear. I'm slowly learning that. So long as you've your beastly rabbits, you don't mind if Tony starves.

LORD LISTER: What? Tony hungry? Have another piece of toast? You're worse than Beecham, Moll. You ought to take a sedative.

LADY LISTER: I sometimes wonder if I didn't take one when I married you.

Lord Lister winces.

I'm sorry, Joe. I'm worried about Tony's future – but it doesn't matter. Will you be a dear – and run along and make the breakfast for my ducks? It's in the scullery. I've got to go and do the laundry—they're coming here today. Oh – and, Joe, poor Clara's not been laying at all well, so give her more than all the others, dear.

LORD LISTER: Yes – rather – yes. Yes – rather – yes. Poor old Clara – of course I will.

Lady Lister has gone out. Lord Lister follows.

TONY: Why's everybody on the hop today?

JUNE: Reaction. Say, what time's your train?

TONY: Nine fifty-five. It only takes four minutes in the car.

JUNE: I'll run you down. You packed?

TONY: Old Beecham's up there now.

JUNE: O.K. I'll finish this and get the car. I'm sorry you're going.

TONY: I'll have leave this week-end.

JUNE: That's swell. And then?

TONY: Oh, I dunno. Maybe I'll stay on in the army, till some foreign gentleman splits my atom – in World War Number Three.

JUNE: You can't do that.

TONY: Why not?

JUNE: Because you've got no cash.

TONY: They pay one in the Army, dear.

JUNE: How much?

TONY: Oh, I dunno. About a mess-bill's worth.

JUNE: Hell, Tony! This is 1945! You've got to roll your sleeves right up – and make a pile of dough.

TONY: What for?

JUNE: For me – I guess.

TONY: I thought you had a lot.

JUNE: You think I'm going to keep you, kid?

TONY: Well, no. I wouldn't put it just like that.

JUNE: How would you put it, then?

TONY: Well – dash it, June. Don't pin me down, old girl. What's the matter with you, June? You've never been like this before. You got engaged to me. You knew I hadn't any money then.

JUNE: It isn't only money that you need.

TONY: Well, what's the matter, then?

JUNE: I guess you need some guts.

TONY: Here – damn it, that's not fair. I don't want to boast, but fellows in the Army thought I had my share. Oh, I know I got the M.C. 'cos I lost myself near Tripoli – and found myself behind the German lines. But still, they said I had a lot of leadership and – drive and – things.

JUNE: Well, why not use them now?

TONY: Well, dash it. You're talking as though I'm the only Tory candidate that's lost his seat. There's hundreds did.

JUNE: I'm not complaining that you lost. You get my goat because you let it get you down.

TONY: I haven't let it get me down. I sang in my bath this morning. At least, I didn't have a bath, because the water's cold. I think I'm being jolly brave. I had to plug a policy that's out of date – –

JUNE: You might have thought of that before.

TONY: I've not had time to think – since 1939 – what with reading maps and kit inspections – taking sand out of one's hair.

JUNE: I guess you haven't got it all out yet. Say, can't you just forget the past – and look ahead?

TONY: What at?

JUNE: At life. At us. At you and me. At lots of yelling children with a father on the dole.

TONY: June, not at breakfast, please.

JUNE: Yes, kid. At breakfast – lunch and tea and dinner – every day and every night. A crowd of hungry little kids – all looking at you with reproachful eyes—and screaming for their ration books. You've got to face it, boy.

TONY (*shuddering*): I can't.

JUNE: You've got to WORK.

TONY: I'm not brought up to work. I'm culture – all the things you Yankees like – that's me! The upper crust that makes the bread of life digestible! The world needs men of leisure – more than ever – in these hectic days. And I was born to be a man of leisure. It's a sin for me to work. It's a betrayal of my birthright. It's – –

JUNE: Say, listen, Tony – don't you want to work for – me?

TONY: What? No.

Her eyes blaze.

I mean – well, if I had to – yes.

JUNE: I'm telling you – you have to.

TONY: But – to work for you – it's – it's – it's taking coals to Newcastle.

JUNE: I guess we needn't bring in Newcastle. I'm telling you – if you don't get a job, you don't get me.

TONY: All right. Well, if you say so – –

JUNE: Good. Then, what's it going to be?

TONY: I'll stay on in the army, if you like.

JUNE: We've had that once – and I don't like.

TONY: Oh, have a heart. It's all that I can do. For five years I've been taught to kill. I did it jolly well. But now – the killing's off. It's dashed bad luck. It leaves a fellow in the air.

JUNE: I'll say it does.

TONY: June – have you got no sympathy? It's all they trained me for.

JUNE: Well, why not start right in and train yourself for something else?

TONY: Well – what?

JUNE: Hell – anything. My father and my uncles – in the States. They only had a hundred dollars to their name when they were kids. Where are they now? They're millionaires – and shall I tell you why?

TONY: No, I can guess.

JUNE: Because they roughed it. And because they worked like blacks. And now – all three of them – are millionaires.

TONY: But I don't want to be a millionaire.

JUNE: I'd say you needn't worry about that. I'll be content if you can make enough to keep yourself in underpants.

TONY: I don't wear underpants.

JUNE: Say, listen, Tony – I'm dead serious.

TONY: I know you are.

JUNE: I'm telling you – if you don't get a job – then our engagement's off. You think that over at the Depot and then give me your decision next week-end. O.K.?

TONY: O.K.

JUNE: I'll go and get the car.

June goes out – leaving Tony in the depths of depression. Bessie comes in to clear away the breakfast.

BESSIE: Oh, I'm sorry, sir. I thought you were finished.

TONY: So I am. You carry on. Er – Bessie, tell me something. How much do you get for doing this?

BESSIE: Two pounds a week, my lord.

TONY: Two – a week. Ah – yes, I see. That isn't very much. (*Pause.*) Do men get more than women for this sort of thing?

BESSIE: Oh, yes, my lord. Men's stronger, see?

TONY: Oh, are they? Yes, I see. Er – tell me – is it very hard – this work?

BESSIE: Oh, no, my lord.

TONY: When do you start?

BESSIE: I'm always up at half-past five.

TONY: Good God!

BESSIE: And, usually, I'm through by – –

TONY: Thank you, Bessie – that's enough.

BESSIE: I'm sorry, sir.

TONY: No, not a bit. If you were married, would you mind your husband not having a job?

BESSIE: Not if I loved him, no, my lord. I'd work my fingers to the bone for him.

TONY: You would?

BESSIE: Oh, yes – my lord. It's only them with too much money who gets martyrs to it, sir.

TONY: I so agree.

BESSIE: My mother always says, 'Poor peoples' happier than rich.'

TONY: She does? Well, why is that?

BESSIE: Because they have to do with all the things that don't need money to be got. And them's the best things in the end.

TONY: Such as?

BESSIE: You can't buy 'appiness, my lord.

TONY: By jove – that's true.

BESSIE: Nor love, my lord.

TONY: Nor love – by jove.

BESSIE (*embarrassed*): I'm talking out of turn, my lord.

TONY: No, rather not. I like talking to you, Bessie. Er – tell me, you're Commonwealth, they say.

BESSIE: That's right. I follow Mum.

> *Lord Lister enters with a plate of duck food in one hand and a highly-coloured book in the other.*

TONY: Oh, yes. And Mum, I take it, is a bit left wing.

BESSIE: I'm sure I couldn't say, my lord.

LORD LISTER: Dashed good book in the scullery. 'She Never Knew What Hit Her.' Wonder whose it is?

BESSIE: It's mine, my lord.

LORD LISTER: Oh, good – I'll loan it from you if I may.

> *Beecham enters. He holds the door open for June, who follows him in.*

JUNE: Come on. You'll miss your train.

BEECHAM: Her ladyship is coming down to say 'good-bye,' my lord. She's in the linen cupboard.

TONY: Good. I'll come along.

BESSIE: Safe trip, my lord.

TONY: Oh, thanks. I hope we meet again this next week-end.

Bessie blushes. June and Beecham react unfavourably.

I'm just off, Dad.

He exits, followed by June and Beecham.

LORD LISTER: Eh? What? Oh, yes, well come back soon.

Bessie gives a sob.

I say – I say, don't do that. No need to worry – he's only going to Aldershot.

He goes out with the plate of duck food and book. Bessie goes on clearing the table. Beecham comes back as the car is heard to drive away.

BEECHAM: 'Safe trip' – indeed.

BESSIE: Well, don't you hope he comes back safe? I'm sure I do.

BEECHAM: That's not the point. It's not your place to say so – see?

BESSIE: No – I don't see. He's nice, his lordship is.

BEECHAM: And what's he got that I've not got?

BESSIE: I wouldn't know him well enough to say. Not yet.

BEECHAM: What do you mean – 'Not yet'?

BESSIE: Just what I says. Not yet.

BEECHAM: Now, don't you get ideas, my girl. You've work to do. And working people can't afford to get ideas.

BESSIE: Why can't they? They don't get much else.

BEECHAM: You looking for a husband, eh?

BESSIE: And if I am?

BEECHAM: And if you are – stop looking for him right above your head. You don't find husbands in the clouds. You may find other things – not husbands, though. A woman finds her husband on the ground – and keeps him there.

BESSIE: I ain't found mine.

BEECHAM: Maybe you haven't looked. Maybe you won't find one until you've learnt to keep your place.

BESSIE: Perhaps I haven't found it yet.

BEECHAM: You found your place the day that you were born. So keep it, see? The world's arranged that way – for all of us. You don't see elephants in trees.

> *He has been getting a little nearer to Bessie. Suddenly the telephone rings. He crosses to answer it.*

Hullo? . . . Yes . . . Mr Cleghorn? . . . You will be delighted to accept for next week-end. I thank you, sir. I'll tell her ladyship.

> *He hangs up and turns to Bessie, who is about to leave the room with the tray.*

That means I'll have to watch the spoons.

> *Bessie goes out. Beecham goes to finish off clearing the breakfast table with a look on his face of mingled resignation, forbearance and disgust. Lord Lister enters through the window, immersed in his book and still carrying the duck food. He comes to his place at the table and sits. Beecham is standing above the table, holding the coffee-pot and milk jug.*

LORD LISTER: Breakfast nearly ready, Beecham?
BEECHAM: You've had it once, my lord.
LORD LISTER: Are you sure?
BEECHAM: Quite sure, my lord.
LORD LISTER: Dammit, there's someone who hasn't – – (*He sees the duck food.*) Oh, yes, of course, those blasted ducks. (*He gets up again to go through the window.*)

CURTAIN

ACT TWO

SCENE 1

The following week-end. Saturday night – after dinner.
Lord Lister is behind the sofa, wearing a day suit. Lady Lister and
Lady Caroline are seated on the sofa. Lady Lister is doing some mending,
and wears a short dress. Lady Caroline is in evening dress. June, in
trousers and a sweater, is sitting in the chair at the desk. Tony, with open
shirt and corduroy trousers, is sitting on the floor beside her. They are
reading letters. Cleghorn, in a dinner jacket, is in the armchair.

LORD LISTER : Dashed sorry, Cleghorn – making you bottle yourself up in that dashed outfit. Beecham should have told you that we
didn't dress.

CLEGHORN : That's quite all right. I always wear it, Lister.

LADY CAROLINE : It's so much nicer changing in the evenings –
after all the heat and dust of the day – the tumult and the shouting.

LORD LISTER : Who's been shouting, Caroline ?

LADY CAROLINE : Joe, I was quoting then.

LORD LISTER : Tell you what I'll do, Cleghorn. I'll put mine on
tomorrow – just for old times' sake. My dear fellow, have a cigarette ?
Tony, get your guest a cigarette. (*He starts to play patience.*)

CLEGHORN : No, please. I never do. (*He takes out a cigar. To Lady
Lister.*) I hope you don't mind these ?

LADY LISTER : No – not at all. No – do go on. My husband loves
the smell.

LADY CAROLINE : Well, Mr Cleghorn – have you bought yourself
a nice job in the Cabinet ?

CLEGHORN (*refusing to take offence*) : Oh, well – I live in hopes. The
Chief approached me on the question when the Coalition first broke up.

LADY LISTER : Oh, how exciting – tell me, which post do you
fancy ?

CLEGHORN : Don't ask me!

LADY LISTER: Why not Prime Minister?

CLEGHORN: Afraid that's booked.

LADY CAROLINE: And, anyway, one needs a wife for that.

CLEGHORN: You think that's an essential?

LADY CAROLINE: Yes, of course. Responsibility doesn't go with bachelordom. What you need is an old Conservative wife to knock you into shape and file the edges down.

CLEGHORN: You find me rough?

LADY CAROLINE: No – just uncut.

LORD LISTER: Tell me, Cleghorn – are you in favour of this State Control?

CLEGHORN: In certain cases, yes.

LORD LISTER: What, all the usual stuff? The mines – the banks – so forth?

CLEGHORN: Yes, broadly speaking, yes.

LORD LISTER: I looked your manifesto through. Not one dashed word about the land.

CLEGHORN: Oh, well. I'm glad I pleased you by default.

LORD LISTER: You didn't please me, man. If someone doesn't take this blasted place away before I die, my wife'll have to walk the streets.

LADY LISTER: Joe, don't be silly, dear. I've got my ducks.

LORD LISTER: You won't have, dear, if I don't shoot that fox. (*To Cleghorn.*) You wouldn't want the land controlled, is that correct?

CLEGHORN: No, rather not. Not yet. We can't sweep everything inside the State at once.

LORD LISTER: But, dash it, man. It's common decency. You tax me nineteen shillings in the pound – and more – and then expect me to keep up a place like Blenheim, Fontainebleu and Versailles all rolled into one.

LADY CAROLINE: Why don't you let it, Joe?

LORD LISTER: Beecham wouldn't stand for it. And, anyway, who'd take it? Takes you half an hour to run your bath. The food's cold when it reaches you. Why, dash it all, you need a horse to get around these corridors.

JUNE: Say, this is good. Say, listen. 'Dear Lord Pym, – May I say how sorry, etc., etc., etc. May I also echo – in the words of your grand old father, quoted in the current *Advertiser* – we must fight back.'

TONY: Here, who sent that?

LADY LISTER: You didn't say that, Joe?

LORD LISTER: Say what, my dear?

JUNE: Say, Joe, have you been spouting to the Press?

LADY LISTER: Of course he hasn't, June; he's only written to the papers once. *The Times*. About young women's toenails.

LORD LISTER: Painting 'em – you know.

CLEGHORN: That's interesting. What line did you take?

LORD LISTER: I merely pointed out that people did it – just before the fall of Rome. Dashed fellow never put it in. He sent it back. He said he thought there were other more strategic reasons why Rome fell. Facetious ass. Of course, they may be better now they're red.

JUNE: What colour were they then?

LADY LISTER: No, dear. He means *The Times*.

Beecham comes in for the coffee-cups.

TONY: Oh, Beecham, could you get the *Advertiser* for this week?

BEECHAM: Yes, very good, my lord.

LORD LISTER: I put it by the raspberries to keep the birds away.

BEECHAM: Oh, yes, my lord.

Beecham goes out.

LORD LISTER (*to Cleghorn*): By the way, talking of the *Advertiser*, I saw a bit last week where you described me as a parasite. Mark you, I'm not complaining. Something in it, I daresay.

LADY LISTER: What nonsense, Joe. It only said the family should not monopolize this Seat.

TONY: By Jove, it's right at that. I couldn't say so, Cleghorn, at the time. But still, I couldn't help agreeing with you all along the line.

JUNE: Stop shooting off your mouth.

TONY: After all, just because one of our ancestors picked up a damned good pocket borough – paid through the nose for it – got a majority of two in an electorate of ten, by bribery – it doesn't mean that I'm prepared to carry on where he left off.

LADY LISTER: But then you didn't, did you, dear?

CLEGHORN: Now, Pym, you shouldn't talk like that. A man in your position's got so much to give.

TONY: Afraid that's where you're wrong. I gave eight hundred quid – and that's the lot.

LORD LISTER: And that was mine.

CLEGHORN: Of course, my party pays its candidates' expenses.

TONY: Really?

CLEGHORN: Yes.

TONY: I say!

Beecham enters through the french windows with the 'Advertiser'.

JUNE: Oh, let me see it, Beecham. Be a pal.

BEECHAM: Would that be the item, miss? (*He gives it to her.*)

LORD LISTER: I want my evening clothes tomorrow, Beecham.

BEECHAM: If your lordship recollects, you gave them to the game-keeper last year.

LORD LISTER: Well, dash it, he won't want 'em every night.

BEECHAM: No, no, my lord. Your lordship gave them to him with a view to scaring off the pigeons from the plums.

JUNE (*who has been reading*): I say, that's swell. That's really swell.

LADY LISTER: What is it, June? Don't keep it to yourself.

JUNE: All tuned in?

Beecham, in the background, listens proudly.

(*Reading.*) 'Lord Lister, in a recent statement from Lister Castle, made the following comment on the defeat of his son, Lord Pym, in the General Election. " – – As Lord Lieutenant, I am neutral. As a man, I feel the situation most acutely. The effect on the human organism of two hundred years' tradition overthrown as suddenly as this is hard to gorge at first – –" '

BEECHAM: 'Gauge,' miss.

JUNE: ' "Gauge" at first – – All I can say is that the mind is numbed, while kindly Nature breathes her healing balm around her stricken child.'

LADY LISTER: Joe, you only had one glass of sherry and a Guinness on that day.

JUNE: This is IT. 'His lordship closed with the stirring call to battle. "We must fight back," he said, "WE MUST FIGHT BACK".' (*Running to Lord Lister and throwing her arms round his neck.*) You sweetie-pie! I wish I was engaged to you instead of Tony.

LORD LISTER: Yes, my dear – so do I. (*He disengages himself.*) Beecham, have I ever written for the *Advertiser*?

BEECHAM: To my knowledge, no, my lord.

LORD LISTER: Well – who the devil has?

BEECHAM: If I may hazard a suggestion, my lord, I would say that the paragraph in question has been contributed by some unknown Elector, with a view to bolstering morale beneath the heavy shadow of defeat.

TONY: Yes, that's the thing. To get a bit of easy cash.

BEECHAM: There are Conservatives, my lord, whose motives on occasion are not prompted by the lust for gold. (BEECHAM *goes out.*)

LADY CAROLINE: How nice he is. He gives one confidence.

LORD LISTER (*to Cleghorn*): My sister's a Conservative, you see. Museum minded. Still believes in aristocracies.

LADY CAROLINE: I'm sure Mr Cleghorn does as well.

CLEGHORN: Oh, no. You saw my speech in Lister Market, didn't you?

LADY LISTER: Of course, that's why I voted for you.

CLEGHORN: What! Against your own son?

LADY LISTER: Oh, yes. We take no part in Party Politics.

CLEGHORN: You sabotage them, eh?

LADY CAROLINE: Why don't you like the aristocracy, may I ask?

CLEGHORN: Oh, many reasons.

JUNE: Because you aren't a belted Earl yourself?

LADY LISTER: Now, June dear, don't be rude.

CLEGHORN: I merely think the aristocracy's out of date.

JUNE: Oh, hell, you make me sick. (*Looking towards the fireplace.*) That picture's old. You don't chuck that away because it's old.

CLEGHORN: That's just an ornament, Miss June.

JUNE: So what! What's wrong with ornaments? I'm one myself.

CLEGHORN: A very pretty one, if I may say so.

JUNE: You think I'm out of date?

CLEGHORN: No, God forbid.

TONY: I do. I never heard such concentrated rot in all my life.

JUNE: You got engaged 'cos I'm an ornament – or was it for my cash?

LADY LISTER: Now, June, don't get so overwrought. You can't turn everything to personalities.

W.D.H.–K

JUNE: You can. That's what they are. That's life. The rest's just fossils and machines.

LORD LISTER: Tory fossils and Socialist machines?

LADY CAROLINE: I really think it's time we went to bed.

The telephone rings.

JUNE (*answering it*): Hullo, who's calling? . . . Yeah, Lister Castle . . . O.K. Who's on the line? . . .

LADY LISTER: I think it's time we all went up. (*To Cleghorn.*) I expect you'll have a lot of all-night sittings in the House.

CLEGHORN: Yes, we've got a lot to do to straighten out the world.

LADY LISTER: Be very careful with it – won't you? It's a little brittle, I'm afraid.

JUNE: Oh, say, HULLO! How are you? What's the story? . . . Yes, I am. American . . . Say, how'd you guess? . . . I'm going to marry a Conservative. Lord Pym. You ever heard of him? . . You have? . . . You think he's good? I think he's dumb. Well, guess you're busy, so I'll pass you on – –Oh, hey! I'm very sorry that you won. (*She turns to Cleghorn.*) A guy called Attlee calling you.

LADY LISTER: Attlee!

Cleghorn rises and takes the receiver.

CLEGHORN: Hullo? . . . Yes, Chief. It's Cleghorn here . . . What's that? . . . I'm very honoured. I'll be delighted . . . Rather. That suits me . . . What's that? . . . No, Clem, no – I can't accept . . . I'm sorry, no. Against my principles.

LADY LISTER: Now, Mr Cleghorn, principles need not be obstacles, you know.

CLEGHORN (*taking a snap decision*): Well, Clem, if you put it like that I can't refuse . . . Well, thanks . . . That's fine. See you next week . . . Good-night. (*He hangs up.*)

LADY LISTER: What is it, Mr Cleghorn?

CLEGHORN: He's offered me the Dominions.

LADY LESTER: Accepted?

CLEGHORN: Yes.

LADY LISTER: You must be pleased. Why did you hesitate?

CLEGHORN: Afraid he made a proviso. Too many Ministers in the Commons. So he's sent me to the Lords.

JUNE: You turned that down?

CLEGHORN: I took it, no.

JUNE: You can't have done. You said just now – –

CLEGHORN (*rather embarrassed*): Well, it was just the way he put it.

JUNE: P'raps the P.M. in Queen Anne's day put it just like that.

LADY LISTER: Not on the telephone, I'm sure he didn't, dear.

LORD LISTER: What'll you call yourself, Cleghorn?

CLEGHORN: Oh, Cleghorn's good enough for me.

LADY CAROLINE: It has to be OF somewhere, doesn't it?

LADY LISTER: I think it does. Where do you live?

CLEGHORN: At Egham, I'm afraid.

LORD LISTER: It can't be helped.

LADY LISTER: That means a by-election, doesn't it?

JUNE: What, HERE?

LADY LISTER: Yes, dear, the sitting Member's gone up to the House of Lords.

JUNE: But Tony here's a Lord.

LORD LISTER: That's courtesy, my dear, that's all. It doesn't count. Eldest son, that's all. He's really Anthony Smith – only some dashed fellow at the College of Heralds wants something to do.

JUNE: A by-election here! Say, Tony, that's your chance. A second chance. Oh, gee!

TONY: I've told you, June – I've had the Tories.

LADY LISTER: Well then, you ought to stand as Labour candidate instead of Mr Cleghorn – don't you think so?

CLEGHORN: That depends on Pym.

TONY: You think that one could change like that?

CLEGHORN: Well, people do.

LORD LISTER: Of course they do. Winston did. I always think chameleons make dashed good M.P.s.

> *Beecham enters with a glass of water on a salver and goes to Lady Caroline.*

BEECHAM: Your glass of hot water, Lady Caroline.

LADY CAROLINE: A little whisky, please – to celebrate.

> *Beecham moves up to get the whisky.*

JUNE: Say, Tony, if you change I'll never speak to you again.

TONY: You told me that I had to find a job.

JUNE: I'm just not kidding, Tony. (*She kisses him.*) I'll NEVER speak to you again.

LORD LISTER: My dear Caroline, I've never seen you touch the stuff before.

Beecham brings the whisky to Lady Caroline.

LADY CAROLINE: My dear Joseph, I've never heard a charming man like Mr Cleghorn so honoured before. (*She sips the whisky.*) It's very strong. I think I'll finish it upstairs. I'm ready now, Molly. Good night.

LADY LISTER: I'm coming with you. Good night, everybody. Good night, Mr Cleghorn. I do hope you'll be comfortable.

CLEGHORN: I hope so.

LADY LISTER: Good night, Joe. Don't sit up too late.

Beecham holds open the door, and Lady Lister and Lady Caroline go out.

JUNE: Say, Beecham, there's a by-election here.

BEECHAM: Has Mr Cleghorn had an accident, then, miss?

TONY: He has. He's going to the House of Lords.

JUNE: Well, Beecham, how's it hit you? Pretty good?

BEECHAM: I understand that Mr Asquith contemplated something similar in 1911, miss – on a somewhat larger scale.

CLEGHORN: Oh, Beecham, I've rather a busy day tomorrow. Could I have an early call?

BEECHAM: I'll mention it to Bessie, sir.

CLEGHORN: Six-thirty?

BEECHAM: Very good, MY LORD.

He goes out with an icy look on his face.

TONY: Have another drink?

CLEGHORN: No, thanks.

TONY: Now, what about this by-election, sir?

CLEGHORN: Well, what about it, Pym?

TONY: If I did stand as Labour . . .

JUNE: Say, Joe, come out around the garden and I'll drive the foxes over you.

LORD LISTER: Eh, what? (*He sees the situation.*) All right – I doubt if I'll hit the beggar on the move and in the dark. (*He picks up his rifle.*) Still, try anything once.

JUNE: It's guys who haven't got the pep to try things twice that get my goat.

> *Lord Lister and June go out through the french window.*

CLEGHORN: You're just a bit unpopular, I think.

TONY: Oh, typical American. Old fashioned – 'Ghost Goes West' – and all that stuff. Now, what about this Seat? You got a candidate?

CLEGHORN (*laughing*): The Labour Party moves quite fast – but not as fast as that.

TONY: Got one in mind?

CLEGHORN: I mustn't give information away to the enemy.

TONY: Don't worry about me. I've had the Right.

CLEGHORN: Then you were serious tonight?

TONY: Of course. So's Father – Mother too. One must progress.

CLEGHORN: Pym, are you genuinely Left? Or are you Left – well, just because the Right's got left behind?

TONY: Oh, no. It's genuine.

CLEGHORN: Quite sure?

TONY: I know I stood as a Conservative, but – dash it all – one must progress. This election's taught me something. Every dashed question had me. 'Why should you be a lord?' Well, why should I? Damn it, they'll ask YOU that tomorrow.

CLEGHORN: Let's stick to the point. Your election address made me think. You didn't what you might call 'quote the Tory Press.' If you'd been a Liberal, I would have said, well – vote-catching. But as you were a Tory, I thought, well – this boy's sincere.

TONY: You did? Well, thank God someone did.

CLEGHORN: Sincere – but not a Tory, do you see. Now, Pym, I'll tell you what I'll do. I'm speaking as a politician now. I'll call the Party Secretary. (*He sits on the desk and takes up the receiver.*) Of course, it's not my pigeon now, but still, I take it I'll still pull some weight. (*Into the telephone.*) Lister 2911, please. (*To Tony.*) You're sure you mean it, Pym?

TONY: Yes, rather, yes.

CLEGHORN: Your fiancée?

TONY: Oh, she'll be all right.

CLEGHORN: She's obstinate.

TONY: Well, damn it, so am I. I'm dashed if I'll live on her.

CLEGHORN: All right. But still, she doesn't look the type who's keen on unconditional surrender – – (*Into the telephone.*) Oh, hello. Cleghorn here . . . Look, I've some news for you. I'm going to the Upper House . . . Dominions . . . Oh, thanks . . . Yes, rather a surprise in a way . . . That's very decent of you – thanks. Now look . . . Exactly . . . Yes, that's what I've called you up about . . .

June has come in and is standing by the window.

Yes, I have. I've thought about it quite a bit . . . Yes, well – well, I suggest young Pym . . . Yes, yes, I think he would. And it would save a contest . . . Quite . . . Yes, National – or something of that sort. The Tories often try that trick . . . Well, anyway, you sleep on it. I'll see you Monday morning . . . Yes, and many thanks again . . . Good night. (*He hangs up and rises.*)

Lord Lister enters through the french window.

LORD LISTER: Well, I'm off to bed. Coming, Cleghorn? Never saw the brute (*Putting his rifle by the window.*) I smelt him, though. I don't suppose it comes out, anyway, until I've gone to bed. You coming up?

CLEGHORN: Yes, rather, yes. Good night, Pym.

TONY: Good night – and thank you.

CLEGHORN: Thumbs up. Good-night, Miss Farrell.

June does not answer. Cleghorn goes out.

LORD LISTER: Don't sit up all night, Tony. And shut that window. Don't want rabbits chewing up the chairs.

TONY: Yes. Good night.

Lord Lister goes out.

(*Going to the table behind the sofa.*) Have a drink?

JUNE (*above the armchair*): You lousy little worm. I wouldn't marry you if I were paid a million dollars down – and free of tax.

TONY: Why? What's the matter now?

JUNE: Say, can't you guess? You surely aren't that dumb!

TONY: Me going Labour, I suppose? So that's it, is it? Silly child.

You know damn all about our politics. The world moves on – that's all.
One either moves as well – or gets moved out. It's providence, this
break. And if they have me I'll be unopposed. Besides, this talk of
party politics is all hot air. They all want just the same – they all want
bread and beer and dollars. The parties are just labels. Labels get worn
out and can – and should – be changed.

June: If there's no difference, why – –

Tony: Don't be a silly kid. I'm doing this for you.

June: For me! That's swell! Say, thanks a lot!

Tony: You told me I must get a job. You told me I must rough it,
like your uncles in the States. And so I've joined the Labour Party.
Damn it – if that isn't roughing it, what is? Come here, don't be a silly
little ass. Come on – let's have a kiss. All right, I'll come to you.

>   *She turns away.*

All right, if you're going to be a child – well, carry on. If one does
something in one's life that one believes in, people always turn against
one anyway. One's got to bear one's cross.

June: O.K. St Anthony!

Tony: June – please – I want to kiss you, please.

June: I wouldn't want to kiss a yellow skunk.

Tony: All right, I'll shoot myself. (*He picks up the rifle.*) You'd
look pretty silly if I shot myself because you couldn't mind your own
business. What would you do?

June: I guess I'd tell your father that another rabbit's had it in the
grounds.

>   *Tony goes out through the french window. June flops down in the
>   armchair. Beecham enters.*

June: Oh, Beecham, come and hold my hand. I want my mum.

Beecham: I doubt if I should be a satisfactory substitute for Mrs
Farrell, miss.

June: Give me a drink. Have one yourself. (*As he hesitates.*) Go on.
Relax. The upper class have gone to bed.

>   *Beecham pours out two drinks.*

You ought to meet my mother, Beecham. You'd be nuts about her.
Doesn't stink of autumn leaves, like all the guys round here.

Beecham: (*crossing to her with the two drinks*): She sounds refreshing, miss. (*He hands her one glass, then lifts the other.*) To your engagement, miss – the union of two great English-speaking Powers.

JUNE: One isn't speaking, Beecham. My engagement's off.

BEECHAM: A lovers' tiff, miss, frequently occurs in the prenuptial period.

JUNE: Say, Beecham, would you marry Tony?

BEECHAM: Well, miss, if I were young and beautiful and rich – –

JUNE: If you wore skirts and he wore pants, would you get hitched?

BEECHAM: I would, miss – on the long view – yes. His lordship is perhaps a trifle immature. The public school system in vogue in this country has a tendency towards prolonging adolescence into early manhood, miss.

JUNE: I'll say it has.

BEECHAM: May I inquire if you feel amatory towards his lordship, miss?

JUNE: Hell, Beecham – cut the parlour talk. You asking – 'Am I nuts about the guy?'

BEECHAM: That phrase contains in essence the embodiment of my inquiry, miss.

JUNE: Oh, I dunno. (*She considers.*) I want to bite his ears till the room spins round and all his ancestors stand up inside their frames and shout out 'Atta girl' – You follow me?

BEECHAM: Quite closely, miss.

JUNE: I want to go away and never see the dope again. I want to hug him – till his ribs are cracked. I want to slap his face and pull his hair and kick him in the teeth. I want – – Oh, Beecham, tell me what I want.

BEECHAM: I think, miss, if you'll pardon me, you want a good night's rest.

JUNE: But do I love the guy?

BEECHAM: His lordship certainly appears to play a major role in your emotional reactions, miss.

JUNE: But if he stands as Labour in the by-election – that's the end.

BEECHAM: I think it most unlikely, miss. His lordship lacks political stability, admittedly – but surely not to that extent.

JUNE: That's what you think. It's all arranged.

BEECHAM (*amazed*): You mean that, miss?

JUNE: Yeah. Have another drink.

Beecham pours himself another whisky.

It knocks Pearl Harbour through the hoop.

BEECHAM: Exactly, miss – that episode assumes the relative importance of a fracas in a public-house.

JUNE: Oh, Beecham. What am I to do?

BEECHAM: I suggest you fight him back, miss.

She looks up.

Remember Lady Astor was a foreigner, and yet she sometimes gained the public ear.

JUNE: But Lady Astor married. I'm a U.S. citizen.

BEECHAM: That's easily adjusted, miss.

JUNE: Say, Beecham, are you doing the big thing?

BEECHAM: No, miss. His lordship was the groom I had in mind.

JUNE: What – board him first – and sink him afterwards?

BEECHAM: Precisely, miss.

JUNE: We aren't on speaking terms.

BEECHAM: I should be very ready, miss, to take the role of go-between.

JUNE: No. Hell, I won't. He's letting down the family – betraying everything he ought to love, including me.

BEECHAM: In that event, miss, nothing can be done. Except to wait and trust to the Electorate to show his lordship that expediency does not always pay.

JUNE: But Mr Cleghorn says he'll be unopposed.

BEECHAM: It's up to someone to oppose him, miss.

JUNE: But WHO?

BEECHAM: I don't know, miss. The situation's terrible. There's nothing I would not do to save his lordship from political advancement at the cost of principle – no, nothing, miss.

JUNE: Say, is that true?

BEECHAM (*surprised at the tone in her voice*): Indeed it is, miss, yes.

JUNE: O.K. Oh, Beecham, you're swell – Beecham. Does your mother call you Beecham too?

BEECHAM: No, miss. She calls me Benjamin. Beecham was my mother's maiden name. My father's name – my proper name – is Charles. Benjamin Charles.

JUNE: That's swell. Why Benjamin?

BEECHAM: My father's father had a great affection for the late Lord Beaconsfield – –

JUNE: Your grandmother?

BEECHAM: I said – grandfather – miss.

JUNE: Oh, yeah. Of course you did. Now, Benjy – we've a secret – you and I – till Nomination Day.

BEECHAM: What secret, miss?

JUNE: His lordship's going to be opposed! That's all. Good night. And keep your chin up. We'll fight them back!

> *June goes out. Beecham picks up his glass and swallows the remainder of his drink. Tony enters through the french window with the rifle.*

TONY: Hey, Beecham, leave that there. I want a drink.

BEECHAM: I thought perhaps you would, my lord. I'll pour it out.

TONY: No soda, thanks. I may be going to fight this seat as Labour – have you heard? Dashed good idea, what?

BEECHAM: That's open to debate, my lord.

TONY: Well, dash it – everybody's Labour now. Call myself National Labour – and get twenty thousand Labour votes – and most of the Conservative. Besides, I'll be unopposed.

BEECHAM: Perhaps, my lord.

TONY: Don't tell me anybody'd be such a silly fool as to fight me and lose his deposit.

BEECHAM: It's the so-called silly fools that often save the world, my lord.

TONY: What for – that's what I want to know – what for?

BEECHAM: Posterity, my lord. Good night.

> *He goes out. Tony goes to the window. After a pause, Bessie enters. She sees Tony.*

BESSIE: My lord. I seen the light.

TONY: You have, by Jove? I've seen it too.

BESSIE: I came to put it out.

TONY: Oh, yes. Well, carry on. (*He puts his glass on the table, switches off the lamp.*) It's nicer in the dark.

BESSIE: I thought that there was no one here.

Tony: Now, don't keep walking backwards, Bessie. You'll have a fall. Sit down and have a chat.

Bessie: Oh, sir, I couldn't, sir.

Tony: Why couldn't you? Come on. Sit down and have a drink.

Bessie sits on end of the sofa. Tony goes to pour out a drink for her.

I want to hear your views on politics. You voted for old Cleghorn, didn't you?

Bessie: I'm sorry, yes, my lord.

Tony: Good show! You've got some sense. (*He hands her the drink.*) That not too strong?

She nods.

(*Sitting beside her, and offering his case.*) A cigarette?

Bessie: No thanks, my lord.

Tony: Don't smoke?

Bessie: No, sir.

Tony: You funny child, what do you do?

Bessie: I do the rooms, my lord.

Tony: Oh, yes, I know you do. Dashed well, as well. There's going to be a by-election here.

Bessie: Oh, yes, my lord.

Tony: I'm going to stand as Labour, possibly.

Bessie: Oh, I'm glad.

Tony: You are? Thank heaven someone is. Now, tell me why.

Bessie: Then I can vote for you, my lord. Just like I wanted to.

Tony: Why did you want to, eh?

Bessie: Oh, sir!

Tony: Because you liked my face?

Bessie: Oh, sir!

Tony: That's awfully sweet. (*He rises and takes her empty glass.*) Another one?

Bessie: Oh, sir – I mustn't, sir.

Tony: Come on. Why not? (*Pouring her another one even stronger than the last.*) Now, Bessie, what's your plan in life?

Bessie: Oh, sir, I haven't thought – –

Tony: Of course you have. All women think – of that. How old are you?

Bessie: I'm twenty-two.

TONY: A boy friend, eh? (*He hands her glass.*)

BESSIE: No, sir.

TONY: A man friend, then. (*He sits beside her again.*) I know all about you. You don't believe in marriage, do you?

BESSIE: Oh, I do.

TONY: You mustn't, Bessie, it's all rot. One can't get unconditional surrender from a woman.

BESSIE: Sir, you mustn't talk like that.

TONY: Why not? It's true.

BESSIE: Miss June – –

TONY: Blow Miss June. She's given me the bird.

BESSIE: I'm sorry, sir.

TONY: How sweet you are. What pretty hands you've got. You mustn't spoil them dusting. (*He tries to take one, unsuccessfully.*) Damn it all, why should you dust? Mother does it, anyway.

BESSIE: I've got to earn my keep.

TONY: I know, it all comes down to that. You don't believe in money, do you, being Commonwealth?

BESSIE: Well, it's nice to have a bit.

TONY: It isn't, Bessie. It can't buy the only thing that matters – which is love. You wouldn't like to hold my hand?

BESSIE: Oh, sir.

TONY: Of course you wouldn't – no. I'm feeling lonely, that was all. You ought to fall in love and settle down. A little cottage – and some flowers.

BESSIE: Yes, sir – it would be nice.

TONY: Don't call me 'sir'. Tony's my name.

BESSIE: Oh, sir – I couldn't, sir.

TONY: Of course you could. You said you couldn't have a drink. You've had two now. (*He takes her glass and puts it on the table behind.*) Come on – say Tony twice.

BESSIE: Tony.

TONY: Again.

BESSIE: Tony. (*She giggles.*) Oh, it's so funny here.

TONY: What's funny? Me?

BESSIE: The place. It's all so big. I live at home in just a tiny cottage. Father, Mother, me – that's all. It's nicer, though. It's much more homely. People are themselves. It's cheaper, too.

TONY: How much?

BESSIE: Well, ours is nine and six a week.

TONY: Good God – can people live in a cottage for nine and six a week?

BESSIE: Of course, you can have smaller ones.

TONY: How sweet and sensible you are. A cottage and some flowers is all one wants. Except, of course, a wife.

BESSIE: That might be more expensive.

TONY: Why? It needn't be. (*He puts an arm round her.*) It wouldn't be – with you.

BESSIE (*getting up*): Oh, sir – I'm going to bed.

TONY (*getting up too*): What's wrong? Don't go. I think you're sweet. (*He suddenly kisses her.*)

BESSIE (*bursting into tears*): Oh, sir.

TONY: What's up?

BESSIE: I didn't ever want to till I met my man.

TONY: Well, p'raps you have. And, anyway, you've got to start sometime.

BESSIE: It's not your fault. I'll just go up.

TONY: No, Bessie, stop. I didn't want to spoil your dream.

BESSIE: I know. But – just the same – it's spoiled.

TONY: Well – if it's spoiled – let's have another one to say 'Good night.' (*He holds out his arms to her and she comes into them.*) Perhaps we haven't spoilt your dream after all.

> *They both sink on to the sofa and continue with the embrace. Lord Lister enters in a dressing-gown, and crosses to the window.*

LORD LISTER: Hullo, Tony. You still up? (*He picks up his rifle.*) Came to get my gun.

> *Tony and Bessie rise.*

Moonlight. I might see something from my dressing-room. (*He discerns another figure.*) Hullo, is that June?

TONY: No, Father. Do you know Miss Sykes? (*Lamely.*) She's Commonwealth.

LORD LISTER (*shaking hands with Bessie*): Oh, how d'you do? Dashed good of you to turn out at this time of night. You politicians never rest. I mustn't hang about, or Molly's sure to see a bat. Molly's my wife. She can't stand bats. She thinks they nest in women's hair. God knows why! I wouldn't like to have my nest brushed twice a day. And hair-pins shoved right through me. Still, one never knows with bats. Well, I'll be off. Call again and meet my wife. (*He goes to the door, then turns.*) Say, tea – or something. Sorry she's not down to see you now. (*He examines his equipment.*) I got everything? Mustn't interrupt you. I expect you want to go on chewing over the Election. Well, good night.

> *He exits.*

CURTAIN

SCENE 2

Nomination Day in the By-election.
The Scene is set for breakfast as in Act One, Scene 2. Bessie, the silver basket on her arm, is putting the finishing touches to the table.
Tony enters in a smart city suit.

TONY: 'Morning, Bessie. (*As she just stands and looks at him.*) What's the matter – have you lost your voice?
BESSIE: I'm sure I don't know what I've lost, my lord.
TONY (*going up to kiss her*): Come on, let's see you smile. I'll be an M.P. by one o'clock.
BESSIE: I thought they had to vote.
TONY: Not when I'm unopposed. Come on, let's have a kiss.
They kiss.
You liked that, didn't you?
BESSIE: I like a lot of things I didn't like before.
TONY: Then you must be in love.
BESSIE: Well, p'raps I am.
TONY: With me?

> *Bessie pulls away.*

What's the matter?
BESSIE (*bursting into tears*): Oh, I don't know. I wish I knew.
TONY: No, Bessie. Not at breakfast, please.

She rushes to the door crying. Beecham comes in with the coffee.

BEECHAM: Here, what's the game?

BESSIE: I've got a headache, sir.

She rushes out.

BEECHAM (*shouting after her*): Well, take an aspirin and get laid down. (*Seeing Tony.*) Good morning, my lord. A most emotional young person. She informs me that she often dreams of Mr Errol Flynn. A Transatlantic cinematograph performer, I believe, my lord.

TONY: The papers come yet?

BEECHAM: No, not yet, my lord.

TONY: It's a lovely day for politics. (*Beecham does not reply.*) You don't approve of Viscount Pym, M.P.?

BEECHAM: I don't like turncoats, no, my lord.

TONY: Oh, come on, Beecham; after all, I'm unopposed. I've saved the Government a bit of cash. Besides, you voted for me as a Tory, so it shows you think I ought to be in Parliament. I've chosen the best vehicle, that's all.

BEECHAM: Talking of vehicles, the tumbril had, at least, a certain dignity, my lord.

TONY: By Jove, a revolutionary! Is that it? Want to guillotine us all?

BEECHAM: Not indiscriminately, no, my lord.

TONY: Damn fools, those fellows. All those French aristocrats. It serves 'em right. They couldn't see the future, that was all.

BEECHAM: Perhaps their lack of foresight might have been less tragic than the vision of the Corsican, my lord.

TONY: What Corsican?

BEECHAM: The Emperor Bonaparte – a somewhat irresponsible young man, my lord.

Lady Lister comes in.

BEECHAM: Good morning, my lady.

LADY LISTER: Good morning, Beecham. 'Morning, Tony.

Beecham exits.

Goodness, you're early. What's the matter? Did you drink too much last night?

TONY: No, Mother, I'm a bit excited, I suppose.

LADY LISTER: Oh, yes, of course. It's Nomination Day. I knew it was, but Joe said I was talking nonsense. Oh ,what squashy sausages! Your father's very worried, Tony dear.

TONY: That means you are. What's the matter? Ducks not laying well?

LADY LISTER: No, June. (*She kisses Tony.*) She seems so strange. She's always telephoning secretly and going out. Your father wonders – are you still engaged?

TONY: I wouldn't know. We aren't on speaking terms.

LADY LISTER: How very childish, dear! You really must grow up – an M.P., too, today. The Speaker couldn't say 'I'm not on speaking terms.'

TONY: If June would keep her fingers out of politics, I wouldn't mind.

LADY LISTER: That's silly, dear – June's an American. She's interested in all old-fashioned things.

TONY: I know – I wish that isolation wasn't out of date.

LADY LISTER: Besides, she does no harm. She's just a child.

Lord Lister enters.

TONY: Children can do some pretty hare-brained things. I wouldn't trust her round the corner till I'm in – she's too dashed rich.

LORD LISTER: Who's rich?

TONY: June, Father.

LORD LISTER: Why, has someone died?

LADY LISTER: No, dear, she's rich, that's all. Some people are.

LORD LISTER: Dashed funny things these death duties. In the old days, when someone died one used to get a bit of cash. Now someone dies and one pays up, as though it was dashed entertainment tax. (*To Lady Lister.*) I saw that fox last night, my dear – twelve thirty-one.

Beecham enters with the daily papers.

TONY: Oh, give 'em here. I want to see what dear Lord Beaverbrook says about me.

Beecham crosses and gives the papers to Tony.

LADY LISTER: You needn't worry about that, my dear. In 1939 he said there wouldn't be a war.

LORD LISTER: Beecham.

BEECHAM: Yes, my lord?

LORD LISTER: Who cooked these sausages?

BEECHAM: Bessie, my lord.

LORD LISTER: She dashed well didn't.

BEECHAM: Very good, my lord.

LORD LISTER: Tell Bessie from me that both sides of a sausage ought to be cooked. (*Handing his plate to Beecham.*) Take 'em back and get 'em done.

BEECHAM: Yes, very well, my lord.

TONY (*leaping up*): My God!

June enters.

LADY LISTER: What is it, dear – one of my pins?

TONY: I'm going to be opposed. Listen. (*He reads excitedly from the 'Daily Express.' Beecham stands listening.*) 'Surprise nomination expected at East Milton. Our Political Correspondent understands that the East Milton Conservative Association have adopted as their candidate in the by-election a well-known local figure.'

LADY LISTER: How exciting, Tony. Is it somebody we know?

TONY: I've never heard of him. A chap called Charles. Benjamin Charles.

Beecham drops the plate and sausages.

LORD LISTER: What the devil are you doing, Beecham? Had a heart-attack?

BEECHAM: No, something burnt my finger-tips, my lord.

JUNE: Come on, I'll help you Beecham. (*Aside.*) Stick it, Benjy. 'On the beaches, in the meadows.' Stick it, Benjy. Show you've got some guts.

LORD LISTER: Leave him alone, June. Damn fellow comes in here and throws the plates about. You wouldn't do that music-hall turn in the pantry, would you, now?

BEECHAM: Not voluntarily, no, my lord.

LORD LISTER: Well, damn it – why try out your parlour tricks in here? Now take 'em out and get 'em cleaned and cooked.

Beecham goes out with the dish and plate, June opening the door for him.

TONY (*taking the 'Daily Mail'*): Let's see what it says here. Ah, here's a photograph.

W.D.H.–L

LADY LISTER : Do have your coffee, Tony. It's all getting cold.

TONY : My sainted aunt! It's Beecham! Mother, look! It's BEECHAM, Father! BEECHAM! June! Here, ring the bloody bell.

LADY LISTER (*taking the paper from him*) : TONY! If you are going to talk like that, you take your breakfast into the smoking-room. I will not have you using filthy words like that before your father. (*She glances at the photograph.*)

LORD LISTER : What's that, dear?

LADY LISTER : He wants to ring the bell.

LORD LISTER : You leave the bell alone. I want my sausages.

TONY : But, Father – BEECHAM! Standing against ME!

LORD LISTER : Dash politics. I want my bloody sausages.

LADY LISTER : Yes, Tony dear, your father wants his sausages. Sit down and have your breakfast, dear. There must be some mistake. Perhaps Lord Beaverbrook has got things wrong again.

TONY : And Kemsley – and Camrose – and Rothermere! Not likely, eh?

LORD LISTER (*who is studying the photo in the 'Daily Mail'*) : Where the devil did old Beecham get that hat?

LADY LISTER : What's wrong with it? It's very smart.

LORD LISTER : It's smart all right. It dashed well ought to be. It cost me forty-seven shillings in St James's Street last year.

LADY LISTER : I gave it to him, Joe, for Christmas – I remember now. It didn't match your suit.

LORD LISTER (*who is still studying the photograph*) : Which suit? (*He points at the photograph with great emotion.*) That suit?

LADY LISTER : Yes, dear, the suit is yours as well. I gave that to him too. Remember when they gave you that material – the year you won the fat-stock prize at Lister Show?

LORD LISTER : What! That was priceless stuff!

LADY LISTER : It may have been – but Beecham thought it was too loud.

The telephone rings. Tony goes to answer it.

TONY (*at the telephone*) : Hullo? . . . Conservative Association? . . . Pym here. You don't want me? . . . I didn't think you would. Who do you want? . . . Miss Farrell? Hold the line. Here, June. (*He holds out the receiver.*)

JUNE (*at the telephone*): Yeah, hullo. A lovely day for politics.
. . . Yeah . . . Yeah. I know. We've hit the headlines quite O.K.
They've done us proud. We've jumped the gun . . . Yeah – he'll be
O.K. . . . Yeah, he'll be there. I'll keep him on the mark . . .
O.K. . . . O.K. Be seeing you. So long.

> *She hangs up and turns to see Tony, who is standing beside her
> with his mouth agape.*

Hullo, you taking off the Loch Ness Monster?

TONY: WELL! Dash it, June, I think you might have told me.

JUNE: I guess I didn't kinda think you thought I was a politician,
kid.

TONY: You little fool! My God, I wish I'd never clapped my eyes
on you.

JUNE: O.K. – Democracy! It isn't your election, Tony. There's a
crowd of other funny little guys who like to have a say. Least, that's
what Lincoln thought.

TONY: SHUT UP!

LADY LISTER: My children, please!

TONY: Go back and live in your stupendous, vulgar, headline-
hitting country – and leave me ALONE.

> *He stamps out through the french window and walks up and
> down outside.*

JUNE: O.K. – then – Garbo. When I've cooked your goose I'll hop
it, kid.

LADY LISTER: Now, children, please don't quarrel. There are more
important things to do. (*To Lord Lister.*) Joe, tell me – what are we to
do? You must DO something, Joe.

LORD LISTER: What can I do? If Beecham wants to stand, it's up
to him. He's twenty-one.

LADY LISTER: But, Joe, he's coming in – at any minute – with the
sausages.

LORD LISTER: I hope he dashed well is.

LADY LISTER: Well, you MUST say something then.

LORD LISTER: Don't worry. If they aren't done right, I'll say a
thing or two.

LADY LISTER: Oh, Joe, what use are you?

LORD LISTER: I take no part in Party Politics, my dear.

LADY LISTER: But, dear, the servant problem isn't politics.

LORD LISTER: Still, 'course I know my duty. As Lord Lieutenant I shall have to ask him here to stay, that's – if he wins. (*Dismissing the matter from his mind.*) I saw that vixen last night, June.

JUNE: You did? You get a shot?

LORD LISTER: No – too dashed dark. Still, I'll get her yet. I knew a fellow once who waited for a buffalo for seven years.

JUNE: He must have been a constant guy.

LORD LISTER: Brute killed him in the end. He climbed a tree – the fella, not the buffalo. It licked his feet right off.

LADY LISTER: Joe, not at breakfast, dear!

LORD LISTER: Eh? Not at breakfast – no. Just before dawn.

> *Beecham enters with the sausages. He crosses to Lord Lister with the plate and dish, puts down the plate before Lord Lister, then lifts the cover of the dish for the inspection of the sausages.*

That's better. Something like a sausage, that. (*He helps himself to a couple.*)

> *Beecham goes to the door. Tony comes in through the french window. They all watch Beecham.*

LADY LISTER: Oh, Beecham.

BEECHAM: Yes, milady?

LADY LISTER: Have you seen the newspapers this morning?

BEECHAM: Not yet, milady, no.

TONY: You're billed to stand against me as a Tory in the by-election.

BEECHAM (*going out*): Very good, my lord.

TONY: Hey, Beecham.

> *Beecham stops.*

Just as well it's out. It gives you time to knock this joker on the head and tell 'em you'll withdraw.

LADY LISTER: You will withdraw, of course. You couldn't want to stand. And as it's clearly someone's joke, we'll say no more about it, will we, Joe?

LORD LISTER: No, rather not. Except, of course, I hope you'll come and stay with us if you get in.

BEECHAM: Most certainly. I will accept with deepest gratitude, my lord.

LORD LISTER: No, not a bit. Be nice to have you – er – er – round the place. (*He picks up 'The Times'.*)

Beecham turns to go once more.

TONY: Here, Beecham, show some sense. You must withdraw.

BEECHAM: My lord, my party comes before my personal preferments. If I'm chosen by the people's representatives, I have no option but to hear their call.

JUNE: Hear! Hear!

BEECHAM: Will that be all, milady?

LADY LISTER: I suppose so, yes.

TONY: I hope you've got a thousand quid to chuck away.

BEECHAM: Crusaders never want for cash, my lord.

He exchanges a look with June and goes out.

TONY (*furiously, turning on June*): You're backing him.

JUNE: So what? I don't see why the Labour boys should sit on all the money-bags.

TONY: Why can't you go away?

JUNE: I guess I will, when Mr Charles is IN.

LADY LISTER: Oh, children, please! Joe, really this is serious. We've only got one servant in the place – –

LORD LISTER: Good thing! He won't be here to chuck the plates about.

LADY LISTER: Oh, what a blessing Bessie's here.

TONY: You won't have Bessie any more.

LADY LISTER: Why not? She hasn't given notice, has she?

TONY: No. I'll give it for her, Mother. I've made up my mind. I'm going to marry Bessie.

JUNE: Tony! You're NOT!

TONY: I didn't think that it'd interest you.

JUNE: You must be NUTS.

TONY: O.K. That's something you should understand.

June snatches her engagement ring off, flings it at Tony and rushes from the room in tears. The ring falls in Lord Lister's sausages.

LORD LISTER (*picking it out*): I say – the butcher forgot to take the ring out of this pig's nose!

LADY LISTER (*taking the ring from him*): Oh, Tony dear, why must you talk like that? You've upset June.

TONY: But, Mother dear, it's true.

LADY LISTER: But, dear, we haven't got a servant in the place.

TONY: I can't help that.

LADY LISTER: Of course you can – you should have thought of that before you put the question, dear. And Caroline and Lord Cleghorn are coming here the week-end after next. Joe, Joe, DO SOMETHING, Joe!

LORD LISTER (*looking up from 'The Times'*): What is it, dear?

LADY LISTER: Tony says he wants to marry Bessie.

LORD LISTER: Who's Bessie?

TONY: Bessie Sykes, Father.

LORD LISTER: Ah, yes. The girl who called that night about the Commonwealth. Dashed pretty girl. Does June agree?

TONY: I don't care what June thinks.

LADY LISTER: But, Joe, Bessie's the maid.

LORD LISTER: What maid?

LADY LISTER: Our maid. She's BESSIE, dear.

LORD LISTER: Well, that's all right, if Beecham doesn't mind.

LADY LISTER: Oh, dear – you are so thoughtless, Tony. You've got no idea how difficult they are to get.

LORD LISTER: What? Maids or wives?

LADY LISTER: Now, don't be silly, dear. I'm really angry now. I'll have to ring the agency.

LORD LISTER: Now stop it, Moll. You married me. Why shouldn't Bessie Sykes get married too? Where's June?

TONY: In hell, I hope.

LADY LISTER: Tony, I will not have that talk. You've upset June, you've upset me. (*Rising.*) I'll have to go and comfort her. You really are too thoughtless, dear. Why these things have to happen when my ducks want feeding, I don't know. (*She exits.*)

TONY: Well, I must go and get the car – I've got to hand my nomination in by ten.

LORD LISTER: You taking Beecham with you?

TONY: Damn it, no.

LORD LISTER: You must. I'm dashed if I'll send two cars these days. (*He rises and rings the bell above the fireplace.*) I'll have him ready on the mat. It's only civil, after all.

> *Tony goes out. There is a pause. Then Bessie comes in to clear the breakfast and answer the bell.*

BESSIE: Did you ring, my lord?

LORD LISTER: Er – yes. Is Beecham there?

BESSIE: He's changing. Says he's going with Lord Pym, my lord.

LORD LISTER: Ah – yes. Ah – good. (*He watches her nervously as she clears the table, then summons up courage and walks across to her.*) Er – are you Bessie – eh?

BESSIE: Yes, my lord.

LORD LISTER (*putting out his hand*): I'm Lister. How d'you do? I hope you'll come and stay with us as soon as you can get away – –

BESSIE (*bewildered*): Thank you, my lord.

LORD LISTER: You give your fortnight's notice in today and come and stay the week-end of the poll.

BESSIE (*still more bewildered*): What, my lord?

LORD LISTER: Er – aren't you Bessie Sykes?

BESSIE: I am, my lord.

LORD LISTER: That's right – I thought you were. Well, you're engaged to Tony.

BESSIE: Me!

LORD LISTER: Yes – hasn't he told you yet?

BESSIE: He hasn't, no, my lord.

LORD LISTER: Oh, well, perhaps he forgot. My family's very absent-minded. Still, you can take it from me you are engaged. Congratulations. We'll have a lot of fun. Well, I'm afraid I must go now. Er – yes. Excuse me. I've got to go and feed those blasted ducks.

> *He goes out. Bessie, rather stunned, turns once more to the table. Then Beecham enters, wearing Lord Lister's very loud suit – Lord Lister's St James's Street hat in hand.*

BEECHAM: Now, lunch at one – if I'm not back – and keep your place – and say 'my lord' – and get the silver cleaned, you understand?

BESSIE: Yes, Mr Beecham, very good.

BEECHAM: I'll trouble you to call me Mr Charles.

BESSIE: Yes, Mr Charles.

BEECHAM (*taking a cigar out of his pocket and lighting it*): And don't let's have you breaking any plates. This place is not a music-hall.

BESSIE: Don't talk to me like that! I'm going to marry Tony.

BEECHAM (*shaken out of himself*): You're what?

BESSIE: I'm going to marry Tony, so don't you talk to me like that – and learn to keep *your* place.

TONY (*off*): Beecham!

BEECHAM (*in a strangled voice which Tony does not hear*): Yes, my lord.

TONY (*shouting louder*): BEECHAM!

BEECHAM (*drawing himself up to his full height, hat on head, cigar in mouth, defiant*). Comin', Pym.

Majestically and slowly he goes out.

CURTAIN

ACT THREE

SCENE 1

The day of the by-election count. Before lunch – a fortnight later.

Bessie, staying here now, is alone and bored. In her 'Sunday best,' she is seated on the sofa, reading 'The Tatler,' which she has obviously read several times before. She throws it down beside her, looks at the telephone, then at the clock and hurries to turn on the news.

The voice of the Radio Announcer comes through.

RADIO ANNOUNCER: This was denied by the Ministry of Food today.

> *Bessie is about to switch off when she hears the following.*

The result of the East Milton by-election has not yet been declared. As listeners to our earlier bulletin were informed, there has already been one re-count and another has been in progress all the morning. There has also been a further examination of spoilt papers and the results may be expected in the early afternoon.

> *Lord Lister enters through the french window and stands listening.*

Our correspondent understands that, while they are awaiting the result, both candidates will be entertained to luncheon at Lister Castle by the Earl of Lister who, as Lord Lieutenant, takes no part in party politics. (*Pause.*) A second denial from the Ministry of Food – –

> *Bessie switches off.*

LORD LISTER: No news?

BESSIE: He says 'expected in the early afternoon.'

LORD LISTER: You seen my wife?

BESSIE (*resuming 'The Tatler'*): She's dishing up the luncheon, I expect.

LORD LISTER: Does she know both of 'em are coming to lunch?

BESSIE: Expect so. Everybody in the country seems to know.

Lord Lister: Oh, yes, my dear. The B.B.C. knows everything. They know it's going to rain before the weather knows itself. I wish you'd run along and tell her what that fellow said – and help her out a bit.

Bessie: Oh, shucks. I helped her with the slops today.

Lord Lister: Oh, really, did you? I didn't know. That puts a different light on it. All right, I'll go myself.

Bessie: You think I'm selfish, don't you?

Lord Lister: What? No, rather not. I see your point. You mustn't overdo it on your first day as a guest.

Bessie: You think that's funny, don't you?

Lord Lister: No, no. Rather not.

Bessie: You do – you're laughing at me. I can tell you it's – it's no fun staying here.

Lord Lister: By Jove, you've said a mouthful there.

Bessie: What? You agree?

Lord Lister: Of course I do. I bet a galley-slave – if one came here to stay – would send himself a telegram.

Bessie (*practically sobbing as the result of this unexpected sympathy*): And Tony wouldn't take me to the count.

Lord Lister: Oh, wouldn't he? P'raps there wasn't room.

Bessie: There's room for June, so why not for me?

Lord Lister: Ah, yes – why not? I'd better slip along and – – (*He starts for the door again.*)

Bessie: I'll tell you why he wouldn't take me. He's ashamed of me, that's why. (*She starts sobbing.*) Oh dear, I wish I was a maid again.

Lord Lister (*startled*): My dear, you don't mean . . .? Oh, yes, yes. A maid.

Bessie: At least I got two pounds a week. And had an overall to wear. Now everybody wants me to keep on working – every minute – in my Sunday best, without a single penny for my pains. It isn't fair.

Lord Lister: Come, come, my dear. We all get used to it in time.

Bessie: I won't. I never won't.

Lord Lister: Oh, yes – you will. The first initial shock – when one starts roughing it – is always worst. I know it from experience. The army taught me that. It doesn't last, my dear. We human beings are adaptable, you know. And Nature helps us to adjust ourselves to all the trials we have to face through life. (*He is getting a little involved, so he pats Bessie's head.*) There, there, my dear. I wish that I were younger. Fifty years ago I would have known the way to brush away those tears. I've not forgotten yet, by Jove. (*He moves away from temptation, however, rises, goes to the radio table and picks up a book.*) Here, have a look at that. It's interesting. It traces rabbits from the Ice Age down to 1939.

> *Nodding kindly to Bessie, he goes out. Bessie flings the book away across the floor. The door-bell rings. She rises and picks it up again. Lady Caroline and Lord Cleghorn are heard off.*

LADY CAROLINE (*off*): What an extraordinary thing. There must be someone in.

LORD CLEGHORN (*off*): Perhaps they've all gone off to hear the count.

LADY CAROLINE (*off*): Whatever for?

LORD CLEGHORN (*off*): Morbidity. To see the last Conservative brought low.

> *Lady Caroline enters, followed by Lord Cleghorn.*

LADY CAROLINE: My dear Lord Cleghorn, you're counting chickens before they're hatched. Ah! Here's Bessie, at any rate. Lord Cleghorn – this is Bessie. I've heard all about you from dear Molly, and I've told Lord Cleghorn EVERYTHING.

BESSIE: How do you do?

LORD CLEGHORN (*not shaking hands*): I think we met a few weekends ago?

BESSIE: Yes. I think we did.

LORD CLEGHORN: I think Lady Caroline would like to see her room.

LADY CAROLINE (*just as Bessie starts scowling*): I know my room. I always have the Purple Room. I've had it since I was a tiny girl. I wonder which is yours.

LORD CLEGHORN: I'm sure Bessie will conduct me there.

BESSIE: Here – don't you start on me as well. (*Putting the book down on the desk.*) I'm staying here, like you.

LORD CLEGHORN: So I perceive. But still, I thought you might be ready to assist a fellow guest to find his room.

Bessie stamps her foot and goes out of the french window.

I call that most uncalled for. What a very common, vulgar little girl.

LADY CAROLINE: I think she's rather sweet. She'll polish up quite wonderfully. She's just uncut.

LORD CLEGHORN (*wincing*): She doesn't know her place.

LADY CAROLINE: Does anyone, these days?

LORD CLEGHORN: Yes, I do. I'm plebeian – and I'm proud of it.

LADY CAROLINE: What – proud of what you were? Or what you are today?

LORD CLEGHORN: Of what I was, of course.

LADY CAROLINE: And not of what you are?

LORD CLEGHORN: I didn't say that.

LADY CAROLINE: I think you're just proud. And that's a failing you must try to cure.

LORD CLEGHORN: I like that! You're far the proudest person I have ever met.

LADY CAROLINE: I'm getting less proud every day. I'd like to be like Joe. He's got no pride at all. I sometimes think that that's the highest state we mortals can attain. The greatest quality tradition has to offer to the world. One generation can't achieve it, though. It's handed down and – thank the Lord – it can't be taxed.

Lord Lister comes in through the french window with a basket of potatoes. Lord Cleghorn rises.

LORD LISTER: Hullo, Caroline. Hullo, Cleghorn. Sorry that I wasn't here to meet you. I've been getting some spuds. Been down to the Town Hall?

LORD CLEGHORN: No – we came straight here from the station.

LORD LISTER: Ah, yes – yes, I see. A fellow told us – on the B.B.C. – that both of 'em are coming back to lunch. Dashed nice of him. Re-count, you know.

LORD CLEGHORN: Re-count! I can't believe it!

LORD LISTER: Well, there it is. Dashed funny things, re-counts. You count the votes once, and you reach a certain total – if you follow me. Then, dashed if you don't count 'em again – and you're hundreds out. Uncanny. How do you explain it, Cleghorn, eh?

LORD CLEGHORN: I can only hazard the suggestion that someone counts them wrong.

Beecham enters, wearing a blue rosette.

LORD LISTER: Ah, here you are. Er – Cleghorn, do you know – er – dash it, Beecham, what's your name today?

BEECHAM: Benjamin Charles, my lord.

LORD CLEGHORN: How do you do?

BEECHAM: Extremely well, my lord.

LORD CLEGHORN: Good weather for a by-election, eh?

BEECHAM: A Tory sun is peeping fitfully through Labour clouds, my lord.

> *Bessie comes in through the french window. Beecham regards her with distaste.*

LORD LISTER (*to fill the breach*): We heard the news. There wasn't any.

BEECHAM: The agent will ring through, my lord, if the result comes through earlier than expected.

LORD LISTER: Is June back yet?

BEECHAM: Miss Farrell is photographing Labour Party slogans chalked on the paintwork of the car, my lord.

LORD CLEGHORN: Good reading, I'll bet.

BEECHAM: I hardly think that statements like 'Old Beecham's heading for the House of Lords as well,' will earn immortal fame in English literature, my lord.

LORD CLEGHORN: How bigoted these people are. Provided that a man can get things done, I have no quarrel with the heights to which he may attain. They never seem to understand that leadership's a quality that's only granted to the lucky few, and then it rightly gains its own reward.

BEECHAM: Exactly so, my lord. (*To Lady Caroline.*) I'll take your suitcase up, my lady.

LADY CAROLINE: Please don't bother – I can manage it.

> *Lady Lister enters wearing an apron. Lady Caroline and Lord Cleghorn rise.*

LADY LISTER: Dear Caroline – how well you look. (*Turning to Lord Cleghorn.*) How are you? Sorry that I wasn't here to meet you, but I couldn't leave the vegetables.

BEECHAM. What vegetables, my lady?

LADY LISTER: Mostly brussels sprouts, I think.

BEECHAM: Here, Bessie – – (*there is a tense hush*) – you hop along and watch the veg. Her ladyship has other things to do.

BESSIE: Pipe down. I'm staying here.

BEECHAM (*quietly*): You heard me, Bess. (*He opens the door for her.*)

> *Bessie exits breaking into a run as she passes the masterful Beecham. Lords Lister and Cleghorn avoid each other's eye.*

Nicely done brussels sprouts are one of the minor rewards of leadership, my lord. Your lordship's room is next door to the Purple Room.

LADY CAROLINE: Come along with me. I know where it is. I'll show it to you, Jackie. (*She goes out.*)

LORD LISTER: Who's Jackie?

LORD CLEGHORN (*embarrassed*): My name is Jackie.

BEECHAM: I'll take your bags up, my lord.

LORD CLEGHORN: No, no, rather not. You stay here. (*He goes out.*)

LORD LISTER: Well, dash it – I'd say that fellow was in love with Caroline – if I didn't know she'd got a face like the back of a bulldozer.

LADY LISTER: Joe – *pas devant* . . .

LORD LISTER: Eh, what – *pas* who?

LADY LISTER: Oh, Joe, be quiet.

LORD LISTER: I won't be quiet. You started it by saying Pas somebody. What the devil is it?

LADY LISTER: Joe, I said BE QUIET. (*She goes out in anger.*)

LORD LISTER (*mystified*): Well, I'm dashed. She's like a scalded cat. Have I done something wrong?

BEECHAM: Her ladyship was talking French, my lord.

LORD LISTER: She can't talk French.

BEECHAM: Her ladyship did not attempt the accent, I admit, my lord. She merely phrased the first two words of the French idiom (*with a beautiful accent*) pas devant les domestiques.

LORD LISTER: What the devil does it mean?

BEECHAM: A hackneyed phrase, my lord – denoting that the subject mooted by some member of the company is scarcely fitted for the servants' ears.

LORD LISTER: Oh, that was it. Oh, thanks. What was the subject, eh?

BEECHAM: Your lordship merely stated that your sister, Lady

Caroline – in your opinion – lacked those qualities that might have launched a Trojan war, my lord.

LORD LISTER: Well, nothing wrong with that.

The telephone rings. Beecham crosses to it. June passes the window and enters.

JUNE: Say, is this IT?

June moves towards the telephone, but Beecham forestalls her.

BEECHAM (*in his butler's voice*). Hullo, sir? . . . Yes, sir. Hold the line a moment, sir, and I will see if he's in.

LORD LISTER: Who is it – me?

BEECHAM: No. It's the Press for me, my lord.

LORD LISTER: Well, get on with it, man.

He crosses and exits with the potatoes.

BEECHAM (*at the telephone – the politician's voice*): Hullo, yes . . . I am Mr Charles . . . An article? Hold on. I'll put you through to my secretary. (*He calls near the mouthpiece.*) Miss Farrell.

JUNE (*near the telephone*): O.K., Mr Charles. (*Into the telephone.*) Yeah – yeah . . . She's speaking . . . An article. O.K. What's its worth? . . . What, fifty pounds? What's that in dollars? . . . Hell – that's chicken feed. Say, listen, do you know we've got a lot to do? We can't waste time on parish magazines . . . I don't care what Lord Beaverbrook says. It's what I say that goes around these parts . . . A hundred. Yeah. O.K. Well, cheery-bye . . . So long, white slave. (*She rings off, sits at the desk and takes pencil and paper.*) O.K., Ben, let's do it now. Say, are you pro- or anti-war?

Beecham looks bewildered.

BEECHAM: What is this about, then, miss?

JUNE: Foreign policy. Sorry, I thought you knew.

BEECHAM: A glass of sherry, miss?

JUNE: No, thanks. Have one yourself. It might ease up the joints.

BEECHAM (*pouring one out*): Will you please take this down, miss.

He takes a sip of sherry. Tony comes in and stands regarding Beecham with distaste.

I do not believe in wars . . .

JUNE: Say, let's have something definite. That's wind.

BEECHAM: All politicians tend to vaporize a little, miss. (*Continuing with a slightly diminished confidence.*) I do not believe in wars . . . (*Pause.*) I do not believe in wars . . .

TONY: You've said that just three times.

Beecham puts down his sherry and draws himself up.

BEECHAM: No doubt your lordship finds it hard to visualize a politician saying anything identical on three consecutive occasions.

TONY: Carry on.

BEECHAM: I believe – – (*To June.*) If you'll excuse me, miss, I do not find the atmosphere conducive to developing my thesis for a working foreign policy. I think I'll go and find a less congested area in which to work. (*He crosses to the french window.*)

TONY: Yes, good idea.

BEECHAM (*stopping on his way out*): Would your lordship care to have a sporting wager on the outcome of the count? I'll lay you nine to four against yourself, my lord.

TONY: Dashed cocky, aren't you?

BEECHAM: Quietly confident, my lord. I'll give you three to one.

TONY: Shut up – you make me sick.

BEECHAM: I offer my apologies, my lord. I always understood finance was uppermost in every Labour politician's mind.

He stalks out through the french window.

JUNE (*after a pause*): Tony.

TONY: Hullo – on speaking terms again?

JUNE: On any terms you like. Please don't be angry, Tony. I just did it 'cos I love tradition and – and all the things you really love and don't quite know you do.

TONY: Then you'd better get around to loving Bessie too.

JUNE (*attempting a light laugh*): Oh, Bessie. She's a silly thing. I don't mind that.

TONY: That's big of you.

JUNE: I know you only did it 'cos you lost your rag. I don't mind that. There's no harm done. It won't hurt you. It won't hurt her – because she's just a silly little flirt.

Tony (*losing his temper*): She's not a flirt. She isn't silly. She's a damn sight more intelligent than you.

June (*losing her temper as well*): Oh, yeah? She is? O.K. Well – marry her. Go on and marry her.

Tony: I'm going to. It'll be in the papers when this dashed result is out. Is that O.K. by you?

June: O.K. – that's swell. (*She is hysterical now.*) You marry her – and have your sausages half done. Go on and marry her – and eat your lousy half-cooked sausages.

Tony (*shouting*): Why don't you go back to the States and stop this bloody row?

He goes out through the french window.

June (*shouting too*): O.K. – I will. (*She rushes to the telephone.*) Hullo! Hullo! I want the American Embassy, London . . . Yeah. I'll hold the line . . .

Bessie enters.

Yeah, yeah. United States Embassy, Grosvenor Square, London, England. Yeah.

Bessie: I hope you're not sore about Tony. After all, a man's allowed to change his mind.

June: I guess he is. Provided he's got a mind to hand in in exchange.

Bessie: Here, give a girl a chance. You don't get much in life if you're a parlourmaid. It's 'Yes, my lord,' the whole damn beastly day.

June: I guess you might try giving 'No, my lord' a break. (*To telephone.*) Hullo, yeah – that the Embassy? . . . Oh, Mr Rogers, please . . . Say, that you, Bolles? June Farrell here. Say, listen, Bolles. I want a passage to the States . . . Right now . . . Say, when's she sail? . . . Tomorrow, that's O.K. You do your best and ring me back at once. Lister one – O-N-E . . . No, I can't hold on . . . (*Angrily.*) No, sir – I'm *not* a bride.

Lord Lister enters just as June slams down the telephone.

Lord Lister: Lunch is nearly ready. Where is everyone? (*To Bessie, who is reading Beecham's election address.*) Hullo – you going Tory, Bessie? Dashed good stuff. (*He crosses to the french window and calls through.*) Hey, Tony, lunch is nearly ready.

W.D.H.–M

TONY (*off*): All right, Dad. I'm coming.

Lady Caroline and Lord Cleghorn enter.

LORD LISTER: Now, Cleghorn, have a drink.

Tony enters through the french window. The telephone rings. Tony picks up the receiver.

TONY: Pym speaking – are you the Town Hall? . . . –What? . . . Who's still on the line? . . . The American Embassy? . . . What's that? . . . The Washington? . . . Southampton. Nine o'clock. Tomorrow night . . . Yes. I'll tell her . . . Thanks. Good-bye. (*He hangs up and turns round to June.*)

JUNE: O.K. I got the message, thanks.

TONY: June – –

June exits. During the above, Lord Lister has handed sherry to Lady Caroline and Lord Cleghorn, who are by the fireplace. He is now determined to cheer things up.

LORD LISTER: Reading your election address in bed last night, Tony. All this talk about capitalism. Dashed rot. Every country's a capitalist country. Just depends whether it's state capitalism or private capitalism, that's all.

CLEGHORN: Exactly – that's our point.

LORD LISTER: But it isn't the point. The dashed point is – whether the private owner or the state are bigger crooks.

LADY CAROLINE: Joe, don't forget you take no part in party politics.

LORD LISTER: That isn't party politics. It's common sense.

The telephone rings.

That damn thing ought to be cut off. (*He gets there first.*) Hullo? . . . Yes, Brown . . . You're speaking from the Town Hall? . . . What? . . . You've got the result and you want a pencil? Surely to God you didn't ring me up for a pencil!

June enters through the french window.

(*In response to various offers.*) No – no – he's got a pencil at the Town Hall. (*Into the telephone.*) Ye-es. I see. You know, of course, I take no part . . . You do? But I'll gladly pass it on to 'em . . . Yes . . .

Thanks. (*A thought strikes him.*) Oh, Brown – I'd like to see you some-time. Any time you're free. About these damn foxes – there are too many of them. I thought we might have a shoot. The Master's in the South of France – so now's the time. . .

Tension is almost at breaking point.

Yes, come and dine one night and we'll have a chat . . . Yes, yes – I'll tell 'em both. Good-bye. Damned good of you to ring up. (*He hangs up.*) Now, Tony, where were we?

JUNE: Joe – did he say who won?

LORD LISTER: Yes – rather – yes.

JUNE: Well – WHO?

LORD LISTER: What? Well, what did he say? Er – dammit, you confuse me so.

Lord Cleghorn crosses to the telephone and lifts the receiver.

LORD CLEGHORN: The Town Hall, please, at once . . .

LORD LISTER (*during the wait for the call*): I know he wants to tell somebody – –

LORD CLEGHORN: Hullo . . . Lord Cleghorn – Lister Castle – here. Have you the result? . . . I thank you . . . Many thanks. Good-bye. (*He hangs up.*) Your butler won by thirty votes.

BESSIE (*breaking the hush*): Oh, goodie. And I voted for him, too.

TONY: You – WHAT?

BESSIE: I voted for him 'cos Mum said you was a Bourgeois.

TONY: This is the end. I'd like to meet a consistent woman for a change.

LORD CLEGHORN (*chivalrously pointing to June*): Well, this is one. (*Going to June.*) Congratulations. You must be feeling very happy now.

JUNE (*looking up for the first time since the news came through*): Oh, God! I wish we had lost!

> *She bursts into tears and goes and rests her head on Lord Lister's shoulder. He accepts the position with mingled pleasure and embarrassment.*
> *The door opens and Beecham enters. Momentarily dismayed by the scene before him, he forgets that he is a guest bearing a*

message to other guests and, despite his rosette, becomes the butler again.

BEECHAM : Luncheon is served.

LORD LISTER (*to June*) : Excuse me, please. (*He gets up and goes to Beecham.*) Ah, Beecham, just in time. Come in, come in, my dear fellow. (*He takes him by the arm.*) I want you all to meet our new M.P. My sister Caroline; Lord Cleghorn; your opponent you know; Miss Sykes and Miss Farrell. May I congratulate you from us all?

There is an unhappy lack of response to this gesture.

Now come along and meet my wife.

He urges him happily towards the door as the Curtain falls.

SCENE 2

Later the same night.

Lord Lister and Lord Cleghorn are at the table, Lord Lister pouring out three glasses of port. Beecham is standing aloof. All are wearing the same clothes as in the previous scene. Cigars have been lighted.

LORD LISTER : Dash it – I wish Molly wouldn't pull the table cloth away before I've had my port. I feel like a displaced person.

LORD CLEGHORN : Still, you've got a lot to be thankful for. Your wife's a wonderful cook.

LORD LISTER : Think so? I didn't think that bit of salmon was born yesterday. Here, have a glass of port. Who the devil are these glasses for? I must be getting like those fellows at the count who couldn't count. I wonder why the devil I brought three.

> *In the background Beecham shifts awkwardly – unseen. Lord Lister sits down on the chair, dismissing the matter from his mind. He and Lord Cleghorn each take a glass.*

Talking about salmon, Cleghorn – their sex life, my dear fellow– quite astonishing. Do you know – the female spawns – and then the male comes along later – when she isn't there, mark you – never meet. Extraordinary! Imagine, my dear fellow! For the sake of argument, my sister Caroline – stayed at Claridge's one night – you know, passing through, shopping and so forth – and then you – or any dashed fellow for that matter, up for a board meeting – stayed there the next night. Well – see what I mean? If you were a salmon – both of you, of course – dashed if the manager wouldn't find his dashed hotel half full of little silver smolts!

BEECHAM: I've always understood that some ninety per cent of the male fish – after the – er – spawn is completed – fail to survive the long trip down river to the sea.

LORD LISTER: Very likely –overdo it, eh? (*Suddenly realizing that Beecham is present and has contributed the last remark.*) What the devil do you know about it, anyway?

BEECHAM: The annual holiday, which you always assumed I spent at Blackpool with my bucket and spade, was, in reality, enjoyed on a Scottish river where I've leased a rod for more than thirteen years.

LORD LISTER: Well – I'll be – – Think you might have told me. Crazy about fishing, after all.

BEECHAM: Exactly, my lord, and it has always been my ambition to assimilate sufficient capital to lease another rod and to invite you as my guest.

LORD LISTER: That's very decent of you. Very decent. Let me see, they hope to raise the M.P.s' salaries this session, don't they, Cleghorn, eh?

LORD CLEGHORN: I've heard the subject mentioned, certainly.

LORD LISTER: Oh, good. Here, Beech – er, Charles, do go and get yourself a glass of port. Expect you've got the cellar key.

Beecham makes towards the door in embarrassment.

LORD CLEGHORN (*tactfully*): I think the port's already on the table, isn't it?

LORD LISTER: Eh, what? Yes – dash it – of course – that glass. (*To Beecham's retreating form.*) Beecham! Here – come here. Sit down and have a glass of port.

BEECHAM (*coming to the table*): Thank you, my lord. (*He takes the third glass.*)

LORD CLEGHORN: Good health!

They all drink. Beecham takes his port to the sofa and sits. There is an awkward silence, broken by: –

Lord Cleghorn: I can't help thinking of June Farrell, Lister.

Lord Lister: Don't blame you. Dashed attractive, isn't she?

Lord Cleghorn: No, no, you get me wrong. I'm sorry that she's going. Though I disagree with her, of course – by gad, she's got some guts.

Lord Lister: All of us have, my dear fellow. Do you know, if you tied one end of your gut – the greater gut, I think it's called – to, well we'll say, for the sake of argument, the middle stump at Lord's – you could walk down to the other end, shake hands with the bowler, and back – round the square-leg umpire – to the wicket? No trouble at all, my dear fellow. Quite interminable. Hard to visualize. I mean to say – take Caroline – thin as a lead pencil – you'd never imagine . . .

Lord Cleghorn: I can think of nothing Lady Caroline reminds me of less.

Lord Lister (*interested*): Than what?

Lord Cleghorn: A pencil.

Lord Lister (*mystified*): Who's talking about pencils?

Lord Cleghorn: I thought you were.

Lord Lister: No, no. Caroline – you know, the one that's washing up.

Lord Cleghorn: Yes, yes – I know.

Lord Lister: Why are you looking at me like my bank manager?

Lord Cleghorn: I merely object to hearing a lady for whom I have the highest regard compared to a lead pencil.

Lord Lister: Well – take my wife – no need to quarrel about her. Now, you'd never imagine to look at Molly that you could wind her round the Albert Hall, take her off to cocktails at the Ritz – without a break. (*He laughs.*)

Lady Caroline enters, taking off an apron. They all rise.

Hullo, Caroline. We've just been talking about you.

Lady Caroline: Oh, pulling me to pieces, I suppose. I've done the washing-up. Now June and Molly've started on the silver. And she wants you to do something to the boiler, Joe.

Lord Lister: By Jove, yes. Needs a shot of coal. I don't know how to do it, though.

Beecham: Permit me to instruct you, then.

LORD LISTER (*as he passes Beecham on the way to the door*): No – not at all. You drink your port.

> *He goes out with Lady Caroline. Lord Cleghorn is left alone with Mr Charles, M.P.*

LORD CLEGHORN: Well, Beecham, how do you like being an M.P.?

BEECHAM: I feel a little out of place, my lord.

LORD CLEGHORN: Oh, well, you've done a goodish job today – apart from all the repercussions in the house.

BEECHAM: You have no bitterness against me, then?

LORD CLEGHORN: No – not a bit. Why should I have? It's my profession – politics. You've done your job and done it well. But now it's done.

BEECHAM: You say my job is done?

LORD CLEGHORN: Well, almost, yes. Not quite. You'll never be a politician, Beecham. No professional at any job is any use in politics – Field Marshals, University Professors, Butlers – none of 'em are any good. You see, a politician does the odd-man's jobs. He lacks the concentration and integrity to specialize. So, Beecham, take my tip and don't degrade yourself. A man who has got a place in life should keep it.

BEECHAM: Then, what should I do?

LORD CLEGHORN: Why don't you do what Lloyd George and Ramsay Mac – their jobs completed – should have done?

BEECHAM: What's that?

LORD CLEGHORN: Resign. Good night.

> *Lord Cleghorn goes out.*

BEECHAM (*wistfully*): Resign!

> *He is left bewildered. Then Bessie comes in through the french window.*

And where have you been?

BESSIE: Walking in the woods.

BEECHAM: Alone?

BESSIE: Of course I was alone. I've had this life. I'm through. Society makes me sick. God – it gets me down. Cold bath-water and moth-balls. I hope you done the washing-up tonight.

BEECHAM: It isn't proper for a man to do them dirty jobs.

BESSIE: My man'd have to do it.

BEECHAM: That's neither here nor there. Are you in love with Pym?

BESSIE: Oh, I don't know.

BEECHAM: Don't you like me a little bit, Bess?

BESSIE: I think you're very strong.

BEECHAM: Well then, don't strong men make fine handsome husbands for nice buxom country girls?

BESSIE: You asking me to marry you?

BEECHAM: Strong men don't fall in love with butterflies. They kiss them sometimes, though. You hear me, Bess? I said, 'they kiss them sometimes, though.'

BESSIE (*very quiet*): I heard you, Mr Charles.

> *She turns her face round to him and he moves towards her. She then rises and breaks away in front of him.*

Don't, Mr Charles. I couldn't never be a politician's wife. They gets above themselves.

BEECHAM: Who says I want to wed you?

BESSIE: Who says you don't? (*She kisses him.*) But you'll have to give up being an M.P. and learn to keep your place – that's straight.

> *She kisses him again. Lord Lister comes in through the french window and coughs tactfully. Bessie flies from the room.*

BEECHAM: Will you permit me to apologize?

LORD LISTER: No, not at all. Still, Bessie seems to get around a bit. Correct me if I'm wrong, but she's engaged to Tony, isn't she?

BEECHAM: The situation is a trifle fluid there. It could be solved by statesmanship.

LORD LISTER: Well, why not go ahead?

BEECHAM: It needs self-sacrifice as well.

LORD LISTER: What rot! (*He digs him in the ribs.*) If I was your age I'd know what to do. Go on, man – go on . . .

BEECHAM (*irresolute – suddenly decides*): Thank you, my lord.

> *He exits. Lord Lister picks up his gun by the window and is going out as Tony comes listlessly in.*

TONY: Dad – –

LORD LISTER (*off*): I've gone out.

Tony sits down on the sofa as June, in her dressing-gown, peeps round the door to see if he is there – and, seeing him, comes in.

JUNE (*crossing to the sofa*): I'm going in the morning.

He doesn't answer.

Write to me, Tony. We've been good pals. You used to like me, Tony. I'm going to kiss you just once more for memory. (*She does – not very successfully.*) I'm sorry, Tony dear, you are Conservative. It's in your blood. It's in your family. It's in your heritage. I know I've lost you, Tony. I was silly. You were stronger-minded than I thought . . . You need your hair cut, Tony dear. (*Emotion overcomes her.*) Say something, please. I can't live without you, Tony. I'm not going to live without you, do you hear? I'm going to die. (*She rushes to where Lord Lister keeps his rifle.*) I'm going to shoot myself. Oh, Tony, don't you want to say good-bye?

TONY: No. See you at the funeral.

June reaches behind the curtain for the rifle. A shot rings out. She screams. Tony rushes to her.

Oh, June. My darling June. You aren't hurt, are you?

JUNE: No. That was Joe, I guess.

TONY: June, my darling, will you marry me?

JUNE: Yes, but you'll have to get that job.

TONY: But, darling – I've been thinking, landowning's a full-time job. When Father's agent dies, I'll take his job and run the good old place. What say you, eh?

JUNE: That sounds all right. How old's your father's agent?

TONY: Twenty-eight. But he gets frightful colds.

JUNE: Oh, Tony darling, you're hopeless. P'raps that's why I love you, though.

TONY: Of course it is – and till then there's always politics.

JUNE: You've had it as a politician, kid.

TONY: Don't you believe it. We Listers always come up more than twice.

JUNE: But where?

TONY: Don't be so practical.

They fall into each other's arms. Lord Lister, with his rifle, enters in high excitement through the french window.

LORD LISTER: Tony, I've got it at last! Saw it in the moonlight, by the cypress tree. Dashed brute – it had a duck right in its jaw.

He leaves his rifle by the window, crosses and rings the bell, then notices June and Tony still locked in each other's arms.

Every time I come in the room this sort of thing's going on. Where's Beecham? I wish he'd hurry up.

Tony and June break up. Lord Lister rings again.

I wish he'd come – the beast may not be dead.

JUNE: It's no use ringing, Joe.

LORD LISTER: Why not?

JUNE: You know, Joe. Beecham's our M.P.

Beecham enters dressed as a butler. There is an electric silence.

BEECHAM: You rang, my lord?

LORD LISTER (*alone unmoved by Beecham's change of costume*): There's a fox and a duck under the cypress tree.

BEECHAM: Alive or dead, my lord?

LORD LISTER: Dead, damn it – fetch 'em quick – before they disappear.

BEECHAM: Yes – very good, my lord.

He goes out through the french window at the double.

JUNE: Joe! Tony! Why is Beecham dressed like that?

LORD LISTER: Like what?

JUNE: In tails.

LORD LISTER: Well, p'raps he likes 'em. P'raps they keep him warm.

JUNE: But, Joe, get hold of something, can't you? Beecham's our M.P.

LORD LISTER: What? Dash it – so he is. See what you mean, – no top hat.

Beecham enters carrying the corpses. Lord Lister hurries to examine them.

BEECHAM: Here we are, my lord.

LORD LISTER: An old vixen, by jove – that'll save a century of ducks.

BEECHAM: The duck was in the snare, my lord.

LORD LISTER: What? Dammit – then you set the thing too high.

BEECHAM: Unless the bird was moving *ventre-à-terre*, my lord.

JUNE (*butting in*): Say, Benjy, why the uniform?

BEECHAM: My name is Beecham, miss. (*To Lord Lister.*) I wonder – might I have your lordship's leave to use the telephone?

LORD LISTER: Yes, rather – ringing up the 'Field' or something, eh? (*Fingering the fox.*) Dashed lovely coat.

> *Beecham places the duck on the table, then goes to the telephone and lifts the receiver.*

BEECHAM: Lister eight-nine, please, miss.

LORD LISTER: If I had that cured, I doubt if Molly'd ever know it wasn't some dashed vermin from a Bond Street store.

> *He goes out through the french window with the fox.*

BEECHAM (*at the telephone*): Hullo? . . . Is that the *Advertiser*? . . . Take a story, please . . . 'Mr Benjamin Charles, M.P., the newly-elected member for Milton East, has decided to abandon the uncertainty of public life in favour of the constancy and unrivalled glory of domestic bliss' . . . Yes, this is Mr Charles himself . . . No – I am not. I had a single port at ten o'clock. Hullo? . . . Quote continues – 'I understand that Viscount Pym will contest the ensuing by-election in the interests of the . . .' Hullo? Hullo? I've been cut off. (*He hangs up.*)

TONY: Dashed good of you to give it up.

Beecham: No – not at all, my lord. I feel that you will make an excellent M.P. The lessons you have learnt will strengthen you on future platforms.

JUNE: Tory platforms, eh?

BEECHAM: Not necessarily – no. I have lately come to the conclusion that provided one's personality is proved, the party one belongs to is quite immaterial, my lord.

JUNE: Oh, Tony – now you've got a job, I will marry you.

TONY (*still worried*): I've got to put things right with Bessie first.

BEECHAM: You need anticipate no trouble on that score, my lord. She has found no difficulty in wiping the whole incident from her mind.

TONY (*stung*): Oh! Still – I'd better see her.

JUNE: I think I'll come and hold your hand.

> *They go out. Lord Lister comes running in through the french window.*

LORD LISTER: Beecham, what about this second rod?

BEECHAM: The money paid by avid newspapers will cover that, my lord.

LORD LISTER: It will, by Jove!

> *Bessie has entered, dressed once more as a maid.*

BEECHAM: I trust your lordship and her ladyship will come to Scotland as (*he includes Bessie*) OUR guests.

LORD LISTER: By gad, yes. When?

BEECHAM: Next month, my lord, if we may take our honeymoon and holiday combined. (*He has again included Bessie in a sweeping and possessive gesture.*)

LORD LISTER: Of course you can. Dashed decent of you. Thanks.

BEECHAM: The pleasure will be ours, my lord.

LORD LISTER: Er – Beecham, er – does Bessie fish?

BEECHAM: Not with rod and line, my lord.

LORD LISTER: Ah – dashed good girl. (*He catches sight of the duck, turns it to examine the profile and recognizes it with horror.*) My God – it's Clara! (*Running across in front of Bessie to the door.*) Molly! Molly!

> *He runs from the room to own up to his wife.*

BEECHAM (*opening his arms to Bessie*): I've come to the conclusion that an odd-man's job is far beneath my dignity. An odd-man is an odd-man, whether he is a politician or he merely carries up the coals. I have resigned my Seat.

BESSIE (*leaping into his arms*). My darling Ben!

> *Beecham swings her off the ground and kisses her. The telephone rings. He puts her down and indicates the duck.*

BEECHAM: Will you take that luckless creature to the larder, love? (*He goes to answer the telephone.*)

> *Bessie picks up the duck and starts to go, but half-way to the door stops to listen.*

(*At the telephone.*) Hullo? . . . What? . . . Yes? The *Advertiser*?

. . . Yes, I know – we were cut off . . . I am applying for the Chiltern Hundreds . . . My dear young man, where is your education? To apply for the Chiltern Hundreds is the only means whereby a sitting Member may resign his Seat – a Parliamentary privilege of which, in my opinion, far too few M.P.s avail themselves. I shall apply tomorrow morning after I have done the washing-up. (*He bows towards Bessie.*)

> *Bessie, hearing this surrender over the washing-up, flits away triumphant.*

My resignation is a purely personal affair. The policy has triumphed – and that is the point . . . What is that? . . . What is my policy? (*Indignantly he draws himself to his full height.*) My policy is this. It is embodied, always and forever, in the phrase – 'They also serve who only stand and wait.' Good night.

> *He hangs up the telephone, and moves with dignity towards his Destiny – –*

CURTAIN

THE
THISTLE AND THE ROSE

THE THISTLE AND THE ROSE was first produced at the
Boltons Theatre, Kensington, on 6 September, 1949, with the following
cast:

A Shepherd's Wife	JANE SAVILLE
Her Son	PETER BRODERICK
King James the Third	THEODORE BIKEL
A Murderer	CARL WILLIAMSON
Lord Angus	HUGH MORTON
The Duke of Rothesay	RAYMOND WESTWELL
Margaret Drummond	ANNE GUNNING
An Armourer	JACK STEWART
Janet Kennedy	HEATHER STANNARD
Doctor West	MEADOWS WHITE
Will Dunbar	MAURICE BROWNING
Princess Margaret of England	DOROTHY TUTIN
Lady Surrey	JANE SAVILLE
Lord Surrey	HENRY FIELDING
1st English Soldier	JACK STEWART
2nd English Soldier	JEREMY HARE
A Highlander	CARL WILLIAMSON
Bishop Elphinstone	ANTHONY SHARP
Alexander Stuart	PETER BRODERICK
Monsieur de la Motte	THEODORE BIKEL
Lady Heron of Ford	JULIA FLAXMAN
Her Daughter	PERLITA NEILSON
Islay Herald	JACK STEWART
Rouge Croix Herald	ALEC MacMUNN
Lord High Admiral	ANTHONY SHARP
Lord Home	MAURICE BROWNING
Lord Lindsay	EDWARD JEWESBURY
English Soldiers Attendant on Lord Surrey	JOHN HESTON / JEREMY HARE
Scots Soldier	JOHN GROVES

The Play directed by
COLIN CHANDLER

THE THISTLE AND THE ROSE *was subsequently presented by Linnit & Dunfee Ltd. at the Vaudeville Theatre on 15 May 1951 with the following cast:*

A Shepherd's Wife . . .	CATHERINE SALKELD
Her Son	DAVID PAGE
King James the Third . .	JAMES THOMASON
A Man	DENIS HOLMES
Lord Angus . . .	ANDREW CRUICKSHANK
King James the Fourth . .	HUGH BURDEN
Bishop Elphinstone . .	BERNARD MEREFIELD
Margaret Drummond . .	JOSEPHINE GRIFFIN
A Douglas Soldier . .	HARRY GWYN DAVIES
An Armourer . . .	ANTONY KEAREY
Janet Kennedy . . .	VALERIE HANSON
Doctor West . . .	FREDERICK LEISTER
Will Dunbar . . .	MAURICE BROWNING
Lady Surrey . . .	CATHERINE SALKELD
Margaret Tudor . .	PATRICIA GILDER
Lord Surrey . . .	GEORGE CURZON
Alexander Stuart . .	MICHAEL MCGRATH
Islay Herald . . .	JAMES THOMASON
Monsieur de la Motte .	KENNETH HYDE
Lady Heron of Ford . .	SONIA HOLM
Her Daughter . . .	VICTORIA GRAYSON
Rouge Croix Herald . .	ERIC DODSON
Sir Thomas Howard . .	DENIS HOLMES
Lord Lindsay . . .	ANTONY WOODRUFF
Lord Home . . .	MAURICE BROWNING
Lord Lennox . . .	HARRY GWYN DAVIES
Lord Huntley . . .	ANTONY KEAREY
Lord Argyll . . .	JAMES THOMASON

The Play directed by
JOHN FERNALD

W.D.H.—N

CHARACTERS

in order of their appearance

A SHEPHERD'S WIFE
HER SON
KING JAMES THE THIRD
A MURDERER
LORD ANGUS
THE DUKE OF ROTHESAY, KING JAMES THE FOURTH
BISHOP ELPHINSTONE
LORD LINDSAY OF THE BYRES
MARGARET DRUMMOND
A DOUGLAS SOLDIER
AN ARMOURER
JANET KENNEDY
DOCTOR WEST, *the English Ambassador*
WILL DUNBAR, *a Poet and Minstrel*
PRINCESS MARGARET OF ENGLAND
LADY SURREY
LORD SURREY
ALEXANDER STUART, *Archbishop of St Andrews*
ISLAY HERALD (*Scots*)
MONSIEUR DE LA MOTTE, *The French Ambassador*
KING HENRY THE EIGHTH OF ENGLAND
THE LORD HIGH ADMIRAL, SIR THOMAS HOWARD
LORD LYON KING-AT-ARMS
LADY HERON OF FORD
HER DAUGHTER
ROUGE CROIX PURSUIVANT (*English*)
1st SCOTS SOLDIER
LORD HOME
1st ENGLISH SOLDIER
2nd ENGLISH SOLDIER
2nd SCOTS SOLDIER

The Memorial to those who fell at Flodden, the battle which was fought on 9 September, 1513, and which resulted in the total defeat of the Scots by the English General, Lord Surrey, is situated on a grassy mound, some three miles into England, south of Tweed, below the ridge of Flodden, near the spot on which King James the Fourth of Scotland lost his life.

THE
THISTLE AND THE ROSE

ACT ONE

PROLOGUE

A shepherd's wife walks across the stage, carrying a bucket. She goes off, and can be heard lowering the bucket away. It splashes into the well. Then she begins drawing it up on a chain.

A small boy, her son, runs on from where she came. He calls to her. He holds another bucket, empty, in his hand. He is looking away, off stage.

BOY: Hey! Mither – mither –
WOMAN: Bring yon bucket, Davie.

He still looks.

BOY: Mither – there's a rider comin' doon the road fra' Sauchieburn.
WOMAN: An' what am I supposed to dae aboot it, Davie!
BOY: Mither – how he's gallopin'! (*He still stares.*) Oh, mither! There's anither rider half a mile ahint him – –
WOMAN: Likely they're soldiers fleein' fra' the wars.

She comes on stage to look. The boy still stares.

BOY: Is there a war the noo?
WOMAN: The noo! There's aye a war, so dinna talk sae daft. Here, Davie, bring yon bucket.

He takes it to her, looking back.

Aye, there's a war a' right. (*She sighs.*) A war betwixt the King and Angus Bell-the-Cat. (*She takes the bucket from him.*) And Angus has the

Duke of Rothesay in his power – puir wee lad. (*She turns back towards the well.*)

BOY: Who is the Duke o' Rothesay, mither?

WOMAN (*turning back towards him*): Ignoramus! He's King Jaimie's eldest son. Puir bairn! (*She sighs again, moving towards the well.*) Ye can thank your mither, laddie – or your mither's lack o' beauty, maybe! – that your feyther's no a King!

BOY (*in wild excitement*): He's turnt. He's off the road. He's gallopin' across the heather noo! Here, mither – look!

He seizes her by the arm. The sound of a galloping horse approaches rapidly and grows in volume. She drops the bucket. The sound of galloping hooves becomes confused. As the bucket clatters on to the stage, a horse whinnies in terror. There is a crash, as of a man in armour falling to the ground.

He's doon. Oh my, he's doon!

There is the lighter sound of a riderless horse galloping away.

Oh, mither, what are we to dae? 'Twas you that gi'ed the horse a fright.

A male figure, in armour and a cloak, half crawls, half drags itself on to the stage.

WOMAN: Here, Davie, get some water.

Davie lingers, fascinated. The Woman turns to the prostrate figure.

Come – lay your heid doon in my lap. An' dinna fret yersel'.

She looks up and sees Davie still staring.

Come, Davie, get a move on, lad.

The figure gasps and groans. Davie runs off.

Will you be from the fighting at the Sauchieburn?

The figure nods. David returns with the bucket.

King Jamie's man? Or Angus Bell-the-Cat's?

MAN (*weakly*): King Jamie's man.

The Man takes some water from the bucket with difficulty in his hand, and drinks it.

Boy (*excitedly*): Sir – did you see the King?

Man (*his voice a little stronger*): Aye, lad, I did.

Boy: Oh, sir – I've wanted all my life to see the King.

Man: Then look your fill on me.

> *There is a tense pause.*

I was your King this morning, boy.

> *Davie starts in surprise. The Woman reacts violently.*

Woman: The King! Run, Davie, and get help – afore the rebels catch the King.

Boy: Yon rider that I saw! (*He stands up and looks towards the Sauchieburn.*)

Woman: Aye – he'll dae.

Boy: He's here! He's lightin' doon from off his horse.

Woman: Thanks be to God.

> *The Boy runs off.*

Boy (*off stage*): Good sir, the King is hurt.

> *A Man, well concealed in a cloak, comes on.*

Man: Where is the King?

Woman: 'Tis he I'm tendin' on. His horse was frighted by ma bucket clatterin'.

King James III: Who is this man?

Man: I am a priest, your Majesty.

Woman: A priest! Then God be praised!

Man (*to the Woman*): The King is wounded unto death?

Woman: Nay, Father – 'tis not so.

King: Yet give me absolution, for I feel my death is nigh.

> *He closes his eyes. The Man, while the King is speaking, draws a dagger from its sheath behind his back.*

If I have sinned in aught, in loving friendship more than power, in loving country less than comfort, music more than State affairs . . .

> *The Man is standing over him now.*

If I have sinned in doing all or aught of this, then shrive me, holy Father.

MAN: This shall shrive thee . . . This shall give thee shrift. Short shrift, I'll warrant you!

He plunges his knife into the King's heart. Then turns, still hiding his face, and runs towards his horse.

WOMAN (*screaming and holding up a bloodstained hand*): The King is dead! The King is dead! The King is murdered, Davie. He has killed the King.

She collapses, sobbing, as the sound of a horse galloping fades into the distance.

The King! The King!

The lights go out.

SCENE 1

The curtain rises on the Council Chamber at Scone. Lord Angus, a tall, dark, black bearded warrior, is pacing to and fro. There is a sound outside.

ANGUS: Who comes?

The cloaked murderer comes in. Through the entrance, with their backs to the room, can be seen Two Soldiers in the Douglas livery on guard. It is Lord Angus' livery. The door closes.

You bring me tidings of the King?

MAN: I do, Lord Angus.

ANGUS: Good or evil tidings?

The Man drops his gaze.

Which?

MAN: Both good and ill, my lord.

ANGUS: Then let me hear the evil first. I do not fear the good.

The Man still hesitates.

Come, let me hear.

The Man stays silent.

What ails you, man? I do not pay my messengers to lose their tongues.

MAN: I am afeared.

ANGUS: Then you have failed? Why then, you have good reason for your fears!

MAN: I have not failed, my lord. (*He starts speaking quickly, excusing himself.*) Your orders were to follow on the King. To give my life – if need – so long as he did not escape. And to deliver him, alive or dead, to you. Were those the orders as you gave them me, my lord?

ANGUS: They were.

MAN: Then are they carried out. I followed him. His horse shied at a shepherd's woman drawing water from a well. He fell. I came upon him lying on the ground, his head within the woman's lap. Then I delivered him to you.

ANGUS: Alive or dead?

MAN: The King is dead, my lord.

There is a pause, then Angus speaks harshly.

ANGUS: Where is the proof?

MAN: The proof is here.

The Man takes out the bloodstained dagger. Angus steels himself and looks at it.

ANGUS: It is no wonder you were feared to tell me this. It is not natural to kill a King. You should have captured him.

MAN: A captive King is troublesome, my lord. I heard you say that once.

ANGUS: Methinks that I have said it more than once.

He turns away and stands in thought.

MAN (*cringing*): Then have I done your will, my lord?

ANGUS: My will! Nay, God forbid! I have no will to have a hand in murdering my King. I have a duty to my country – that is all. Yet never did I will his death. (*He turns to the Man, picking a bag of money from the table.*) Yet do not fear. You did your duty, too. 'Tis possible you have exceeded it – and yet 'twere better that than failure. Now your task is done. (*He throws him the money bag.*) The hardest task is mine – to tell the Duke of Rothesay that his father's dead.

There is a sound of soldiers saluting outside.

Begone, and fare thee well.

As the Man turns to go, the doors are thrown open. The Two

Soldiers stand at the salute. The Man throws his cloak across his face and hides his money bag. The Duke of Rothesay, young, handsome, dignified, comes in and stands in the doorway. Lord Angus and the Man both bow.

JAMES : Lord Angus, who is this?

Angus makes no reply. The Man moves towards the door. James turns to him.

Do you bring tidings of my father, sir?

The Man stops, but does not speak.

Then is he well?

Still no answer. James turns angrily to Angus.

Lord Angus, do you bid this fellow speak!

As he turns to address Angus, the Man slips away. James turns again, sees that he has gone and shouts:

Guards, stop that man!

The sentries do not move.

Go! Bring him back to me.

They stand motionless. He runs up to the Soldiers and speaks furiously to one.

Run! (*To the other.*) Run! (*He loses his temper and shouts at them.*) I order you on pain of death. The Duke of Rothesay orders it!

They still stand motionless, as motionless as Lord Angus watching the scene.

Then are you deaf?

He looks at them, from one to the other, as though he would strike them. Then he turns, deflated and weary, back into the room.

Not deaf, alas, but disobedient!

He sits dejectedly, while Lord Angus watches him in silence. Then he speaks half to himself.

I am no prince, it seems – but only prisoner.

ANGUS: Those soldiers are both Douglases, your Grace.

JAMES: Your soldiers, aye. Do I not know it! Am I not beset by Douglases on every side. And you – my jailer – Angus Bell-the-Cat!

ANGUS: Your Majesty will soon have soldiers of your own.

JAMES (*scarcely hearing him*): What use are soldiers to a prisoner? (*Suddenly his mind reacts to Angus' words.*) What said you then, my lord?

ANGUS: I said – your Majesty will soon have soldiers of your own.

JAMES: My lord, I am the Duke of Rothesay. Why then call me Majesty?

Is Angus about to speak?

I will by no means wear the crown so long as my dear father lives.

ANGUS: That time is past, your Grace.

JAMES: What mean you, Angus?

Angus stands with bowed head.

Is my father dead?

Angus still stands silent. James moves over to him.

Lord Angus, is my father dead?

Angus remains silent. James moves away and speaks with his back to Angus.

How did my Royal father die, my lord?

ANGUS: He fell from off his horse at Beaton's Mill. A woman with a pitcher frighted it.

JAMES: My father fought on foot.

ANGUS: It was Lord Lindsay's horse.

JAMES: Did Lindsay give the King his horse to carry him to safety?

ANGUS: Aye, your Grace.

JAMES (*very quietly*): I would I had been he. (*To one of the guards.*) Go fetch me Bishop Elphinstone.

The Soldier does not move until he gets a nod from Angus.

Where is Lord Lindsay now?

ANGUS: He lies here under guard, your Grace.

JAMES: Send for him here.

Angus hesitates.

Send for him here, Lord Angus. Am I not the King? You told me so yourself!

ANGUS (*to the other sentry*): Go – bid your Captain bring Lord Lindsay here.

The Soldier goes.

Lord Lindsay is on trial for his life, your Majesty.

JAMES: And who shall be his judge?

ANGUS (*hesitating*): Your Majesty – –

JAMES (*cutting in*): Yes, I shall be his judge, my lord.

Enter Bishop Elphinstone.

BISHOP: You sent for me, your Grace.

JAMES: Good Bishop Elphinstone, I would hear masses for my father's soul.

BISHOP: Your Majesty, I offer you my humble sympathy.

JAMES: I do accept it, Bishop Elphinstone. It comforts me to be befriended by a man of God. With you, my lord, I'll pray forgiveness for my father's death from Him who could forgive the evil and misguided men who brought about his own.

He and Lord Angus exchange a glance of hatred mixed with fear. The Soldiers bring Lord Lindsay in. Lord Lindsay looks at Angus coldly, with disdain. Only when James speaks does he realize the King's presence, and then bows with reverence.

Why do you hold Lord Lindsay prisoner, my lord?

ANGUS (*reading the charge*): For that he gave your father counsel to devour your Grace – for that he gave to him a horse to fortify himself against his son. Your answer, David Lindsay of the Byres?

LINDSAY: My answer, Angus, is that I did all these things right willingly and with a loyal heart. And though I stand on trial for my life, yet is my conscience clear, because what guilt may be in this affair lies with my master's enemies and murderers, and not with me.

BISHOP: Your Grace, this man's beside himself.

JAMES: Good Bishop, let him speak. Did he not owe allegiance to an earthly King like that you owe to God – the more intensely, possibly, because his King had urgent need of him!

BISHOP: I will prepare the Chapel for your Grace.

The Bishop goes. Lord Lindsay breaks out.

LINDSAY: Beware your Grace! Beware of men who murder kings. He will not rest till he be King himself. Beware, your Grace, Lord Angus plans your death.

ANGUS (*sharply*): Enough! (*To James.*) A man will talk thus wildly when he faces death.

LINDSAY: I have no fear of death. I only fear my conscience and my God.

JAMES: You will have justice, David Lindsay – never fear of that!

LINDSAY: 'Tis you I fear for, sir.

ANGUS: Remove him hence.

The Soldiers start to drag him out, then stop when James speaks.

JAMES: Lord Lindsay, in my father's name I thank you for your loyalty. Methinks that I will send you into Rothesay Castle for a twelvemonth, till the storm is past. In Scotland there is need of men like you.

Lord Lindsay bows and the Soldiers drag him out.

I would that I had been with Lindsay at my father's side against the rebel lords. Then would my conscience be at peace.

ANGUS: You joined the rebels of your own free will, your Grace.

JAMES: I joined them, aye. As salmon join a net that circles them about. Or as a rabbit joins a snare. (*His voice rises.*) I joined you, my lord Angus, when you told me that my father must be taught to rule aright. I never heard you say he must be killed.

ANGUS: Your father fell from off his horse, your Grace. You surely do not blame yourself for that.

JAMES: How learnt you of his fall?

ANGUS: By messenger, your Grace.

JAMES: And was your messenger the man who would not let me see his face?

ANGUS: I cannot answer that.

JAMES: You cannot answer that! I may not know who brought you tidings of my father's death! Is there some mystery? Was there, perchance, foul play?

ANGUS: The messenger was passing Beaton's Mill. It is not in his interest to disclose his name. The country folk will publish and embroider tales.

JAMES: What kind of tales have you in mind?

ANGUS: There is no limit to the tales that country folk invent.

JAMES: What kind of tales, my lord?

ANGUS: Fantastic and unfounded tales, your Grace.

JAMES: Perchance such tales as this? (*He talks intently, fixing Angus with his eyes.*) The King was thrown at Beaton's Mill – from off Lord Lindsay's horse – and while he lay another horseman, cloaked and daggered, came – dismounted – and then stabbed him unto death. Such tales as that, my lord?

ANGUS: 'Tis possible, your Grace. A tale like that will ever gain a certain currency. Yet none will give it credence.

JAMES: I believe it utterly. (*He goes up to Angus and speaks straight at him.*) I trust your lordship paid your messenger according to his worth.

> *Margaret Drummond bursts into the room. She is young and beautiful.*

MARGARET: My lord – –

> *She sees Lord Angus and stops short.*

JAMES: What is it, Margaret?

MARGARET (*speaking hesitantly*): There is a rumour that the King is dead, my lord. 'Tis surely but a rumour.

JAMES: 'Tis the truth.

MARGARET (*horror-struck*): No, no, my lord!

JAMES (*in a tired voice*): Then ask Lord Angus, do you doubt my word.

> *Margaret turns fearfully to Angus.*

ANGUS: The King was thrown from off his horse by accident.

MARGARET: 'Tis as I heard – by accident.

JAMES: Then, Margaret, you did not hear aright.

ANGUS: I do not doubt that Mistress Drummond, in her wisdom, heard aright.

> *She looks at him and hears the sinister note in his voice with sinking heart. He shortly turns to James.*

I will retire, your Grace. What solace you will find to ease your grief will be in lighter company than mine.

> *He turns for the door.*

JAMES (*stopping him*): My lord, no earthly company will ever ease the burden of my guilt.

> *He looks at Margaret and feels a weakening, and speaks more violently.*

But, lest it should, lest dalliance should bring forgetfulness, I'll wear an iron belt about my waist. And to it will I add one ounce in weight for every year that God permits a father's murderer to live.

> *Angus turns away.*

I'll bid the armourer prepare me such a belt – or better, will you order him, my lord? Perchance the armourer's a Douglas, too.

> *Angus goes.*

Who can I trust? In all my kingdom, is there anyone that I can trust?

MARGARET: You can trust me, my lord.

JAMES: I can trust you – who fawns and simpers when Lord Angus lies!

MARGARET: 'Tis wiser so to do.

JAMES (*he seizes her wrist*): For why? Is Angus aught to you?

MARGARET: What should he be? Lord Angus pays his court to Mistress Kennedy.

JAMES (*still suspicious*): Is Mistress Kennedy as beautiful as you?

MARGARET: I cannot say, my lord.

JAMES: I do not think it possible she is.

> *He melts and seizes her in his arms and kisses her. Slowly the present reasserts itself.*

My father has been murdered, Margaret.

MARGARET: Such news flies fast, my lord.

JAMES: And yet 'twas Bell-the-Cat that heard it first.

MARGARET: Why is he called that name, my lord?

JAMES: For what he did at Lauder, Margaret.

MARGARET: What did he there, my lord?

JAMES: He rose against my father. He was jealous of his favourites. Lord Angus said their power must be curtailed. The nobles met in

Lauder kirk – and then Lord Gray stood forth. He said such talk was like the mice who feared the cat and wished to hang a bell about her neck to warn them of her coming – but there was no mouse that dared. Then Angus cried 'I'll bell the cat.' And then he hanged my father's favourites from the bridge at Lauder.

Margaret shudders involuntarily.

MARGARET: I am afraid.

JAMES (*protecting her in his arms*): Be not afraid – I will protect you now I am the King.

MARGARET: I would I were at home, my lord.

JAMES (*protecting her still more*): At home! Beside the Tay! I would that I were with you there.

>*He looks round his cold surroundings and his voice assumes a longing note.*

To see the salmon splashing in the stream – and hear the wildfowl calling in the starlit sky – (*He seems to be listening for them.*) The wild geese will have travelled north by now . . .

MARGARET: Three months ago, my lord.

JAMES: But they will come again. One night, in mid September, you will stir upon your pillow and your ears will hear their music as they circle over Stobshaw when they come to Tay again. My father used to take me out to see the geese. He loved their music, Margaret. As I loved him. (*His voice breaks.*) Yet now he's dead – and I am King, among his murderers.

MARGARET: Hush, hush, my lord.

>*She puts a hand over his mouth, but he brushes it away.*

JAMES: They are. All murderers. And I, his son, his Royal murderer. I would I had been born to till the fields beside the Tay, and, in the evening, walk with you along the riverside. (*He turns and speaks passionately.*) With you I could be strong. Alone, I am a prey in every fear. (*He lays his head on her breast.*) Oh, Margaret, I do not want to be a King.

MARGARET (*stroking his hair*): Your Grace should go to rest.

JAMES: I cannot rest. I cannot rest alone. The only peace I ever knew was in a woman's arms. My mother first – then you . . . (*He looks up.*) Do you not fear to be the favourite of a King?

MARGARET: What should I fear, my lord?

JAMES: Lord Angus is not wont to let a favourite live too long.

MARGARET: Though Angus took my life, my lord, he could not kill my love.

The bell starts tolling as he kisses her.

THE CURTAIN FALLS

SCENE 2

A Douglas Soldier enters hurriedly. He is like Lord Angus's messenger in the previous scene. He shouts towards the noise of hammering whence the glow of firelight flickers on to the stage.

SOLDIER: Ho, Armourer!

The hammer stops, then starts again.

Ho, Armourer!

ARMOURER: What's a' the noise aboot?

He comes out of the off stage forge, carrying an iron belt.

SOLDIER: I'm wanting this cleaned up. (*He holds out a dagger.*)

ARMOURER: I canna dae it now.

SOLDIER: 'Tis but a minute's job.

ARMOURER: What is't that's wrong? (*He takes it.*)

SOLDIER: The blade's a wee bit dulled.

ARMOURER: I dinna like yon stain.

SOLDIER (*dismissing it*): Och, that! 'Tis but a rabbit's blood I skinned and ate upon the road.

ARMOURER (*disbelieving him*): I canna dae it now. I'm workin' on King Jamie's belt.

SOLDIER: Is Jamie grown o'er big around the middle, then?

ARMOURER: Nay, man. I'm addin' weight. Each year I've this to dae. There's twelve ounce mair than when I shaped it first. (*He balances it in his hand.*) How would you like yon resting on your hips?

W.D.H.–O

He hands it to the Soldier.

I'm thinking if he lives the normal span o' life, he'll no be verra comfortable at a'!

SOLDIER (*trying its balance*): Man, it's an awfu' weight.

ARMOURER (*taking it back*): Aye – is it not.

SOLDIER: Will Jamie wear yon fearful thing to bed at night?

ARMOURER: Aye, man. He never takes it off – but once a year when I'm at work on it. I'm thinkin' 'twill be inconvenient like in certain circumstances. (*He winks at the Soldier.*) Still, it seems that Mistress Drummond doesna mind the thing at a'. Ah well! There's nae accountin' for a woman's taste.

He turns back towards his forge, but the Soldier stops him again.

SOLDIER: You burnish up yon skian-dhu – and I'll pay ye for it wi' a piece o' news. That dae?

ARMOURER: Och, get away wi' ye! I never heard a piece o' news I couldna dae wi'out.

SOLDIER: I've ridden wi' it – all the way fra' Mistress Drummond's hame.

ARMOURER: Fra' Mistress Drummond's hame . . .?

SOLDIER: There's nae a body kens a word about it – but Lord Angus an' meself. An' maybe you.

ARMOURER: What is't?

SOLDIER: 'Tis this – that Mistress Drummond's dead.

ARMOURER: Lord save us, how? Is the King informed?

SOLDIER: There's naebody informed – but Angus and meself an' you.

ARMOURER: I'd no be minded to inform the King.

SOLDIER: Old Bell-the-Cat'll dae it fine. He's no afeared o' kings. Now – will ye dae the job?

ARMOURER: I'll dae it – aye. (*He takes the dagger unwillingly.*)

SOLDIER: Then I'll awa' an' feed ma horse. (*He goes.*)

ARMOURER: Puir Jamie! (*He looks at the dagger stain.*) Puir wee rabbit! Never did a body any harm at a'.

He goes off to his forge, muttering sadly and shaking his head.

THE CURTAIN RISES

SCENE 3

The Council Chamber, Lord Angus is in earnest conversation with Janet
Kennedy, young and pretty Court lady.

ANGUS: Well, then – what say you, Mistress Kennedy?

JANET: My lord, I know not what to say.

ANGUS: Then, shall I speak again?

JANET: I do not doubt your lordship will.

ANGUS: The day I overthrew the former King at Sauchieburn, I
swore that you would be my wife. But then – my wife still lived. Ten
years and more I've loved you. Is not that enough?

JANET: I never thought to see Lord Angus overcome with love.

ANGUS: Why do you jest?

JANET (*in wide-eyed surprise*): I do not jest, my lord. Your eye
misleads. 'Tis possibly because I have a roguish smile. At least, so say
my friends.

ANGUS: What friends?

JANET: My lady friends, my lord.

ANGUS (*making a gesture of impatience*): Come, Mistress Kennedy,
your answer – yes or no?

JANET: Perhaps.

ANGUS: 'Perhaps' is neither yes nor no.

JANET: Exactly so, my lord.

ANGUS (*with difficulty curbing his temper*): I am a soldier, Mistress
Kennedy. I use a soldier's bluff, straightforward speech. I am not used
to play with words. I ask a question of my soldiers and they always
answer yes.

JANET: Is it a wife that you are looking for, my lord, or but a new
recruit?

ANGUS: A woman ever treats a man who loves her thus.

JANET: You love your country, do you not, my lord? And yet 'tis
said you treat it thus!

ANGUS: Then, Mistress Kennedy, if you will not say yes, I'll take
it that 'tis no.

JANET: 'Tis as you wish, my lord.

ANGUS: Methinks you have another suitor kneeling at your feet.

JANET: Another, sir! Does that imply a suitor at my feet already? Is there one? (*She looks down, mockingly.*) Alas! I did not think there was.

ANGUS (*throwing himself at her feet*): Sweet Janet!

JANET: Fie, my lord! Your ardour takes away my breath!

ANGUS (*rising again and thwarted*): It seems the rumour that you love the King is true.

JANET (*looking amusedly at his back, where he stands sulking*): Should all of us not love the King, my lord?

ANGUS: In moderation, certainly. I've watched you sometimes look towards the King.

JANET: What woman would not sometime look toward the King?

ANGUS: To do so may be dangerous.

JANET (*opening her eyes wide*): How mean you – 'dangerous', my lord?

ANGUS: An English Embassy is come to offer Princess Margaret to his Majesty. The House of Stuart and the House of Tudor, in alliance, will bring peace to Scotland, Mistress Kennedy. 'Tis therefore very dangerous to look toward his Majesty, and tempt him thus to cast away the safety of the realm.

JANET: Your words should be addressed to Mistress Drummond rather than to me, my lord.

Lord Angus turns away.

The King has loved her, as you know, ten years and more. 'Tis said that he intends to marry her.

ANGUS: He cannot marry her.

JANET: Methought the King could do what he desired, my lord.

ANGUS: Not always, Mistress Kennedy, as he will shortly learn.

A trumpet sounds outside.

The English Embassy has come. (*He moves towards her.*) Your answer, Mistress Kennedy?

JANET: 'Twere wise my answer should be yes, my lord.

He tries to take her in his arms. She draws away in fear, then recovers her courage.

Perhaps!

He follows her towards the door. Enter the King.

JAMES (*speaking back out of the door*) : Bring in the English Embassy.

Janet curtsies. Angus bows. The King smiles, looking at Janet.

And does Lord Angus seek to find his youth again ?

Janet pouts and runs out.

ANGUS : Your Majesty – –

JAMES : I have but little time to waste, my lord. I have a ship to see
this afternoon, at Leith.

*With a flourish of trumpets the English Ambassador, Doctor
West, comes in and bows low to the King.*

Be seated, sir. I do not know your name.

WEST : My name is Doctor West – so please your Majesty.

JAMES (*in good humour with this cheerful Ambassador*) : I cannot say
it pleases me. Nor yet that it displeases me. (*He looks at Doctor West's
cheerful countenance.*) Suffice it that it evidently pleases you !

WEST : It satisfies me, sir.

JAMES : You would not be an Englishman were you not satisfied.
How does your Royal master ?

WEST : He sends greetings to your Majesty.

JAMES : And I return him mine. And is Lord Surrey well ?

WEST : He ages, sir. He suffers in the joints.

JAMES : When we were fighting in the Borders, did he catch a
'Border chill' ?

WEST : I've heard him hazard that suggestion, sir.

JAMES (*jestingly*) : Then will he not be hot to travel north again
in haste.

WEST : I trust the need will not arise again, your Majesty. Our
countries are at peace.

ANGUS : Amen.

WEST : And should your Majesty show favour to the purpose of
my mission – may I make so bold as to express the hope that peace may
be perpetual ?

JAMES : What is your mission, Doctor ?

WEST : To inquire if Princess Margaret's hand in marriage would
be likely of acceptance by your Majesty.

JAMES: The Princess Margaret Tudor . . . Is she pretty, Doctor West?

WEST: Her mother hath a pleasing countenance, your Majesty.

JAMES: Her mother! What is that to me?

WEST: I mean, sir, that the Princess Margaret's future beauty should not be in doubt. Your Majesty must recognize she is but just turned ten.

JAMES: Just ten! I have a child of nigh that age.

WEST: I offer my congratulations, sir.

JAMES: There is no need. It came to me quite naturally. Have you a miniature?

WEST: I have, sir. (*He takes out the miniatures of Princess Margaret.*) Two.

JAMES: Methinks, from what you say, one will suffice. (*He looks at the miniature.*) My age is eight and twenty, good Ambassador. And you have come to offer me a child of ten.

WEST: I act upon my Royal master's orders, sir.

JAMES (*looking at the miniature again*): What should I do with her?

WEST: Be patient, sir!

JAMES: It is not in my nature to be so.

WEST: Then can your Majesty not – farm your patience out?

JAMES: Do you advise me as a doctor – or an Englishman?

WEST: As an Ambassador, your Majesty.

JAMES (*putting down the miniature, and shaking his head*): King Henry doth not know my character, it seems.

WEST: My master is aware you are a Stuart, sir.

James looks up.

And therefore understands your love of – chivalry.

JAMES (*smiling*): That were a kindly choice of word.

WEST (*smiling too*): Then may I take it, sir, that you accept the Princess Margaret's hand?

JAMES: You may do no such thing. (*He suddenly becomes stern.*) I have no will to wed this sickly child. I grow embittered by these crude attempts to captivate my heart. Since I assumed the throne I've heard of nothing else. Cecilia was first – and then a young princess of Spain. And now this latest offering! I will not wed for politics. But like the meanest of my crofters in the Western Isles I'll exercise my right to wed for love.

WEST: 'Tis possible the Princess Margaret might be worthy of your Grace's love.

JAMES (*he throws down the miniature*): Were Princess Margaret beautiful beyond belief, Ambassador, yet could I not present her with my love – because it is no longer mine to give.

> *Angus stiffens.*

Go tell your master, Doctor West, King James hath lost his heart and he will wed the woman who has captured it.

WEST: And may one know this lady's name, your Majesty?

JAMES: Why not? (*He looks defiantly at Angus*): For all the world will know it soon. Her name is Margaret Drummond.

ANGUS (*starting forward*): Sir – –!

JAMES: Lord Angus, this is surely no surprise to you.

ANGUS: Your Majesty, a messenger – arrived an hour ago – –

JAMES: A messenger, my lord!

> *He sees the look on Lord Angus's face.*

I recollect another messenger – – What message did he bring?

ANGUS: That Mistress Drummond died this day.

JAMES: That Margaret died! That Margaret died! How could she die, my lord? She is too young and beautiful to die – –

ANGUS: In Scotland there are many who showed Mistress Drummond jealousy – –

JAMES: Name one! Then name me one, Lord Angus. (*He is almost screaming at him.*) Name me *one*!

ANGUS: Your Majesty, this surely is a private matter not to be discussed before a foreign Embassy.

> *James hides his face in his hands.*

WEST: I beg leave to withdraw.

> *James nods acquiescence without looking. The Ambassador bows and moves towards the door, then turns.*

(*To Angus.*) Will his Majesty not sign?

> *Angus shrugs and turns away. Doctor West diffidently approaches the King.*

Your Majesty – –

> *James does not look up, but Doctor West persists.*

My master bid me ask your Majesty to sign the Treaty.

JAMES (*looking up, dazed*): Treaty?

WEST (*patiently*): Treaty, sir, 'twixt England and your realm.

JAMES (*taking it and then pushing it away*): I cannot see the writing.
Read it me.

> *West starts to read. The King, thinking only of Margaret, stares
> straight before him.*

WEST (*reading*): 'First, that in all time to come there shall be a
sincere, complete and inviolable peace, friendship and league between
the most illustrious and excellent prince, James, King of Scotland – and
Henry, King of England, King of France – –'

JAMES (*starting up, and glad to vent his spleen on something*): Since
when was Henry Tudor King of France?

WEST: He is styled so, your Majesty.

JAMES (*seizing the parchment*): He is not King of France. Nor shall
be – while *I* live. (*He strikes out the offending phrase.*) 'Twere better
far – for all of us – could England leave the French alone. (*He looks
down at the Treaty.*) 'Inviolable peace'! I would that I could suffer it.
(*He hands back the Treaty.*) Yes – it will do.

WEST: But will your Majesty not sign?

JAMES: I will not sign, Ambassador. I give my Royal word.

> *Doctor West picks up the miniature, and turns.*

Show me that miniature again. (*He looks at it, talking almost to himself.*)
But ten years old! They surely could not murder such a child!

> *He looks up as West reaches the door.*

Ambassador – go tell King Henry that I take the offer of his daughter's
hand. I cannot wed the woman that I love, so I will wed the wife who
may be useful to my realm.

> *Doctor West bows himself out. James turns to Angus.*

Give me one name, Lord Angus. Give me *one* name – other than your
own!

> *He looks at Angus in hatred, but Angus stares back. The King
> drops his eyes, his head drops into his hands and his shoulders
> heave. Lord Angus gravely bows, and turns and goes.*

THE CURTAIN FALLS

SCENE 4

BEFORE THE CURTAIN

A minstrel singing. It is Will Dunbar.

DUNBAR: 'Oh, fairest fair of every fair,
Princess, most pleasant and preclare,
The loveliest that on earth there been –
Welcome in Scotland to be Queen.

'Sweet lovely imp of beauty clear,
Most mighty monarch's daughter dear,
Born of a princess most serene,
Welcome in Scotland to be Queen.

'Welcome the Rose, both red and white,
Welcome the flower of our delight,
Our spirit, rejoicing from the spleen,
Welcome in Scotland to be Queen.'

During the last verse – the curtain rises.

SCENE 5

A room in the Palace of Dalkeith, outside Edinburgh. Lady Surrey, the elderly wife of the Princess Margaret's escort commander, and the ten year old Princess Margaret, petulantly toying with the cards, are seated at a card table. The song ends, and Lady Surrey claps her hands.

LADY SURREY: It is a mighty pretty song. Is it your composition, sir?

DUNBAR: Aye, ma'am.

LADY SURREY: What is your name?

DUNBAR: My name is Will Dunbar.

LADY SURREY: It is a mighty pretty song.

She speaks as though she wished the Princess to echo her sentiments, but all to no avail.

DUNBAR : I trust her Royal Highness found it pleasing too.

Margaret looks up, still disconsolate.

LADY SURREY : Aye, so she did. Her Royal Highness is quite overcome. Begone, good sir. Refresh yourself and then return.

Dunbar, who is, after all, the Court Poet, looks at her in some surprise.

I thank you for your pains.

She gives him some money. Dunbar departs, displeased.

'These Scotsmen, Lady Surrey,' says my lord to me each day, 'will ever value money more than Englishmen – and therefore are content with less.' 'Tis evident my lord was wrong! (*She turns to the Princess.*) You do not seem in sorts, my lady. Are you overtired, perhaps?

MARGARET : I'm cold. These Scotsmen do not heat their houses overmuch.

LADY SURREY : 'Tis August, ma'am.

MARGARET : 'Tis cold enough for February.

LADY SURREY : Then place this wrap around your shoulders, ma'am. (*She removes her wrap.*)

MARGARET : Then will not you be cold?

LADY SURREY : Nay, ma'am. I'll tell you something that I would not tell you – were it not I wish to see you smile. (*She leans over and whispers.*) I have my winter woollies on! (*She imparts another secret.*) And furthermore, I do not mean to take them off until I cross the Tweed again.

Margaret smiles at this against her will, and Lady Surrey goes on triumphantly.

But do not tell Lord Surrey so, I pray you, ma'am. 'Twould make him ardent, so I fear. 'Tis only when a soldier knows a citadel is well defended that he feels in honour bound to lay a siege.

MARGARET (*cheering up a little*) : What thinks Lord Surrey of the Scots?

LADY SURREY: My lord is prejudiced. He swears his bones are filled with Scottish damp. He says the Scots are cold and fierce and treacherous – a fit companion to their climate, ma'am.

MARGARET: What thought he of the King?

LADY SURREY: He did not meet the King, as I recall.

MARGARET: Is he too cold and fierce and treacherous – and damp?

LADY SURREY: Nay, ma'am – a King has qualities his subjects do not share – –

MARGARET: What qualities?

LADY SURREY: I hear his Majesty is warm and generous at heart – too generous at heart, some say! Though what they say in London may be better left unsaid in Edinburgh!

MARGARET: I've heard 'tis said in Edinburgh as well.

LADY SURREY: Yet, ma'am, 'tis not to be despised. A man who gives his heart to women easily will scarce withhold it from his wife. 'Tis said that he loves music, too.

MARGARET: My brother Henry told me there was little difference 'twixt the Scottish music and the squealing of a slaughtered pig.

Lady Surrey laughs.

My brother said that when one heard that sound it was the prelude to a massacre.

LADY SURREY: 'Tis nonsense, ma'am.

MARGARET: He told me that the Scots ate porridge always – plunging in their forearms to the elbow in an oatmeal bowl. He said they went abroad half naked. Yet I have not seen a single one the least bit naked yet.

LADY SURREY (*twinkling*): I counsel patience, ma'am.

This joke passes over Margaret's head.

MARGARET: He also said they sleep with heather for their sheets. And that they eat the bladder of a sheep – all raw, with burning spirits. And – he said – they go abroad with knives stuck in their legs. (*She becomes petulant again.*) My lady – how will I exist with such barbarians!

LADY SURREY: Come, ma'am, your Royal brother has been wanton with his tales. Or else he spoke about the northern parts – the Lowlanders are better civilized. Although, it's true, the Romans must be thanked for that.

MARGARET: What? Are there Romans here as well?

LADY SURREY: Nay, nay, sweet child. The Romans are all dead and gone.

MARGARET: All massacred!

Lady Surrey laughs again, but Margaret bursts into tears.

My lady Surrey, take me home again.

LADY SURREY: Come, come – it is not fair that you should give me orders that I cannot carry out.

MARGARET: Please take me home again.

LADY SURREY: What would your Royal father say? An English Princess frightened of the Scots! Come, let us play at cards.

MARGARET: I do not want to play at cards!

LADY SURREY: My lady, do not fret. In two days' time – when you have met the King in Edinburgh – your fears will all be gone.

MARGARET: Why did he not meet me? He would have met me at the Border – were he not uncivilized! Instead, 'tis said he goes out – hawking!

LADY SURREY: Ma'am, you must not blame him thus. Lord Surrey and the Scots Commissioners have planned your coming so. The Lyon King-at-Arms received you at the Border – as is proper – brought your litter to Dalkeith. And here 'tis planned that you should rest – and get some colour to your cheeks – before you ride to Edinburgh to meet the King.

MARGARET: I do not *want* to meet the King. I do *not want* to meet the King. (*She stamps her foot on the ground and throws the cards on the floor.*) I'm going home! I'm going home! I will *not* meet the King.

LADY SURREY: My lady – hush! The minstrel will return ere long. It is not right he hear such words.

MARGARET (*shouting*): I do not care who hears? I'm going home. I do not care who hears!

LADY SURREY (*sternly*): Then will I fetch Lord Surrey to you, ma'am.

MARGARET: Then fetch him. I am not afraid of him! I shall command him that my escort be prepared to take me home again. Go, fetch him! And right quick!

Lady Surrey goes. Margaret, in a temper, starts tearing up the cards left on the table. The bagpipes suddenly start playing. She stops, listens, looks and screams. Then she puts her hands over her ears and runs. She meets Lady Surrey and Lord Surrey at the door.

My lady Surrey! Oh, my lady Surrey! 'Tis a massacre! My lady Surrey, save me! (*To Lord Surrey.*) Oh, my lord, it is a massacre! Lord Surrey, save me! I am so afraid.

LORD SURREY (*in a fatherly way*): 'Tis not a massacre, my sweet Princess. 'Tis but the Scottish pipes.

LADY SURREY: 'Tis what thy Royal brother calls a squealing pig!

MARGARET: Why do they play it here? I cannot bear the noise. 'Tis unendurable! Why do you let them play it here, my lord? (*Imperiously.*) Go – bid the piper cease.

LORD SURREY: It is not in my power to do so, ma'am.

MARGARET: I order you, my lord.

LORD SURREY: I cannot hear your order, ma'am.

Will Dunbar returns. Margaret turns to him.

MARGARET: Whose piper plays without?

DUNBAR: The King's, my lady.

MARGARET: What! The King's! What does his piper at Dalkeith?

DUNBAR: He's aye beside the King.

He resumes his seat where he played.

MARGARET: Beside the King! What! Is the King here at Dalkeith? Is this then true, my lord?

Lord Surrey nods.

My lady Surrey, is this true?

Lady Surrey inclines her head. Margaret seizes her hand.

Quick! To my chamber with me. I must comb my hair and clean my face. Come, let us run!

LADY SURREY: I am six times your age, my lady. Sakes!

They run towards the door. The pipes increase in volume. Margaret, dragging Lady Surrey by the hand, meets a figure in the door. She tries to get round it without looking up. The noise of the pipes is deafening, as the piper passes the door outside and turns and stops. Angrily, Margaret looks up at the figure blocking her progress, about to rebuke it. She sees, tall above her, carrying in his

*hand a hawking lure, the King. Lady Surrey sees him too, releases
Margaret's hand and curtsies. Lord Surrey and Dunbar both
bow. The pipes still scream. Then Margaret realizes it is he. He
stares at her until she drops her eyes and curtsies too. He stoops
and takes her hand and kisses it. The pipes stop. The King turns
to Lady Surrey.*

JAMES : My lady Surrey. (*He kisses her cheek.*) My lord Surrey.

He takes Lord Surrey's hand. Then he turns back to Margaret.
And my well beloved bride.

He kisses Margaret tenderly.

MARGARET : I do not like your beard.

LADY SURREY : She is a little overtired, your Majesty.

MARGARET : I am not tired. And still I do not like his beard.

JAMES (*good humouredly*) : What is it that you do not like? Its
shape – colour – or its size?

MARGARET : It tickles me.

JAMES : All beards do that.

MARGARET : Then I dislike all beards.

JAMES (*patiently, as though talking to a child – as, indeed, he is*) : But
'tis the very latest fashion with the French.

MARGARET : I do not like the French.

JAMES : Would you not have your husband always wear the latest
beard – as he would always have you wear the latest gown?

MARGARET : Not if it tickled, no.

JAMES : So. If your dressmaker devised a gorgeous gown of cloth of
gold, you would reject it – just because it tickled you!

MARGARET : I would insist my dressmaker adjust it, sir.

JAMES : And – if the tickle were removed – then would you be
content?

MARGARET : If it were quite removed.

JAMES (*to Lady Surrey*) : Have you the wherewithal to clip my beard?

LADY SURREY : I have some scissors, sir.

JAMES : Then please to operate.

*He sits down in a chair. She picks up the shawl, from which
flutter bits of cards. Margaret turns away and blushes, not un-
noticed by the King. Lady Surrey puts the shawl about his neck.*

LADY SURREY: How much, sir?

JAMES: Why – as close as may be.

> *He throws back his head. Lady Surrey starts clipping.*

LADY SURREY: Your minstrel has been entertaining us, your Majesty.

JAMES: Who, Will Dunbar – my minstrel!

LADY SURREY: Is he not a minstrel, sir?

JAMES: He is a poet and a priest.

LADY SURREY: My lord – to think that I rewarded him with money from my purse, and he a priest!

JAMES: No doubt he took it as a poet. There is no harm done. (*To Margaret.*) And do you like the bagpipes, ma'am?

> *Margaret does not answer.*

SURREY: She finds that she grows used to them, your Majesty.

MARGARET: I have not found it yet.

JAMES: (*to Dunbar*): Go, Will – and bid the piper go below and quench his thirst.

> *Dunbar starts to go.*

Do you like Scotland, ma'am?

MARGARET: 'Tis very damp.

JAMES: (*to the departing Dunbar*): Some whisky, Will. (*To Margaret.*) 'Tis only medicine. (*To Lord Surrey.*) My lord, I welcome you to Scotland on this happy embassy. Or does it irk you – coming as a man of peace?

> *All these remarks, due to Lady Surrey's hairdressing, are directed at the ceiling, rather loudly.*

SURREY: Nay, sir. Like every soldier, I would rather exercise my art in peace. 'Tis only men of peace who fancy war.

LADY SURREY: Will that suffice, your Majesty?

JAMES (*to Margaret*): What think you, ma'am?

> *He leans over and kisses her, before she suspects the move. In spite of herself, she is enchanted by it.*

MARGARET: 'Twill do for now.

JAMES (*jumping up and throwing off the shawl*): My thanks. (*To Margaret.*) Now let us have a game of cards.

She hesitates.

Come, ma'am.

He takes her hand and sits her down.

The cards are all destroyed. Has someone lost their patience, then?

Margaret looks shyly away from his teasing.

Some music, then. (*He jumps up.*) Come, ma'am, let us dance.

MARGARET: Nay, sir.

LADY SURREY: She has not danced with men, sir, yet.

JAMES: Then shall she dance with you.

MARGARET: The minstrel is not here.

JAMES: Then shall I take his place.

He picks up the minstrel's instrument and plays, Margaret watching him in admiration.

LADY SURREY: Come, ma'am.

She startles Margaret out of her star-gazing. They dance while the King plays. Dunbar brings the whisky in. He takes it to the King, who waves him away and goes on playing. Margaret takes some first, then Lady Surrey, then Lord Surrey.

MARGARET: Oh dear! 'Tis very strong.

The King smiles.

But very warm. And very good!

While they drink, he sings the last line of Dunbar's song — 'Welcome in Scotland to be Queen'. Margaret looks at him with love dawning in her eyes. He finishes and jumps up.

JAMES: I must be gone. The hunt is still abroad and I must ride to Edinburgh ere dark.

SURREY: I'll see your Majesty to horse. (*He goes out.*)

JAMES: My lady. (*He kisses Lady Surrey's hand.*) Ma'am. (*He kisses Margaret too.*)

MARGARET: My lord —

The King stops on his way to the door.

I pray your Majesty to call me Margaret.

His face clouds and his jaw contracts.

JAMES: How does the beard? It does not tickle you so much? (*He kisses her tenderly.*)

MARGARET: Please – call me Margaret.

JAMES: I must be gone.

He runs out. She stands looking after him.

LADY SURREY: My lady – are you still desirous to go home?

MARGARET: Oh no. I love him utterly. And yet – he would not call me Margaret.

THE CURTAIN FALLS

SCENE 6

BEFORE THE CURTAIN

A street in Edinburgh.

Two English Soldiers, of the Princess Margaret's Escort force, slightly the worse for drink. One of them is more than slightly drunk.

SOLDIER: Aye, 'twas a pretty sight, I'll warrant you. Yet never did I see a wedding yet – and I not shed a tear. Where are we going, Corporal?

CORPORAL: Home.

SOLDIER: What – home! Tonight! To London – nigh four hundred miles with Scottish whisky in your boots.

CORPORAL: Nay, fool, to billets. Sergeant does not drink. He will be waiting up for us.

SOLDIER: Not he. There's other things to do at night in Edinburgh but drink.

CORPORAL: What things?

SOLDIER: You ask the sergeant in the morning, lad. (*He winks.*) Or if he do that neither, then maybe you'd better ask the King of Scots. I doubt the Queen'll scarcely know what's what.

He is puzzled.

A Highland soldier in a kilt walks by.

W.D.H.–P

Good evening to you, lady.

>*He walks on.*

CORPORAL: 'Lassie,' try.

SOLDIER: Good evening to ye, lassie! 'Tis a pleasant night.

>*The Highlander stops.*

Could you and me not take a walk – to see the sights.

>*The Highlander growls in half Gaelic.*

What's that? You understand the lady, Corporal? Dratted if I do.

HIGHLANDER (*speaking in clear Scots*): I'm no a lady, mon.

SOLDIER: What's that she says?

CORPORAL: She says she's not a lady.

SOLDIER: Aye, I thought 'twas that she said. Well, that'll suit me fine. I'll see you in the morning, Corp.

>*He lurches over to the Highlander.*

Come, lassie, show me where you live.

HIGHLANDER: I'm ga'in' to ma bed alone.

SOLDIER: What! On the wedding night! And you're going to your bed alone! Shame on you, lassie.

HIGHLANDER: I'm no a 'lass'.

SOLDIER: I'm full, maybe, but not so full that I can't see a skirt – and shapely legs as well.

HIGHLANDER: You keep your fingers to yersel.'

SOLDIER: She's hairy knees! Look, Corporal, strike me dumb if she ain't hairy knees! By God – she's not! She has and all! (*Feeling.*) She's got a beard.

>*The Highlander draws his skian-dhu.*

CORPORAL: Stand back, it's not a lady. She's a Highlander. Stand back – she'll knife you else. (*To Highlander.*) I'm sorry, sir, my friend's a bit the worse for drink.

HIGHLANDER: I'm no fou' mesel'. You take him home – –

>*He digs the Corporal in the ribs with his dagger, returns it to his stocking, and goes.*

SOLDIER: Man, did you ever see the like. A woman – with a beard and hairy knees? And carryin' a knife!

CORPORAL: Come on – 'tis time you were in bed.

SOLDIER: What – not with that!

CORPORAL: Nay, friend – we're going home to billets.

SOLDIER: Billets. Aye – She'll not molest me there. By God – but 'tis a fearsome country this!

They stagger off.

SCENE 7

The Great Chamber in Holyrood.

A long oak table, and in the background, a large State bed, curtained. The room is hung with red and blue. There is a fresh tablecloth and rich dresser. A carpet by the bed – elsewhere, rushes on the floor. The King is wearing 'white damask, figured with gold and lined with sarsnet: jacket, with leaves of crimson satin, hints of black velvet: doublet of cloth of gold: scarlet hose: shirt embroidered with thread of gold: bonnet, black with a rich ruby'. The Queen, 'hair loose, under a rich coif'. Lord Surrey, Lady Surrey, Bishop Elphinstone, Lord Angus are seated at the table. The meal is finished. The Queen sits on the King's right. Janet Kennedy stands behind the Queen's chair, Lord Angus's eyes upon her.

A MINSTREL (*singing off*):
> 'Welcome to be our Princess of honour,
> Our pearl, our pleasure, and our paramour,
> Our peace, our play, our plain felicity.
> Christ thee comfort from all adversity.'

SURREY (*rising to his feet*): Your Majesties, we have been royally entertained. (*He drinks to them.*) And when my lady and myself return to London, we will tell his Majesty, with pride, to how much pageantry and festival – to how much generosity and love – his Embassy was treated here in Scotland by his Royal son-in-law. I thank your Majesties – officially and personally – for England, for myself, and for my wife.

LADY SURREY: And to Lord Surrey's words, your Majesties, I add my humble gratitude and thanks.

JAMES (*rising*): I thank you both with all my heart. In you, my lady Surrey, have I found a gay and cheerful friend. 'Tis said, my lord, you are the greatest soldier in all Europe. Therefore am I proud to think that in the Border Wars I stood in arms against you, and survived. (*His voice becomes serious.*) And therefore, too, I pray – with all my heart – your realm and mine may never take the field again in war.

BISHOP : Amen to that, your Majesty.

JAMES : Good Bishop Elphinstone, I wonder – do you raise that loud 'Amen' because the Christian Gospel holds that warfare be a crime? Or, with less honesty but more expedience, because Lord Surrey is an English General?

Lord Surrey laughs.

BISHOP : I am a friend to England and a man of peace, your Majesty.

JAMES : And I.

BISHOP : If Heaven hear my daily prayers, your Majesty, why then you are – a thousandfold – –

LADY SURREY : The Queen is sleepy, sir.

James looks down at Margaret, where she is trying hard but unsuccessfully to keep awake.

SURREY : What! Sleepy on her wedding night!

LADY SURREY : I would you had been so, my lord. I never thought to see the dawn alive!

They laugh and Margaret wakes.

QUEEN : Why! Have I been asleep?

JAMES (*tenderly*): You have been dozing, sweet. Now Mistress Kennedy and Lady Surrey will conduct you to your bed.

LADY SURREY (*rising and taking her hand*): Aye, let me take you to your bed, your Majesty.

QUEEN : I bid you all good night. (*To James.*) Save you, my lord. 'Tis early yet to say good night to you. (*With childish charm.*) My lord, when I am put to bed, I pray you – come to me.

JAMES : Aye. Gladly will I come to you, my love.

She goes with Lady Surrey and Janet Kennedy, rubbing her eyes. She disappears behind the curtain of the great State bed, where Lady Surrey will undress her out of sight of those at table still.

Good Bishop, is St Andrew's See not vacant yet?

BISHOP : It is, your Majesty.

JAMES: Then shall it soon be filled. 'Twill suit my son right well. What think you, my lord Angus?

BISHOP: It were over-generous, methinks, to make a babe Archbishop ere it has been born.

JAMES: Nay, nay. I mean the son that I already have. 'Twill suit my little Alexander well. (*To Surrey.*) I would that you had met my son, my lord. He is a pretty child.

SURREY: What age is he, your Majesty?

JAMES: Some six or seven years. (*To Angus.*) Then do you not approve my choice, my lord?

ANGUS: 'Tis possible there would be those might look on him as passing young.

JAMES: Among them Bishop Elphinstone?

BISHOP: Your Majesty – I cannot help but feel that he might lack experience of Church affairs.

JAMES: He will, my lord, and all the better for it too. For what he lacks in guile, he will make up in innocence!

BISHOP: Your Majesty, I beg to take my leave.

JAMES: More wine?

The Bishop declines with a nod.

For you, my lord.

SURREY: Nay, sire, I have an early ride tomorrow morn.

JAMES: Well, then, good night.

He returns the Bishop's bow and shakes Lord Surrey's hand.

My lord, 'tis my most earnest hope that we may meet again.

SURREY: And mine, your Majesty.

Surrey bows and the Bishop and he go out. Angus is about to follow them when the King stops him.

JAMES: A toast, my lord. (*He raises his glass.*) To Margaret.

He looks into Angus's eyes. He drinks. Angus bows and goes. Janet Kennedy comes in.

Are you not yet betrothed?

JANET: To whom, your Majesty?

JAMES: Lord Angus, Mistress Kennedy.

JANET: We have not spoken of it recently, my lord.

JAMES: For why?

JANET: Lord Angus is a jealous man, your Majesty. He told me once I looked too much toward the King.

JAMES: What did you answer him?

JANET: That everyone should love the King, my lord.

> *There is the dawning of a look between them as Lady Surrey appears from behind the State bed.*

LADY SURREY: The Queen awaits your Majesty.

JAMES: Good night.

> *Lady Surrey curtsies and goes out. Janet is about to go but when the King turns and walks up to the bed, she stops and watches him. He gently draws the curtain back.*

(*To himself.*) She is asleep. (*He mutters to himself.*) She asked me why I would not call her Margaret.

> *He slowly draws the curtain back, turns and comes back into the main room.*

Poor child, she is too young to understand.

> *He turns and sees Janet Kennedy still standing there.*

But you are not.

> *He moves over to her and takes her in his arms to protect himself from loneliness.*

Sweet Janet – you are not.

> *Angus comes in, looking for Mistress Kennedy, sees them and withdraws again.*

THE CURTAIN FALLS

SCENE 8

BEFORE THE CURTAIN

Lord Angus, with a look of anger on his face, is waiting in the corridor. Mistress Kennedy passes him before she sees him.

ANGUS: Mistress Kennedy.

JANET: (*she stops, surprised*): You startled me, my lord.

ANGUS: (*moving towards her*): You walk like someone in a dream – (*Still nearer.*) – With buoyant step and starry eyes – for all the world – as though you were in love.

JANET: And if I am, my lord?

   She is backing away.

ANGUS: Why, if you are, 'twere better you abandon it.

JANET: Is it a sin to be in love, my lord?

ANGUS: That will depend on whom it is you love.

JANET: Not you, my lord, I'll warrant you.

ANGUS: Then who?

JANET: I am in love with – life, my lord.

ANGUS: With life! Why, then, 'twere wise you do my will, lest you should lose your love.

JANET (*frightened*): What is your will, my lord?

ANGUS: My will is that you leave the Court and never more return.

JANET: My lord!

ANGUS: 'Tis little use entreating me. I am resolved to move you into Galloway.

JANET: To Galloway?

ANGUS: To Whithorn – aye.

JANET: To Whithorn. Is there not an Abbey there, my lord?

ANGUS: Aye – so there is. The Holy Friars will offer spiritual comfort for a broken heart.

JANET: And should his Majesty refuse to let me go?

ANGUS: You will not see the King again.

   Janet looks up and sees two Soldiers at either end of the corridor.

JANET: And should he ask where I have gone?

ANGUS: He will be told you have removed to Galloway.

JANET: And should I still refuse to go?

ANGUS: Then will you go elsewhere.

JANET: You would not dare!

ANGUS: There's nothing that I would not dare for Scotland, Mistress Kennedy.

JANET: For Scotland – pshaw! 'Tis due to jealousy, my lord, because I will not marry you.

ANGUS: 'Tis I that will not marry you.

JANET: Yet 'tis the same result. We are not wed.

ANGUS: I will not marry you because you have a mind to give yourself in wantonness as mistress to the King.

JANET: My lord – a woman's love is never wanton. Women love by instinct. Men, methinks, as oft as not, to satisfy their lusts.

ANGUS: I care not how you love, and so you love alone in Galloway.

He turns on his heel and goes, and leaves her standing there.

⋅ THE CURTAIN RISES

SCENE 9

Seated, the Archbishop of St Andrews, Alexander Stuart (the illegitimate son of the King). He is between ten and fifteen years of age. He is seated over his books, his elbows on the table, paying scant attention to Will Dunbar, who is giving him a history lesson. Among his other activities Will Dunbar combines that of being a non-operational priest.

DUNBAR: Well, then – what have we now? The Pope and Maximilian grew mortally afraid of Charles of France. They formed a league against him, called the League of Venice – –

The boy flicks something perilously near to his tutor.

Now, my lord Archbishop, pay attention please! (*He carries on.*) In 1498 – twelve years ago – Charles died by accident. And who succeeded him?

ARCHBISHOP: The present King of France.

DUNBAR (*sarcastically*): Aye, right – but safe! King Louis Twelfth succeeded him, who married Charles's widow – –

ARCHBISHOP: Anne of Brittany.

DUNBAR: Precisely, Anne of Brittany. And then yon League broke up.

ARCHBISHOP: I thought that they were married still.

DUNBAR: I'm talking of the League of Venice, not of Anne and Louis's conjugal relationship.

ARCHBISHOP: I'm sorry.

DUNBAR: Will you please to give me your attention, or I'll keep ye in an extra hour.

ARCHBISHOP: My father said I could go hawking with him, when I've had my dinner.

DUNBAR: I'm sure he didna, wi' the Prince sae poorly!

ARCHBISHOP: What can father do about it?

DUNBAR: Do about it! He can fall upon his knees an' pray to God that yon wee bairn willna die, that health and happiness be showered upon her Majesty the Queen, and on the new-born heir to Scotland's throne. And you, my lord Archbishop, would do well to pray the like.

ARCHBISHOP: Then will you let me off my history, if I go and pray?

DUNBAR: I'll not! I dinna trust ye, lad. And that's a fact! In 1502, eight years ago, King Louis made an effort to dissuade his Majesty from marrying the Princess Margaret, since he thought that it would neutralize the Scots and thus disturb the balance of the Powers – –

ARCHBISHOP (*yawning*): And did it?

DUNBAR: No. Because his Majesty's a friend to France, in spite of being married to an Englishwoman – or, maybe, because of it! The Pope – to try to split the Franco-Scots alliance – sent your father here a jewelled hat and sword, and named him the Protector of the Christian Faith. I'm thinking wi' a Pope like yon, it maybe needed one! But still, your father wouldna break his faith with France.

ARCHBISHOP: Will, can't *we* have a break?

DUNBAR: A break! These matters are of verra intimate concern.

ARCHBISHOP: Read me some poetry.

DUNBAR (*trying to ignore this*): On April 22nd of last year the Seventh Henry died. His son, King Henry Eighth, the brother of your father's queen, refused to send her Majesty some jewels and a legacy her father left her in his will. And so relationships with England grew much worse.

ARCHBISHOP: I do so love your poetry!

DUNBAR: Three months ago Sir Thomas Howard, the Lord High Admiral of England's Fleet, attacked your father's ships and slew Sir Andrew Barton, as you know. In consequence there's tension with the English. Doctor West is here just now in Edinburgh. All this concerns the fate of Scotland very closely – –

He looks round and sees the Archibishop eating an apple, concealed behind the flap of his desk.

Rather more, it seems, than it's concerning you!

ARCHBISHOP (*wheedling*): Read me the Thistle and the Rose.

DUNBAR (*tempted, but still adamant*): And then, last year, occurred a glorious event. And will ye tell me what it was?

ARCHBISHOP: My tiercel killed two herons at Craigmillar.

DUNBAR: No!

ARCHBISHOP: He did. I found them both near Carberry.

DUNBAR: I'm thinking of another matter – more important possibly. Though maybe not so thrilling to your Reverence! But no less glorious.

ARCHBISHOP: The Queen fell ill!

DUNBAR: I canna find much glory in that sad event. But why did she fall ill?

ARCHBISHOP: Because of jealousy and Janet Kennedy.

DUNBAR: My lord, how dare ye say such things!

ARCHBISHOP (*realizing he has gone too far*): Because of Arthur, I suppose.

DUNBAR: Aye, ye suppose correct. The glorious event of which I'm speaking was the birth of Arthur – son and heir to Scotland's King. I think ye might have recollected that – above your tiercel's barbarous activities.

ARCHBISHOP: He's never killed two herons in one day – before or since. And father's had a lot of children in his day!

DUNBAR: But not a son and heir.

ARCHBISHOP: I thought I was his son.

DUNBAR: Aye, you're his son all right, but no his heir.

ARCHBISHOP: I don't see why I shouldn't be. Why shouldn't I?

DUNBAR: Because, in law, the heir must needs be born in certain circumstances, and through certain – channels, shall I say? Conditions which did not prevail when you, my lord Archbishop, came into the world.

ARCHBISHOP: Why didn't they?

DUNBAR: Suffice it that they didna, lad. The why and wherefore's no concern o' mine.

ARCHBISHOP: It surely is of mine.

DUNBAR: Well, I'll no enlighten ye.

ARCHBISHOP: Have you had many mistresses?

DUNBAR: My lord Archbishop, is it proper ye should ask a priest that question?

ARCHBISHOP: If the answer's not improper, there's no harm in it. (*He speaks wistfully.*) I hope I'm going to have a lot. A new one every year, like worn out shoes!

DUNBAR (*hastily*): You asked to hear my poetry.

ARCHBISHOP: Yes, please – the Thistle and the Rose.

DUNBAR: Och, no – ye've heard that oft enough. I've got a new one in ma heid. I'll gie ye just one verse.

He recites.

> 'I that in health was and gladness,
> And troublit now with great sickness
> And feeblit with infirmitie,
> *Timor mortis conturbat me.*'

ARCHBISHOP: I like that, Will. *Timor mortis conturbat me.* Are you afraid of death?

DUNBAR: Aye, like all men.

ARCHBISHOP: I'm not. And shall I tell you why? Because Archbishops go to Heaven, Will Dunbar!

DUNBAR: Aye, do they so! Then maybe I'll prefer the other place.

ARCHBISHOP: That's jealousy.

DUNBAR: An' if it is! I've served his Majesty – year in, year out— and never once has he suggested me for any Bishopric at all.

ARCHBISHOP: You'd never make a bishop, Will.

DUNBAR: The competition's no so strong.

ARCHBISHOP: You mustn't talk like that. I'll have you burnt!

DUNBAR: Aye, so ye would, ye little de'il. To gi'e yersel' a right good laugh! Och, maybe I prefer the Court at that. Maybe it's better to be happy on this earth than fallin' on one's knees an' seekin' for the doubtful chance o' it elsewhere!

The King comes in.

What news, sir? Is Prince Arthur mending?

JAMES: Thank you, Will, for your concern. God grant his health improves.

DUNBAR: Amen.

JAMES: God grant it soon, before his strength is gone too low. How goes the history lesson, Alexander?

ARCHBISHOP (*decidedly*): It is finished, sir.

JAMES: And did you learn all Will intended that you should?

ARCHBISHOP: Yes, sir.

JAMES: What did you learn?

ARCHBISHOP: I learnt that Anne of Brittany was married twice, to Charles and then to Louis.

JAMES: Did you also learn that she is very beautiful?

ARCHBISHOP: No, sir.

JAMES: Then store it in your memory. Such women – in high places – have a mighty influence in world affairs.

ARCHBISHOP: Like Helen, sir.

JAMES (*to Dunbar*): The boy is quick. Nay, God forbid she be like Helen, son, for Trojan Helen caused a war. Pray God that Anne of Brittany do no such thing as that.

ARCHBISHOP: Can we go hawking, sir?

JAMES: Go hawking? (*Playfully.*) Should you not be posting to St Andrews to your See? Methinks I will displace you, and make William here Archbishop in your stead!

Dunbar looks awkward.

Hence, Will – and summon me the English Embassy.

Dunbar goes. He turns to Alexander.

Go hawking! Nay, I fear me not. 'Tis now five days that Doctor West has waited, and I fear he grows irate. Sweet son, the world is full of hawks, and all more fierce than yours – and hungrier. Nor do they stoop at larks and pipits and wild ducks. Instead they stoop at France. And if they have their kill, they all will stoop at Scotland next.

A trumpet sounds.

Stay here with me. Then will you learn why – even had I leisure – I would scarce go hawking with you now. 'Twould be plain agony to watch the quarry twist and turn to cheat the thunderbolt. And all in vain.

The trumpet sounds just outside. Enter Doctor West. He is angry.

West: I must protest, sir, that an English Embassy has waited for an audience for five long days.

James: I will not hear your protest, sir.

West: I make my protest in the name of his most Christian Majesty of England.

James: Christian Majesty indeed! That braggart boy! How Christian is the man that steals his sister's legacy?

West: I do not understand your meaning, sir.

James: You understand me perfectly, did you so wish. The legacy that Henry's father left my Queen. The Jewels that Prince Arthur – her dead brother – left her too. Where are they, Doctor West?

West: They are quite safe, your Majesty.

James: Quite safe! Is that the answer of a thief when he is questioned? 'What I stole, I kept quite safe'! (*Furiously.*) How dare King Henry send an Embassy, without he send the jewels as well. 'Tis plain outrageous, sir – to hoard his sister's legacy against her father's will. 'Tis said the Scots are hoarders of their money, but the money that we hoard is ours – we are not thieves!

West: I cannot stay to listen to these insults to my master, sir.

James: Then go – –

West: I have my orders to fulfil. King Henry bid me say he finds himself concerned by Scotland's attitude to France.

James: 'Tis no concern of his. Since when was Scotland's choice of friends the business of England's King?

West (*speaking calmly, in opposition to the King's anger*): My master is concerned, your Majesty, that if a situation should arise obliging him to move against the French – should such a situation come, I do not say it has, but should it come – my master is concerned that Scotland should be neutral, sir.

James: That he may ravage France in peace.

West: That he might save his country from the French, your Majesty.

James: France does not threaten England, Doctor West. If England war on France, 'twill be because the English ever look for betterment at the expense of weaker nations – like my own.

West: Your Majesty is less than just.

James: And is it justice when the Lord High Admiral attacks my ships and slays Sir Andrew Barton? Is that justice, sir?

WEST: The Lord High Admiral had thought that they were pirates, sir.

JAMES: My sailors are not pirates, sir. They sail the seas 'neath Scotland's flag.

WEST: 'Tis possible the High Admiral had thought Sir Andrew Barton was conveying reinforcements into France.

JAMES: I am not like your master, Doctor West. I do not war when I am still at peace. If I decide to aid the French, you may be sure King Henry will be told of it. I have not so decided, but my patience can be overtaxed.

WEST: My master finds it hard to understand your friendship for the French, your Majesty.

JAMES: 'Tis no surprise to me. His understanding is not great.

WEST: He grows more angry towards Scotland every day, your Majesty.

JAMES: And I no less toward him. In youth, I found it prudent to restrain my wrath, Ambassador. I durst not leave the throne untenanted, were I to die. But now I have an heir, Prince Arthur, Doctor West. Go tell King Henry this – that Arthur, heir to Scotland's king, stands counter to his tyrannous ambition, as King Henry's brother Arthur stood 'twixt him and England's throne.

WEST (*quietly*): Until he died, your Majesty.

JAMES: What mean you, sir, by that?

WEST: You spoke of Arthur, sir – King Henry's elder brother – and as all the world's aware, Prince Arthur died, and then King Henry sat upon his father's throne. 'Tis all my words intended, sir.

JAMES (*white with passion*): You have been listening about the Court, Ambassador.

WEST: No, sir.

JAMES: The gossip-mongers have been talking of the illness of my son.

WEST: I've heard he is not well, sir, certainly.

JAMES: You have not heard that he is dying of a wasting sickness?

WEST: No, sir – God forbid!

JAMES: You have not heard that Bishop Elphinstone prays hourly by his crib?

WEST: Nay, sir, I have heard none of this.

JAMES: Then do not listen, should such rumours tend to fly about the Court before you leave. There are too many people hereabouts with naught to do but talk. Go tell King Henry, Doctor West, Prince Arthur's well.

> *Unseen by the King, Bishop Elphinstone comes in.*

That he will grow in stature while his father stands against the enemies of Scotland unto death.

> *Bishop Elphinstone whispers in the King's ear.*

Why do you wait, Ambassador? Go, tell King Henry that Prince Arthur's well.

> *His voice breaks on the last word, but he holds his pose until Doctor West has gone.*

ARCHBISHOP: Can we go hawking, father, now?
BISHOP: Your Grace, Prince Arthur hath this moment died.
ARCHBISHOP: But father said that he was well.

> *James looks at him, but does not rebuke him, and turns to the Bishop.*

JAMES: I will be with you in the Chapel presently.

> *The Bishop goes.*

Come hither, Alexander.

> *Frightened, the little Archbishop goes towards him, and James gently takes him by the arm.*

I would I could go hawking, Alexander. But I go to pray for little Arthur's soul – to ask forgiveness, lest his weakness can be laid to my incontinence. Poor Arthur, what a little time to live!

> *The bell starts tolling.*

Yet God decreed that I must lose a son. And – if it must be so – 'twere better he than you – –

> *He pauses, while the bell tolls on.*

– For you were born of love.

> *He turns and kisses him.*

THE CURTAIN FALLS

ACT TWO

SCENE 1

The Queen, now about twenty years old, is dictating a letter to Doctor West, the English Ambassador.

QUEEN (*dictating*): ''Tis now two years and more that this dispute remaineth unresolved.' Is that not so? Aye, surely 'tis two years. You came here from my brother last the year that Arthur died – –

WEST: I recollect that sad occasion, ma'am, with tears unto this day.

QUEEN: I fear my husband quarrelled with you bitterly. But he was overwrought and anxious for my little Arthur's health. And – as I hope – a little for my own.

WEST: I understood his Majesty's unhappiness full well.

QUEEN: But did my brother understand?

WEST: King Henry was concerned about his sister's health, your Majesty.

QUEEN: Dear Henry! Loves he still the Spanish Catharine?

WEST: With all his heart, your Majesty.

QUEEN: With all his heart! Why, then, methinks, he cannot love her much. I would not be his wife, had I the choice. His love might turn too suddenly to hate and then – I would not be his wife. (*She turns, after a faint shudder, to Doctor West.*) But let us get this letter to my brother writ. Where are we got to now?

WEST (*reading*): ''Tis now two years and more that this dispute remaineth unresolved.'

QUEEN (*reminiscent again*): How much has happened in those years! My Jamie born and strong. I did not think to have a child that would survive above a year. My husband almost had despaired as well. Yet was he kind to me. The more especially because the fault was wholly mine. There could be no disputing that, because my husband's potency hath never lacked the proof! Come, Doctor, let us write this letter to my brother and then talk.

WEST: I am awaiting your dictation, ma'am.

QUEEN (*dictating*): 'Our husband knows the legacy withholden for his sake – and therefore will he recompense us. Our husband is ever the longer the better to us, as God knows. Your loving sister, Margaret.' 'Tis done. It is degrading, Doctor West, this petty quarrel over jewels and a legacy. I do not understand the meaning for it.

WEST: Ma'am – (*he looks round to see that he is not overheard.*) – my master said he would not hesitate to send the jewels, provided that his Majesty sit in his chair.

QUEEN: Sit in his chair?

WEST: He means, your Majesty, that should he go abroad – as, in your private ear alone, he doth intend – he would require the King of Scots to make no move across the Border.

QUEEN: And to that, with all my heart, I say Amen.

WEST: Can you restrain him, ma'am?

QUEEN: I fear me not. He hath a destiny. His soul is eaten by a sense of guilt that he was instrumental in his father's death. Thus, all the more, he seeks to wash away that stain by sacrifice.

WEST: My master hath a mind to make him Regent in his absence overseas, and to create him Duke of York.

QUEEN: And have you told my husband so?

WEST: Not yet. But I am bound to do so, ma'am.

QUEEN: I fear my brother does not know my husband, Doctor West. Alas, I often wonder if I know him either – as a wife should know the man whose children she has borne. He does not live entirely in this world. There is a part of him I cannot catch. Or, if I catch it sometime, then it slides as suddenly from out my grasp.

WEST: It must be soul-destroying, ma'am.

QUEEN: No, rather is it wonderful! A woman loves a man like that. Because a woman only loves what is elusive. 'Tis because the things she cannot hold she cannot break. And therefore are they ever tempting her.

WEST: You must persuade him, ma'am.

QUEEN: Of what, good Doctor? That I love him so?

WEST: You must persuade him that he sit upon his chair.

QUEEN: It is not possible.

WEST: Then can Lord Angus not persuade him, ma'am?

QUEEN: Nay, Doctor, for the people love my husband now, since

W.D.H.–Q

Jamie's birth. And thus Lord Angus dare no longer challenge him.

WEST: Then, if he cannot be persuaded, ma'am, there will be war.

QUEEN: Two nations cannot go to war about some jewels and a legacy.

WEST: Your Majesty, the jewel that your brother casts his eyes upon is – France.

QUEEN: Doth Henry really mean to sail for France?

WEST: If he is not already sailed.

QUEEN: Already sailed! Then what will Scotland do?

WEST: The King of Scots alone can answer that.

QUEEN: We must not go to war! It is plain folly to begin the Border quarrels once again.

WEST: It is not England's wish they should begin again, your Majesty.

WEST: Then let my brother send the legacy – and thus placate my husband.

WEST: When I left your brother, ma'am, he was not in a placatory mood.

> *During the next speeches the King comes in, unseen, and overhears.*

Indeed, his words were these – 'that if the King of Scots persist in war, the King of England will not only keep the legacy, but take from him the best towns that he hath in Scotland.'

QUEEN: Do you mean to tell my husband that!

WEST: My orders are to speak, if he is adamant.

QUEEN: Then God help Scotland, Doctor West.

WEST (*persuasively*): It only needs a sentence from the King to say that he will stay in Scotland and – the legacy is yours.

JAMES: The legacy is hers already, as I understand it, Doctor West.

WEST (*taken aback, standing up and bowing*): Your Majesty . . .!

> *The King moves angrily forward and confronts the Ambassador.*

JAMES: Is this the way King Henry's Embassy conducts its business! By whispering in women's ears and dangling temptation at your finger tips! Is bribery the latest weapon in your English armoury?

WEST (*standing up to him*): Nay, sir – it is the pike.

JAMES: The pike! Then would I rather that you brought your escort here to Holyrood, and bade them raise their pikes above my head and cry 'Submit' – 'Twere better far than underhand dishonesty.

WEST: I was not so instructed, sir. When force prevails the function of Ambassadors is past.

JAMES: Aye, then methinks that I would welcome an appeal to force. I am grown sick of Embassies and bribes. 'Tis time that you in England understood that Scotland is a nation having interests and loyalties no less exacting than your own. What was the Royal edict that I overheard?

WEST: One sentence, taken from its context, often is misleading, sir.

JAMES: The sentence that I overheard I scarcely could have misinterpreted. Nor can I see what context could have cloaked so bald a threat! Your master said that if I go to war he will not only keep the legacy, but ravage and destroy my country. Did I hear aright?

WEST: You heard but half, your Majesty.

JAMES: Yet have I heard enough.

He turns away in disgust, but Doctor West tries again.

WEST: You did not hear my master's offer to instal your Majesty as Regent in his absence overseas – –

JAMES: Since when has he been purposed to be absent overseas?

WEST: The plan was in debate in Parliament when I departed sir.

JAMES (*with sarcasm*): And is King Henry journeying, perchance, on a Crusade?

WEST: Sir, some might call it so.

JAMES: Into the Holy Land?

WEST: No, sir.

JAMES: Then where?

WEST: To France, your Majesty.

JAMES: To France! And he would have me Regent while he wages war upon the French!

WEST: I am instructed further, sir – in order to facilitate the Regency, and to extend your power in England, sir – his Majesty would willingly create you Duke of York.

JAMES: He would create me Duke of York! And to extend my power in England! I can think of other ways of doing that.

WEST: 'Twould be the greatest honour to be Duke of York, your Majesty.

JAMES: An honour, think you! 'Tis an honour for the King of Scotland to be bribed with titles, and his Queen with jewels! It seems the honour of an Englishman much differs from mine own – I beg you, sir, permit me to retain my own conception of the meaning of that word, though you permit me not to keep my towns! I give you leave, good Doctor, to withdraw.

WEST: Your Majesty – –

He bows and backs towards the door.

JAMES (*shouting after him*): Were Scotland utterly destroyed, your master never could destroy my honour, sir.

Doctor West is shown out by a Herald.

(*To the Herald.*) Go summon Bishop Elphinstone and my lord Angus here.

The Herald goes. The King turns back into the room.

QUEEN: My lord, I pray you not to quarrel so with Doctor West. For never was a man less quarrelsome. He loves his country, sir – as you love yours – and I love mine. Or both of mine.

JAMES: It is not at the Doctor that my barbs are aimed, but at your headstrong brother, ma'am.

QUEEN: My lord, I scarcely think that insults – proudly hurled from side to side the Tweed – are fitted best to ease the tension that exists between my brother and yourself.

JAMES: What would you have me hurl at him? A flight of spears?

QUEEN: Nay, God forbid!

JAMES: Then would you have me send the Lyon King-at-Arms, with money, to his court – and bribes! What would you have the Lyon say? 'The King of Scotland will create you Duke of Rothesay if your Majesty will keep the peace'! Or would your brother, madam, deem such words an insult, think you, as I do myself?

QUEEN: I own my brother wild and overbearing, sir. But he is young. While you, compared with him, are old in judgement and experience. (*She appeals passionately.*) My lord, there never was a situation in the world so warlike or so dangerous but cool and level-headed statesmen could control it, if they willed to do so in their hearts. I pray you to be temperate.

JAMES: I cannot stand aside if Henry march on France.

QUEEN: Why, then beseech him not to march on France, but do not answer him the more.

JAMES: A man may not beseech another man to anything – and still retain his manhood.

QUEEN: Then 'tis time that women held the reins of government, my lord.

JAMES: If Scotland go to war – and I should die – as die I will, for God will surely recompense me for my father's death – then will you have your wish – – You will be Regent in my son's minority.

QUEEN: My lord, you must not go to war. Nor shall you die. I cannot have you die. I shall not let you die.

Lord Angus, followed by Bishop Elphinstone, comes in. They bow.

ANGUS: An Embassy from France is just arrived, your Majesty.

JAMES: Who leads the Embassy?

ANGUS: A General La Motte, your Majesty.

QUEEN: I will be gone.

JAMES: I have no secrets from the Queen.

QUEEN: Yet will I go, with your permission, sir. Then can you speak of England as you will. Nor shall I be offended when I cannot hear your words. Besides, in Bishop Elphinstone I know I leave behind an eloquent and noble advocate for peace. And in Lord Angus, too.

ANGUS: I ever was a friend of England, ma'am.

QUEEN: Then can I go, with easy conscience, and prepare my son for sleep. (*To James.*) My lord, if your deliberations here – and with the French Ambassador – do not last overlong, I know the Prince will sleep the sounder could you come and say good night to him.

James inclines his head in assent.

And, when you come, I pray you bring us word that Scotland will not go to war.

BISHOP: Amen, your Majesty.

The Queen curtsies and goes.

JAMES: 'Tis not with prayers we will restrain her madcap brother, Bishop Elphinstone.

BISHOP: The power of prayer is limitless, your Majesty.

JAMES: And so is his ambition! Still, good Bishop, do you pray. I am no enemy to prayer.

JAMES : My lords, I am informed King Henry means to march against the French.

ANGUS : Then I, for one, would let him march.

JAMES : I did not think that you would pray, my lord. Yet never did I think to hear you use such words.

ANGUS : Yet have I used them, sir.

JAMES : I heard you tell her Majesty you were a friend to England, yet I cannot think you are a friend to Scotland too. Are we not allied with the French? Can Scotland lightly lay aside her friendship for the only European power that checks the English – and thus keeps them south of Tweed.

ANGUS : I do not see the French in any danger, sir. King Louis should not, in my estimation, fear the English – even though they sail for France.

JAMES : Why should he not? There never was a country in such mortal danger as is France today. As you are well aware, the Holy League – so called – is formed against the French. The Emperor Maximilian – with Spain and Venice and the Pope – all leagued against the French. And England, too – preparing to attack. And yet – you say King Louis need not be afraid! I am not much inclined to fear myself, and yet I would not face that combination of the European powers with confidence – nor equanimity. Methinks you are too brave, my lord – or too attached to England – to have read the situation right.

BISHOP : If I might speak, your Majesty.

JAMES (*wearily*): Good Bishop, speak your fill.

BISHOP : Lord Angus and myself do not believe that Scotland should involve herself upon the Continent. Admittedly, the Holy League is formed against the French. But, sir – 'tis not by any means the first League formed in Europe, nor – I'll warrant you, the last. Such Leagues have ever had high sounding names, but seldom have they had long life. The League of Venice in my memory did not survive above a year or two. And therefore, sir – 'tis folly, in my view, to be embroiled upon the Continent. Assuming that we went to war with England – God forbid it should be so, I say so only for the sake of argument – supposing that we did, your Majesty, who knows what might occur? The League might break asunder – France might join the Emperor, or Spain, or England, too conceivably – then where would Scotland be, your Majesty?

JAMES: She would not be dishonoured, my lord Bishop, anyway.

BISHOP: Yet might she be the victim of a crowd of angry powers – the wrath of England pouring on her head, her countryside destroyed, and all for . . . what? To save King Louis from a nameless fear!

ANGUS: Stand fast, your Majesty! Keep Scotland strong and see what may befall.

JAMES: I like your council less and less, my lords. If Scotland hold her hand, allowing Henry to invade the Continent – and should he gain against the French – and he return inflated in his victory – then who shall say him 'Nay'?

He turns to the Bishop.

The very fears that you express, my lord, will be fulfilled. The pride of England, thirsting evermore for blood, will fall upon our land . . . our countryside will be destroyed to make an English holiday. And if that happens, history will recount that Scotland was well served, because she sat, alone, in fear and durst not save her last ally, the King of France.

ANGUS: Your Majesty, you are not strong enough to war with England – even were it necessary – which I deny.

JAMES: Since when was duty measured by one's strength? The thing that's right – is right. 'Tis not success or failure that should be the guiding principle in men's affairs – but what is right.

ANGUS: Men's actions should depend on what they may achieve, your Majesty. 'Tis madness to involve this realm in war and thus to court disaster for no visible reward.

JAMES: I do not seek rewards, I seek two things. Politically, I seek security. And morally, I seek to hold my head on high. It is not in my nature to forsake a friend in need.

BISHOP: You talked of history, sir. 'Tis possible historians will say that Scotland struck her neighbour in the back, when she was struggling elsewhere.

JAMES: I do not doubt the English histories will say such things. Yet is it false. Nor am I frightened by the contents of a history book. 'Tis not the truth that England's struggling elsewhere. King Henry hath no need to sail for France. 'Tis all because he hath a wish to style himself the King of France, as his poor foolish father did. There is no shadow of excuse for England – that she land upon the Continent.

BISHOP: Assuming that your Majesty was killed . . .

JAMES (*angrily*): God knows there is enough to bear me down, without you talk about my death. (*He stands up.*) Good Bishop, think you in your heart, I shall be killed?

BISHOP: No, God forbid, your Majesty.

JAMES: I do. I know it in my heart. Methinks that I have always known it in my heart.

His voice and face are strange. Lord Angus smiles.

ANGUS: Then is your Majesty afraid of death?

JAMES (*banishing his tell-tale horror*): Afraid! You ask the King is he afraid!

ANGUS (*quietly*): Of death, your Majesty.

JAMES (*quietly too*): Of death. Why, yes. I am afraid of death. Is it not natural, my lord?

ANGUS: 'Tis instinct certainly. All animals fear death.

JAMES: All men, as well.

ANGUS: Not I, your Majesty.

JAMES: Then are you not a man.

They look at each other with renewed hatred. The Bishop intervenes.

BISHOP: I was about to lay an argument before your Majesty.

JAMES: Then speak.

BISHOP: I did intend to say – if something untoward should happen to your Majesty – if you were captured by the English, say – (*he adds that qualification hastily to avoid touching on the subject of death*) – the Prince is only one year old, my lord – the Queen is English – and a Regency would raise again the factions that your Majesty has tamed with such forbearance and success.

JAMES (*with sarcasm*): Then doubtless, would my lord of Angus take control. As I remember it, he hath a most persuasive way with youthful kings.

ANGUS: 'Tis clear that my opinions and my presence are offensive to your Majesty. Yet 'tis my duty to oppose you, sir, in this. 'Tis madness, in my view, to go to war.

JAMES: I noted your opinion earlier, my lord. It will not gain in weight by repetition – rather will it lose. The less your love for

England be impressed upon my ear, the more unlikely is it I shall doubt your loyalty.

> *Enter a Herald.*

Who comes?

HERALD: The French Ambassador, your Majesty.

JAMES: I will receive him now.

> *The Herald bows and goes.*

Your lordships will remain. I would not have it said I have a secret understanding with the French. Not even in the history books your lordships fear so much!

> *Enter General de la Motte, the French Ambassador. He bows, in Continental fashion, to the King.*

I welcome you in Scotland, Monsieur de la Motte.

DE LA MOTTE: I thank you, sire.

JAMES: Lord Angus – Bishop Elphinstone.

> *He waves his hand in introduction. De la Motte bows again and addresses Lord Angus.*

DE LA MOTTE: You have a reputation with my countrymen, my lord.

JAMES: 'Tis flattering, I hope!

DE LA MOTTE: We know Lord Angus as a warrior. And as a power in Scotland's counsels, sir.

ANGUS: I am most honoured, sir.

DE LA MOTTE: And Bishop Elphinstone. Your Scottish Bishop of Moray – whom Louis hath made Bishop of Limoges – hath told me how you raised the University of Aberdeen. And of your interest in the education of the people, to such purpose, so 'tis said, the Scots will soon be better educated than my countrymen!

JAMES: I pray you, sir – be seated!

DE LA MOTTE (*seating himself*): Sir – –

JAMES: What news from France?

DE LA MOTTE: King Louis bade me give his fondest greetings to your Majesty and to affirm his lasting gratitude that Scotland has remained aloof from those who plot to bring about the fall of France.

JAMES: And does King Louis know that England purposes to sail on France?

DE LA MOTTE: I understand the English have already sailed, your Majesty.

JAMES: Already sailed! Then is the English Embassy a liar and a cheat!

DE LA MOTTE: All Englishmen are surely that, your Majesty!

ANGUS: Does Monsieur not forget our English Queen?

DE LA MOTTE (*equal to this*): I said all English*men*, my lord. All women are angelic – be they English, Scots or French – above all, French!

BISHOP (*tactfully*): I trust you had a pleasant voyage, sir.

DE LA MOTTE: It was exciting, most assuredly. I brought four English ships to Leith.

JAMES: Four English ships. You captured them?

DE LA MOTTE: It was a mere coincidence, your Majesty. My guns were pointing at them – where we met upon the ocean – and they turned about – and sailed before me into Leith! 'Tis my desire your Majesty will take them as a gift from France.

JAMES: With all my heart, Ambassador.

ANGUS (*stepping forward*): Your Majesty, should you accept these English ships from France, 'twill almost constitute an act of war.

JAMES: I take them in exchange for jewels and a legacy, my lord.

ANGUS: 'Tis very dangerous.

JAMES: Did you not teach me at a tender age, my lord, that life was dangerous? Both at my father's death, and then again when Margaret Drummond died? And now you preach me caution. Are you getting old, my lord? What think you, my lord Bishop – is he past his best!

BISHOP: I cannot but agree with my Lord Angus, sir. We cannot risk the wrath of England for a paltry prize.

JAMES: Four ships!

BISHOP: We have a mighty fleet. We have the great St Michael, sir. Beside, four English ships are lost to England, if they be imprisoned by the French. So, 'tis not necessary – in any case – to add them to our fleet, and thus precipitate a war.

JAMES: What think you to these arguments, Ambassador?

DE LA MOTTE: The war is started, sir. 'Tis past the time for talking of activities that might enrage the enemy – or, if one does, 'tis well
to plan for more!

ANGUS: Your enemy, La Motte. Not ours.

DE LA MOTTE: The enemy of both of us. Your country is allied
to France. The League between us was renewed in Edinburgh – this
very town, my lord. Do you not recollect it then?

ANGUS: I do. But, by its instruments, we are not bound to go to
war against the English.

DE LA MOTTE: Yet 'tis in the instruments that you are bound to
help us.

BISHOP: Help you, aye. And yet, 'tis possible to help a friend without one join his quarrel, Monsieur, is it not? Indeed, 'tis more than
probable that Scotland, standing strong and watchful, in neutrality,
may be well placed to bring about an early peace between your country
and the English King.

DE LA MOTTE: Your Majesty, do these, your counsellors, express
your country's policy?

BISHOP: We put the arguments in favour of remaining neutral – as
our duty is.

DE LA MOTTE: Yet can I not believe your Majesty accepts these
arguments.

JAMES: 'Tis very clear, Ambassador, that you do not.

DE LA MOTTE: I never shared with any man opinions based on
fear.

ANGUS: I trust you did not come to Scotland to insult us, sir. Or,
if you did, 'twill scarcely serve you well.

DE LA MOTTE: I came to Scotland to fulfil the wishes of my King.
He did not bid me stand upon the violence of my words. (*He turns to
the King.*) I came to Scotland, sir – to seek a friend. (*He becomes impassioned and eloquent.*) I came to Scotland, sir – convinced that here, in
Edinburgh, my cry for help – the cry of France in agony – would
scarcely go unheard. What do I find instead? (*He shrugs, hopelessly.*)
The Bishop, talking in a cautious vein, about neutrality. Yet, could I
almost stomach that – for Bishops have a spiritual obligation to be
prejudiced for peace – though few of them indulge it publicly. (*He
turns to Angus.*) But you, my lord! I did not think to hear soft counsel
from Lord Angus-Bell-The-Cat!

He includes them all in his appeal.

The war is started, gentlemen. King Henry sails towards the coast of France. The Holy League encircles us. 'Tis not the time to bandy words and platitudes. 'Tis action that will save my country now. And yours! For Scotland surely will be England's victim next – if France should fall.

He turns to the King, and fires a Parthian shot.

Your Majesty, you would not have me sail for France and tell King Louis that the King of Scotland sits – on English Henry's orders – in his chair.

JAMES: I take no orders from King Henry, sir.

ANGUS: Nor do we take them from the King of France.

La Motte, thwarted, plays his last card as romantically as he knows how.

DE LA MOTTE: Then will a woman's prayers not move your Majesty?

JAMES: What woman do you speak of, pray?

DE LA MOTTE: Her Majesty the Queen of France.

JAMES: Of Anne of Brittany.

His voice softens and La Motte is swift to follow up his advantage.

DE LA MOTTE: I have a letter from her Majesty.

JAMES: What doth this letter say?

DE LA MOTTE: 'Tis sealed, your Majesty.

He hands it over.

She bade me give it you in person, sir.

JAMES (*after reading*): She bids me, for her sake, step three feet into English ground. (*He looks up.*)

DE LA MOTTE: Her Majesty has sent this ring.

JAMES (*taking it*): A turquoise ring! 'Tis very beautiful!

DE LA MOTTE: 'Tis but of little beauty, sir – compared to Anne of Brittany.

JAMES (*half to himself*): She bid me – for her sake – step three feet into English ground.

His eyes kindle. The Frenchman watches him and knows that he has won. Then the King turns to Angus and Elphinstone.

My lord, I would not be a Stuart King, were I not moved by this request.

BISHOP: A woman's counsel is not always practical, your Majesty.

JAMES: I would not have it otherwise. I would not have a woman practical if, being practical, implies that they should be like men. A man relies too much upon his brain, which always is imperfect – while a woman lives by instinct, which is God's.

He comes to a decision – the decision which decreed that Scotland never more should be a first-class power.

My lords, it is not in my nature to ignore this plea.

ANGUS: 'Tis weakness, sir, to be so moved.

JAMES (*turns to La Motte*): If then 'tis weakness, 'blessed are the weak', say I. Ambassador, go tell the Queen of France the King of Scotland is not yet too old for chivalry.

DE LA MOTTE: Most gratefully will I send word, your Majesty. But, for myself, I purpose staying here in Scotland, sir. It is my wish to join your army on the march.

JAMES: 'Tis well and bravely said. (*He looks at Angus.*) Perchance you will inspire my nobles with your selfless zeal. Then send your mistress word that Scotland will not fail.

ANGUS: Your Majesty – –

JAMES: I will not hear you, sir.

BISHOP: I pray your Majesty – –

JAMES: Yet will I make one further move for peace. I'll send the Lyon King-at-Arms to Henry. If he bring his army out of France, I will not march on English soil. But, if he stay – why, then – (*He turns to La Motte.*) – I pledge my country, Monsieur de la Motte. I will make war.

DE LA MOTTE: Your Majesty has earned the lasting gratitude of France.

He bows and goes.

JAMES: Lord Angus, bid the Constable array the might of Scotland on Boroughmuir. And have my horse prepared that the Ambassador and I may ride through Edinburgh. Thus will we let the people see how Scotland keep her word. Our audience is ended, gentlemen.

Angus bows and goes. The Bishop follows him to the door and then turns.

BISHOP: Your Majesty – –

JAMES: I give you leave to go, my lord. I have no stomach for your cold and passionless advice.

BISHOP: 'Tis not of that that I would speak.

JAMES: What is't?

BISHOP: The Pope – –

JAMES: The Pope!

BISHOP The Pope hath excommunicated you, your Majesty.

JAMES (*stunned*): The Pope hath excommunicated me! When came this news?

BISHOP: Today.

JAMES: What hour?

BISHOP: This morning. I withheld it till your Majesty had seen the French Ambassador.

JAMES: The Pope has excommunicated me! I am accursed! Is that not so? I am accursed! The Cross of Christ is washed from off my brow. And, when I die, my body may not lie in consecrated ground. Is that not so, my lord?

BISHOP: 'Tis so, alas.

JAMES: Then stay you not in audience. Begone lest you should be defiled. It is not fitting for a Bishop to rub shoulders with a heretic. Begone, I say, Begone!

The Bishop hesitates, and then moves towards the door.

Do you accept this Papal Bull, my lord?

BISHOP: I have no option – sir – –

JAMES: Although you know the Pope hath excommunicated me because I will not join his cursed League? Are Scotland's Bishops so weak-livered they support the edict of a foreign Pope against their King?

BISHOP: Against the world, your Majesty.

JAMES: Then am I not a King! 'Tis but a mockery – the Pope is King!

BISHOP: The Papal power is spiritual, your Majesty.

JAMES (*losing his temper*): I will not give my soul to any Pope. It is my own. 'Twas given me by God. 'Twill be returned to God by me. And God alone will judge me for my actions here on earth. I will no longer tolerate the interference of the Pope. I tell you, Bishop Elphinstone, I snap my fingers at your Pope.

> *The Bishop bows and goes – with dignity – without a word. The King shouts after him.*

I snap my fingers at your Pope!

> *Alone, he crosses himself. Then he looks at the ring on his finger from Anne of Brittany, and mutters to himself:*

She bid me for her sake step three feet into English ground.

THE CURTAIN FALLS

SCENE 2

The English Camp at Teroenne. King Henry VIII and the Lord High Admiral of England, Sir Thomas Howard. An English sentry stands on guard. The King is reading a letter.

HENRY VIII: It doth surpass all else that I have ever read in insolence. (*To Soldier.*) Go you and fetch the Herald of the King of Scots.

> *The Soldier goes.*

'Tis you who are to blame, my lord High Admiral. My sister's husband hath not yet forgot the day you took Sir Andrew Barton prisoner with all his ships. Methinks my sister hath a wretched and unhappy life among these rude barbarians.

> *Enter the Lyon King-at-Arms.*

LYON: Your Majesty.

HENRY VIII: Lord Lyon King-at-Arms – –

> *The Lyon bows.*

I note with pleasure that your manners are much better than your King's! We have considered his request to us with all the calmness that we could command. Now take this answer back. Say this to thy good master, Lyon King – 'tis I that am the holder of all Scotland, and not he. He holdeth it of me, by homage. And moreover, as he doth rebel against me now, I shall at my return – and with God's help – expel him from his realm. And so tell him. Well, then – begone.

LYON: I will not tell him so, your Majesty.

HENRY VIII: What's this! You will not tell him so! 'Tis my command.

LYON: There is one King, your Majesty, and only one, to whose commands I give obedience – the King of Scots.

HENRY VIII: Then wherefore came you here?

LYON: I came to give your Majesty the ultimatum from my master.

HENRY VIII: Will you take no answer to it then?

LYON: I will not take that answer, sir.

HENRY VIII: You will not take that answer! 'Tis the only answer you will get. Pray tell me, Lyon King, what answer would you have?

LYON: There is no answer I require, save one. That you return immediately home.

HENRY VIII: 'Odsblood! Were I at home, your master would not beard me thus. I will return – in my good time, and at my pleasure – to your damage, never fear. Not at your master's summoning.

LYON: Is that your final answer, sir?

HENRY VIII: It is. Begone, I do not like your manner. First you will not take an answer. Then you question any answer that I give. Begone – and tell your master I have left a nobleman at home who will not suffer insults to my subjects from your Scottish King. Begone.

The Lyon goes.

The King of Scots must learn his lesson, Thomas Howard.

HOWARD: I do not doubt my father will provide him with a salutary lesson, sir, if he dare cross the Tweed.

HENRY VIII: I have a mind to send you with some reinforcements to your father, Thomas Howard.

HOWARD: There's naught that I would welcome more, your Majesty.

HENRY VIII: So be it, then. And do you sail with all despatch. I do not trust the temper of the King of Scots. (*He takes Howard's arm.*) Methinks 'twere kindness to my sister to dispose of him. 'Tis sometimes soothing to the spirit to be ridded of a husband, so 'tis said. I know 'twould soothe me famously, could I be ridded of my wife!

They stroll off.

THE CURTAIN FALLS

SCENE 3

BEFORE THE CURTAIN

There is a sound of trumpets. King James, in armour, strides along the corridor, his helmet in his hand. The Queen runs after him.

QUEEN: My lord!

He turns.

My lord, I have but just this moment heard what happened at the Cross last night.

JAMES: What happened there?

QUEEN: The Devil spoke – a ghostly voice – from out the midnight sky.

JAMES: The Devil or the Pope – 'tis all the same to me.

QUEEN: He bade his servants all appear before his throne – one month from now. He named them all.

JAMES: What names?

QUEEN: Your own, my lord. He summoned James, the King of Scotland, to appear – and Crawford and Glencairn – Montrose and Forbes and Lennox – and a host of other names, my lord.

JAMES: Did he not speak the name of Angus Bell-the-Cat?

QUEEN: My lord, 'tis not a jest. For many citizens have heard this ghostly voice. They cannot all have been deceived.

JAMES: I'll warrant you you cannot tell me one.

QUEEN: One Richard Lawson heard it. And he called his servant, and he heard it too. He hurled some money at the Cross, and as it fell he cried, 'I do appeal against your sentence.' Then came there a silence – like the grave.

JAMES: I will inquire of Richard Lawson on the Boroughmuir.

QUEEN: You will not find him on the Boroughmuir, my lord. So frighted was he at this voice, he swore he would not go to war. Nor must you go, my lord.

He turns impatiently. She seizes hold of him.

I will not let you go.

W.D.H.—R

JAMES (*holding her off*): Your brother cannot hold me. Are you stronger then than he?

> *A trumpet sounds.*

I must begone.

> *He turns to go. The Queen loses her temper.*

QUEEN: Why is it you prefer to please the Queen of France – and yet you please not me, your loving wife, the mother of your son!

JAMES (*patiently, as she holds on to him*): 'Tis not the Queen of France that makes me go to war.

QUEEN: Lord Angus thinks 'tis so.

JAMES: Lord Angus thinks too much – and never thinks with charity.

QUEEN: I will not lose my lord for any Queen of France.

> *One remembers the petulant child at Dalkeith.*

JAMES (*taking her by the wrists*): I tell thee, love – 'tis not for her I go to war.

QUEEN: And yet you wear her ring!

JAMES: I wear her ring because she gave it me.

> *The Queen starts to cry. He does not yet notice it.*

I go to war because the honour of my country is at stake. I never more could raise my head – were I to break my faith with France. And therefore do I go to war – whatever it may cost!

> *He knows what it will cost. In the pause he hears her sobs and tries to comfort her. He kisses her.*

Have faith in me, sweet Margaret.

> *He goes.*

QUEEN (*looking after him*): He never called me Margaret before.

> *She turns slowly on her heel and walks back from whence she came, as the trumpets sound – and sound again more faintly still.*

THE CURTAIN RISES

SCENE 4

Ford Castle in Northumberland. Lady Heron, thirty-four or thereabouts, young and beautiful, is seated. Near her is a harpsichord or clavichord. Beside her, her fifteen year old Daughter – promising equal beauty – stands, her hand upon her heart. The roar of cannon shakes the room.

DAUGHTER: Oh, mother, I am frightened.

LADY HERON: Frightened! Was an Englishwoman ever frightened of the Scots before!

DAUGHTER: I do not know – but I am! How I wish my father had been here.

LADY HERON: I would he had been here as well. Your father could have held this castle 'gainst the Scots. He ever says that Ford can stand a siege. But he is prisoner in Scotland, and we needs must give it up.

DAUGHTER: Why is he prisoner? He did not slay Sir Robert Kerr.

LADY HERON: Nay – but his brother did. Sir Robert was the Warden of the Scottish Marches. And the King of Scots was fearfully enraged. He took your father – as he could not take John Heron – –

DAUGHTER: John! Is John my father's brother?

LADY HERON: Aye – you know full well he is.

DAUGHTER: You told me once he was my father's father's bastard son.

LADY HERON: Sakes – what a memory you have, my child. And so he is.

DAUGHTER: Then he is not my father's brother. (*Decidedly.*)

LADY HERON: Nay – if 'tis your purpose to be obstinate. He is half brother to your father.

DAUGHTER: Well – a half is not a whole!

LADY HERON: My child! (*She sighs, but half amusedly.*) A moment since we were united in the wish Sir William were at Ford today – and now we are in argument about the indiscretions of your grandfather! And all the while King James' army marches ever nearer Ford – –

A cannon roars, much louder than the rest.

Hark! Almost are they at the gates.

> *There is a less loud but closer crash. She gets up and looks out or listens.*

DAUGHTER: Why must the Scots come here? Why can they never stay where they belong? I heard the drawbridge fall. There is a horseman in the courtyard.

> *The girl runs to her mother.*

Mother, they'll murder us!

LADY HERON: Nay, they will not. You are too pretty to be murdered, child.

DAUGHTER: Then they will murder you.

> *Lady Heron can afford to laugh at this. A Scots Herald, Islay, appears.*

ISLAY: My lady Heron?

LADY HERON (*clasping her frightened child*): At your service, sir.

ISLAY: The King of Scots hath sent me with his compliments. He hath a wish to lie at Ford tonight – and so your ladyship agrees.

LADY HERON: And I agree! Methinks I have but little choice.

ISLAY: His Majesty hath ordered me to say he will by no means come to Ford against your will.

LADY HERON: And if I say him nay?

ISLAY: Then will he stay in camp, beside his army, as he hath each night since we have crossed the Tweed. His Majesty hath ever paid attention to the wishes of a lady, ma'am.

LADY HERON: Aye, so 'tis said!

ISLAY: Then am I to return and tell his Majesty that Lady Heron hath no wish for him to lie at Ford tonight?

LADY HERON (*after a pause*): Aye, tell him that.

> *The Herald bows and goes*

(*Half to herself.*) Then will he surely come.

DAUGHTER (*overhearing this*): We cannot have the King of Scots at Ford.

LADY HERON: My daughter – be not so impetuous! Your father, my beloved husband, lies a prisoner in Scotland. 'Tis reported that the King of Scots hath taken Norham, Wark and Etal, while Lord Surrey lies at Alnwick still with thirty thousand men. Perchance 'tis just the moment to approach the King of Scots and beg him for a favour – for my husband's sake.

DAUGHTER: And do you think the King would let my father free?

LADY HERON: That will depend on the approach.

DAUGHTER: How mean you to approach him, mother?

LADY HERON: Do not ask so many questions, child. Besides, it may be possible to learn the disposition of the Scottish force – and thus Lord Surrey will be well prepared. (*She is eminently satisfied with herself.*) Ah yes, 'tis very wise to entertain the King of Scots.

DAUGHTER: Then why did you inform the Herald that you did not wish the King to lie at Ford tonight?

LADY HERON: Because, my dove – as you will learn when you are older – men are minded most to lie where they are not invited to.

> *The bagpipes sound outside. There is the sound of a horse's hooves.*

I hear a horseman in the courtyard once again. Do you sit down, my child, while I will play upon the clavichord – and sing. Thus may we both compose ourselves.

> *They both sit, making an unconscious – or a conscious? – tableau. Lady Heron sings a verse or two of 'Young Lochinvar' or some old Scots ballad. As she sings the King and the Archbishop of St Andrews, in full armour, appear. Lady Heron, with her back to them – but knowing they are there – sings on. Her daughter, fascinated by the Archbishop's appearance, tries not to look at him, but he – with no such inhibition – stares at her. The King seems equally entranced by Lady Heron, or her song. She sings a verse or two, then drops her hands.*

JAMES: My lady Heron.

> *Lady Heron feigns surprise, jumps up and curtsies low.*

I never yet heard voice and song so sweet in unison.

LADY HERON: You are most kind, your Majesty.

> *Her daughter curtsies, still looking at the Archbishop, a fact James notes and finds amusement in.*

JAMES (*introducing him*): The Lord Archbishop of St Andrews, Alexander Stuart – and my well-beloved son.

DAUGHTER (*involuntarily*): Your son, my lord?

JAMES: Why, yes. I think so, child. Why – doth he look so old?

DAUGHTER: Methought your son was little more than one year old, my lord.

JAMES: That is another son.

DAUGHTER: My mother told me once your Majesty had not been married much above ten years.

JAMES: Nor have I, child.

DAUGHTER: Then is the Lord Archbishop of St Andrews not yet in his teens?

LADY HERON: Be silent, child.

She whispers in her daughter's ear, while the King smiles at them.

DAUGHTER: Oh, yes – I see! Like Uncle John and Grandpapa! (*She turns to the King.*) I do apologize, my lord. I did not understand.

JAMES: Then go you with her, Alexander, and enlighten her some more. For I would talk with Lady Heron here alone.

They go out shyly.

LADY HERON (*with mock concern*): I trust my daughter will not come to harm – alone with the Archbishop, sir.

JAMES: She is no more in danger than her mother is.

LADY HERON: Then must I fear for her.

JAMES: And no less able to defend herself.

LADY HERON: Where Norham, Wark, and Etal fell before your Majesty's assault, methinks my own defence would stand but little hope of holding off the King of Scots – should he desire to take me, sir.

JAMES: I would Lord Surrey's force were equally accommodating, ma'am.

LADY HERON: My husband is your prisoner, my lord.

JAMES: I know it, ma'am.

LADY HERON: Yet is he innocent.

JAMES: And that I know as well.

LADY HERON: Why does your Majesty imprison innocence?

JAMES: Your husband is a hostage, ma'am. His bastard brother slew Sir Robert Kerr – and did escape my hand. I hold your husband in his stead.

LADY HERON: I pray you, let him go.

JAMES: I cannot let him go. Sir Robert was my friend.

LADY HERON: Exchange him, then.

JAMES: With whom? With you?

LADY HERON: King Henry holds Lord Home and George, his brother, doth he not?

JAMES: 'Tis true enough.

LADY HERON: I pray you ask Lord Surrey to effect exchange of prisoners.

JAMES: I cannot beg a favour from Lord Surrey, ma'am.

LADY HERON: Do you but signify your willingness, then will I beg Lord Surrey on your Majesty's behalf. It is a woman's privilege to beg.

JAMES: Lies he at Alnwick?

LADY HERON: So 'tis said.

JAMES: How shapes his army?

LADY HERON: Ill, my lord, by all accounts. But 'twas my husband we were talking of. I pray you, do as I beseech you, sir. I pray you, sir.

JAMES: Then if Lord Surrey will return Lord Home and George, his brother, to my army by September fifth – –

LADY HERON: That is next Monday, sir.

JAMES: Aye – so it is.

LADY HERON: Could I but see Lord Surrey and persuade him to it – –

JAMES: If thou canst – then is Sir William free.

LADY HERON: My lord, was ever woman so in debt to any man?

JAMES: 'Twere easy paid, my lady, did you let the Lord Archbishop of St Andrews and myself lie here tonight.

LADY HERON: With all my heart, my lord.

JAMES: Did not my Herald bring me word you would not have me here?

LADY HERON: My lord, I had not met you when your Herald came.

A trumpet sounds. The King looks round. The English Pursuivant, Rouge Croix, appears.

ROUGE CROIX: I bear a message from Lord Surrey to the King of Scots.

JAMES: Then speak your message, sir.

ROUGE CROIX: Lord Surrey challenges the King of Scots to battle, and it please your Majesty.

JAMES: It pleases me full well. Did I not come to England for that very purpose, sir? Though I had been in Edinburgh, I would have left all other business to meet Lord Surrey here. (*He shouts.*) Where is the Islay Herald to be found? (*To Rouge Croix.*) How doth my lord of Surrey?

ROUGE CROIX: He is well, your Majesty.

JAMES: Did I not hear he travels in a chair?

ROUGE CROIX: My lord is three score years and ten in age. Yet what he lacks in strength he gains in vigour of his mind. The Lord High Admiral hath likewise sent a message to your Majesty.

JAMES: Sir Thomas Howard? Methought he was in France.

ROUGE CROIX: He hath but lately joined his father, sir.

JAMES: What saith Sir Thomas Howard?

ROUGE CROIX: He bade me tell your Majesty that he is here to answer for the pirate Andrew Barton's death.

JAMES: How dare you bring that message, sir?

ROUGE CROIX: 'Tis not for me to choose the messages I bring, your Majesty.

JAMES: 'Tis true. I cannot lay the blame to you, but to Sir Thomas Howard. Then tell the Lord High Admiral the King of Scots will surely see he answer for Sir Andrew Barton's death.

ROUGE CROIX: And to Lord Surrey's challenge will your Majesty give answer?

JAMES: Aye. My Herald will attend him straight. Then go you now and seek refreshment from my escort here.

ROUGE CROIX: Your Majesty, Lord Surrey bid me say no quarter will be given – saving for the King himself.

JAMES: Then tell my lord that I would rather die at mine own hand than be the prisoner of England. Go.

Rouge Croix goes. Islay Herald passes him, coming in.

Go you and seek Lord Surrey in his camp, and bear him word the King of Scots accepts his challenge. I will meet him on the ninth.

ISLAY: Your Majesty. (*He bows and goes.*)

JAMES (*turning to Lady Heron*): My lady, would that I had not been born to be a King. There are so many better things in life than war.

LADY HERON: Such things, my lord?

JAMES: Why, such as women. Women never go to war – and yet they ever win the fight.

THE CURTAIN FALLS

SCENE 5

BEFORE THE CURTAIN

The English Camp at Barmoor. Lord Surrey, carried on by two English Soldiers in a sedan chair, with the Lord High Admiral, Sir Thomas Howard (or – if this is impracticable – moving over to a chair outside his tent, supported by Howard). The latter wears a snow-white uniform.

SURREY (*indicating a letter carried by Sir Thomas*): Now do you read it back to me, good Thomas, ere we send it.

HOWARD: (*reading*): 'Barmoor – the eighth day of September, at five of the clock in the afternoon.'

SURREY (*making an impatient gesture*): 'Tis but the end that is of first importance.

HOWARD (*reading*): 'Albeit it hath pleased you to put yourself into a ground like a fortress, I desire now of your Grace you will dispose yourself tomorrow, with your host – likewise as I shall do for mine – and shall be with the subjects of my Sovereign Lord on my side of the plain to give you battle betwixt twelve of the clock and three in the afternoon, upon sufficient warning by you, to be given by eight or nine of the clock in the morning.'

SURREY: Dost thou think that readeth well, my son?

HOWARD: It readeth famously, my lord.

SURREY: Then is the Herald here?

HOWARD (*shouting*): Ho, Herald!

ROUGE CROIX (*off*): Here, my lord. (*He comes on.*)

SURREY: Pray take this letter to the King of Scots where he lies camped on Flodden Ridge.

ROUGE CROIX: My lord. (*He goes.*)

HOWARD: I doubt he will not come down off the Ridge.

SURREY: And yet I think he may. I found him ever chivalrous when I escorted Princess Margaret into Scotland.

HOWARD: Many years have passed since then, my lord.

SURREY: Methinks he hath not changed in chivalry. But, lest it should be so – why, then we must persuade him to abandon it. To-morrow will we march to Berwick!

HOWARD: Berwick, sir!

SURREY: Aye, Berwick! First, the baggage train – escorted by a reasonable force. The Scots on Flodden Ridge will see it go.

HOWARD: I scarce can credit that you do not mean to fight the Scots.

SURREY: Were you a Scot, good Thomas – –

HOWARD: God forbid!

SURREY: Well, then – were you an Englishman, on Flodden Ridge. And did you see the English army, marching east-north-east for Berwick – what would you assume, my son?

HOWARD: I would assume my father had grown over-cautious – and was frighted by the Scots.

SURREY: Yet if you knew your father as you do – as Scotland knows him too – –

HOWARD: As England's greatest general – –

SURREY: You are too dutiful, my son! Then, did you know Lord Surrey was not frighted, what would you assume?

HOWARD: Perchance I would assume Lord Surrey meant to gain the Lowlands without battle – and then march on Edinburgh.

SURREY: Exactly so. Then – were you Scotland's King – what action would you take?

HOWARD: I should retire across the Tweed.

SURREY (*shaking his head in disagreement*): You do not know the King of Scots, my son. He will not easily retire. What other action might you take?

HOWARD: I would make every preparation to retire – then wait and see what might occur. (*He gives it up.*) I cannot think what I should do, my lord.

SURREY: You would do just as you have said. The King of Scots will do the like. Observe the baggage train – then strike his camp upon the Ridge and come down on the plain. Then, should I follow on the road to Berwick with my army, he will cross the Tweed and get 'twixt me and Edinburgh. Aye – is that argument not sound? Methinks 'tis very sound.

HOWARD: Then – if 'tis sound – what purpose in your march to Berwick, sir?

SURREY (*turning to one of the Soldiers.*): Unroll that map.

The second Soldier holds it with him.

I do not mean to march on Berwick, son – save only with my baggage train. You see – –

> *He turns to the map, which is very large and shows Flodden, the Tweed, Till and Berwick.*

The while the King of Scots hath left the Ridge, and hesitates upon the plain, and watches for my army on the Berwick road – then you, my son, will be across the Tweed at Twizel Bridge, beneath the contour of the slope – between the King of Scotland and the Tweed. Thus have we circled him. (*He smiles triumphantly at his son.*) You see? Yourself and Edmund – here – to cut the Scots' retreat. Myself and Dacre – hid beside the Till – to come and strike the centre, when you've headed them. I shall expect a message from you when the moment's ripe for me to move Lord Stanley over Ford and Etal Bridge – and strike them in the rear. And thus, their backs against the Ridge of Flodden, will they be destroyed.

> *He beckons to the Soldier to roll up the map.*

What think you of my plan?

HOWARD: 'Tis marvellous, my lord. Yet – if the King of Scots should stay on Flodden Ridge . . .?

SURREY: Why – then the plan has failed.

HOWARD: And then?

SURREY: Why, then we must attack him on the Ridge.

HOWARD: And suffer a defeat?

SURREY: 'Tis more than possible. Yet must we fight.

HOWARD: Why must we fight?

SURREY: For many reasons, son. The autumn comes apace. I cannot keep my army here – our fortresses all captured, saving Berwick – on the open field. Yet can the Scots, for they are hard and thrive upon the cold, and dance to see the wind is in the east. Yet still you lack the soundest argument of all. (*He leans forward and speaks in a mock whisper.*) The army hath but three days' ration left of beer.

> *Howard and the Soldiers laugh.*

'Tis laughable, perhaps! Yet there's the reason that we have to fight. So much for generals, my son!

He beckons to his Soldiers and they pick up his chair.

It is not I who rule my army's destiny. It is the hop! And therefore must I try the plan. Lead on.

His Soldiers start to carry him off. As they go he turns to Howard, who follows by his chair.

I'll tell thee this, my son. I fear me less to die on Flodden Ridge – than to command an English army without beer!

They go off.

THE CURTAIN RISES

SCENE 6

The Scots Camp. Flodden Field. Friday, 9 September, Lord Angus's pavilion. Present: Lord Angus, Lord Home, Lord Lindsay and others who, if named, would be Lennox, Crawford, Argyll and Huntly. Two Scots Soldiers stand, their backs to the company, outside the open tent on either side of the aperture.

ANGUS (*to the Soldiers*): Give ample warning if the King should come in sight.

SOLDIER: Aye, sir.

The Second Soldier indicates assent. Angus returns to the centre of the tent and addresses the company.

ANGUS: My lords, the King has sent the Islay Herald to Lord Surrey. Thus, without consulting us, his Majesty commits us all to fight this day.

LINDSAY: 'Tis folly so to do.

ANGUS: 'Tis worse than folly – 'tis plain suicide.

LINDSAY: Then must we stop the King.

ANGUS: 'Tis not so easy done. Yet must we do our best. Then who is with me?

LINDSAY: I.

ANGUS: I thank you, Lindsay of the Byres. Your counsel well may influence the King. He hath a feeling in his heart for you since Sauchieburn. Who else?

There is silence.

Then may I take your silence as consent?

HOME: Nay, Angus Bell-the-Cat. My Borderers are hot to try their strength against Lord Surrey's host. And I as well.

ANGUS: It seems your memory is short, Lord Home. A prudent man would heed the recollection of the ambush that you suffered little o'er a month ago. 'Twas said you lost five hundred men.

HOME: Yet have I twice and thrice the men that would avenge that raid.

ANGUS: My lords, I am not young and headstrong, as are some of us. Old age hath tamed my spirit and matured my judgement – therefore do I beg you hear my words. The English army at the present time can muster all its strength. Lord Surrey challenged us to battle therefore, knowing well that after mid September 'tis most dangerous to go campaigning in the north. 'Tis playing in his hands to fight him now.

HOME: What would you else?

ANGUS: I would retire. I would retire and lie upon the northern bank of Tweed, and let the English army seek supplies in vain.

HOME: 'Tis treason so to talk.

ANGUS: Since when was caution treason, my lord Home? I am a soldier, tried and true. 'Tis not 'twixt loyalty and treason that the fate of Scotland swings this day. 'Tis sober judgement and sound strategy against the headstrong folly of the King. The first will save our country – and the second ruin it.

HOME: 'Twere better should you lay these views before the King himself.

ANGUS: 'Tis useless so to do – without his Captains give me their support.

HOME: And – did we give it you?

ANGUS: Why, then – 'twere time enough to tell the King.

HOME: And did we give you our support – and did we go before the King – and did the King refuse to hear us, as is more than probable – what then?

ANGUS: It will be time enough to think of that when it occurs.

> *The Second Soldier on guard throws down his spear and turns to face the tent. All recognize the King.*

JAMES: It *has* occurred! The King is here!

> *In the dead silence that ensues, he moves slowly into the middle of the tent.*

The King has heard your arguments. The King has listened to the Captains of his host in secret conference against his Royal will. Now, Angus-Bell-the-Cat – how answer you the King?

ANGUS: I answer you with humble but impassioned words, your Grace. I beg you to return your army into Scotland, sir. Then were we clear of my lord Surrey and his host. Thus would we gain a bloodless victory.

JAMES (*with a sarcastic laugh*): A victory, think you?

> *He looks round to share the joke with the other Captains, but they evade his gaze.*

ANGUS: With Norham, Wark and Etal in our grasp, your Majesty, methinks that we have done enough for honour – –

JAMES: So! And think you, if we crossed the Tweed, Lord Surrey would not take them back again? 'Tis not a Border raid we are engaged upon, my lord. 'Tis war.

ANGUS: I never heard your Majesty had been engaged in war at Ford.

JAMES: What mean you, Angus?

ANGUS: While your Majesty hath sat at Ford, in dalliance – 'tis not my phrase, my lord, I heard it so described about the camp, or nearly so – your troops have lost their fire, and some of them have crossed the Tweed again.

JAMES: We have an army still – some thirty thousand men.

ANGUS: Lord Surrey will have more.

JAMES: I am informed that he hath less.

ANGUS: And I that he hath more. I have been active in reconnaissance, your Grace, while you have been at Ford. (*He cannot resist a cut.*) It seems my lady Heron told your Majesty Lord Surrey led a foray, when in fact he leads an English army at full strength. (*There is an angry pause.*) Methinks she well deserves to have her castle burnt before her eyes. I would she had not first had time to lay a screen of smoke before your own.

JAMES: I do not like your tone, my lord.

ANGUS: I do not like your strategy, your Majesty.

JAMES: Methinks that age hath marred your intellect.

He turns from Angus to the other Captains.

My lords, Lord Surrey sent his Herald – as your lordships know –
requiring me to leave the heights. I did refuse. We are invincible on
Flodden Ridge. 'Twere madness to abandon it – or worse.

*He looks at Angus with cold hatred and suspicion. One recalls
the Duke of Rothesay's hatred of Lord Angus in his early days.
The Archbishop of St Andrews, running, appears before the
entrance to the tent.*

ARCHBISHOP: I seek the King.

SOLDIER: Within, my lord.

He runs in and addresses the King breathlessly

ARCHBISHOP: The English army marches on the road to Berwick,
sir. The sentinels have seen the dust.

JAMES: To Berwick! Is it possible?

ANGUS (*quietly*): 'Tis as I thought.

JAMES (*furiously*): 'Tis as Lord Angus thought. It seems Lord
Angus hath the second sight.

ANGUS: I would have done the like – had I been Surrey, sir.

JAMES: Aye, so you would. I do not doubt you would. Old men
have this in common – be they Scots or English – that they run before
a fight.

ANGUS (*stung*): There is a limit to my patience, sir.

JAMES: Yet none to your disloyalty.

HOME: The English army turns and runs, my lord – and you
announce 'tis no surprise!

ANGUS: Lord Surrey hath not turned and run.

JAMES: Then have you better eyesight than my sentinels.

ANGUS (*ignoring this*): 'Tis true the English army marches on the
Berwick road. 'Tis false to say Lord Surrey runs away.

HOME: What does he then?

ANGUS: He marches on the road to Berwick – leaving us encamped
on Flodden Ridge. 'Twere better far that we should cross the Tweed
and get 'twixt him and Edinburgh. (*He appeals again to the King.*) I
beg you get the army on the move, your Majesty – before it is too late.

JAMES: What think you all, my lords?

HOME: I would not wish an English raiding force in Coldstream, while I kick my heels on Flodden Ridge. I would breathe happier upon the northern bank of Tweed, your Majesty.

LINDSAY: And I, with all my heart – and all the army too.

James looks at them, nonplussed, then turns to the Archbishop.

JAMES: Go, Alexander – bid the French Ambassador attend us here.

The Archbishop goes. Angus starts forward in anger.

ANGUS: Since when has Scotland needed foreigners to fight her wars, your Majesty?

JAMES: Perchance since Scotsmen lost the will to fight, my lord.

ANGUS: There is no wonder that the French Ambassador would have us fight. 'Tis no strange thing to find him prodigal of Scotland's blood – who works alone for France.

JAMES: He doth not work alone for France. He works against the English. 'Tis a point of view that you, my lord, would scarcely understand.

Enter De la Motte, in armour, followed by the Archbishop. De la Motte bows.

DE LA MOTTE: Your Majesty – my lords – –

JAMES: I am impatient for your counsel, sir. It seems the English army will not do us battle here. My sentinels report their presence on the Berwick road. (*He looks round scornfully.*) My Captains, led by my Lord Angus here, would have me move my army back across the Tweed. They fear Lord Surrey means to march on Edinburgh. What think you of their fears, Ambassador?

DE LA MOTTE: 'Tis but a feint, your Majesty.

ANGUS: A feint! How so?

DE LA MOTTE: I read the situation thus. Lord Surrey wishes you to think he marches into Berwick. Thus he hopes your army will be ordered back across the Tweed. Then, while you march, he will return and do you battle on the plain below the Ridge.

ANGUS (*scornfully*): The while his army is beyond the Till!

DE LA MOTTE: Are there not bridges o'er the Till, my lord?

HOME: 'Tis true. At Twizel and at Ford.

JAMES: Well, then Ambassador . . .?

DE LA MOTTE: Then stay – and fight, your Majesty. 'Tis folly, in my view, to listen to the counsel of Lord Angus, sir.

ANGUS: 'Tis treason, in my view, to listen to your own.

DE LA MOTTE: Then let us leave it to the King to make his choice.

They all look at James.

JAMES: Methinks there is an argument to either side.

DE LA MOTTE: 'Tis surely not the King that speaks! Should you retire across the Tweed, your Majesty, I nevermore will dare to raise my head in France. The greatest army Scotland ever raised – an army led by Scotland's greatest King, the flower of chivalry, the friend of France, the wearer of a ring from Anne of Brittany – in full retreat across the Tweed, like children running from a frightened cur. Your Majesty, is this the King of Scotland who is loved by Anne of Brittany, and by all France?

ANGUS: A pretty speech, as well becomes a Frenchman, sir. The sort of speech, methinks, that courtiers – aye, and ladies – would applaud. But we are soldiers, sir. We do not deal in rosy words. We deal in deeds. (*He turns deliberately to the King.*) I speak for all of us when I insist your Majesty remove the army back across the Tweed.

CAPTAINS: Aye, so you do.

JAMES: 'Insist', my lords!

CAPTAINS: Aye, aye – insist!

James looks at them and realizes he must compromise.

JAMES (*speaking with dignity*): I have attended to your counsel, my lord Angus, Monsieur de la Motte, my lords. Nor will I hide it that 'tis given to a foreigner to speak my inner thoughts. Yet am I not a tyrant. Therefore will I compromise. (*He pauses.*) I will strike camp.

DE LA MOTTE: Your Majesty . . .!

JAMES: Yet will I not return across the Tweed.

De la Motte heaves a sigh of relief.

I will array my army on the plain, and thus – if Surrey really march to Berwick – we may move, before 'tis night, to Scotland and remove the threat to Edinburgh. If, on the other hand, he turn and do us battle, then will we do battle with him on the plain. How say you to that plan?

ANGUS: 'Tis neither one thing nor the other, sir. 'Tis folly to prepare to march and then – not march!

JAMES: 'Tis equal folly to retire before 'tis necessary.

ANGUS: 'Tis necessary now, your Majesty.

JAMES: My lords, I have arranged to battle with Lord Surrey in the afternoon. I would not have the English say I had not stayed to fight. And therefore do we stay this side of Tweed.

ANGUS: 'Tis suicide.

JAMES: 'Tis my command!

ANGUS (*trying a last appeal*): I beg of you to cross the Tweed, your Majesty.

JAMES (*mockingly*): Then are you feared?

ANGUS: I never was afeared in all my life.

JAMES: Then fear has come upon you now – in your old age.

ANGUS: That any man should speak such words!

JAMES: Yet I have spoken them. You are afeared! Go home, old man. There is no place for aged cowards here.

Angus, struck dumb, moves towards the door, then turns.

ANGUS: I would you had not called me coward, sir. I never spared myself for the defence of Scotland and the honour of my King. Now – seeing that my counsel has no place – I go. Yet will I leave my sons – the surest pledge that I can give of my affection to your Majesty.

He pauses and looks at them squarely, with his head held high. His voice is broken, though.

And I pray God, your Majesty, my lords, my prophecy may be proved false, than that these things should happen which I think I see before mine eyes.

Lord Angus goes, a broken, tired old man. The King, who has stood with bowed head since his outburst, speaks – still without looking up. He has been moved as well.

JAMES: Lord Lindsay of the Byres – do you not go as well?

LINDSAY: I have not the excuse of age, your Majesty.

JAMES: 'Tis well. For did you go – and I return to Scotland – I would hang you from your gate. (*He addresses them all.*) Then are you all with me, my lords?

There is silence.

Then will we draw the army up – beneath the Ridge, prepared to stand – or march – as may befall. Lord Home, Lord Huntly, do you take the left – or, if we march, the van. Lords Crawford and Montrose, the centre – there shall I be too. Lords Lennox and Argyll, the right – and if we march 'twill be your duty to protect our rear. (*He looks round.*) Are we disposed of now?

DE LA MOTTE: Not I, your Majesty.

JAMES: (*smiling at him in a friendly, lonely way*): Good sir, 'tis not the function of ambassadors to fight.

DE LA MOTTE: I am a soldier, sir.

JAMES: Well said! Then go you on the right, with Lennox and Argyll. Begone, my lords. And fortune favour you.

They go. The King and the Archbishop remain. The King's spirit seems to flag: his fear of death grows more acute. The Archbishop moves over to where he sits, dejected.

ARCHBISHOP: Lord Angus hath disturbed your peace, my lord.

JAMES: Aye, so he has. And more than that. As I arose this morning, Alexander, in my tent, I saw a stain upon the canvas – –

ARCHBISHOP: 'Twas the dew. I saw it too.

JAMES: 'Twas much like blood! And then I found the buckle of my helmet – and the leather – torn away.

ARCHBISHOP: 'Twas only mice, my lord.

JAMES: Aye, so it was. Such creatures eat away the trappings of a King. First mice – then Angus Bell-the-Cat!

ARCHBISHOP: There's nothing to such superstitions, sir.

JAMES: Then, while Lord Angus ranted here and I stood guard without – a hare leapt up and started o'er the Ridge. These omens bode not well.

ARCHBISHOP: I would my greyhound had been there, my lord.

James looks up at him.

JAMES: You are too young to feel the touch of death upon your brow. I should have left you safe at Ford. You are too young to die.

ARCHBISHOP: Why think you so of death?

JAMES: There never was a moment in my life I did not think of death – save in a woman's arms. In Margaret's arms – beside the banks of Tay – –

> *A trumpet sounds without. James stares before him, with memories of Margaret Drummond and the Tay.*

ARCHBISHOP: I must begone.

JAMES (*seeing him at last*): Aye, go – if go you must.

> *He moves to him.*

Farewell, my most beloved son.

> *The Archbishop runs out. James looks after him.*

Farewell. *Timor mortis conturbat me.*

> *He crosses himself, then falls upon his knees.*

Take me, oh God – but spare the innocent.

> *Leaving him praying there – –*

THE CURTAIN FALLS

SCENE 7

ON RIGHT OF STAGE

There is the roar of cannon and the clash of weapons.

SCOTTISH VOICES (*shouting*): Lord Surrey's o'er the Till! Lord Surrey's o'er the Till!

> *The smoke clears. Lord Surrey is seated in his chair. An English Soldier stands beside him, looking through the dusk.*

SURREY: How goes the battle?

SOLDIER: Hard to see, my lord. The light is gone.

SURREY: The moon will soon be up. I pray the Lord High Admiral does well upon the right.

> *There is a sound of running feet*

Who comes?

> *A Second English Soldier runs on.*

2ND SOLDIER: The Lord High Admiral hath sent me, sir.

SURREY: What news?

2ND SOLDIER: He stands betwixt the Scottish Army and the Tweed.

SURREY: Ah, very well.

2ND SOLDIER: He is beset by Home and Huntly. Huntly – as I left the field – was slain. But Home is pressing hard upon him, sir.

SURREY: What would he have me do?

2ND SOLDIER: Attack the centre of the Scots.

SURREY: Their army is not past him, then?

2ND SOLDIER: Nay, Home and Huntly are the van. Their army is encircled utterly.

SURREY: Then speed you to the Lord High Admiral and tell him I attack. (*He turns to the 1st Soldier.*) You – seek Lord Stanley on the left, and bid him fall upon the Scottish rear.

> *They both go.*

(*To himself.*) Then have we utterly destroyed the Scots.

> *The light dims still further. Lord Surrey's outline disappears.*

SCENE 8

BEFORE THE CURTAIN

There is the sound of weapons clashing and the roar of cannon – this time louder. Again the smoke clears. The King appears lying beneath the Royal Standard, with Lord Lindsay holding it aloft. He is sorely wounded and his head rests on Lord Lindsay's knee.

JAMES: Is Huntly dead – and Lennox and Argyll – and de la Motte – and Crawford and Montrose? Then who still lives but I?

> *A Scots Soldier runs past.*

Halt you!

> *The Soldier stops unwillingly.*

Were you not with the Lord Archbishop of St Andrews?

SOLDIER: Aye.

JAMES: Then why have you forsaken him?

SOLDIER: The Lord Archbishop's killed.

JAMES: What? He as well!

He seizes the Soldier by the shoulder.

The boy I loved above all others in the world. Above my son and heir – above the Queen – and all, save Margaret Drummond!

'The Flowers of the Forest' starts playing very low. He shouts after the soldier.

Do you say he's dead?

SOLDIER (*terrified*): Aye, sir.

The Soldier is gone.

JAMES: Then all I love is gone. And I must die – as I have lived – alone.

The King's head falls back as he speaks the word 'alone'. Lord Lindsay, who is already kneeling, bows his head. 'The Flowers of the Forest' grows in volume.

On the other side of the stage the English flag flies bravely and beneath it sits Lord Surrey, with his head uncovered, in his chair. Between these two tableaux – the English tableau on the one hand, and on the other, James lying dead beneath the drooping Standard of the Scots, the Memorial to Flodden can be dimly seen.

The rising moon, climbing the Memorial, illuminates the inscription:

TO THE BRAVE OF BOTH NATIONS

'The Flowers of the Forest' fades away in the distance as – the curtain falls.

THE BAD SAMARITAN

THE BAD SAMARITAN *was first produced at the New Theatre, Bromley on 2 September 1952, with the following cast:*

Little Alan	. . . .	KENNETH ROBINSON
An Italian Priest	. . .	JEFFREY SEGAL
Brian	. . . .	JOHN BENNETT
Veronica	. . . .	NANCY MANSFIELD
Jane	. . . .	PAT SANDYS
Mrs Foster	. . .	BARBARA BOLTON
The Dean	. . .	JOHN CAREW
Alan	. . . .	ALAN EDWARDS

The Play directed by
GEOFFREY EDWARDS

Subsequently the play was presented at the Criterion Theatre on 24 June, 1953, with the following cast:

Brian	. . . .	MICHAEL DENISON
Jane	. . . .	HEATHER STANNARD
Mrs Foster	. . .	JESSIE WINTER
The Dean	. . .	GEORGE RELPH
Alan	. . . .	RONALD LEWIS
Veronica	. . . .	VIRGINIA McKENNA

The Play directed by
MURRAY MACDONALD

Note: In the version played at the Criterion the Prologue and Epilogue were omitted

CHARACTERS

LITTLE ALAN, the Dean's grandson
AN ITALIAN PRIEST
BRIAN, the Dean's eldest son
VERONICA
JANE
MRS FOSTER, the Dean's wife
THE DEAN
ALAN, the Dean's youngest son

SYNOPSIS OF SCENES

PROLOGUE
Outside a Church in Italy, 1959

ACT ONE   The sitting-room in an English Deanery.

TIME   Around 1950. Summer. Saturday afternoon.

ACT TWO
   Scene 1.   The same. Saturday night
   Scene 2.   The same. Sunday morning.

ACT THREE The same. Some months later. Afternoon.

EPILOGUE
Outside a Church in Italy, 1959

THE BAD SAMARITAN

PROLOGUE

Outside a Church in Italy, 1959.

The church is situated half-way up a mountain on Lake Como, opposite Bellagio. On one side of the stage is the white-washed wall and the entrance to a small church. Across the stage centre runs a wall, beyond which is the sky and, possibly, a mountain-top or two — beyond the lake. On the other side of the stage, steps run away down to the lake-side, a few hundred feet below.

The curtain rises on a small boy, Alan — aged about seven. He is wearing an English school cap, and he is listening to the music, which comes from the organ in the Church.

After a moment, he turns and shouts back over the wall — downwards.

ALAN: Come on, Daddy! You're nearly there. (*He raises his voice.*) Come on, Mummy. You're miles behind!

> *He stands on tip-toe, looking down over the wall. An Italian priest, with a beard, comes out of the church and stands, looking at him, unseen. The organ goes on playing.*

PRIEST: Good morning, little boy.

> *Alan turns round — looks frightened — and retreats towards the steps.*

But do not run away! It is a long climb, is it not? But worth it. Worth it — every time.

> *He looks out, over the lake, while Alan moves in closer to study him.*

ALAN: Are you a clergyman?
PRIEST: I am.

Alan looks doubtful.

At least, I am a priest.

ALAN (*relieved*): Oh, yes. That's different, isn't it? I thought you couldn't be a clergyman. At least, a proper clergyman. Because they don't have beards. My Grandpa's one.

PRIEST: When you grow up, you will discover that all men have beards. Yes, even clergymen!

> *Alan looks like arguing this out, so the priest goes quickly on.*

But, unlike me, your Grandpapa no doubt removes his beard every day.

ALAN (*his imagination fired*): Can you do that?

PRIEST: Can I do – what?

ALAN: Take off your beard.

PRIEST (*apologetically*): I'm sorry – no.

ALAN (*magnanimously*): Well, never mind! Detectives and – well – spies and things – are just about the only ones who can. And not a lot of them.

PRIEST (*gravely*): You comfort me.

ALAN: Do you live here?

PRIEST: No, there. (*He waves his hand across the lake.*) Bellagio.

ALAN: Oh! We're staying there.

PRIEST: Indeed! You like it – no?

ALAN (*mistaking his Italianism*): Yes, why? Don't you?

PRIEST: It is my home.

ALAN: And do you climb up here each day?

PRIEST: Yes – sometimes even twice a day.

ALAN: All by yourself?

PRIEST: All by myself.

ALAN (*pointing at the music*): Then, that's the B.B.C.

PRIEST (*looking round and then laughing*): Oh, no – today I have a friend. A fellow-priest. He is on holiday. Like you.

ALAN: Has he a beard?

PRIEST (*with the same apologetic tone*): I'm sorry – no. I have to cross the mountains to a shepherd, who is very ill. My friend has come to help me out.

ALAN: What! Is he going to carry you!

PRIEST (*laughing again*): Am I so old to you? No, no – he will stay here while I am gone, to guard my little church. You like it – no?

ALAN (*again misunderstands his Italianism*): Oh, yes – don't you?

PRIEST: I am beginning to. (*Tenderly.*) Perhaps I have got used to it. I have been here for thirty-seven years.

ALAN: Have you climbed up this hill – each day – for thirty-seven years?

PRIEST: Ah, yes. It takes me longer every day. But you are young. (*He pats Alan's head.*) You do not feel it – no?

ALAN (*getting it this time*): No. Not a bit. But Daddy does – and Mummy too. Are you Italian?

PRIEST: I am.

ALAN: Oh – then you must have shot at Daddy in the War.

PRIEST: Priests do not shoot.

ALAN: Not even birds – and things!

PRIESTS: Not even birds.

ALAN: And where's the goat?

PRIEST (*mystified*): The goat . . .!

ALAN: Yes, Daddy said to Mummy – when he read a telegram at breakfast – 'all right, darling – we'll go straight up and see if the old goat's still there.'

PRIEST: Indeed!

ALAN: Well – is it here?

Panting, and mopping his cheerful face with a handkerchief, Brian appears at the top of the steps. He wears a blue tennis-shirt and white flannel trousers. The priest looks up.

PRIEST: Ah, Capitaine!

He advances towards Brian with outstretched hand.

BRIAN: Hullo. Just fancy you remembering! Since 1945.

PRIEST: It's Captain Brian Foster, is it not?

BRIAN (*mopping his brow again*): It is – what's left of him! Phew – what a climb! I'm not as young as I was – well, how long ago?

PRIEST: The War – I have forgotten it! But none of us get younger any more. And do you still reside in Italy?

BRIAN: No – London now. Worse luck! It's only wars that give a chap like me a holiday.

ALAN: Daddy!

BRIAN: I'm stockbroking. You know – a *criminale financale!*

ALAN (*pulling at his trouser-leg*): Daddy!

BRIAN: What is it, Alan?

ALAN: Daddy – where's the goat?

BRIAN: What goat?

ALAN: The 'old goat' that you brought Mummy to see.

BRIAN (*embarrassed*): You run along and play, young man – and don't talk nonsense.

PRIEST (*laughing and seizing him*): I will show you him!

> *He puts his hands over little Alan's eyes.*

The goat! Imagine him! What does he have – the Goat? He has the beard, of course! Now! Look!

> *He spins Alan round, and then removes his hands when Alan's facing him.*

Viola! The Goat!

> *The Priest laughs uproariously at Alan's bewilderment and Brian's embarrassment. Veronica appears at the top of the steps and smiles at the scene. Brian sees her.*

BRIAN: Oh, Father – meet my wife.

PRIEST (*going forward, as if he knew her*): Ah, it is good. (*He stops.*) But, you have changed so much.

BRIAN: She has. It's someone else. (*He turns to Veronica.*) He thought that you were Jane. We used to come up here a lot. (*He turns back to the priest.*) It's quite all right. Jane's always been Veronica's best friend. (*To Veronica.*) Look, darling, I'll take young Alan to the top – and then you two can have a chat. (*To the priest.*) If you can spare a moment?

PRIEST: Certainly.

BRIAN (*to Veronica*): All right?

VERONICA: Yes, darling.

BRIAN (*pointing at the bench against the wall*): You'll find us waiting here when you come out. (*To Alan.*) Come on, young man. I'll give you 'goats'!

> *He chases Alan up the steps. The priest is laughing as they watch them go.*

PRIEST: He is a comedy, that one! He used to sit up here, beside your friend, Miss Jane. She was a Red Cross nurse. And, when I passed them, he would say, 'Father, look the other way. You mustn't look at two romantic children, terribly in love, because it's sin! So, get along inside your church, and thank God for the atom bomb!' He is a comedy, that one! But he is settled now. I'm glad. You have a lovely little boy.

VERONICA: Yes, isn't he?

PRIEST: We have had much to say. He tells me that his grand-father's a clergyman. Without a beard! (*He laughs.*)

VERONICA: He was. He's dead. We had a telegram today. We haven't told him yet.

PRIEST: How sad. His father's father?

VERONICA (*after a momentary pause*): Yes.

PRIEST: Too bad. And you it was that wished to see me – no?

VERONICA: Yes, Father. Will you hear my confession?

PRIEST: Alas! I have to cross the mountain now. To see a dying man.

VERONICA: But we're travelling tonight – and I – – You see, I've been outside the Church for seven years, and – –

PRIEST: It is quite all right. I have a colleague here from Rome.

VERONICA: Is that him playing?

PRIEST: Yes.

VERONICA: How beautifully he plays.

PRIEST: Go in, and he will finish presently. And now, I have to go.

He senses her unhappiness and lays a hand upon her head.

Go in, and give your burden up to God.

He turns away. She follows him in desperation.

VERONICA: What use is it – confessing – Father!

PRIEST (*turning away*): Child – you ask me that. Where is your Faith?

VERONICA: Oh, yes – I know – forgiveness comes from God – I know all that. But how can I find peace if – if there is someone else – who can't forgive me – just because he doesn't know the truth?

PRIEST: Where God forgives – then all forgive.

VERONICA: That isn't true! How can it be?

PRIEST: Go in, my child – the ways of God are strange.

*She stands and watches him as he walks away. Then she turns
and goes into the church. Little Alan runs down the steps and
crosses up to the church door, and peeps through. Brian comes
down, more slowly, and sits on the bench. The music stops.*

ALAN: Oh, Daddy – come and look. She's kneeling by a box with
curtains round it, with her eyes shut. What's she doing, Daddy?

*He does not answer, but sits looking straight in front of him.
Alan pulls his sleeve.*

BRIAN (*coming out of his reverie, and looking round at him*): Doing,
Alan? Living through the past again – that's all.

*He looks in front of him again, as the lights fade and go out.
Organ Music, and the sound of boys' voices, singing, are heard in
the darkness, as the*

CURTAIN FALLS

ACT ONE

*The sitting-room of an English Deanery. A Saturday afternoon. Summer.
Time: Around 1950.*

*The Curtain rises on the sitting-room of Dean Foster's house, in the Close of
an English cathedral town. It is a summer afternoon, and through the
open windows – beyond the Cloisters – can be seen the outline of the cathedral.
The sound of the organ and the voices of the choirboys at their singing
practice meet our ears.*

*Seven to ten years younger than in the Prologue, Brian, still white-
flannelled and wearing a coloured tennis-shirt, stands kissing Jane – blonde
and very pretty – dressed in tennis shorts and shirt.*

*The voices in the Cathedral rise to the climax of their anthem. Jane
looks up at Brian with a smile.*

JANE: Bri – were you ever in the choir?

BRIAN: No, dear. I've always been a base. (*He kisses her again.*)
The basest child that ever sprang from out the loins of a Church of
England clergyman – and that is saying some!

The singing and the music cease.

Old Alan must be giving them a break for lemonade and lollipops. (*He
walks away from her to the window.*) To think those flawless sounds
should be produced by twenty vicious, spotty little boys! How like the
world! Deceptive and illogical and vile!

He returns and automatically takes hold of Jane.

BRIAN: Sweet child, I love you.

JANE: No, you don't.

BRIAN: I know I don't. That's why I'm base. (*He kisses her again.*)
Because I stand here, holding beauty in my arms, and giving nothing
back. You shouldn't let me do it, Jane.

JANE: I like you doing it.

BRIAN: That makes it all the worse. My father says a Christian's

W.D.H.–T

greatest privilege is to resist the things he likes. But, then I'm not a Christian.

JANE: Yes, you are.

BRIAN: No – not according to the books, I'm not. And not according to my Very Reverend Papa, the Dean – and Chapter – what a Chapter! Nor, according to my saintly little organ-grinding brother, and his Choir of razor-slashing Cherubim. I must sit down. My knees are giving out. (*He sits down on the sofa and enlarges on his theme.*) You see, dear Jane – in my humble philosophy of life – evolved after five years of war to perpetuate war – I reached the conclusion that there were only two kinds of people in this world. Those who are good enough to think they're wicked – and those who are wicked enough to think they're good! I salute the former and mistrust the latter. Father does exactly the reverse.

He holds out his hand.

Come here, sweet child.

He is suddenly serious.

You mustn't be in love with me.

JANE: Why not?

BRIAN: Because you're far too good. My definition – not the Dean's. Too honest and too beautiful. And I'm a tiny bit in love with someone else.

JANE: What time's she getting here?

BRIAN: At half-past five. Be nice to her. (*He pulls her down beside him on the sofa.*) She's very young and very innocent.

JANE: Will you be sitting here, like this – with her, tonight?

BRIAN: Good God, no, Jane.

JANE: Why ask her, then?

BRIAN: Hope springs eternal!

JANE: Why ask me?

Brian shrugs his shoulders.

To make her jealous?

BRIAN: No – she couldn't be.

JANE: Then why?

BRIAN: To make a four at bridge!

JANE: Oh, yes!

BRIAN: And also to stop brother Alan cutting out Sir Galahad. You know he met me with her once in London. Then, he took her out to lunch alone. Not once, but twice! I mean to say – he hasn't lunched alone with any woman since he lunched with Mother, when he was a baby, and he hadn't any other choice.

JANE: So this week-end's for Alan's benefit? (*She is pulling his leg.*)

BRIAN: Well, not entirely – no. But, still – two glorious young women, sitting round, like sirens, through a whole week-end, may save him from becoming an intolerably sanctimonious and boring saint.

JANE: You mistrust saints as well?

BRIAN: Of course, I do. A saint, without experience, is like a tank that's never left the drawing-board. A theoretical perfection. Cardboard armour-plate – and tracks of celluloid. Take Lancelot and Galahad. Well, Lancelot was grand, because he had his old Achilles' heel. But Galahad went rushing round behind the Holy Grail, and never had a single human weakness. Well, it isn't natural! I bet he pulled the wings off flies for fun!

JANE: I think that Alan's rather sweet.

BRIAN: Well, you can have him, dear!

JANE: I don't think brothers ever see each other with a charitable eye.

BRIAN: No, he's all right. Hats off to chaps like that! That's what I say. Teetotallers the same. They don't know what they miss, but one respects their point of view.

JANE (*mockingly*): You are broad-minded, aren't you?

BRIAN: Possibly – or merely lazy. It's an almost indistinguishable substitute.

JANE: So Alan's passed to me for entertainment – that the plan?

BRIAN: Yes – if Veronica's not too fed-up with me.

JANE: And if she is?

BRIAN: Then you and I will go off playing golf, and leaving her and Alan playing Galahad and Joan of Arc.

JANE: Is she an atheist, like you?

BRIAN: Good lord, no – Roman Catholic.

JANE: Where did you meet her, Bri?

BRIAN: In Schmidt's – in Charlotte Street. She's learning acting at a drama school. She won't be any good. She's too sincere. She doesn't like it, anyway. Her father pushed her in.

JANE: And did you just accost her?

BRIAN: Jane! No, I was dining there. And so was she – with her papa. He paints, that's why he dines in Charlotte Street. Or else he paints because he dines in Charlotte Street. She wore my regimental badge. And so I said 'Hullo.' Then, it transpired I knew her brother in the war. He trod on something in a field in Sicily, and disappeared in smoke. He always wore a little crucifix. I used to see it in the showers in Cairo, just before El Alamein.

JANE: And, so – you said 'Hullo'. What did she say?

BRIAN: I think she said, 'Hullo', as well.

JANE: Love at first sight!

BRIAN: No, second – I'm afraid. The first time I was far too tight.

JANE: And then?

BRIAN: That's all. I've never even kissed her.

JANE: Have you tried to?

BRIAN: Yes, of course. That was a silly question, wasn't it?

JANE (*sadly*): Yes, I suppose it was.

BRIAN: She says she's anti-kissing people, when she's not in love. She's not like me.

> *He kisses Jane again, but cannot see her face – as we can – and the pain that flits across it suddenly.*

You see, with her, the Soul leads Sex by half-a-length, at least. She thinks Sex doesn't stay. I told her that it could be trained to win the National.

JANE: What did she say to that?

BRIAN: She said she wouldn't know.

JANE (*wistfully*): I rather envy her.

BRIAN: You don't!

JANE: I do. It's lovely – waking up – but how it hurts. And, I'm afraid the hurt lasts longer than the loveliness.

BRIAN (*struck by remorse*): Jane – darling – you aren't saying you regret our little interlude?

JANE: Oh, no – life's far too short for that. If one's prepared to hit one's head against the stars, one may as well accept a nasty bump each time one reaches them.

BRIAN: Some star! (*Gently.*) You calling me a star? (*She turns away.*) A fallen star!

He gets up and walks to the window in an attempt to avoid the emotion that it is his aim in life to escape.

JANE (*following him*) : Please, Brian – if Veronica holds out against you promise you'll stay with me. I don't mean marry me. I wouldn't marry anyone who didn't love me back.

BRIAN (*standing with his back to her*) : Gosh! What a cad I am!

JANE : And I'm – –

BRIAN (*turning round and putting a gentle hand over her mouth*) : – A beautiful, unselfish, and uncalculating little child.

JANE : Your father wouldn't think that – if he knew.

BRIAN : He doesn't know. (*He walks back to the sofa.*) It isn't good for clergymen to know. Both clergymen and children flourish on a diet of deceit. That's why I don't believe in God.

JANE : God doesn't choose the clergy, Bri.

BRIAN : He tolerates them, though. He never strikes them with a murrain or with sores. Instead, he turns them out with curly, silver hair – a lovely gaitered leg – and with a handicap of six. And then provides them with a faithful wife, like Mother, and a handsome son – like me! And even Alan – who'll be a curate, when he's done his course – looks rather like Apollo after a cold bath!

He reaches out a hand for Jane, and pulls her down and kisses her.

Oh well, they always say that the wicked shall flourish like a grey bean tree.

MRS FOSTER (*off*) : Brian.

BRIAN : No, that can't be right! What is it? Father's always weighing in with that.

MRS FOSTER (*off*) : Is anybody there?

BRIAN (*shouting*) : Yes, Mother, coming!

He disentangles himself from Jane, who gets up and tidies her face. Brian goes to the door.

Got it. It's a green bay tree.

MRS FOSTER (*as he opens it, shouting*) : Will somebody, please, open the door?

BRIAN : Let me take the tea-cakes. Let the clutch in slowly.

Mrs Foster wheels in a wheeled tea-table.

I'll take over now.

Mrs Foster, an elderly woman, with a cheerful, homely face, takes the tea-cakes back, just before Brian drops them on the floor.

I thought that driving this was Father's job. Where is he anyway?

Mrs Foster: He's walking round the garden with the Bishop's wife.

Brian (*nipping to the window*): What! Is she coming in to tea? I'll have to wear a tie.

Mrs Foster: No, dear – she's going back to tea. The Bishop's just like any other man. He has to have a woman there to pour it out.

Brian: Is that the only function of a Bishop's wife?

Mrs Foster: Yes – that, and darning socks.

Brian: Do they wear socks? Whatever for?

Mrs Foster: Well, did you win the tennis, Jane?

Jane: No, I'm afraid I didn't – Brian's much too good for me.

Mrs Foster: Well, what can you expect? You get tired out with nursing all the week – while Brian only puts his feet up on his city desk – and drinks unending cups of tea.

Brian: It's funny, Mother, isn't it?

Mrs Foster: What's funny, dear?

Brian: It makes one think. The Bishop and his wife were married back in 1910.

Jane: How many handsome sons have they?

Brian: They haven't any – that's what makes one think.

Mrs Foster: Well, dear – it's nice to think that something does.

Brian: I'm not sure someone shouldn't tell him. P'raps it's not too late.

His face lights up, as the Dean –tall, distinguished, grey-haired – comes in. He wears a tweed coat, a clerical collar, grey flannel trousers. He smokes a pipe.

I think it's Father's duty!

The Dean, accustomed to Brian's irreverence and irrelevance, displays no interest in this statement. He seats himself and selects a piece of toast. Brian, however, persists.

Brian: We've decided you must tell him, Father.

DEAN: Who? And tell him what?

BRIAN: The Bishop, Dad. The facts of life.

DEAN: I sometimes wonder if there aren't advantages in missing some of them! (*He turns to Jane.*) Well, Jane – and how's the Hospital? I shouldn't think you've ever met another patient half as troublesome as Brian was in Italy.

JANE: Oh, I don't know. He made me laugh.

DEAN: Oh, really! That's a side to Brian's character I've never felt the impact of. But then, I don't like *Punch*!

BRIAN: I wrote a limerick last night. What was it? In my bath. Oh, yes – it's coming back. (*He looks round and sees no interest displayed in any quarter.*) Tell us, Brian – DO!

MRS FOSTER: Well, I suppose so – if you must.

BRIAN: It isn't dirty, Mum. It's wh-wh-whimsical. Old Barrie might have written it – if he'd written verse.

DEAN: He did.

BRIAN: Oh, well – perhaps it's cribbed from him.

JANE: Come on, then, Brian. We can't wait.

MRS FOSTER (*just as he opens his mouth to start, and the Cathedral clock strikes the quarter*): Your friend should be here soon.

DEAN (*as Brian makes a second attempt to start on his limerick*): Your mother and myself are dining with the Bishop. Will she think us rude?

BRIAN: No – not a bit.

DEAN: What are you going to do with her?

BRIAN: I thought we'd take her to the flicks.

DEAN: You ever met her, Jane?

JANE: No, never – but I've heard a lot about her recently.

DEAN: Is Brian walking out with both of you?

BRIAN: Now, really, Father – you're talking like the Oxford Group.

DEAN: Be careful Alan doesn't cut you out. Facetiousness is not a quality that women find endurable for long.

BRIAN: I have my other points.

DEAN: Such as?

BRIAN: My profile and my love of poetry. (*Suddenly his mind reverts.*) Ah, yes. I've got it now. Hold everything! (*He holds the muffin-plate and starts reciting.*)

> When the Suffragan Bishop of Leeds
> Was clearing his garden of weeds,
> He found the Dean's gaiters
> Among his potaters
> And – his wife's favourite necklace of beads!

How's that?

MRS FOSTER: Dreadful!

DEAN: Inaccurate as well. There is no Suffragan in Leeds.

BRIAN: Poetic licence, Father.

DEAN: That's another way of saying 'ignorance'.

BRIAN: Well, you improve on it.

DEAN: Most certainly.

> When the Suffragan Bishop of Jarrow
> Was tending his vegetable marrow – –

JANE: Oh, that's much better.

DEAN: I agree.

BRIAN: I don't. If he was tending his vegetable marrow, why should he do it among the potatoes?

DEAN: Most clergymen are incompetent gardeners.

BRIAN: Poetic licence, I suppose!

DEAN: Or benefit of clergy!

BRIAN: Well – you try and finish it.

DEAN:
> When the Suffragan Bishop of Jarrow
> Was tending his vegetable marrow,
> He found the Dean's gaiters
> Among his potaters – –

BRIAN: Go on!

DEAN: He had bullied the Dean when at Harrow.

BRIAN: No, no – that won't do.

DEAN: Of course it will. The moral is 'Deans never forget!'

Alan comes in. He is Brian's younger brother – good-looking, aesthetic and shy.

BRIAN: Hullo, Sir Galahad – have one, before I clear the plate. (*He offers him a muffin.*)

ALAN: Thank you, Brian.

DEAN: How's the choir?

ALAN: Oh, all right, Father, thanks. They sang quite beautifully.

BRIAN: Was Tompkins Major sucking lollipops? And Simpkins Minor flicking ink at Jenkinson? And Roberts trying not to dribble down his tie?

ALAN (*smiling*): I didn't notice – I expect they were. I found the organ took up all my time.

JANE: Was that you playing, when the choir was singing?

ALAN: Yes, the organist's on holiday.

JANE: How beautifully you play!

BRIAN: I say! I've never had a compliment like that about my tennis yet.

JANE: I mean that, Alan.

ALAN: It's the mood one's in, I think.

JANE (*quietly*): I was just in the mood.

BRIAN (*declaiming*):

> If Music be the food of Love,
> Play on.
> Give me excess of it, that – surfeiting –
> The appetite may sicken, and so – die . . .

He reaches out a hand towards his Mother.

– that strainer again.

She pours him another cup of tea, while the Dean shudders at this ghastly pun.

DEAN: To think that I produced a child like that!

BRIAN: I know! You must be jealous of the Bish. If he's done nothing else in life, he's proved that fellow in the right – who said, 'Where ignorance is bliss, 'tis folly to be wise.'!

MRS FOSTER: Dear Brian, how your mind does run along! Now, Alan, have another cup of tea.

ALAN: No, thank you, Mother. I must go and get Dad's letters ready for the post.

BRIAN: Veronica's arriving any moment now – so don't be long.

ALAN (*who is going towards the door of the Dean's study, turns and looks at him a little strangely*): I'm sure that you can entertain her, Brian. Play a single against her and Jane.

BRIAN: I wanted you to handicap me!

ALAN (*smiling*): Oh, all right – if I can get away.

He goes out.

BRIAN: If he can get away! He can't, poor devil – he's been trapped. It isn't decent for a chap to get religion till he's over thirty, Father. It's like letting little children smoke cigars. It makes them sick. And it affects their hearts for ever. Damn it all, it isn't fair.

MRS FOSTER: Dear Brian – what a lot of funny theories you've hatched today.

DEAN: He's nervous of the imminent arrival of his lady-friend. It does no harm to let him get it off his chest.

BRIAN: I'm not.

DEAN (*pulling Brian's leg*): Oh yes – you are. You're trying to build up an atmosphere, congenial to her exotic worldly personality – her brittle and theatrical approach to life. I have no doubt, like you, she's made the latest intellectual decision that there is no God – thus travelling full-cycle backward to the same conclusions reached by prehistoric man. I have a feeling Alan will be good for her.

BRIAN: I rather fear that she'll look on Alan as a fraud. (*He is now pulling the Dean's leg.*) You see – she's genuine – the proper article. She's Roman Catholic – I thought I told you, Dad.

DEAN: You didn't – no.

BRIAN: Oh, didn't I? It must have slipped my mind.

DEAN: Yes, very possibly.

BRIAN: Well, anyway, she is. Don't fight the whole week-end – for heaven's sake – and mine!

MRS FOSTER: What should they fight about?

BRIAN: Oh, I don't know. Whatever Protestants and Catholics do fight about. It's always been a mystery to me. (*He turns to the Dean.*) You ought to know – I mean to say – they've trained you for it, haven't they? The Pope and – well – all that – –

DEAN: The Pope's a very estimable man. I met him once – oh, years ago. He's done extremely well – according to his lights. He leads the strongest force the world – at least, the white man's world – has ever seen united in one creed. But, whether it's a force for good or evil is no subject for a tea-time talk.

BRIAN (*with emphasis*): Nor a week-end.

DEAN: Nor a week-end.

MRS FOSTER: But, Brian dear, you mustn't marry her. Your father would be very angry if you did.

JANE: Why should he be?

DEAN: I don't suppose you know my views about the Roman Church.

BRIAN: Who doesn't, Dad!

DEAN: I don't suppose Jane does.

JANE: What would you do, if Brian did?

DEAN (*pretending to be puzzled*): What would I do – if Brian did – –

BRIAN: He'd take away my widow's mite.

JANE (*bursting out*): But that's so horrible and so unfair. I know there's nothing in it, but suppose there was. Suppose that she and Brian fell in love. You mean to say you'd cut off Brian – just as if he'd done some crime?

DEAN: I don't remember saying so.

JANE: Well, then – what would you do?

DEAN: I've never given such a doubtful possibility much thought. I'm not a pessimist. I don't believe in planning for disaster, until it comes.

BRIAN: You know, you almost make me WANT to marry her. To tweak you where you need it most.

DEAN (*smiling*): And what if I should tweak you where you need it most – inside your pocket-book!

BRIAN: Oh, Mother – save me from this wicked man!

MRS FOSTER: Bri – don't be rude.

BRIAN: I'm sorry, Father.

DEAN: Sorry for my views about the Church of Rome? I've never been so optimistic as to think that you would understand them, Bri.

BRIAN (*getting up*): How right you are! I'm just a good broad-minded child of nature, without prejudice. Poor Alan! I'd go crazy if I had his job. It's 'Love your neighbour' – 'Hate your neighbour' – 'Kiss your neighbour' – 'Curse your neighbour'. Come on, Jane – let's go and have another set.

JANE: All right.

The front-door bell rings.

MRS FOSTER: Oh, Brian – there she is. Run down and let her in.

Brian goes towards the door.

I'm glad we had this argument BEFORE she came.

BRIAN (*turning in the doorway*): And, Father – (*He wags an admonitory finger at the Dean.*) – please remember that Veronica is no more to blame for being a Roman Catholic than you are for being a Protestant. Neither of you can help it – because it's Original Sin!

The Dean smiles, and Brian runs out, down the stairs.

DEAN: I wish that boy would settle down. Whenever I have nightmares they inevitably come through dreaming Brian is my stockbroker!

MRS FOSTER: It isn't very easy for young men to settle down.

DEAN: I can't see why. I was a curate long before I reached his age.

MRS FOSTER: But Brian's got imagination, dear.

DEAN: Oh, thank you very much!

MRS FOSTER: Perhaps he ought to write.

DEAN: Yes, that's a good idea! 'Denunciations of the English Church' – by a Dean's son.

Enter Brian, followed by Veronica. She is pretty in a quiet way.

BRIAN: Come on in. (*He introduces her.*) My mother – –

VERONICA: How do you do?

MRS FOSTER (*shaking hands*): Do have some tea. You don't mind having it before you go and tidy. I'm afraid it's getting rather cold. (*She pours it out.*)

BRIAN: My father – –

DEAN: Very glad to meet you. Any friend of Brian's is a friend of mine.

BRIAN: Except my bookmaker! And Jane – –

JANE (*shaking hands*): Hullo.

BRIAN: I've told you all about her, haven't I?

JANE (*smiling*): The least unpleasant things, I hope!

VERONICA: He told me – if you'd lived four hundred years ago – they would have burnt you at the stake.

JANE: Oh, dear! Because I was a witch?

VERONICA: Because you were a saint.

JANE: He did! And then he tells me that he's 'anti-saint'.

BRIAN: Not saints who've won their spurs.

MRS FOSTER: Well, now you've met us all – do have a piece of cake.

BRIAN: There's Alan still to meet. But, then – you've met him, haven't you?

VERONICA: Yes. How is Alan?

BRIAN: Very well. (*He waves a hand towards the Dean's study.*) He's closeted in there. He's studying to be a clergyman – I don't suppose he's told you 'cos he never speaks. – At Cambridge – in the School for budding Bishops – In the Hols. he's bottle-washer to His Reverence the Dean. The Bishop's wife's in love with him!

DEAN (*to Veronica*): Where did you meet this crazy boy of mine?

VERONICA: In Charlotte Street.

DEAN: By chance!

VERONICA: My brother knew him in the war.

JANE: And then he took you out to dine and talk about himself.

VERONICA: How did you know?

JANE: He did the same to me! You listen well?

Veronica smiles.

Yes, so do I.

BRIAN: Do stop them, Mother! They'll make me blush.

MRS FOSTER: I haven't seen you blush for years. I don't believe you could.

BRIAN: No – nor do I – my blood-stream isn't what it was!

DEAN (*to Veronica*): Have you been down this way before?

VERONICA: No, never – but it's lovely, isn't it. The change from London. So extreme – it makes one catch one's breath.

DEAN: You live in London?

VERONICA: Yes, in Chelsea – for my sins. My father's had a studio down there since Mother died.

DEAN: Your sins must all be very minor ones. I don't think Chelsea's changed at all, since we were there. We had a little church down Tite Street way.

BRIAN: I came along, when they were there. Symbolic, wasn't it!

DEAN (*getting up and filling his pipe*): I sometimes miss those days. The town lives at a higher tempo. Good and evil painted in more striking colours. Nothing ever seems to happen here. It does, of course. But colours merge together here. And saint and sinner wander through the cloisters arm-in-arm, both unidentified, both mellow, and both drunk with sunshine and green leaves. In London, one must fight.

The clash of steel goes on incessantly – exhilarating, dangerous, progressive and alive. Down here, one bivouacs without a guard and goes to sleep.

BRIAN (*bored with this*): You like a set of tennis, Jane?

JANE: If no one else does. Wouldn't you, Veronica?

VERONICA: No, thank you. I'd like to tidy up. And then I'll come and watch.

MRS FOSTER: Jane, darling, show Veronica her room before you start. It's next to yours.

JANE: I know the one.

MRS FOSTER: I'll clear away the tea.

JANE (*to Brian*): I'll be down in a minute.

> *As Jane and Veronica are going to the door, Alan comes in from the Dean's study. He sees Veronica and looks at her for a long moment, until Brian speaks. Veronica returns his gaze.*

BRIAN: Ah, Sir Galahad! You know my brother Alan. Yes, of course you do. He plays the organ like Beethoven, sings like Mr Crosby, preaches like John Knox – and takes two lumps of sugar in his tea!

> *Veronica goes forward and takes Alan's hand.*

VERONICA: Hullo. How are you, Alan?

BRIAN: He's all right. He's very shy. But, when we had him looked at, all the doctors said that he was quite all right.

ALAN (*smiling*): I'm only shy with people I don't understand. (*He takes her hand and holds it.*) I've never been the least bit shy with you.

> *Veronica goes out with Jane. Alan still stands, looking after her – while Brian watches, quizzically.*

MRS FOSTER (*removing tea-table*): Door, Brian.

BRIAN: All right, Mother. (*He opens it.*) Come along.

> *She disappears in the direction of the pantry.*

DEAN: I like that girl.

BRIAN: You like all girls. Like me. Heredity will out.

DEAN: She has repose. Unusual beauty. Physical and mental.

BRIAN: What a pity she's a pagan, isn't it?

DEAN: Well, Alan here must try his hand. All missions don't start overseas! Now, where's the crossword-puzzle? Ah! (*He finds it and takes it.*) Has anybody done it? No. That's good. (*He moves towards the study door.*) I've got to do my sermon-notes. Now, Brian, don't swear too much on the tennis-court.

BRIAN: You'll never notice, Father. You'll be asleep.

The Dean goes into his study. Brian paces about. Alan looks dreamily out of the window.

You see, that's the big question, old chap. Can one be in love with two women at once? Of course, you wouldn't know. It's driving me mad – I don't mind telling you. For God's sake, Alan, help me to make up my mind.

Alan looks round, and is about to speak, when Brian rattles on.

This is the situation in a nutshell, dear boy, since you ask me! When I'm with Jane, I'm in love with Jane. When I'm with Veronica, I'm in love with Veronica. And, when I'm with both, I'm damn well in love with both. Alan, is it possible, old boy? Cutting out all this ecclesiastical rot about monogamy, is it possible for one natural man to be in love with two women?

ALAN (*who is clearly thinking of something less confused*): I suppose it is – in different ways.

BRIAN: Ah, yes – you've got it there – in different ways. What I call 'upstairs' and 'downstairs' love. Jane is 'upstairs' love. It's all right old chap, she wouldn't mind me saying so. She knows it's damn well true. One automatically associates her, because she's so beautiful, with eiderdowns and breakfast trays and bath-salts – you know, all the light romantic things of life. Then, there's Veronica – she's 'downstairs', isn't she? Good books, kind friends and children, playing on the kitchen floor. You know, old man – eternity, domestic bliss. You know exactly what I mean. You bet you do! (*He looks round at Alan, who is staring at him.*) Don't sit there, like an Inquisition curate! Pray for me, old chap. I'm sitting half-way up the stairs – and looking down – and looking up – and getting dizzier and dizzier. I'll end by falling through the banisters and dying of a broken neck.

ALAN (*smiling*): Downstairs!

BRIAN: Yes. Still, it's no use then. Of course, it's safer downstairs, isn't it? But, would one ever see the stars? Conversely, if one lived upstairs with Jane, one might get sick of seeing stars! Oh damn it, Alan – give me some advice. I'll put ten shillings in the plate to-morrow if you hand me out some good advice – I will – I promise – won it down at Newmarket last week. Come on, I'm sitting at your feet.

ALAN: Well, I should cut out the 'upstairs' and the 'downstairs' tenants. Then, wait until you find somebody who'll love you, on one floor – with your feet on the ground and your head in the stars.

BRIAN: Me! Wait! I'm thirty-four! I'm nearly done. Besides with two such women in the house, you bid me spurn them and seek some-one else! I'm not ascetic, Alan, like yourself. I'm flesh and blood – and pretty largely flesh. (*Compassion for Alan? or is it for himself –– sweeps over him.*) My dear old chap, you don't know what you miss. When, suddenly, after months of flat inaction, deadly sameness, some girl comes, perhaps to tea. And, suddenly, an arrow darts across the table – plunges in your heart – and fills you with ecstatic, God-like, agony. I tell you, Alan, no religion's worth a damn that cuts that out. No man exists – or has a right to – if he hasn't stopped that bloody barb. I know, old chap – I have experience – I stop a couple every day! When two meet in one's heart and grind away against each other, it's too much to bear. But, seriously, I'm perturbed about you, Alan. You're a decent, handsome, well-proportioned chap. And, yet – you might as well be – – Sorry, Alan, I've offended you.

ALAN: You couldn't do that, Bri – you're too spontaneous. And, anyway, let's concentrate on you. You must find somebody to fall in love with – physically and mentally – apart from yourself!

BRIAN: Cad!

ALAN: Well, that's the dictum of an acting-unpaid-curate, just for what it's worth.

BRIAN: It isn't worth a damn, old man. (*He pats his shoulder, turns away – then turns back again.*) Just wait till you get struck. (*He laughs at the thought – but Alan doesn't.*) We won't have all these platitudes, this sanctimonious advice. It's chaps like you who get it worse than anyone. They spend a dozen years on ice – get hooked – rush off and shoot a lion – then hurl themselves beneath a Watford or a Stanmore train! You watch your step, old chap.

JANE (*calling off*): Brian.

BRIAN (*on his way to the door*): It happens very suddenly.

ALAN (*half to himself*): There I agree.

JANE (*coming round the door*): Come on – I'm ready, Bri.

BRIAN: I hope so too. The way you women talk!

> *Brian and Jane go out. Alan rises, thoughtfully – goes to the piano – starts playing gently. Mrs Foster comes in.*

MRS FOSTER: Has Father gone to watch them playing, Alan?

ALAN: No, he's in his study – writing out his sermon notes.

MRS FOSTER: Oh dear – I'd better go and help him with the anagrams.

> *Mrs Foster goes into the study. Alan resumes his playing, till Veronica comes in again. She stands there watching him. He sees her, suddenly, and stops. There is a pause, as Alan looks down at his idle hands upon the keys.*

VERONICA: How beautifully you play.

> *He does not answer, but starts playing again gently.*

You play as if you were in love.

ALAN (*abruptly and decisively*): I am.

VERONICA: And do you always speak the truth?

ALAN: I try to, yes.

VERONICA: How very frightening! It makes life far more difficult.

ALAN: But more worthwhile

VERONICA: You must be very brave.

ALAN: Why don't you ask me who it is I love?

VERONICA: Perhaps because I'm not so brave as you.

ALAN: I think you are. (*He stops the shadow of a tune he has been playing.*) Come here.

> *She moves towards him, and he swings on the stool, and takes hold of her wrists.*

I want to look into your eyes. (*He does so, with intent seriousness.*) Of course, you are. (*He drops her wrists, but she does not move away.*) And, anyway, you didn't need to ask. You know.

VERONICA: Yes, Alan. But it's silly. It's too sudden, when we've only met each other twice.

ALAN: Three times.

VERONICA: But only twice alone.

W.H.D.–U

ALAN: That doesn't matter. It's the sudden things in life are genuine. They give no time to puny little human intellects to twist their simple meaning and distort their fundamental truth. (*Very quietly.*) I want to kiss you, please.

VERONICA (*after a long pause, and equally quietly*): Why don't you, then?

ALAN (*looking up at her*): I've never kissed a woman in my life.

VERONICA (*gently mocking*): Not brave enough!

ALAN (*experiencing a feeling that he never knew existed*): Veronica! (*He takes her in his arms.*)

ACT TWO

SCENE 1

The Deanery sitting-room. The same night.

The Dean and his wife are dining out with the Bishop, and have not returned as yet. It is about ten-thirty. Alan is playing the piano, meditatively, stopping sometimes and gazing in front of him, deep in thought. The front door opens and Brian's loud and cheerful voice can be heard, singing, 'There's nothing left for me – Of days that used to be –' In the hall. Alan closes the piano, gets up – and goes into his father's study. In a moment, Brian, Jane and Veronica come in.

BRIAN: Thought I heard the piano. Must have been a ghost. Or p'raps it was old Alan playing in his room.

VERONICA: Has Alan got a piano in his room?

BRIAN: Yes, rather. I believe he sleeps in it. A drink?

JANE: Yes, please. Some lemonade.

BRIAN: Veronica – – ?

VERONICA: Yes, please – the same.

BRIAN (*as he pours them out*): I wonder if the Very Reverend the Dean is home. Or do you think he's swilling port, while Mother's playing patience with the Bishop's wife! (*He takes the drinks over.*) I wonder where old Alan is. Hullo – the light is on in there. (*He opens the study door.*) Oh, pardon me – I trust I haven't wrecked your theme. (*He shuts the door again.*) Old Alan – hammering the keys for all he's worth. (*He pours himself a drink and talks on.*) He is a bit stand-offish, isn't he? I don't believe he likes us!

JANE: What's he doing at this time of night?

BRIAN: It's Father's sermon, I expect. The higher that one rises in the English Church, the more Divine assistance rallies round to turn one's sermons out. There's Father – dining out with Mother at the Bishop's tenement, and, all the while, his sermon for tomorrow drops – direct from Heaven – via Messrs Underwoods supreme invention, on to half-a-dozen sheets of virgin foolscap. Talk of miracles and writings-on-the-wall and all that slap-stick stuff!

VERONICA (*smiling*): I'm sure your father writes his sermons by himself.

BRIAN: You've never heard them, dear – I have! (*He moves over with his drink.*) In consequence, my filial devotion stops me entertaining such disloyal doubts.

JANE: Bri, don't be silly – Alan doesn't write them.

BRIAN: No – he puts the flabby periods inside a verbal truss. He binds the split infinitives in splints. He stiffens up the sentiment. You see – unlike his father – Alan's not a sentimentalist. He's hard and cold and razor-edged. He flickers with blue flame. That's why old Alan couldn't ever marry. Gosh, I'm talking well! I must be rather tight.

VERONICA (*quietly*): Why couldn't Alan ever marry, Bri?

BRIAN: Well, damn it all – imagine it – it's obvious. I mean to say, he'd love his girl-friend with a holy, shining ardour, till he found that sex's a thing that can't be sublimated on one's wedding-night. And poor old Alan thinks that everything that's not sublime is sin. Well, what'd happen then? He'd bash his head against the wall – and stone himself – and sit on rows of red-hot pins. And, generally make himself a nuisance round the house. No woman's going to stand for that.

JANE (*smiling*): What nonsense you do talk.

BRIAN: It isn't nonsense, Jane. That's why those saintly fellows always live alone. St Francis, for example – look at him! He shared a cabin with a lot of rooks and seagulls! Why? Because it took an utterly insensitive and noisy bird to tolerate the poor old chap at all. (*He goes to get another drink.*) And, anyway, they only rolled up for the grub. What brought this subject up? Ah – yes – my father's sermons. Father isn't steel you see, he's clay. The difference between Father's brain and Alan's is the same as that between a lady of the town and Joan of Arc.

JANE: I've often heard you speak in favour of the ladies of the town.

BRIAN: I know – forgive me, Jane. I let my love of metaphor outweigh my sense of loyalty. Experience has taught me that the ladies of the town are apt to be extremely kind and understanding – and completely without guile. Those qualities, in my opinion, are the prizes that a Christian of discernment ought to covet most. (*He clears*

his throat and walks to the open window, and listens.) I heard a nightingale out there last night. (*He turns round and looks at them.*) Who's
going to come outside and make it sing until it busts itself?

VERONICA: How does one make them sing?

BRIAN: By making rude, discordant noises underneath the tree.
There's nothing jars a nightingale so much as loud, untutored sounds.
How sad that Father doesn't preach at night! Come on, who's going
to brave the bats? (*He takes out a coin and spins it.*) Veronica.

VERONICA: Can't Jane come out as well?

JANE: No, I'll stay in reserve.

VERONICA: Come on.

JANE: No, really – I'd rather not. I'll hear it just as well from here
– and I'm so comfortable.

> *Brian and Veronica go out. When they are gone, the smile fades
> from Jane's face. Alan comes in from the study and, on seeing
> her, makes to withdraw again.*

JANE: Hullo.

ALAN: I thought I heard you all go out.

JANE: I'm sorry. I'm still here. Were you avoiding us?

ALAN: No, I've been working. Where's Veronica?

JANE: She's just gone out with Brian to wake up the nightingale.

> *He looks quickly towards the window, and then changes the
> subject abruptly.*

ALAN: Do you like staying here?

JANE: Of course.

ALAN: When Brian's nice to you, all's well.

> *Jane looks at him, surprised at this new interest.*

JANE: All's nearly well.

ALAN: Poor Jane!

JANE: Please, Alan, don't start being sympathetic or I'll cry.
What's happened to you, anyway? I never thought that you acknow-
ledged human weaknesses like love.

ALAN: Perhaps I'm growing up.

JANE: Don't, Alan, then. Take my advice and don't.

ALAN: Can I do anything to help?

JANE: Yes, Alan – take me off your list of charities.

He looks hurt.

It's very sweet of you, but there is nothing you can do. I'm just the sort of woman you could never understand. I love too easily, you see. And that, to you, is weakness – if it isn't worse. Since Brian met me in the war in Italy – oh well, there isn't any use in talking.

ALAN: Yes, there is – it always helps.

JANE: That's true – it does. But pouring out one's sorrows is a little self-indulgent, isn't it?

ALAN: Go on.

JANE: I've never thought of anything but Brian, since we met near Como, in Bellagio. We used to row across the lake and go up to a little church – and sit up there and watch the deep blue water of the lake. I never knew it possible such happiness could be. You see, I hadn't ever been in love before. Since then, I haven't had a single thought that hasn't been of him. Not one. You think that's silly, don't you? P'raps it is. But women can be silly, and I'm possibly a little sillier than most.

ALAN: I don't think that it's silly, Jane.

JANE: He loved me then, you see. He loves me still, I know, but only in a certain way – just physically. I wouldn't ever blame him for it. People can't help things like that. They happen and there's no use trying to pretend they don't. I'm just a useful antidote to loneliness and Brian – underneath his superficial cheerfulness – is just a lonely and bewildered little boy. He's always searching for a kindred soul. He doesn't realize that souls are never made to match. He's out there, searching now.

ALAN: And do you think he'll find what he is looking for?

JANE: Of course he won't. Veronica's a mystery to him. She represents the opposite extreme to me. Where I am obvious, she's utterly elusive. Where I'm only lovely on the surface, she has inner beauty. Where I'm weak, she's unassailable. Where I surrender wholly to an overwhelming love, she'd fight it back and win. And Brian thinks she's what he's looking for. He's wrong, of course, because she doesn't love him. Not a bit. And Brian is the kind of man who can't exist unless he's loved. He's like a window-box that must be watered every day, or else it dies. I'm sorry. I'm a bore.

ALAN: Why don't you try Veronica's technique and keep him at arm's length?

JANE: Because I love him, Alan.

ALAN: Yes, I asked a silly question, Jane.

JANE: And, anyway, it's far too late. He knows how weak I am. There's not a hope that Bri would ever marry me. I've given him, well – everything. So what's he got to gain?

ALAN: I see.

JANE: We went to Como – to Bellagio – from Rome. It started there. That shocks you, doesn't it?

ALAN: Tremendously.

JANE: But even so, they happen, things like that – especially in Italy. (*Her thoughts are on Bellagio again.*) You couldn't love a girl like me. Not ever, could you?

ALAN: Never, I'm afraid. I feel an overwhelming pity for you, though.

JANE: That's nice of you. And Brian? Do you think he feels the same?

ALAN: No – not the same.

JANE: What do you think he feels?

ALAN: A dreadful trinity. Desire, and Pity, and Contempt.

JANE: Oh, Alan – how I hope that isn't true. I can't change like you said. It's far too late.

ALAN: It isn't, Jane. It's never that.

JANE: A woman who's in love is lost. We think of every known excuse for what we do, when we're in love. But, actually, we just can't help ourselves.

ALAN: Please try. I'll pray for you.

JANE (*touched*): Dear Alan! I'm afraid I gave up praying long ago.

Veronica comes in.

VERONICA: Jane, Brian wants you to go out and listen for the nightingale. It wouldn't sing for me.

JANE: How warm is it?

VERONICA: It's lovely. Brian said that he would cry if you refused to go.

JANE: Oh dear – I'd better go. He's far too old to cry before a nightingale.

She goes. Veronica sits down. There is a pause.

ALAN: Did you enjoy the film?

VERONICA: Yes, very much. I wish you had been there.

ALAN: What was it?

VERONICA: Oh, American. A sentimental tale. They do those things so well.

ALAN: Tell me the plot.

VERONICA: Oh, well, the usual thing. Two people fall in love quite suddenly. They can't be married for some reason – I forget exactly why. And so, they do the normal thing instead.

ALAN: What did they do?

VERONICA: They went to San Francisco.

ALAN: Do Americans do that when they are crossed in love?

VERONICA: Well, these two did.

ALAN: I wonder what the special healing qualities for broken hearts – peculiar to San Francisco – are!

VERONICA: Large comfortable hotels – large sunny bedrooms, with communicating doors.

ALAN: I see.

VERONICA: It sounds a little commonplace. It didn't in the Odeon. The two of them seemed noble, dignified, and almost qualified for martyrdom.

ALAN: A martyrdom a little less exacting than the stake.

VERONICA: Perhaps, in this case. But it needn't be.

ALAN: You haven't had experience of that?

VERONICA: Oh, Alan – what a question! Did I speak as though I had? How frightening!

ALAN: Why – frightening?

VERONICA: It must have been a shadow.

ALAN: There's no need to be afraid of them.

VERONICA: They sometimes fall in front of one – across one's path.

ALAN: Come back to San Francisco.

VERONICA: San Francisco?

ALAN: Where those two did – 'just the normal thing to do.'

VERONICA: Did I say that?

ALAN: Initially, I don't suppose you did. It sounded just like Brian.

VERONICA: Yes, I think it was.

ALAN: I'm sure it was. Old Brian loves the under-dog. It's there-

fore quite inevitable he should be the doughty champion of sin. Did
Brian try to kiss you in the garden?

VERONICA: Yes.

ALAN: And did you let him?

VERONICA: No.

ALAN: Why not?

VERONICA: Because I'm not in love with him.

ALAN: But you let me.

> *She does not answer him. He walks to the window, as the night-*
> *ingale starts singing. They listen in silence, till it stops.*

VERONICA: Now, Brian must be making loud, discordant
noises!

ALAN (*coming back from the window*): Veronica, I want to talk to
you.

VERONICA: Please play instead.

ALAN: I fell in love with you today. And you with me.

> *She does not deny this.*

I know it's sudden as you said. But still, it's true. It's wonderful –
supremely wonderful – but shattering as well. I hardly understand it
yet. (*He is talking half to himself, half to her.*) You see, emotionally,
I'm still a child. Intentionally, as well. I say 'intentionally', because an
adult introduction to the world is apt to hurt. And I have always
thought, maybe, I wasn't strong enough to walk with life, without a
loss of faith. And so, when I left school, I said, 'I'll give my life to God.'
I said, 'This is the only love in life – the love of God – the only worthwhile love.' 'All else,' I said, in my sublime intransigence, 'is cheap
and hollow, pomp and vanity and flesh.' Since I left school, I've lived
on that philosophy. That's why old Brian calls me Galahad. I've
thought myself a saint, you see. But now – since meeting you – I've
learnt that I was just a saint without a soul – a self-recruited young
disciple without understanding – an intolerant, conceited, priggish
little tin-pot God. Since meeting you, I know for certain that the life
I've always meant to lead was not a life at all.

VERONICA: Don't be too sure.

ALAN: I've never been so sure of anything. No man has any right
to think he can exist alone. It's merely sanctimonious to think that one

can do without the love of fellow creatures, like yourself. I know that –
without you – I must be incomplete.

VERONICA: Please play the piano now.

ALAN: I haven't finished yet. Veronica, you know you feel the
same.

VERONICA: I feel how good you are.

ALAN: Much more than that.

VERONICA: What is there more than that?

ALAN: There's love.

VERONICA: The love you've lived on all these years. Dear Alan,
surely that's enough.

ALAN: It's not. I've learnt that now. It's founded on an inhibition.
It's a missing out of an essential link. It's like a climber, trying to
attain the highest peak, without a rope attached to a companion with
the same invincible determination as himself. It can't be done. I've
thought it out. That's why I didn't come tonight. I stayed back here to
think. It's all clear now. Veronica, I'm going to marry you.

VERONICA: You can't, my darling Alan.

ALAN: Yes, I can.

VERONICA: You know you can't. A Church of England clergyman,
and I'm a Roman Catholic.

ALAN: I'm not a clergyman.

VERONICA: You will be soon.

ALAN: I won't.

VERONICA: You don't know what you're saying, Alan.

ALAN: Yes, I do.

VERONICA (*hopelessly*): Why say it, then?

ALAN: I always say exactly what I feel.

VERONICA: That leads to misery – or martyrdom – or both.

ALAN: It won't this time. It's leading straight to happiness. I love
you, don't you understand? I love you more than anything I've ever
loved before.

VERONICA: How can you know? We've hardly even kissed each
other.

ALAN: This is spiritual love.

VERONICA: There's no such thing between a man and woman.

ALAN: Yes, there is. I love you with my soul, for ever – don't you
understand?

VERONICA: Please go and play the piano now.

ALAN (*ignoring this*): It's just a hollow fraud for me to go on serving in the Church, when I'm in love with you. If you were Protestant, then we could marry and be happy as we are. But then, it's God's will that you shouldn't be. And so, I've got to make a sacrifice. I wouldn't try to make you change your faith, because it's obvious that faith is not a transitory thing with you. And so, it's up to me – –

VERONICA: It's weakness, Alan.

ALAN: No, it's not. It's taken out of me. I have no hand in this. I love you and – that's all.

VERONICA: You idealize too much.

> She sits, staring in front of her, neither encouraging him nor discouraging him, while he gently kisses her.

VERONICA: Dear Alan, promise me one thing.

ALAN: Yes, anything.

VERONICA: Don't tell your father about this.

ALAN: I must.

VERONICA: No, Alan – please.

ALAN: I must.

VERONICA: Oh, Alan. Well, then – if you must – tomorrow. But don't tell him anything tonight.

ALAN: He might be mellower tonight.

VERONICA (*desperately*): Please, Alan – promise. Not tonight.

ALAN: All right, I'll tackle him tomorrow. (*He kisses her again.*)

VERONICA: Go and play the piano now.

> He walks over to it, leaving her unwillingly, and starts playing gently.

Forget me, Alan, please.

ALAN: Impossible.

VERONICA: It's wrecking your career.

ALAN: It's finding one. A selfless love, in loving you.

VERONICA: No woman's worthy of such love.

ALAN: You are.

VERONICA: I'm not. No woman is. We can't live up to it. A woman's love is simple, earthy, physical. It wouldn't satisfy you, Alan. You, of all men, seek a higher destiny than that.

ALAN: It isn't natural to try to climb too high.

VERONICA: Some people can't live any lower than the mountain-tops. And you are one of them. Don't do it, Alan.

ALAN: I've made up my mind. I feel inspired. I'm going to play the piano all night long.

VERONICA: Will that be popular?

ALAN: No, in my room. I've got a piano in my room.

VERONICA: Where is your room?

ALAN: Come here.

She goes over to the window and he takes her hand.

You see – beyond that tomb. That little door. Well, that's my room. It used to be an office in the Cloisters. Then my mother thought that Father wouldn't sleep, if I played here all night. Whereas, from there, he can't quite hear it in his bedroom. So, I'm banished there. But I don't mind. I love my little room.

VERONICA: When can I come and see it, Alan?

ALAN: Any time you like.

VERONICA: And will you play?

ALAN: Of course.

VERONICA (*with half a breath*): Tonight?

ALAN: Oh, how I wish you could. I shall imagine it. When I'm alone and playing – that you've come tonight. When all the rest have gone to bed, I shall imagine you are slipping through the garden – past the grave-yard wall – and through the Cloister door. And, I'll go on playing.

VERONICA: Brian wouldn't go on playing.

ALAN (*brought up short*): What a funny thing to say.

VERONICA: I'm sorry, Alan. It was just a thought I spoke aloud.

ALAN: Poor Brian – he can't help himself. The devil always gets the upper hand with him.

VERONICA: The devil gets the upper hand with all of us at times.

ALAN: But not with you.

VERONICA: Yes, Alan, yes. You don't believe it, do you?

ALAN: No, of course I don't.

VERONICA: That's why you love me, isn't it? Because you think I'm perfect? I'm like any other woman really, Alan.

ALAN (*smiling*): You'll have to prove it to me, I'm afraid.

VERONICA (*deadly serious*): Yes, I'm afraid of that as well. I'll have to prove it to you, Alan – just to disillusion you. I've got to stop you worshipping a heathen god.

ALAN (*seeing Brian out in the garden*): Here's Brian, coming in. I think I'll go. I don't feel like a leg-pull now. Good night, Veronica.

> *He takes her in his arms. This time, she kisses him, intensely, deliberately. He tries to draw away.*

What shall I play? You'll hear me in your room.

VERONICA: Play anything you like.

> *She kisses him again, influencing his passions in a way she has never done before. He turns and goes. She walks to the window and looks out, in thought. She hears Brian's 'Good night, old chap', and waves to Alan as he crosses the garden, kissing her hand to him. She breathes in the night air, and turns as Brian comes in – her mind almost made up.*

BRIAN: Hullo – not gone to bed!

VERONICA: Where's Jane?

BRIAN: She's gone to roost. (*He goes to get a drink.*) We had a row.

VERONICA: Oh, Brian – please don't make her more unhappy than you need.

BRIAN: I couldn't help it. Damn it, there we were – the roses stinking like a mannequin – an orchestra of nightingales – illuminations thoughtfully provided by the stars. And, then I'm damned if she'd let me kiss her.

VERONICA: So you had a row!

BRIAN: Well, naturally, I felt a little bit inhibited.

VERONICA: That always makes you miserable.

BRIAN: I'll say it does. I mean to say, it's not as if I hadn't known her long. Well – dash it all – I've known her ever since I can remember!

VERONICA: Did she give a reason?

BRIAN: No. Well, yes. She said she thought it wrong to go on like we have. And so, it's got to stop.

VERONICA: How right she is!

BRIAN: But – damn it – without warning! It's a little steep. It's just like letting down a fellow's chair.

VERONICA: How cruel men are. One gives them everything, and they give nothing back – except the doubtful compliment of wanting more.

BRIAN: That's human nature, isn't it? Of course it is. A little boy wants chocolates. Stupid mother says, 'No dear – they won't be good for you'! Result – he wants them all the more. Wise mother gives the little beast a box. He wolfs the lot. And then he's sick. And then he doesn't want his chocolates any more.

> *He goes to replenish his glass, and the piano in Alan's room starts to play.*

It's nature's cure, Veronica. Indulgence is the only medicine that cures desire. The only guaranteed, infallible and total cure for Homo Sapiens in love . . .

VERONICA: What's 'Homo Sapiens'?

Brian (*walking back towards her*): A less offensive way of saying 'Homo Sap'. Don't play old Alan up too much. He's not like me. He doesn't bounce.

VERONICA: Supposing Alan fell in love, I wonder if your cure would work.

BRIAN: Good Lord, of course it would. If he idealized a woman, and she took advantage of it, he'd never touch the ground again. He'd never touch a woman either. He'd finish up as Cardinal, Archbishop, Pope, Chief Rabbi – all rolled into one. You see, he's got a one-track mind. And that is very dangerous. Like living in a house without a fire-escape. But still, I wouldn't let it worry you. The day old Alan lets a woman spoil his beauty sleep, I'll eat my father's gaiters, buttons, straps and all – in Worcester sauce.

> *Mrs Foster comes in.*

MRS FOSTER: We thought you would all have gone to bed by now.

BRIAN: Well – Mother – was it fun?

MRS FOSTER: Yes, I suppose it was.

BRIAN: Did he bring out his vintage port?

MRS FOSTER: I think he must have done. Your Father seemed to like it anyway.

BRIAN: Where is he?

MRS FOSTER: Shutting up the car.

BRIAN: Mum, have a drink?

MRS FOSTER: No, thank you, Bri. I had a tiny glass of port. I think that's quite enough. I really ought to go to bed and sleep it off. I do hope Alan goes on playing. It's so nice to go to sleep to. Well, Veronica, I'll say 'Good night'. (*She kisses her.*) Good night, my dear. I hope you liked the film.

BRIAN: We thought that Father ought to show it at the Sunday School.

MRS FOSTER: Was it religious?

BRIAN: No, American.

MRS FOSTER: Good night, you silly boy. (*She kisses him. To Veronica.*) I hope your room's all right.

VERONICA: Yes, lovely, thanks.

The Dean comes in.

DEAN: Now, Jean – it's time you were in bed.

MRS FOSTER: Now, Albert, don't you bully me.

BRIAN: Dutch courage, Mother!

DEAN: I'll have one more drink and then come up.

MRS FOSTER: Well, only one. Remember – Sunday is your working day. Good night.

She goes.

DEAN: Where's Alan?

VERONICA: Playing in his room.

DEAN: And Jane?

VERONICA: She's gone to bed.

DEAN: Does Alan know he's playing at the early service?

VERONICA: Yes, I think he does.

DEAN: The Bishop thinks a lot of that young man.

BRIAN: Of me?

DEAN: No – if he's wise – he doesn't think of you at all.

VERONICA: Of Alan, do you mean?

DEAN: Of Alan, yes. (*Proudly.*) He thinks he's got a great and useful life before him, after he's been called.

BRIAN (*humming*): 'I hear you calling me!'

The Dean reproves him with a look.

I think the Bishop's right. I've just been saying so.

DEAN (*with friendly sarcasm*): That follows, doesn't it? (*To Veronica.*) The Bishop's very interesting. A first-class judge of men. He said, if Alan wasn't side-tracked, he'll finish up at Canterbury.

BRIAN: What's 'side-tracked' mean?

DEAN: You ought to know. He might meet some young woman who'd knock him off his course. (*Looking sideways at Veronica.*)

BRIAN: Well, you met Mother once, and you're on the 'up and up'.

DEAN: But, I'm not Alan. He's a zealot.

BRIAN: What's a zealot?

The nightingale starts singing again.

DEAN: An enthusiast. Like that.

They listen. Veronica gets up.

VERONICA: Good night.

DEAN: You going? Well, good night, Veronica.

BRIAN: Good night. Sleep well.

Veronica goes out.

DEAN: Are you in love with her?

BRIAN: Don't be so forthright, Father. You'll never be a Bishop till you learn to exercise restraint.

DEAN: Why don't you marry Jane and settle down?

BRIAN: You like her, Dad?

DEAN: Yes, very much. It's also pretty clear that she likes you. And what about Veronica?

BRIAN: Well, what about her, Dad?

DEAN: How often's Alan met her?

BRIAN: Once or twice.

DEAN: Through you?

BRIAN: I introduced them to each other – why?

DEAN: I wondered. Even Bishops have the right to wonder, Brian. Is she staying long?

BRIAN: Till Monday, I believe.

DEAN: I see. Well, I'll be off to bed. A lovely night. (*He goes and knocks out his pipe at the window.*) Hullo!

BRIAN: What's up?

DEAN: There's someone in the Cloisters, standing opposite that tomb. I haven't got my glasses. Come and look.

BRIAN: There's no one there.

DEAN: I could have sworn there was.

BRIAN: A shadow, Dad. (*He moves away from the window.*) One often sees them when the liver's carrying a heavy load of port. There's nothing there.

DEAN (*moving away*): Oh, well – I wish I had your eyes. Good night.

BRIAN: Night, Father. (*Watching him to the door.*) Considering the seas you've shipped, I think your steering's jolly good. Perhaps a tiny list to port, that's all.

DEAN: Turn out the lights.

BRIAN: Yes, Father.

DEAN (*coming back to him as though to speak, and then thinking better of it*): Good night, Bri.

> *The Dean goes. Brian turns back to the window. Alan's piano still plays. He stands for a moment looking out. The piano stops. He shrugs his shoulders. Then he turns out the light and goes.*

SCENE 2

The next morning (Sunday). Breakfast time.

The Dean, wearing his cassock, and Mrs Foster are seated at the breakfast table.

They have long since finished their breakfast, and the Dean has practically finished the crossword in the 'Sunday Times'. No other breakfasters have yet arrived downstairs. It must be after half-past ten.

MRS FOSTER: Dear, don't be angry with him. I expect he overslept.

DEAN: Why should he oversleep? For thirty years, I've taken Early Service – every Sunday morning of my life – except when I've been ill – and never overslept.

MRS FOSTER: Yes, dear – I know. But Alan's young and children need a lot of sleep. And yesterday, he looked so very tired, poor boy.

DEAN: I'm overworking him! Is that your theme?

MRS FOSTER: I don't think Alan's very strong. I hope these things

W.D.H.–X

are keeping hot. These children sleep so peacefully – I envy them.

DEAN: They ought to go to Early Service. All of them. It's utterly disgraceful. Everybody knows – the Bishop knows – I told him so myself last night – that Brian and that girl are staying here. And yet, they don't show up – lie hogging it in bed instead. How can we seek a better world? How can we hope for Peace and the Millennium, when Brian lies asleep at half-past ten – instead of asking God's forgiveness for his sins?

MRS FOSTER: I don't think Brian's sins are very scarlet ones. It isn't in his nature to do anything unnatural. And sin is always that.

DEAN: I'll let that quite inaccurate and typically irrelevant remark go by. The point is this. It isn't only Brian. It's that girl as well.

MRS FOSTER: She's Roman Catholic, my dear.

DEAN: Not her. The other one. The one that looks at Brian like a spaniel looking at a piece of cake.

MRS FOSTER: Now don't be silly, Albert.

DEAN: It's a fact. She ought to go as well. She must have been confirmed. These modern girls – they think of nothing but their faces and their hair. They won't have hair or faces – on the day of reckoning.

MRS FOSTER: I always think that – if God made one beautiful – ignoring all these things is just ingratitude.

DEAN: I really don't know why I married you. You're just a pagan, Jean.

MRS FOSTER: Perhaps I have to be. To make the perfect antidote to you. True harmony can only be achieved by opposites.

DEAN: You know – I'm worried about Brian and that girl. I saw him kissing her – when was it? – yesterday when they were playing tennis after tea. He kissed her after every game he won.

MRS FOSTER: I'm sure he won them all. How nice for both of them. I wish that they'd get married.

DEAN: Well, why don't they, Jean? I don't believe in all this modern freedom. In my day, one never went round kissing girls on tennis courts.

MRS FOSTER: I'm sure we would have liked it if you had.

DEAN: When people get too intimate the line is very difficult to draw between an innocent flirtation and a wanton crime.

MRS FOSTER: My darling, it's quite frightening what Early Service does to you! You come back here to breakfast, purged of sin, prepared to start afresh – then sit behind a coffee-pot and snipe at two delightful children, in the most un-Christian way. And all because poor Alan must have overslept.

Jane comes in.

JANE: Good morning. Isn't it a lovely day? I am so sorry I'm so late.

MRS FOSTER: That's all right, dear. I hope it's all still hot.

DEAN: Have you seen Alan?

JANE: No, not yet. I'm only half awake. I haven't really seen you yet. (*She sits down and smiles serenely at the Dean's frosty countenance.*) You look as though you had been up for hours. Oh, yes – of course, it's Sunday, isn't it! You've been to Church – or haven't you!

DEAN (*shortly*): I have.

JANE: The Early Service, wasn't it?

DEAN: It was. (*There is a frigid pause.*) I rather hoped that I should see you there.

JANE: I nearly went.

DEAN: How nearly did you go? One eye, half open – and a struggle with your conscience in a comfortable bed.

JANE: Oh, no – I wasn't called.

DEAN: I see – unconscious conscience trouble!

JANE: No – I really told myself last night I wouldn't go. I didn't think that I was good enough.

DEAN: The very time to go.

JANE: Oh, no – I don't agree.

MRS FOSTER: Well, I must go and tidy up for church.

DEAN (*as she goes to the door*): If you see Alan, send him in to me.

MRS FOSTER: Yes, dear. Don't hurry, Jane. Unless you want to go to Church. It's Albert preaching, but if you decide the garden's nicer, he'll understand.

She goes out.

DEAN: And may I ask exactly why you don't agree?

JANE: With what?

DEAN: With my contention that the time to go to church is when one isn't feeling good enough to go.

JANE: Oh, I dunno.

DEAN: I thought that must be it!

JANE: At least I do.

DEAN: Oh, now you do!

JANE: You see, I always think Communion's a sort of – well, confession and rebirth. Well, that's all right – but then it says 'Ye that do earnestly repent of your sins' – well, you know it, don't you? Well, it's that that puts me off, because – however much I mean to do it, I know very well I never will, because I'm far too weak.

DEAN: Then why not go and pray for strength?

JANE: I do – at Matins – sometimes – if it's raining hard. But that's quite different, 'cos you see I feel that anyone can go to Matins and not feel a cheat.

DEAN: Are you so wicked then?

JANE: Yes, terribly. A loose, immoral, wanton girl. I'm sure you knew it all the time. I saw it in your face – when you were watching Brian on the tennis court last night. Remember?

DEAN: I don't think so, no.

JANE: Not when I kissed him after every game? Sheer primitive, primeval lust.

DEAN: So that's your weakness?

JANE: That and other things.

DEAN: Such as?

JANE: I wouldn't dream of telling you. You might be shocked.

DEAN: It's part of my profession to be shocked.

JANE: Oh, is it? Oh, I didn't realize.

Brian comes in.

DEAN: Good afternoon.

BRIAN: Good morning, Father. Morning, Jane. By Jove, it's pretty warm for early dawn. (*He lifts the dishes.*) What have we here today?

DEAN: Have you seen Alan?

BRIAN: No. He went to church.

DEAN: He did not go to church.

BRIAN: I say! He must have had a heart-attack. He's never missed before, since he went bathing in the Font.

DEAN: I didn't see you there.

BRIAN (*helping himself*): I'll second that!

DEAN: You ought to go – you never seem to think of me.

BRIAN: Oh, Father – don't be sentimental, when it's hardly light.

DEAN: Of course, I don't expect it, but at least one would have thought you would have done it for your mother.

BRIAN (*sitting down with his breakfast*): Done what for me mum?

DEAN: Attended church sometimes.

BRIAN: I do. I went in 1939 – September Three. I prayed for peace and got five years of bully beef. (*He turns to Jane.*) Hey, golf this morning, Jane.

JANE: Yes, if you like.

BRIAN: O.K. We'll start around eleven hundred hours.

DEAN: I think it's very bad that you should play when church is going on.

BRIAN (*humouring him*): Don't worry, Father – I won't slice my drive.

DEAN: Besides, perhaps Jane wants to go to church.

JANE: I thought of it. But it's so lovely out. It's a sin to be inside.

BRIAN: And Father says it's sin to be outside! This sin would seem to get around a bit! It's everywhere – 'Within' – 'Without' – 'At Home' – 'Away'. Jane, pass the marmalade. (*He helps himself, then decides to clear his father's mind.*) I'm sorry, Father, I'm afraid your anti-ball game views just leave me cold.

DEAN: So I perceive.

BRIAN: I blame it on the war. For five years I spent Sunday mornings marching up and down – or driving up and down – in jeeps, and fifteen hundred-weights, and tanks. I spent them listening to sergeant-majors demonstrating how to drive a bayonet home in someone else's guts. And how to twist it, when it's in. And, not content with that – exactly how to take it out again! I've fired an ordnance piece – at Matins time – towards a lot of Germans I had never met. And, possibly, I blew them all to Hell – at Matins time. The war went on, dear Father – Africa and Italy and Normandy and on the Rhine – on Sundays, during Early Service hours and Morning Service hours and, for the lucky ones, through Evensong. The milk please, Jane. And mark you, Father, during all those years, I never heard one single, solitary cheep of protest from one single, solitary little English clergyman. The Pope, admittedly, occasionally remarked, 'I say, chaps, turn it in', or words to that effect! But not the dear old Church of England – oh dear, no. So Sunday went to Hell.

The sugar please.

It went to Hell beneath the Spitfires and the mortars and the tracks of tanks, because the Lord's disciples hadn't got the guts to say, 'Put up your swords' – but waved 'em round their heads instead: and screamed for blood. And now, you sit here in an ecstasy of holy but post-dated zeal, and curse me! Why? Because I want to spend a peaceful Sunday morning playing golf with Jane – eight shots a hole, and pickings-up-if-no-one's-looking – really it's too much!

DEAN (*smiling*): Have you quite finished?

BRIAN: No. I want another cup of tea. (*He gets up to lubricate his failing vocal chords.*) And then, you wonder why it is, whenever I see clergymen – I roll my eyes and tear my hair and turn a double somersault.

> *Veronica comes in.*

VERONICA: Good morning.

DEAN: Oh, good morning.

BRIAN: Oh, good afternoon.

VERONICA: I'm sorry I'm so late.

BRIAN: Here, have some tepid tea. (*He pours it out for her.*) Have you seen Alan?

VERONICA: No.

BRIAN: Papa is worried. Alan cut his Early Service – and he's going to get a hundred lines – 'I mustn't be a naughty boy, or else I'll never be a clergyman.'

VERONICA: He didn't go to Early Service?

DEAN: No.

BRIAN (*to Veronica*): Don't look so sad. You should be pleased. One heretic has hurried from the flames!

VERONICA (*ignoring this*): Shall I go out and look for him?

DEAN (*irritably*): No, no – it's too late now.

BRIAN: He's sure to come and get his oats. He never misses breakfast. Jolly warm today. (*He walks to the window.*) Hold everything – he's coming through the rye. (*He leans out and shouts.*) What ho, old Alan – come along. Papa is sharpening his cane. (*He turns back into the room.*) He looks like hell, he must have had a visitation in the night.

VERONICA : Oh, Brian, please don't bully him. Perhaps he isn't well.

BRIAN : That's passed to you for action, Father.

DEAN : If he's got a good excuse, I won't say any more.

BRIAN (*to Veronica*) : Are you going to Mass ?

VERONICA : I think so, Bri.

BRIAN : Well, me and Jane'll drop you in the car. It's on the way to golf.

VERONICA : That's lovely. Thanks.

> *Alan comes in. He does not say 'good morning' to anyone. He walks to the table, pours out a cup of coffee and then sits down. The Dean rereads his Sunday paper, while his irritation grows.*

DEAN : Well – Alan – –?

ALAN (*in a dead voice*) : Sorry I'm so late.

DEAN : I think that we'll discuss it when we're alone.

BRIAN : Come, Jane – our exit line. (*He gets up.*) Veronica – –

> *As he and Jane go out, he makes an exit gesture at her.*

VERONICA : I haven't finished yet.

BRIAN : Well, don't be long.

> *He casts an ominous glance at the Dean, and – with Jane – goes out of the room.*
> *Veronica deliberately slow – finishes her cup of tea, watched by the Dean. Alan sits, staring straight before him, sipping his coffee. Veronica gets up and goes to the door.*

VERONICA : If you want me, Alan – I'll be in my room.

> *Alan pays no attention to her, and she goes out. There is a long silence, until the Dean puts down his paper.*

DEAN : Well, Alan – are you ill?

ALAN : No.

DEAN : What's the matter, then?

ALAN : I'm very tired, that's all.

DEAN : Why so? Have I been overworking you?

ALAN : I don't think so. I couldn't sleep. I never slept a wink all night.

DEAN : And so, you felt too tired to come to Early Service – is that it?

ALAN: One reason, yes.

DEAN: And what about your playing at the Morning Service? Will exhaustion override your sense of duty in that instance too?

ALAN: No, I'll play this morning, if you like.

DEAN: I'm glad to hear that anyway.

The Cathedral bells start ringing.

And, for the Bishop's sake – I hope that you'll play as well as last time.

ALAN: I'll do my best, but not entirely for the Bishop's sake.

The Dean, who has reached the door of his study, looks round.

DEAN: What do you mean by that?

ALAN: I mean I'll do my best, because I won't be playing any more.

DEAN: Why not? The organist's away another fortnight.

ALAN: I'm afraid I can't help that. I can't go on. I'm sorry, Father – but I can't go on.

DEAN (*coming back into the room*): What is it, Alan?

ALAN: Nothing. I've just had as much as I can bear. I'm telling you, I can't go on.

DEAN: Yes, yes – but calm yourself. Remember that I'm wholly in the dark. If I can help, then take your time – and calm yourself. And try to tell me what it is that is on your mind.

ALAN: I can't. You wouldn't understand.

DEAN: Condemning me without a trial – is that fair?

ALAN: You couldn't understand. As well expect a King to comprehend the motives of a regicide. The things you stand for – and stand by – mean nothing, less than nothing to me any more.

DEAN: What things?

ALAN: The things you represent.

DEAN: Such as Christianity?

ALAN: I don't mean that. Oh, yes, I know you stand for that – according to your lights. I don't mean that.

DEAN: Well, then what do you mean?

ALAN: I mean the English Church. The state of tepid compromise – the serving of two masters.

DEAN: Just a minute – if you can't be calm – at least be fair.

ALAN: I'm being fair. I'm trying to excuse you all along the line. I can't.

DEAN: I'm sorry to hear that! Two masters! What exactly do you mean by that?

ALAN: It doesn't matter.

DEAN: On the contrary, I think it matters very much.

ALAN: All right, I'll tell you what I mean. (*It pours out wildly.*) You can't give all your life to God – and have a woman in your life as well. It isn't possible. And, even if it were, it isn't right. You either give your life to God, or else you give it to your wife. That's if you're in the Church. If not, you parcel out your love as best you can. The layman isn't under any obligation to be wholly spiritual.

DEAN: No more are you – no more am I.

ALAN: We are. We pose as spiritual advisers – as interpreters of holy writ. And, if we don't interpret it aright, within our own exist- ence – we're frauds.

DEAN: And you've decided that we don't!

ALAN: I know we don't.

DEAN: Why 'we'? I see that you have suddenly developed a dis- taste for married clergymen. That – incidentally's – a state I've been in now for thirty-seven years. It seems a little hard that I should have to face exposure and denunciation now! But still, you haven't answered me. Why 'we'? Are you a fraud yourself?

ALAN: I am.

DEAN: Why? Are you contemplating matrimony?

ALAN: No.

DEAN: Well then. Have you been crossed in love?

ALAN: In love! Don't talk to me of love!

DEAN: I rather thought you indirectly brought the subject up.

ALAN: I'm giving up the Church. I can't go on.

DEAN: Who put you up to this?

ALAN: No one.

DEAN: Veronica?

ALAN: No one, I said.

DEAN: I ask, because these views of yours are not original, you know. The Roman Church supports your somewhat tardy views on married priests. Be careful, Alan, of these Roman Catholics. They cast their bait in most unlikely pools and sometimes have an unexpected catch. Are you in love with her?

ALAN: I hate her – – (*It bursts out before he can stop it.*)

DEAN: Alan, what has happened to you – tell me?

ALAN: No. I can't.

DEAN: Well – can I guess? You thought yourself in love with her? You went so far as to propose to her. A little prematurely, in my view. You hadn't known her very long. But still, the world moves fast these days. And, when she turned you down – you lost your head. Is that correct?

ALAN: If you say so.

DEAN: I thought that would be it. Poor Alan – what a pity you lack Brian's elasticity! (*He pats his shoulder.*) If this had happened to him, he'd be barking up another tree by now. Don't let it prey on you – ridiculous! This talk of giving up the Church! I understand you, luckily. Don't say it to the Bishop – he might take you at your word!

ALAN: That's what he's got to do – and you as well.

DEAN (*a little less confidently, but hurried, as the bells have been going for some time*): Ridiculous! For one young girl. A nice girl I agree. A girl you hate! (*He laughs.*) We'll say no more about it, Alan. You'll laugh at all this nonsense when you've had a bit of sleep tonight.

> *The bells stop.*

Come in and have a chat tomorrow morning. We'll have a pipe and a long talk.

> *The Dean moves away to his study door.*

ALAN: I won't be here tomorrow morning. I'll be away tonight. If I stay here, I think I might go mad.

DEAN: Where are you going to?

ALAN: Oh – anywhere.

DEAN: I see. To 'anywhere'! And when do you come back from 'anywhere'?

ALAN: I don't know, Father. Not until I've worked things out.

> *Brian pops his head round the door.*

BRIAN: Hullo, the U.N.O. meeting over? Nearly time for church, Papa.

DEAN: I know. I've had an argument with Alan. Knock some sense into him, Brian. I'm afraid I can't.

> *The Dean goes into his study.*

BRIAN: Did Father give you hell?

ALAN: No. He was very nice.

BRIAN: Yes. I suppose he is – beneath his plumage! Possibly, a rook has lots of charm, when it's been plucked! You haven't seen Veronica? We ought to go.

ALAN: I think she went upstairs.

BRIAN: Cheer up, old chap. Don't worry about Father. It's the weather gets him down. No wonder – wearing gaiters in a temperature of sixty-eight. He's bound to over-boil!

Veronica and Jane come in.

Ah – here we are. Let's go. There'll be a crowd on Sunday morning.

Alan gets up and goes to the door.

VERONICA: Alan – –

He stops.

I think – I think that I'll go back to London after Mass. Good-bye.

ALAN: Good-bye.

Without another word, he goes.

BRIAN: He's like a walking thunderstorm. What's bitten him?

JANE: He's acting organist today. He's late – that's all.

VERONICA: I've packed my suitcase, Brian. I'll take it with me.

JANE: We can drop it at the station.

BRIAN: Surely you're staying till tonight?

VERONICA: No, Bri.

BRIAN: It's very rude to go!

JANE: Bri – don't be difficult.

VERONICA: Thanks, Jane.

BRIAN: I'll go and get the clubs lined up.

He goes.

VERONICA: I went to talk to him. I only went to talk to him. To tell him not to tell his father he was giving up the Church. And then – he kept on saying that he loved me. So I thought, what Brian said, I thought I'd teach him not to love me. And I have. (*She almost cries.*) Do you believe me, Jane? Because I don't believe myself. I don't believe I thought of anything, except that I was with him in his room. And now, he hates me. Just because he doesn't understand. And I can never tell him why. Jane – I can never tell him why.

Mrs Foster comes in.

MRS FOSTER: Is Brian taking you to Mass?

VERONICA: Yes, thank you.

JANE: We're dropping her.

MRS FOSTER: And lunch at one.

VERONICA: I'm sorry, Mrs Foster – I'm afraid I must go back to town.

MRS FOSTER: Oh dear, how sad!

VERONICA (*lamely*): My father's very keen that I should meet some friends of his tonight.

Brian blows the horn outside.

JANE: I'll just run up and get your case.

Jane runs out. The Dean comes out of his study in full regalia.

MRS FOSTER: Veronica is going back to London.

DEAN: Oh, I'm sorry. Brian been too much for you?

VERONICA: Oh, no. (*She tries to smile, without success.*) And thanks so much for everything. You've all been very nice to me.

DEAN: We like you, dear. That's why. (*He turns to Mrs Foster.*) Now, come along, my dear. The Bishop will be looking at his watch. (*To Veronica.*) Come back and see us soon.

VERONICA: I'd love to. Thanks.

The Dean goes out. His wife lingers.

MRS FOSTER: Does Alan know that you are going?

VERONICA: Yes.

MRS FOSTER: I see.

VERONICA (*looking up, and trusting her*): Look after him. Don't let him lose his head.

DEAN (*calling, off*): Jean, come along.

MRS FOSTER (*calling*). Just coming, dear. (*She turns to Veronica.*) Good-bye. (*She kisses her.*) God bless you both. I'm sure He never meant religion to be quite so complicated. Still, I know I mustn't talk like that on Sundays!

Mrs Foster hurries out. The bells give a final, frenzied ring, and stop. The horn of Brian's car sounds again.

Veronica starts to move towards the door. Then, in the Cathedral, across the cloisters, Alan – at the organ – starts to play the same tune that he played the night before. She listens for a moment – turns – and slowly leaves the room.

ACT THREE

Some months later. The room is empty, but the telephone is ringing.

BRIAN (*off, in garden, shouting*): Telephone!

> *He comes bounding in.*

(*At telephone.*) Hullo – who is it? Alan! You! My dear old boy! Where have you been? We thought that you were dead. To Italy? I know, your letter came from there. But, why come back to this benighted spot? Oh, yes, I see. He has been – I dunno. A breakdown, sort of – too much of the Bishop's port. He's on the move again. He's sitting in the garden now. Yes, basking in the sun. Just like a lizard at a funeral. How did you hear he had been ill? The *Continental Daily Mail*! I say – that's fame! Where are you? At the station! Damn it – at the station – here! Well, don't keep chattering. I thought you were at Domodossala! I'll come and get you in the car. Two minutes – maybe three.

> *He hangs up. Then, he turns to Jane who has come in while he was telephoning.*

He's at the station now. (*He runs to the window and shouts out.*) Oi! Mother – Father. Alan's at the station. He's come all the way from Italy to see you, Dad. He read the *Continental Daily Mail*. He thought that you were dying – and he didn't want to miss the free-for-all! (*He turns back into the room.*) You coming, Jane?

JANE: No, I'll stay here and meet Veronica.

BRIAN: All right. (*He bounds towards the door.*)

JANE: Bri – don't tell Alan that she's coming here.

BRIAN: Why not? He's bound to meet her.

JANE: Yes, I know. But let him get here first.

BRIAN: All right.

> *Brian runs out. Jane sits for a moment, looking after him. The front door bell rings. Mrs Foster's voice is heard from the garden.*

MRS FOSTER (*off*): Brian! Brian!

JANE (*shouting*): He's gone to pick up Alan.

MRS FOSTER: Oh. I heard the bell, I think.

JANE: Yes, that'll be Veronica. I'll go and let her in.

> *She turns to make her way downstairs, as Veronica comes through the door.*

VERONICA: Bri let me in. He's in an awful hurry – was he going to a fire?

> *She makes the joke, but there is no laughter in her voice. She kisses Jane.*

Dear Jane! (*She looks round the room.*) Where's everybody – Evensong?

JANE: Not yet. It's only half-past four. The Dean and Mrs Foster are out in the garden. Brian's ––(*She checks herself.*)

VERONICA: How is the Dean?

JANE: Much Better.

VERONICA: Was it Alan?

JANE: Yes. The doctor says it's 'anno domini'. It's really Alan, though. He's never had a moment's happiness since Alan went away. Maybe, his coming back will do the trick.

VERONICA: Is Alan coming back?

JANE: He's at the station. Brian's fetching him.

VERONICA: He's coming here? Today?

JANE: Yes, Brian's fetching him.

VERONICA (*sitting down heavily on the arm of a chair*): You should have told me, Jane.

JANE: I didn't know. He's just got back from Italy. He's only just rung up. He's like that, as you know. Impetuosity and suddenness. He saw a continental newspaper and found out that his father had been ill. Don't look so miserable. I'm sure he's quite got over everything by now. Do take your coat off and relax.

VERONICA (*irritably*): No – I'm all right. Oh, how I wish I hadn't come. Jane, can't I slip away? There's no one knows I'm here.

JANE: Yes, everybody does. They heard the bell. Now, don't be silly. After all, the world's too small for isolation wards. If you don't meet him now, you'll meet him somewhere else. At Harrods, or at Wimbledon, or Oxford Circus in the Underground. Veronica, if I'd

known, I would have put you off. (*She is moved by Veronica's despair.*)
But we've not heard from him, except he wrote to Brian once – about
a month ago – gave no address, then suddenly – –

VERONICA: Did he say anything to Brian in his letter?

JANE: Only that he had decided not to go on training as a clergyman at Cambridge.

VERONICA: Is that true? Or one of Brian's jokes?

JANE: It's true. I read the letter. That's what broke his father up.

VERONICA: You should have told me, Jane.

JANE: How could I have? If you persist in touring Scotland by
yourself, and leaving no address – you can't expect to hear the stop-
press news.

VERONICA: Did he say why?

JANE: No. P'raps he's found he can't get on without you.

VERONICA: If I thought that that was true, I'd die of happiness.

JANE: Come on. Let's put that coat away.

VERONICA: No, Jane. I want to keep it on.

JANE: It's far too hot.

VERONICA (*crossly*): Don't fuss me so.

JANE: I'm sorry, but you roused my nursing instinct. I don't think
you look too well. You ought to see a doctor, dear.

Veronica looks angry.

I'm sorry. I'm off duty. I won't say another word.

VERONICA: I saw a doctor yesterday in Newcastle.

JANE: And what did he prescribe?

VERONICA: He wished me every happiness. He said my husband
would be very proud of me. I had announced myself as Mrs Foster.
I suppose I couldn't think of any other name. I'm sorry, boring you
like this. I couldn't keep it to myself a minute longer, Jane.

JANE: Poor darling, what a time you must have had!

VERONICA (*in a dead voice*): I went through Perth and Stirling,
then through Edinburgh. I tried to force myself to go. I couldn't make
myself. I simply couldn't make myself believe that it was me. It seemed
so silly. Just the sort of thing that happens in a play – and not at all the
sort of thing that ever happens to oneself. And then, in Newcastle, I
picked a doctor from the telephone directory. His name was Morris –
he was very gay and very young and very nice. He told me all about a

football match that he was going to at Murrayfield on Saturday. Jane, what am I to do? Jane, tell me, what am I to do?

Mrs Foster comes in, pushing the tea-table.

MRS FOSTER: Veronica! How nice to see you after all this time. It's ages since you came down here. You've heard that Alan's back?

VERONICA (*pulling herself together*): Yes, Jane just told me.

MRS FOSTER: Albert will insist on coming in to see you. He's much better now. He's had a little breakdown. But this weather's what the doctor ordered, isn't it? So very warm. Do take your coat off, dear.

VERONICA: No, thanks. I'm quite cool really. I – I've got so little on.

MRS FOSTER (*looking at her*): I had to keep my coat on once – right through the Bishop's Garden Party – on a boiling day. I'm most ashamed to say that I arrived – quite unintentionally – without my stays. And Albert was so cross. He said I let him down. *I* let *him* down!

The Dean comes in.

Ah, Albert – here's Veronica.

DEAN: And how's Veronica?

VERONICA: Quite well. But how are you?

DEAN: Much better.

VERONICA: I'm so glad.

DEAN: Is Alan here?

MRS FOSTER: No, Brian hasn't been gone long. (*To Veronica.*) I hope you had a pleasant drive.

VERONICA: Oh, lovely – thanks.

MRS FOSTER: Where did you stay last night?

VERONICA: In Newcastle.

DEAN: By choice!

VERONICA: I had to see – somebody – there.

DEAN: Where were you coming from?

VERONICA: From Scotland, Oban – Inverness and Sutherland.

DEAN: All by yourself.

Veronica nods.

How wise! On any holiday, one's best companion is oneself. I always say that to my wife.

MRS FOSTER: And he believes it too! I dread to think what he'd do

W.D.H.–Y

without me, though. He's never even learnt to pack. He puts his muddy shoes inside his shirts. He's worse than Brian – if that's possible! Except that Brian always leaves his shirts behind. It keeps them clean, I know – but then, they aren't much use to him!

DEAN: I don't think you've been here, since Alan went away.

VERONICA: I haven't, no.

DEAN: You've heard he's given up his training for the Ministry?

VERONICA: Jane told me that just now.

DEAN: A tragedy! I set my heart on seeing Alan in the Church. And then, this letter came. Oh, well, perhaps he's changed his mind again. He's so impetuous. He's maybe on another tack by now. I'll never really understand what set him off. (*To Veronica.*) Will you?

VERONICA (*quietly*): Yes, I can understand. He fell in love with me.

DEAN: My dear – I was aware of that. At least, my wife informed me of it. But I think it's foolish to assume that any woman, even you, Veronica, could possibly deflect a boy like Alan from the straight and narrow path. To me, it's quite incredible.

VERONICA: I don't suppose you've ever been in love.

DEAN (*smiling*): I'll leave my wife to answer that. I have some work to do.

After kissing Mrs Foster, and realizing Veronica's emotionalism may lead her to say things she will regret, he goes into his study.

VERONICA: I'm sorry, Mrs Foster. I just couldn't stop myself. Forgive me, please.

A car is heard outside.

Mrs FOSTER: There's nothing to forgive. I always used to think that no one in the world had ever been in love – but me. But, that's love's most bewitching quality. Why don't you slip upstairs and have a rest, you look so very tired. You must have driven much too far.

VERONICA: I'm quite all right.

Mrs FOSTER: No, I insist. When Alan comes, you can come down again. (*She leads her to the door.*) Jane's room is full of sun.

Veronica goes out, and Mrs Foster comes back into the room.

Poor child! (*She looks at Jane's face.*) She's told you, hasn't she? I'm glad. Those secrets are too terrible to bear alone. Poor child!

JANE: How did you know?

MRS FOSTER: My dear – one sees a lot of life when one is married to a clergyman. Poor child! (*She goes towards the study door.*)

JANE: You mustn't tell the Dean.

MRS FOSTER: Don't worry, Jane. In thirty-seven years, I've learnt the things to bring to Albert's notice and the things to hide from him. And this – I think is numbered with the great majority!

She smiles and goes into the study. Brian comes in.

JANE: Where's Alan?

BRIAN: He's gone off to see his piano, and to tell it all about his trip.

JANE: How is he, Bri?

BRIAN: He never spoke the whole way in the car. But then, that's nothing new. He never was much of a chap for light and airy talk. Veronica arrived?

JANE: Yes, she's upstairs. She's very tired. She's motored all the way from Newcastle.

BRIAN: And Pa and Ma?

JANE: In there. (*She waves a hand towards the study.*)

BRIAN: That's good. I want to talk to you.

JANE: What is it, Bri?

BRIAN: I've thought a lot since Alan went away. It's changed me, Jane.

JANE: You couldn't ever change.

BRIAN: I don't mean that I limp, or that my voice has gone falsetto. I mean inward change. Old Alan pushing off – Veronica's unhappiness, and Father being shot away. It's made me see how much there is in life that's sad.

JANE: You've always seen that, haven't you? That's why you joke about it, isn't it?

BRIAN: Yes, I suppose so. But, it's made me realize that kindness is the only thing that counts. And then, my thoughts went further – strange to say – and then, I realized that you were kinder than the sum of all the people I had ever met.

JANE: Please don't be serious. It doesn't suit you, Bri.

BRIAN: I'm fishing for your sympathy.

JANE: That's not the way to get it. Clowns get sympathy – so be yourself.

BRIAN: Jane – will you marry me?

JANE: No, Brian. No, I won't.

BRIAN: What! Did my ears deceive me? Did I hear you say 'I won't'?

JANE: You did.

BRIAN: That's what I thought. I say – perhaps you didn't catch the wording of my opening remark. It ran as follows, 'Will you, Jane, take me, Brian, to be your wedded husband – –'?

JANE: No. I'm sorry, but I won't. But, thank you very much for asking me.

BRIAN: Well, damn it – what do I do now?

JANE: Ask someone else, of course – like any other normal man.

BRIAN (*ignoring this*): Why won't you, Jane?

JANE: Must we go into that again?

BRIAN: Yes, please.

JANE: Because you aren't in love with me.

BRIAN: I am.

JANE: I don't agree.

BRIAN: But, damn it – I should know.

JANE: You should, but – true to type – you don't.

BRIAN: Jane darling, if I don't know that, I don't know anything.

JANE: That's taking the discussion further than we need.

BRIAN: Don't laugh at me. I'm serious. I'm asking you to marry me.

JANE: I know. Now, give me just one reason why I should.

BRIAN: Because I – –

JANE: No, you don't. Another one.

BRIAN: Because I'm beautiful. Because I've got long eyelashes and silky hair. And skin as velvety as water on a blue lagoon. Because we never quarrel – much! Because you like the way I kiss you, and the strange and absent-minded way that I make love. Because I'm fascinating, in that I'm half a naked pagan, dancing in a woodland glade – and half a gaitered Dean! Because the whole gamut of man's emotions – good and evil, high and low – run through me at a breakneck pace, and never stop too long. Because I never bore you. And because you love me very much indeed. (*He walks towards her.*) Or did. Until you jumped into the frigidaire – the week-end Alan ran away.

He tries to kiss her.

JANE: Don't, Brian, please. I'm still inside the frigidaire.

She walks away from him.

Those reasons aren't sufficient, I'm afraid.

BRIAN: Why not?

JANE: I'll tell you just why not. Because a lot of men have silky hair and velvet skin – although they don't discuss it quite so openly. And one of them might come along one day, and love me in return. Why don't you ask Veronica to marry you?

BRIAN: So that's why you insisted I should ask her here today?

JANE: Of course it's not. She wrote and told me she was passing through. She's very lonely, judging by her letter – and I thought that you'd cheer her up.

BRIAN: No, Jane. It isn't any use. I thought I loved her once. I told you so. But, whether it was true or not, I lost her on that afternoon she came to tea. My younger brother made a cuckold of me. It's a risk one always has to take with women who don't love one. But, with you it's different.

JANE: Why?

BRIAN: Because I know you love me – and the only thing I need in life is love.

JANE: And when you get it, you don't like it. Men take ill to being loved.

BRIAN: Not men like me.

JANE: Yes, Brian, men like you. You sigh and sob, and tell the world about your loneliness. But then you wouldn't lose it – not for anything.

BRIAN: I need you, Jane! I'm telling you.

JANE: You think you do. But all you really need's a nurse. One doesn't marry nurses though. One just engages them, until the fever's past. And then they go elsewhere. And one is very glad to see them go. I'll nurse you, Brian – if you like.

BRIAN: Well, let me kiss you then.

JANE: No, Bri.

She turns from him, so that he cannot see how much he's hurting her.

BRIAN: Remember Como – and Ballagio. You liked me then. Do I repel you now?

JANE: Oh, don't be silly, Bri.

BRIAN: Well, let me kiss you then.

JANE: Spoilt, beastly, sulky, selfish little boy – –

She kisses him, passionately.

Good-bye, my darling Brian. Thanks for asking me to marry you – and thanks for everything.

She turns towards the door, and opens it, as Alan comes in.

JANE: How nice to see you, Alan.

ALAN: Hullo, Jane.

He moves into the room. Veronica appears.

BRIAN: Well, here's Veronica. Hullo.

ALAN: You never said Veronica was here.

BRIAN: I kept it up my sleeve. I thought that it'd be a nice surprise for you.

There is a silence.

JANE: Bri, have you put the car away?

BRIAN: Not yet.

JANE: I left my golf-clubs in the boot this morning. Come and help me take them out.

BRIAN: Yes, rather.

ALAN: Bri, is Father in?

BRIAN: Yes, closeted in there.

Brian and Jane go out. Alan moves towards the Dean's door.

VERONICA: I'm sorry if my presence here upsets you.

ALAN: That's all right.

VERONICA: Still suffering remorse?

ALAN: I'm better now. Since I confessed.

VERONICA: I didn't know you did that in your Church.

ALAN: One can. Few people do. The atmosphere is wrong.

VERONICA: But you did.

ALAN: No.

VERONICA: You said just now that you confessed.

ALAN: I did. I have become a Roman Catholic. (*He walks over to the window.*)

VERONICA (*vainly endeavouring to control her heart-beats*): Since when?

ALAN: Since I arrived in Italy.

VERONICA: Oh, Alan – not for me? (*Almost in a whisper.*)

ALAN: No, not for you. Because of you perhaps.

VERONICA: And are you happy now?

ALAN: Almost.

>   *He turns and looks at her, and she misunderstands his 'almost'.*

Except for one thing. And I've tried so hard, but it's no use. I can't forgive myself. That wouldn't matter quite so much. What matters is, I can't forgive you either. We were wanton.

VERONICA (*in a whisper*): Alan, please don't talk like that.

ALAN: I'm telling you the truth.

VERONICA: Love's never wanton.

ALAN: Was it love?

VERONICA: Oh, Alan – yes. There's nothing wanton about love. There may be weakness, yes – but nothing wanton.

ALAN: One should not indulge in weaknesses.

VERONICA: Oh, Alan – don't you understand? Humanity is weak. And your own weakness is that you do not allow for that.

ALAN: One can't allow for sin.

VERONICA: Don't talk about it, Alan, please. Agree to disagree.

>   *She tries to take his hand, but he removes it and walks away to the window again.*

You disappoint me, Alan. You are arrogant. The cure for that is love – unselfish love.

ALAN: Where does one find it?

VERONICA: I could show you, Alan.

ALAN: That's impossible.

VERONICA: It's not, you know.

ALAN: It is, Veronica.

VERONICA: Not now you are a Roman Catholic.

ALAN: It is. More so than ever now.

VERONICA (*fear dawning in her eyes*): Why, Alan. Tell me why?

ALAN: Because I'm going to be a priest.

He says this with his back to her, still looking out of the window. She sits quite still. Mrs Foster comes in.

MRS FOSTER: My darling boy! (*She kisses Alan.*) How wonderful to have you back. And aren't you looking well?

She holds him at arm's length, then unselfishly lets him go.

Run in and see your father. Run along. I mustn't keep you from him.

Alan goes into the study.

VERONICA: He says he's going to be a priest.

MRS FOSTER: A priest – oh, Albert will be pleased.

VERONICA: No – Alan's joined my Church – the Roman Church – to be a priest.

MRS FOSTER: My dear – – (*She goes to Veronica.*) I've often thought that that would happen. P'raps it's for the best, if it makes Alan happy. That is really all we want – the two of us – just Alan's happiness.

She looks towards the study door.

I think I'd better go in there, and smooth things down for Albert. Youth can be so terribly abrupt.

She runs into the study, while Veronica tries, without success, to hold back her tears. She fails and Brian, coming in, finds her in tears.

BRIAN: Here! None of that!

She cannot look up, so he moves towards her.

Instead of sitting there like that, you ought to dance and sing and make 'whoopee'. Just think how much the Bishop's wife would give to be in your condition.

Veronica looks up.

She's been barren since the Flood.

VERONICA: Jane's told you!

BRIAN: Yes.

VERONICA: How cruel of her!

BRIAN: No, pardon me – how sweet of her. You know, you ought to get your Church to sanctify that girl. She's given me the impetus that I've been needing all these months. I hadn't got the guts to do it on my own. Veronica, I'm weighing in and asking you to marry me.

VERONICA: No, Bri – –

BRIAN: I knew that you'd refuse. What self-respecting woman could do otherwise? Confronted by a poisonous young man like me!

VERONICA: It's wonderful of you to think of it.

BRIAN (*clearly and deliberately*): And still more wonderful of you to take me on, Veronica. I'm asking you – officially – to marry me.

VERONICA: No, Brian, no.

BRIAN: All right.

> *He gets up and walks slowly to the door of the Dean's study. He lays his hand on the door-handle and then turns.*

VERONICA: What are you going to do?

BRIAN: Old Alan's through that door. If you refuse to marry me, I'll tell him all.

VERONICA: You couldn't, Bri!

BRIAN: Oh, couldn't I? You watch me do it then. And make the whole thing useless – setting all the noble, crazy things you've done at naught. It's up to you, Veronica. You owe it to the child. It's got to have a name. And mine's as good as any other. Just as good as Alan's anyway.

VERONICA (*weakening*): Your father – –

BRIAN: What about my father?

VERONICA: I'm a Roman Catholic.

BRIAN: Oh, no – you're not. Papa has got too much already on his plate. Until he dies, you fade out of your Church.

VERONICA: I couldn't.

BRIAN: Yes, you could. You must.

> *He moves nearer to her – away from the door.*

You've had bad luck, Veronica. I'll grant you that. A million, twenty million less deserving people would have got away with it. But – maybe just because it meant so much to you – you've got to pay. When Father dies, you can go back. And both go back, for all I care. But, up till then, the Roman Church is out.

VERONICA: No, Brian, I won't do it.

BRIAN: Any moment now – old Alan's coming out. It's up to you, Veronica.

VERONICA: No, Bri – I can't.

BRIAN: All right then! Wreck the boy's career – and ruin Father's life – and damn the child. Ye Gods – how selfish women are!

The study door opens and Alan comes out.

ALAN: I'm going, Bri. I've got to catch my train.

BRIAN: Your train! But, damn it – you've just come!

ALAN: I know. But, If I stay here, Father's nerves will be unnecessarily strained. And so, I'm going back to London now.

BRIAN: And when will you be Pope, old chap?

ALAN: I'll be a priest in seven years.

BRIAN: And is that really what you want?

ALAN: It's all I live for, Bri.

BRIAN: I'll run you to the station.

ALAN: Thanks. (*He turns to Veronica.*) Good-bye.

VERONICA: When do we meet again?

ALAN: We don't. I go to Rome next week. Good-bye.

He tries to think of something more friendly, but fails. He turns towards the door.

BRIAN: Ah, Alan – by the way – –

ALAN (*stopping*): Yes, Bri?

BRIAN: I think you ought to know before you go, about Veronica –

Veronica almost faints at his cruel but deliberate pause. Then he goes on.

– and me. We are engaged.

There is a silence. He turns to Veronica.

Or have I got it wrong?

VERONICA (*without looking up*): No, Bri. You've got it right.

She turns and looks at Alan and is terrified at his expression.

Oh, Alan – don't think ill of me.

ALAN: And you said it was love. (*There is scorn in his voice.*)

VERONICA: You hate me, don't you?

ALAN: Yes.

VERONICA: You shouldn't be a priest, with hatred in your heart.

Alan turns towards the door.

Please, Alan – kiss me once before you go. Please, Alan – one forgiving kiss. (*He still walks on.*) Please, Alan. (*No response. She speaks
despairingly.*) Alan – I'll explain – –

ALAN (*stopping and speaking without turning round*) : Well, do so –
if you can.

VERONICA : No, no. I can't. I can't.

ALAN : That's what I thought.

He goes out and her broken voice follows him.

VERONICA : Good-bye.

BRIAN : I'd better take him to the station, poor old chap.

Mrs Foster comes in.

Veronica and I are getting married, Mother.

*Mrs Foster goes to Veronica. The Dean comes in and stops Brian
in the doorway.*

DEAN : Brian. I blame you for this, he never would have thought of
joining Rome, except for you. You put it in his head to criticize the
English Church. Your flippancy and irresponsibility – your blasphem-
ous and foolish criticisms of my Cloth – have undermined his loyalty
and his respect for sacred things. May God forgive you for your
selfishness.

*He looks at Brian, expecting him to answer back, he is in his
cassock and the bells have been ringing for a long while.*

I can't.

He goes out, past Brian, to Evensong.

BRIAN : Well, I must go and run old Alan down.

He turns in the doorway.

I'm sorry, Mother. Seems I'm not much use.

MRS FOSTER : No, dear. But do drive carefully.

EPILOGUE

Outside a church in Italy, 1959.

Brian, in his white flannel trousers, is still seated on the bench. Little Alan is peeping through the church door again. Soon, he returns to Brian.

ALAN: She's still there, Daddy. By that funny box with curtains round it. (*He is getting very bored.*) Oh, Mummy, do come on. (*He stamps his foot.*) I want my lunch.

BRIAN: Run and look for goats.

ALAN: No, not today. It's much too hot for them. There aren't any.

BRIAN: Yes, there are. There's one. (*He whips Alan's cap off his head. He throws the cap behind the seat.*) It's butted off your cap.

ALAN (*very seriously*): You must behave yourself.

BRIAN: Yes, so I must.

Veronica comes out of the Church.

ALAN: Here's Mummy. (*He runs to her.*) Can we have our lunch down by the lake?

VERONICA: Yes, darling. Yes, of course.

ALAN: Why are you crying, Mummy?

BRIAN: Go and find those goats. I saw one going down the steps. Look! There he goes, with a long white beard. Hi – after him.

Alan runs off down the steps and Brian turns to Veronica.

Feel better now?

VERONICA: What use is it? What use is it confessing?

BRIAN: Darling, surely it must help?

VERONICA: It may help me. That's not the point. The point is Alan hates me still. And always will. Because he doesn't know the truth. Oh, Brian, when I was in there, I thought of Alan all the time. I thought I heard his voice, forgiving me. I think I'm going mad.

BRIAN (*tenderly*): Come on. Let's go before that child wolfs all the sandwiches.

He puts his arms round her and leads her down the steps. The priest comes out of the church and stands – with his back to them – looking out over the lake. Little Alan comes back, and starts to look for his cap. And then he sees the Priest.

ALAN: I'm sorry. I was looking for my cap.

The Priest turns round.

What's happened to your beard?

PRIEST (*smiling*): Don't mind about my beard. Your cap's what we're looking for.

ALAN: Oh, you must be the other one.

The Priest starts looking round.

ALAN: Oh, thanks – it's blue and white – my school cap. (*He indicates a rock behind the bench.*) Please can I get up here?

PRIEST: Of course you can. Be very careful though. (*He helps him up.*)

ALAN: Oh, thank you, sir. (*Looking over the wall, and holding on to the Priest.*) Ooh! There's the lake. Right underneath. Miles – miles – down there. How many miles is that?

PRIEST: About five hundred feet.

ALAN: How small the water looks! (*He sees the cap, and jumps down and picks it up from behind the bench.*) I've got it, thank you, sir.

PRIEST: Are you here all alone?

ALAN: No. Mummy's starting lunch down there with Daddy. Mummy's been in there for hours. (*He jerks his thumb towards the church and the Priest's suspicions are confirmed.*) You see, while we were waiting for her – Daddy threw – I dropped my cap. I must be going now.

PRIEST: Don't go. Is this your first trip here?

ALAN: Yes. (*Refusing to be delayed.*) I'll be late.

PRIEST (*talking to stop him*): And do you like it here?

ALAN: Oh, yes. But not so much as home.

PRIEST: You like your home best.

ALAN: Oh, yes. Don't you?

PRIEST: Yes, I do, too.

ALAN: My home's in England. Have you ever been there?

PRIEST: Yes.

ALAN: Well, then, you know. You get out at the station and you walk along. Just opposite the road to the Cathedral.

He is down on the ground, drawing out this very conversational map in the dust with his finger. The Priest is standing looking down at him — at him — not at the map.

ALAN: Well, then — beyond the sweetshop there's a little house. Aunt Jane lives there — and Uncle Jim — he plays the organ very well in the Cathedral — he's jolly good at cricket, too. He hit two sixes in one match once, and then, beyond their field, there's us.

Alan looks up. The Priest tries to concentrate on his words.

ALAN (*standing up*): Well, then, that's where we live. Please will you come and stay sometime? Oh, no — you're a Roman Catholic. And Grandpa doesn't like them. P'raps you hadn't better come.

He tries to comfort him, having withdrawn his hasty invitation.

Have you got any boys like me, 'cos if you have, give them my love. Oh, no — of course you haven't. Mummy says that priests can never marry. Are you very lonely?

PRIEST: Sometimes. Everybody is.

ALAN: I'm not — with Mummy. Never, ever, not.

PRIEST: Well, you're a very lucky little boy.

ALAN: Please don't be lonely. Promise! I know — when I see some goats I'll tell them all to come and talk to you. Would you like that?

PRIEST: Yes, very much.

ALAN: All right. I'll send them all.

Veronica's voice is heard — down the steps — calling 'Alan'. The Priest hears it, so does the small boy.

ALAN: There's Mummy. I must go.

PRIEST: Don't go. Stay for a moment (*desperately.*) Wasn't that a goat?

He points, and Alan looks that way as Veronica appears.

VERONICA: What are you doing, darling? Have you found your cap?

ALAN: Yes, Mummy — here it is.

The Priest turns and walks, with his back to Veronica — towards the church.

VERONICA: Poor Father.

The Priest stops.

VERONICA: I'm so sorry if my little boy's been – (*Her voice dies away in surprise.*)

The Priest turns and looks at her.

VERONICA (*without taking her eyes off him*): Alan, say good-bye and run along to Daddy. I'll follow in a minute.

Alan walks over to the Priest.

ALAN: Good-bye, Father.
PRIEST: Good-bye.

He lays a hand on Alan's head. Alan turns and walks towards the steps.

PRIEST (*under his breath*): Son.

The Priest turns his head and looks at Veronica. They stand for an eternity looking at each other. The Priest walks slowly up to her, leans forward and kisses her forehead. Veronica moves involuntarily towards him but he turns and walks back towards the church. Her arms go out towards him. He goes through the church door into the church. Her hands drop to her sides.

ALAN (*off*): (*Shouting upwards.*) Do come, Mummy. Daddy's eating all the sandwiches.
VERONICA: I'm coming, darling.

She turns towards the steps as the organ starts playing. She stops and looks back.

ALAN (*off*): She's coming, Daddy. (*He turns and shouts upwards again.*) Come on, Mummy.

Veronica still at top of steps listening to the music.

ALAN (*off*): Mum – do come on.

Veronica drags her head away from looking at the church. She looks down the steps and waves and smiles. Then, with one last look back, she turns and starts her journey down the steps, at peace at last.
The music swells in volume as she goes.

THE
RELUCTANT DEBUTANTE

THE RELUCTANT DEBUTANTE *was first produced in London at
the Cambridge Theatre on 24 May, 1955. It was presented by E. P. Clift
in conjunction with Anna Deere Wiman, with the following cast:*

Jimmy Broadbent	WILFRED HYDE WHITE
Sheila Broadbent	CELIA JOHNSON
Jane	ANNA MASSEY
Mabel Crosswaite . . .	AMBROSINE PHILLPOTTS
Clarissa	ANNA STEELE
David Bulloch	PETER MYERS
David Hoylake-Johnston . .	JOHN MERIVALE
Mrs Edgar	GWYNNE WHITBY

The Play directed by
JACK MINSTER

CHARACTERS

JIMMY BROADBENT

SHEILA BROADBENT, his wife

JANE, his daughter

MABEL CROSSWAITE

CLARISSA, her daughter

DAVID BULLOCH

DAVID HOYLAKE-JOHNSTON

MRS. EDGAR

The action of the play takes place in Jimmy Broadbent's flat off Eaton Square in June.

ACT ONE

    Scene 1. Breakfast time.
    Scene 2. Cocktail time, the same evening.

ACT TWO

    Scene 1. Early the following morning
    Scene 2. Breakfast time.

THE
RELUCTANT DEBUTANTE

ACT ONE

SCENE 1

The scene is laid throughout in the sitting-room of the Broadbents' flat in London. This flat, which has been rented for the London season, is clearly not their home.

Through a window on the left can be seen roof-tops. On R., *a service door leads into the kitchen. Back-stage* L. C. *is the sitting-room door, leading into the passage, in which all doors, bathroom, cupboard, etc., are situated.*

Jimmy and Sheila Broadbent are seated at breakfast. Sheila is opening letters.

SHEILA (*opening a letter*): Lord and Lady Aspath. Who on earth are they? July the seventh. The Hyde Park Hotel. (*She puts it down and opens another.*) Mrs. Arthur Milligan. I've never heard of her.

Jimmy covers his plate with his side plate.

What is the matter, darling?
JIMMY: My poached egg . . .
SHEILA: What's wrong with it?
JIMMY: I just don't like the way it's looking at me.
SHEILA: Well, drink your orange juice.
JIMMY: I can't. It lowers my morale.
SHEILA: Well, have some coffee, then.
JIMMY: That's not a bad idea. I don't know how you do it, darling. You look marvellous, considering we weren't in till three.

Sheila rises with two envelopes, crosses to wastepaper basket behind sofa and tears up the envelopes.

SHEILA: Give me some, too. What were you drinking last night, Jimmy?

JIMMY: Anything that I could lay my hands on: champagne, whisky, cigarette ash, lipstick, lemonade . . .

SHEILA: Why can't you stick to one thing or the other?

JIMMY: Well, the thing that I was sticking to ran out. So I went over to the other, until that ran out as well. And then I had to scavenge round among the empties.

SHEILA: Don't . . .

JIMMY: I'm sorry, darling, but you asked. Bring me *The Times*, will you?

Sheila collects 'The Times' from back of sofa.

SHEILA: We mustn't let that happen at our dance.

JIMMY: It's bound to, if I'm going to keep awake.

SHEILA: No, darling, I'm not talking about you. We must lay in an adequate supply of drink.

JIMMY: Don't worry about that: I'll lay on everything from vodka down to hashish; I'm aiming at complete unconsciousness.

SHEILA: Jimmy, it's on the thirtieth. Three weeks, Jimmy. Oh! Isn't it exciting? Only three weeks, Jimmy!

JIMMY: Only three? I doubt if I'll live to see it.

SHEILA: Don't be silly, darling.

JIMMY: I'm not being silly. This damned racket's killing me. In three weeks I'll be nothing but a walking ulcer in full evening dress.

SHEILA: Well, anyway, it's bringing lots of invitations in for Jane.

JIMMY: What is – my ulcer?

SHEILA: No, our dance.

JIMMY: Oh, good! Let's have it on my tombstone: 'By his Death, My Much Beloved Husband Brought a Lot of Invitations in for Jane.'

SHEILA: Now, Lord and Lady Aspath: who are they?

JIMMY: Why?

SHEILA: Well, they've asked us to a dance.

JIMMY: Well, he was Bobby Nicholson before his father became a peer.

SHEILA: Why did he get a peerage?

JIMMY : Long time ago. The river Itchen ran through his garden, and the Prime Minister was fond of fishing. Something of that sort.

SHEILA : And who was she?

JIMMY : Oh, London-Irish.

SHEILA : What on earth is that?

JIMMY : She worked in poor old Florrie's night club.

SHEILA : Oh yes, I know who you mean. She waved to me last week at Newmarket. She looked simply sweet.

JIMMY : She is sweet, so they say.

SHEILA : The dance is for their daughter, Mary Anne; I wonder what she's like?

JIMMY : I hope she's like her mother, for her sake. I was at school with Bobby Nicholson. Do you know, I saw him the other day at Black's and he looked exactly the same as he did his first term at Ludgrove, except that he had trousers on instead of shorts?

SHEILA : Well, as we know them both, I think we must accept. We owe it to our darling Jane.

Sheila picks up another invitation as Jimmy returns to 'The Times.'

SHEILA : Now Mrs Arthur Milligan. Who's she, Jimmy? Jimmy!

JIMMY : I'm reading about Mr Nehru, darling.

SHEILA : You can do that in the office. Pay attention, now. Who's Mrs Arthur Milligan?

JIMMY : I've never heard of her.

SHEILA : Oh dear, I haven't either. Ought we to accept it?

JIMMY : What's it for?

SHEILA : A dance – the twenty-eighth.

JIMMY : Where?

SHEILA : River Room. Savoy.

JIMMY : That sounds all right.

SHEILA : What does?

JIMMY : Well, the address. It might have been the Albert Hall.

SHEILA : But darling, what about her husband?

JIMMY : What about him?

SHEILA : He's not on the invitation card.

JIMMY : Perhaps she hasn't got one.

SHEILA : But she must have one. The daughter's called Belinda.

JIMMY: That's no proof she's got a husband.

SHEILA: But she must have had one some time, Jimmy.

JIMMY: Perhaps he's dead.

SHEILA: Oh what a good idea. I never thought of that. I'll say 'Yes' on the understanding that he's dead. We owe it to our darling Jane. Oh, here's another one (*Reading.*) The Duke and Duchess of . . . Good heavens, what's come over Sylvia? Oh no, it's only cocktails. I was going to say if Sylvia's persuaded Tom to give a party for those horse-faced girls, she ought to get a medal. But she hasn't. It's just cocktails. Well, she'll never get them off on gin. (*She gets up to put the cards on the mantelpiece.*) It's a disgrace.

JIMMY: What is?

SHEILA: Tom's attitude. He's as rich as Croesus and he's won the Derby twice, and he won't lift a finger for those wretched girls.

JIMMY: He should have run them in the Oaks.

SHEILA: Well anyway, that's two more.

JIMMY: How many nights of purgatory does that add up to?

SHEILA: Thirty-one.

JIMMY: How many of 'em do we know?

SHEILA: Sixteen.

JIMMY: That's not a bad percentage in these days.

SHEILA: It'll be thirty-two, with ours.

JIMMY: Don't, Sheila, don't!

SHEILA: You don't think people will be bored with the River Room by the thirtieth? I mean, if they've just been there on the twenty-eighth?

JIMMY: I hope so.

SHEILA: Jimmy! We're giving it for dearest Jane.

JIMMY: And dearest Mary Ann. And dearest Mrs Arthur Milligan, and all the dearest debutantes in London. You're telling me they're dearest. They're so damned dear they're going to cost me fifteen hundred pounds. And all for what? Eleven-thirty until four-thirty — five interminable hours at three hundred an hour! What's that a minute? Knock off a nought. Six into thirty. What's that, darling?

SHEILA: Oh, I shouldn't think it's very much!

JIMMY: It's five. Five pounds a minute.

SHEILA: Well, put it down to entertainment, Jimmy.

JIMMY: Entertainment!

SHEILA: What a good idea! He's so nice, your accountant, if you took him out to lunch occasionally – –

JIMMY: He's not as nice as that, my dear. If he was only half that nice he'd find himself in Wormwood Scrubs.

SHEILA: Well, business. I'm sure it's business.

JIMMY: It's that all right. But I'm afraid the Inland Revenue are still sufficiently romantic about marriage to regard it as an institution rather than a business.

SHEILA: An institution – well, let's call it that. Like military service is for men.

JIMMY: It doesn't matter what you call it, darling. It's a bloody menace.

SHEILA: Well, it's only going to happen once.

JIMMY (*going out to bedroom for coat*): Thank goodness for that. Five pounds a minute! All for what?

SHEILA: I've told you, dear. For Jane.

JIMMY (*off*): She isn't worth it. No one is.

SHEILA: Of course she is. Let's work it out. (*Rises and crosses to bedroom door.*) What does she cost to keep?

JIMMY (*off*): Five hundred a year.

SHEILA: Well, there you are. Five hundred into fifteen hundred. That's three. In three years' time, if Jane's not married you'd be out of pocket, if you see what I mean. Do you see what I mean?

JIMMY (*re-enters*): Yes. Do you?

SHEILA: No, but I did a minute ago.

JIMMY: Well, what you mean is based on sand. You're arguing on the assumption that giving a Deb dance for Jane will get Jane married.

SHEILA: It might.

JIMMY: And it might not.

SHEILA: Well, even if it doesn't, it's our 'thank-you' for the other dances.

JIMMY: An expensive thank you, thank you very much.

SHEILA: Please, not all that again. It's not only a 'thank you' for the other dances, it's a 'thank you' for the whole season during which Jane has been given the chance to meet lots of nice young men, one of whom may marry her.

JIMMY: Good – well, let's hope one of 'em does.

SHEILA: Oh, Jimmy, don't you think one will?

JIMMY: I wouldn't be surprised. She's not repulsive.

SHEILA: Isn't she? Oh, Jimmy, isn't she?

JIMMY: You sound as if you thought she was.

SHEILA: I just can't judge. I've seen too much of her.

JIMMY: No more than I have.

SHEILA: No, but you're a man. And you'd know.

JIMMY (*pulling her leg*): Well . . . I'd say she was attractive – like her mother.

SHEILA: Thank you, darling . . .

He gives her a kiss.

JIMMY: What's the orders for tonight?

SHEILA: Drinks, sevenish. And, as we're dressing, please don't hang about in Black's.

JIMMY: Who's coming?

SHEILA: Mabel and Clarissa.

JIMMY: Not those spots!

SHEILA: She isn't spotty any more. At least, not superficially.

JIMMY: Oh, good. Why dress?

SHEILA: Because we're dining out.

JIMMY: With them?

SHEILA: No. Just ourselves and Jane. We've got to go to Rhoda Gregson's dance.

JIMMY: Oh Lord, I haven't slept since Sunday night!

SHEILA: I know, my darling. But you mustn't give in now.

JIMMY: What number is tonight?

SHEILA: Nineteen.

JIMMY: That's thirteen more to go. I used to keep a calendar at school. I haven't got the nerve to now. Where shall we dine?

SHEILA: Oh, anywhere.

JIMMY: I'll get Miss Grey to get a table somewhere.

SHEILA: Yes.

JIMMY: How many? Three or four?

SHEILA: Three, I'm afraid.

JIMMY: What? No young man?

SHEILA: No. Are you in a dreadful hurry, Jimmy?

JIMMY: Yes.

SHEILA: Well then, sit down a minute. I'm extremely worried about Jane. I've got to tell you, Jimmy.

JIMMY: Why, what's wrong?

SHEILA (*rises and crosses to telephone*): You won't believe me, but I've literally been hanging on that telephone for weeks.

JIMMY: I will. I got the bill this morning.

SHEILA: Nobody'll come. But nobody. I went down Rhoda Gregson's list from A to Z – and not one single solitary man will come and dine tonight. There must be something wrong with Jane.

JIMMY: There may be something wrong with Rhoda Gregson's list.

SHEILA: Of course there isn't, Jimmy! Everybody's on it. Everybody. No, Rhoda Gregson's list's all right. It's Jane. She isn't any good with men. She doesn't know any. She doesn't want to know any.

JIMMY: Wise girl!

SHEILA: No, Jimmy. It's not funny. No, it's not. It's very, very worrying. You've got to talk to her.

JIMMY: Me? Why on earth should I?

SHEILA: Well, you're a man – you can tell her what the young men want.

JIMMY: My dear!

SHEILA: Now, don't be silly, but of course you can. You were a young man once. And you can tell her what the young men want. I'm sure they don't change much.

JIMMY: You bet they don't!

SHEILA: Well, will you talk to her?

JIMMY: No, I will not.

SHEILA: Oh darling, don't be selfish! Surely you could do just that! I watched her all last night. Where were we?

JIMMY: River Room.

SHEILA: Well, she was terrible.

JIMMY: I never noticed anything.

SHEILA: Of course, you didn't notice anything. You stood there by the bar for three hours and talked to all your men friends. I do think you might have had the grace to introduce her to a few young men.

JIMMY: I don't know any.

SHEILA: Well, a few old men.

JIMMY: You told me not to when I did the other night.

SHEILA: Well, he's notorious.

JIMMY: I don't know any young men, Sheila. All the men I know are middle-aged and don't like dancing. Anyway, I went round with her twice myself. Well, give me that, at least!

SHEILA: I saw you. And what happened? She came limping back the first time with her shoestrap broken, and one stocking laddered. And the second time you missed her feet completely and just tore her shoulder-strap.

JIMMY: I think you're overtired. You should have stayed in bed.

SHEILA: I can't. I've got to get a man for dinner, if it kills me.

JIMMY: Why not hire a gigolo?

SHEILA: I doubt if I could find one.

JIMMY: Shall I get Miss Grey to try and trace one?

SHEILA: Jimmy, don't be silly. Everyone at Rhoda Gregson's dance would know that he was one. Jimmy, it's so worrying! She may turn out like your Aunt Eileen, living in a flat in Gloucester Gate with a bull terrier.

JIMMY: Darling! Aunt Eileen's eighty-two. Jane's seventeen. That gives her sixty-five years weight for age. I wouldn't let it get you down quite yet, if I were you.

SHEILA: But she's exactly like that photograph of your Aunt Eileen playing croquet in your mother's book.

JIMMY: No one could be quite like that photograph. Not even my Aunt Eileen.

SHEILA: And Jane loves animals.

JIMMY: Yes, horses. But I doubt if she'd be allowed to set up house with one in Gloucester Gate.

SHEILA: And dogs.

JIMMY: Darling, everybody loves dogs, but it doesn't stop them marrying – the people or the dogs. Now don't be silly, darling. I thought Jane was doing pretty well last night.

SHEILA: Oh yes. She danced with lots of people. Once.

JIMMY: Well, why not ask one of them?

SHEILA: I did. I asked them all when they had finished with her. No, I didn't. I missed one. I'll run and ask her who he was. (*Starts towards the door.*) Yes, I remember perfectly. He went off somewhere when they finished dancing, and just left her standing there. (*Calling through the door.*) Jane darling – Jane, are you awake?

JANE (*off*): Yes.

SHEILA: Where are you? Oh, Jane, who was that young man you danced the foxtrot with?

JANE (*off*): Which, Mummy?

SHEILA: Darling, that's exactly what I'm asking you.

JANE (*off*): Which foxtrot, Mummy?

SHEILA: The one where Lady Price fell down.

JANE (*off*): Oh, David.

SHEILA: David who?

JANE (*off*): I wouldn't know.

SHEILA (*returning*): She really is too casual for words! Imagine dancing with a total stranger and not asking what his name is . . .

Jane comes in in dressing gown.

JANE: What's the flap for, Mummy? Hello, Daddy. (*Kisses him.*)

JIMMY: Hallo.

SHEILA: Jane, who introduced you to this David?

JANE: Daddy.

JIMMY: Me, Jane? When?

JANE: When you were dancing with me.

SHEILA: What's he look like?

JANE: Goofy. (*Kisses Sheila.*)

JIMMY: I know who she means. There was a fellow dancing alongside us, so I introduced her.

SHEILA: Did you know him?

JIMMY: Not from Adam! I just did it out of bonhomie. He didn't seem to mind!

Jane looks at new invitations on shelf.

SHEILA: Who was he dancing with?

JIMMY: The girl we talked about just now, who isn't spotty any more.

SHEILA: Clarissa!

JIMMY: That's right – Mabel's girl.

SHEILA: Well, let's get on to Mabel now; she's sure to know. Now what's her number?

JIMMY: Don't ask me, my dear!

SHEILA: Jane darling, who's Aunt Mabel under now?

JANE: Sir Charles Munro.

JIMMY: Jane!

JANE: What's the matter, Daddy?

JIMMY: Well . . .

SHEILA (*telephone book in hand*): That's right – she took his flat last winter when he went to Paris. (*Puts telephone book on back of sofa.*) M for Mountjoy, Munro, Murgatroyd . . . oh dear, I've jumped it. M-U-N . . . Yes, here we are. Munro, Sir Charles. Sloane 7381.

JIMMY: Well, I must go. See you tonight.

SHEILA: Oh darling, please don't interrupt. Jane dear, what did I say?

JANE: Sloane 7381.

> *Sheila dials.*

SHEILA: Good-bye, darling. And don't be late. Remember about Mabel . . .

JANE: Mummy . . .

SHEILA: Yes, what is it, darling?

JANE: Daddy's gone.

SHEILA: Yes, darling, I expect he has. Why, did you want him?

JANE: No, but couldn't you stop talking to him when he isn't here?

> *Jane drinks orange juice and glances at two letters which she opens.*

SHEILA (*on telephone*): Hullo? Mabel? Darling, yes, it is. Mabel darling. Tell me, who was that young man Clarissa danced the foxtrot with last night? Which one? Well, the one where Lady Price fell down. I know, my dear – poor Harold really ought to keep an eye on her. I know. Too dangerous for words. My dear – and did you see the French Ambassador? He had to literally hurdle her, with Eileen Privett in his arms. I know – and she's no midget, is she? Yes, poor man, I do hope that he hasn't strained his heart. Well, Mabel, what did I ring up about? Oh yes, of course – Jane says his name is David. I don't know. I'll ask her. (*To Jane.*) Darling, Mabel says do you mean David Bulloch?

JANE: Ask her if he's goofy-looking.

SHEILA (*at telephone*): Jane says is he goofy-looking? (*To Jane.*) Yes, a little, dear. (*At telephone.*) No, no, of course it doesn't matter. Do you know where I could get hold of him? Yes, please do, Mabel –

that's too kind of you. (*To Jane.*) She's sent Clarissa up to get her book. (*At telephone.*) Yes, wasn't it too lovely! Did you? Oh, how sweet of you. I simply must tell her at once. I know she'll be thrilled. (*To Jane.*) Jane darling, Mabel says you looked too wonderful for words last night.

Jane puts out her tongue.

(*At telephone.*) She's thrilled. And what about Clarissa? Did she like it? I'm so glad. I thought that she was looking simply radiant. She is so sensible not dancing all the time. Oh, has she? . . . Oh, I see, her shoe's been rubbing her – poor thing! Oh, Mabel, by the way, who was that very dark young man Clarissa danced a waltz with? Sunburn, was it? David Hoylake-Johnston. Where's he come from? Oh, two years. The lucky boy. I always think Majorca's too divine. Oh, Malaya!–poor dear boy. Not so dear! But what do you mean, Mabel? If he's not all right, why ever did you let Clarissa dance with him? No – I suppose you couldn't, if they met at dinner. No – no – Mabel – no! (*To Jane.*) Jane – run into the kitchen and ask Mrs Edgar for some more hot milk.

JANE: There's lots here.

SHEILA: It's cold surely, darling.

JANE: That won't matter. There's no coffee left.

SHEILA: Jane, do as you're told.

Jane goes out with coffee pot.

Yes, Mabel, do go on. I've sent Jane to the kitchen. Oh, my dear – so that's why Brenda Barrington went off to ski in May. He was the man. But didn't you just say that he was in Malaya? Oh, I see – his leave had started then. I know, my dear. That always seems to make them so impetuous.

Jane returns with coffee pot.

(*At telephone.*) Well, Mabel, till tonight, and you must tell me all. (*She hangs up.*) Oh bother. I haven't got the number now!

JANE: It serves you right. You shouldn't gossip so.

SHEILA: But, darling, I was doing it for you.

JANE: I don't want David Bulloch for a partner, thank you.

SHEILA: Why not, darling? Mabel says he's charming.

JANE: Everybody knows he's goofy.

SHEILA: Nonsense, Jane. Now. What was Mabel's number?

JANE: I've forgotten.

Sheila goes to telephone book on back of sofa and looks it up again.

You're only asking him because he's going to be a peer.

SHEILA: A what?

JANE: A peer. You know what peers are, Mummy. David's going to be Lord Cirencester.

SHEILA (*feigning ignorance*): Who told you, Jane?

JANE: He did.

SHEILA: How very vulgar he must be.

JANE: Well, it's no more than someone saying he's going to be an engine driver.

SHEILA: No one ever says that, darling.

JANE: I expect engine drivers do.

SHEILA: When they've been asked, perhaps. I hope you didn't ask him, darling.

JANE: No, he told me straight out of the blue – just like you might say, 'Jane is coming out this year,' he said, 'I'll be Lord Cirencester one day actually'.

SHEILA: And what did you say?

JANE: Oh, I said it couldn't bore me more.

SHEILA: How very rude.

JANE: He quite agreed. He said it couldn't bore me more than it bored him.

SHEILA (*she has found the number*): Oh, did he, darling? He sounds fun. Sloane 7381. We really ought to write it down somewhere. (*She dials.*)

JANE: I can't see why.

SHEILA: Well, darling, after all, Clarissa is your greatest friend.

JANE: She's not.

SHEILA: Of course she is.

JANE: She's all right in the country, but she's horrible in London.

SHEILA: Horrible? Of course she isn't.

JANE: Yes, she is. She's always giggling and looking sideways.

SHEILA: Nonsense, darling. That's just your imagination.

JANE: No, it's not. It's hers.

SHEILA: Engaged. (*She replaces the receiver.*) Did you like any of the young men that you danced with last night, darling?

JANE: No.

SHEILA: You must have found some of them nicer than the others?

JANE: No, I didn't. They were all the same.

SHEILA: Darling, how absurd, no two people are the same!

JANE: They are.

SHEILA: What did they talk to you about?

JANE: Oh, Ascot, Wimbledon and Goodwood. And the dance the night before, and then the dance the next night. It's so boring I could scream.

SHEILA: But you like dancing, don't you?

JANE: Not with them.

SHEILA: Why not?

JANE: They're all so young.

SHEILA: You mean they don't dance properly?

JANE: Oh yes, they do. That's just what's wrong. They couldn't dance more properly.

SHEILA: Darling, what do you mean?

JANE: Oh, Mummy, you know quite well what I mean. They dance just like two people going for a walk, except that *you're* walking backwards. Well, that's not what dancing's for. I mean, when natives dance a love dance out in Africa, it means something.

SHEILA: Oh! What does it mean, darling?

JANE: Well, they're making love.

SHEILA: Jane!

JANE: I don't mean literally. It's in the early stages still.

SHEILA (*relieved*): Oh.

JANE: But they're hotting up for it. That's why they do it. Otherwise they wouldn't do it. They'd go out for a walk instead.

SHEILA: But, darling, they're primitive!

JANE: Well, love is primitive.

SHEILA: Oh, is it, darling?

JANE: That's just what I like about them. They're honest and we aren't. They know what dancing's for. And if it's not for that, it's not for anything.

    Sheila laughs.

What are you laughing at?

W.D.H.—AA

SHEILA: Oh, nothing. (*She laughs again.*) I just had a vision of your father bounding up and down in feathers in the River Room.

JANE: Well, it'd do him much more good than propping up the bar all night.

SHEILA: There I agree.

JANE: I knew you would.

SHEILA: Only about Daddy, darling. I still disagree in principle. I must try Mabel for that young man's number now. (*She gets to the telephone again.*) Just think! I danced with two M.P.s last night, one Minister, two Colonels and the Air Attaché from the Swedish Embassy. Well, if one only danced as a preliminary to making love, my goodness! I wouldn't have much reputation left this morning, would I? (*She has got through at last and takes telephone round to end of sofa and sits on sofa.*) Oh, Mabel, darling, we were cut off. It's too annoying, isn't it? Now, Mabel, did Clarissa get the . . . Oh, how kind of you! (*To Jane.*) Write it down. And stop picking your nose. (*At telephone.*) No, Mabel, don't be silly. I was talking to Jane. You were, too? What a strange coincidence. Yes, yes, I'm ready. (*To Jane.*) Now, darling, write it down. (*In telephone.*) Yes? Mayfair 6384. (*To Jane.*) Thank you so much.

Jane writes it down with a fork on the table cloth.

What's that? Eileen? In the London Clinic! Strained her what? My dear, I hope the French Ambassador's all right. I just can't wait to hear.

JANE: Gossip – gossip – gossip!

SHEILA (*at telephone*): Mabel darling, keep it till tonight. Goodbye, my darling. (*She hangs up.*) Jane, don't be so rude. She might have heard.

JANE: Well, really, Mummy. It's so boring. How I wish I was with Tommy!

SHEILA (*lighting up*): Tommy, darling? (*Rises.*) Oh, that horrid horse!

JANE: He isn't horrid, and he never gossips, and he must be getting far too fat. (*Turns on gramophone.*)

SHEILA: Oh, darling, how I wish you weren't quite so fond of animals. It sometimes frightens me.

JANE: You always frighten me. You do. These days – since we

came up to London you've changed altogether. You're like, well –
you're like the Games Mistress at school – without the games.

SHEILA : Now don't be silly, darling – you're tired.

JANE : Well, whose fault's that? I wanted to come home last night
at one, and you refused to let me come till three.

SHEILA : That wasn't my fault, darling.

JANE : Well, whose was it, then?

SHEILA : Your father's. He saw lots of his old friends. Now, come
along, that number. Did you write it down?

JANE : Yes.

SHEILA : Really, Jane, on the table cloth. Now what will Mrs Edgar
say? What is that thing, a two or three?

JANE : I don't know, Mummy. I've been picking at it, I'm afraid.

SHEILA : You really are too trying, Jane! I'll try 6284. (*She goes
back to the telephone.*)

JANE : I don't know how you've got the nerve to ring him up
when you don't know him.

> *Sheila sits on end of sofa and starts dialling.*

SHEILA : Nonsense, dear. Of course I know him, now I come to
think of it. (*Dialling.*) His mother and I came out the same year.

JANE : I'll bet she's dead by now.

SHEILA : Jane! (*At telephone.*) Hullo. Oh, David, is that you? I'm
Sheila Broadbent. I'm quite sure you won't remember me. Your
mother and I both came out together. What? – I beg your pardon!
No – I don't require a taxi, thank you. (*She hangs up.*) Really, Jane,
it's all your fault. What did we try that time? 6284?

JANE : Yes.

SHEILA : Then it must be three. (*She redials.*) That man was very
rude.

JANE : What did he say?

SHEILA : Never you mind. He almost made me think that I was on
the golf-course with your father. Engaged. Oh dear, it's sure to be
some beastly woman asking him to dine.

JANE : Oh, Mummy, do relax.

SHEILA (*forgetting the last number*): Darling, what have I been
trying?

JANE (*looking at her with interest*): You know, you're perfectly all right at home in the country, Mummy. You behave absolutely normally from morning till night. One wouldn't suspect a thing. Then the moment you come to London you go completely berserk, like a cow when it smells blood.

SHEILA: Of course I can't think why your father and I do all this for you. I really can't. All you deserve is to be left behind to stagnate in the country.

JANE: Can I go back and stagnate then, Mummy?

SHEILA: No, you can't. How can you be so utterly ungrateful, Jane? Your father's taken this flat for you at crushing expense to bring you out and give you every chance. We sit up every night for you until all hours. We both sat up till three last night on your account, and neither of us gets a word of thanks.

JANE: I've told you once, I didn't want to.

SHEILA: I know, don't repeat it. I can't bear it. It just goes to show what an ungrateful little girl you are. Just think how all your country friends are envying you!

JANE: I can't think of one.

SHEILA: Of course you can – the Burrell girl.

JANE: Her! She's a Communist.

SHEILA: What nonsense, dear. Her father's our Chief Constable.

JANE: I can't help that. She sent a Christmas card to Bulganin* last year.

SHEILA: Well, then, those poor fat creatures at the Vicarage.

JANE: You know they've both gone up to Oxford, Mummy. And what's more, I heard a rumour last week-end that Janet's going steady with a Rugger Blue.

SHEILA: Jane, darling, really! 'Going steady'! (*She starts dialling.*)

JANE: Well, as steady as he'll let her. He's South African. His father owns a lot of mines. With diamonds in them.

SHEILA: Money isn't everything.

JANE: I never said it was. I'm only trying to point out that people can get married without passing through the River Room department first.

SHEILA: Hush, darling. (*She turns to telephone.*) Hullo – is that Mayfair 6384? Oh, at last! Is that you, David? My name's Sheila

*Or the name of any topical Russian leader.

Broadbent. I'm quite sure you won't remember me – your mother and I both came out together, and I knew you when you were a tiny little boy. Tell me, are you going to Rhoda Gregson's dance tonight? Yes, aren't they boring? I do so agree. Besides, I'm quite sure you're quite flooded out with invitations. Do forget them all, and come and dine with us! It's just a tiny party. Me – my husband, Jimmy Broadbent – I expect you've met him in some of your Clubs – and Jane, our daughter. She's just coming out this year. (*Signs to Jane to take her feet off the table. Jane doesn't see.*) I think you danced with her last night. Yes, yes – of course there are. How could you possibly remember! Yes, she did. Yes. Every minute of it. Wildly. But, then she's very young. You will! How wonderful! Well, let's say sevenish for seven-thirty. Fourteen Victor Court – you know, just off Sloane Street, the end of Eaton Square. Well, we'll be looking forward to it quite immensely. And we'll have a lovely talk about your mother. By the way, how is she? In the country? How I envy her. Well, when you're telephoning to her next, do give her Sheila's love. Well, good-bye till seven-thirty. (*She hangs up.*) He's coming.

JANE: No, you don't say so!

SHEILA: Charming manners, and a simply charming voice. I've simply got to look him up and see exactly who his mother was.

JANE: You mean to say you didn't know her?

SHEILA: Very likely, darling. I'll tell you in a minute. (*She goes for 'Who's Who'.*)

JANE: When's he coming?

SHEILA: Seven-thirty. We'll all go out. Oh dear, I'll have to telephone to Jimmy now about the table. Will he be there yet? (*Picking up 'Who's Who'.*)

JANE: Mummy, I'll have a nervous breakdown if you don't sit still.

SHEILA: It's all for you, my darling. Take your feet off. (*Jane takes her feet off.*)

JANE: Thanks for nothing.

SHEILA: Nonsense, he's a very nice young man.

JANE: I hate young men.

SHEILA: Darling, I really do begin to think there's something wrong with you.

JANE: I know there's something wrong with him. He paws.

Sheila begins to dial, having put 'Who's Who' on table in front of sofa.

SHEILA: Oh, so you disapprove of that?

JANE: Well, really, Mummy, what a question.

SHEILA: Oh, I am so glad. I was afraid that you might look on pawing as a sort of early form of native dancing.

JANE: Not his sort of pawing, Mummy.

SHEILA (*at telephone*): Hello, Miss Grey? Good morning. Has my husband . . . oh, he has. Yes, please. Oh, Jimmy, we've got David Bulloch dining now. So make it four. And Jimmy – don't ring off. I can't remember who his mother was. His father is Lord Cirencester, so Jane says. Rose Fripp? But Rosie died before the war. What do you mean, 'that's right'? I've just been giving her my love. In what? A séance? – Oh, Jimmy, this is serious. He's gone. (*She seizes* 'Who's Who'.) It couldn't have been Rosie Fripp. He said that she was in the country.

JANE: P'raps she's buried there.

SHEILA: I sent her my love.

JANE: Well, there's no harm in that.

SHEILA: I've got it. Cirencester, John David Wilberforce, born 1911, married 1931 Rose Fripp, died 1937. It's true, Jane, it's too, too terrible. He must have thought me mad. I'll have to ring him up again. (*She seizes the telephone as it rings. At telephone.*) Hullo! Who do you want? Miss Broadbent? Oh, yes, who is speaking? I'm her mother. David Bulloch? Yes, I'll tell her. Jane, it's David Bulloch.

Jane gets her hand on the telephone as Sheila snatches it back again.

What – David Bulloch! (*At telephone.*) Oh, David, this is Jane's mother again. I am so sorry to be such a bore. About your mother. I'm so sorry. Yes, I know she's dead. Yes, yes, I know it was. But I'm so sorry about asking you to give my love to her just now. (*To Jane.*) He says he can't because she's dead. (*At telephone.*) I know. That's why I'm so sorry. A long time ago! (*At telephone.*) Yes, David, it was a silly mistake to make. She couldn't help it. No, I made the mistake. When? Well, just now. You know I talked to you just now. But you must remember. (*To Jane.*) He says he hasn't spoken on the telephone – he must be goofy! You talk to him, Jane.

JANE: (*at telephone*): Hullo! Yes. Don't mind Mummy – she's all steamed up this morning. When? Tonight? But aren't you dining here? Oh. Hold on. I'll ask Mummy. (*To Sheila.*) He wants me to dine with him tonight.

SHEILA: But darling child, he's dining here with us.

JANE: But he says he's not.

SHEILA: Has everyone gone mad? Jane, let me speak to him again.

JANE (*at telephone*): Hold on. Here's Ma.

SHEILA (*at telephone*): David darling. This is Jane's mother. I'm sorry to be such a bore. I don't quite understand. I see. You wanted her to dine with you for Rhoda Gregson's dance. But, darling boy, you said that you'd dine with us. When? Five minutes ago. Excuse me, but you did. I talked to you for hours. That's when I spoke to you about your mother. David, I must know if I spoke on the telephone or not. I got your number from Mabel Crosswaite. (*To Jane.*) What number was it, Jane?

JANE: Oh, Mummy – Mayfair 6384.

SHEILA (*at telephone*): Mayfair 6384. That's not yours! Are you sure, David? My dear boy, do check up on the dial. You're at Caterham? (*To Jane.*) My dear, there's been some terrible mistake. (*At telephone.*) Oh, never mind the Sergeant-Major. David, are you there? Hullo! Are you quite sure you're David Bulloch? He's rung off! (*She replaces the telephone.*)

JANE: No wonder. He must think you're crackers!

SHEILA: What is Mabel's number?

JANE: Sloane 7381.

SHEILA: What can have happened, Jane?

JANE: I wouldn't know.

SHEILA (*dialling*): If David Bulloch isn't dining here, who is?

JANE: I wouldn't know. You know, you ought to see a psycho-analyst. You really ought. You go round sending love to corpses on the telephone. You're half-way round the bend.

SHEILA (*replacing phone*): Engaged! (*The telephone rings.*) (*At telephone.*) Oh, Jimmy. Yes – Quaglino's. No – no, David Bulloch isn't coming now. There's been a terrible mistake. No, no! We'll still be four. I don't know, Jimmy. I don't know, I tell you. No, I'm perfectly all right. Please ring off, Jimmy. I must use the telephone. (*She replaces it, then picks it up.*) Sloane 73 – –

JANE: – 81.

Sheila dials.

You ought to try that place at Tring if they'll have you, Mummy. Otherwise you'll find yourself inside a padded cell.

SHEILA (*at telephone*): Hullo! Oh, Mabel, this is Sheila. Your line's been engaged. Oh, has he? How nice! (*To Jane.*) David Bulloch's asked Clarissa out tonight. (*At telephone.*) But yes, darling, of course. Do bring him round for drinks. Oh, Mabel, by the way, I mustn't be a bore, but are you sure the number that you gave me did belong to David Bulloch? Not a bit. It doesn't matter. Still, just for fun, do ask Clarissa whose it was. (*To Jane.*) She's asking her. (*At telephone*). *Whose?* David Hoylake-Johnston's? Really, how funny! Yes, wouldn't it have been? Good-bye! (*The forced laugh dies on her lips as she hangs up.*) What's the number, Jane?

JANE: The one Mabel gave us?

SHEILA: Yes, of course – –

JANE: Mayfair 6384, Mummy.

SHEILA (*dialling*): I'll have to put him off.

JANE: Mummy, it's awfully rude.

SHEILA: I can't help that. He's – he's – he's not reliable. (*Listening into telephone.*) There's no reply.

JANE: Oh good.

SHEILA: I'll have to send a telegram.

JANE: But what's the matter with him, Mummy?

SHEILA (*re-dialling*): Everything. Aunt Mabel's told me all about him!

JANE: What?

SHEILA: I couldn't tell you, possibly . . .

JANE: Oh, Mummy!

SHEILA (*at telephone*): Hullo – is that telegrams? I'm Sloane 8479. To David Hoylake-Johnston – I don't know – but does it matter? Well, then, put a 't' in it if it makes you happy. No, I'm not being sarcastic. I'm extremely worried. No – no – not about the spelling. (*To Jane.*) What's the number, Jane?

JANE (*deliberately*): Mayfair 6284.

SHEILA (*at telephone*): Mayfair 6284. Regret must cancel invitation for tonight. Signed, Sheila Broadbent. With a 't'. What? I've just told you. Oh, my own? Oh, how I wish I could remember numbers. (*She looks on the dial.*)

JANE: Yes, it is a help.

SHEILA: Sloane 8479. Good-bye. (*She sinks back, exhausted.*) Oh Jane, my darling child, I nearly made a terrible mistake.

JANE (*comforting her with a nice twinkle*): It's all right, Mummy. Everybody makes them sometimes – even me!

Jane goes out, happy. Sheila sinks back exhausted.

CURTAIN

SCENE 2

The same evening. It is well past cocktail time.

Sheila, in a house-coat, is standing by the bedroom door looking off. The sitting-room door is open.

SHEILA (*shouts*): Jane, darling.

JANE (*off*): What!

SHEILA: Where are you?

JANE (*off*): In the bath.

SHEILA: Well, hurry, darling. Mabel and the others will be here at any minute.

JANE (*off*): All right. Don't flap, Mummy.

SHEILA (*shouting*): Don't forget that David Bulloch's coming round with Mabel, darling.

JANE (*off*): How I wish I could.

SHEILA: Now, don't be silly, darling. And hurry up.

The telephone rings and she picks up the receiver.

Hello, Mrs Broadbent speaking. Who? Business . . . I see. He'll be a little late. Thank you very much . . . Oh, and would you ask him to ring me as soon as he's dummy. (*She slams down the receiver.*)

Mrs Edgar opens the door.

MRS EDGAR: Lady and Miss Crosswaite, madam.

Mabel comes in, followed by Clarissa, who isn't spotty any more.

MABEL: Sheila, we're here. How are you, darling? (*Mabel and Sheila kiss.*)
Are we much too early?

SHEILA: No. Would you believe – Jimmy is still playing bridge at Black's. And how's Clarissa?

She kisses Clarissa.

CLARISSA: All right, thanks, Aunt Sheila.

SHEILA: What a pretty dress! Wherever did you get it?

MABEL: From a little woman down in Pont Street.

CLARISSA: Mummy, she's the most enormous woman that I've ever seen – –

MABEL (*sitting down*): We've had a simply dreadful day. I'm quite exhausted.

SHEILA: What have you been doing? Tell me, I just long to hear –

MABEL: Well, hair this morning. Twelve till half-past one – –

SHEILA (*sweetly, to Clarissa*): And what did you do, darling?

CLARISSA: Hair as well.

SHEILA (*politely disbelieving*): Oh, really. Well, go on. (*Offers Mabel cigarette from box.*)

MABEL: We didn't lunch till two. Where did we snatch it, darling, in the end? (*To Sheila.*) We had to grab it where we could.

CLARISSA: The Ritz.

MABEL: Oh, yes that's right. And in the afternoon, Clarissa simply dragged me round that most exhausting exhibition.

SHEILA: What did you think of it?

MABEL (*takes cigarette*): Quite terrible – although I must admit it made the Private Viewers look comparatively nice – –

CLARISSA: You didn't understand the pictures, Mummy.

MABEL: Well, thank goodness for that. That sheep with seven eyes!

CLARISSA: That was symbolic.

MABEL: Yes, you've told me that before. (*To Sheila.*) She keeps on saying that, but when I ask her what it was symbolic of, she doesn't know.

CLARISSA: I do!

MABEL: Well, tell me, darling.

CLARISSA: I've already told you.

SHEILA: Well, tell me. I'm simply dying to be told.

CLARISSA: It represents the beast in love.

SHEILA: My dear, how thrilling!

CLARISSA: And the green is envy. And the seven eyes are meant to be the seven deadly sins. And they're where they are because . . .

SHEILA: Where are they, darling?

MABEL: Anywhere but in the head, my dear!

SHEILA: It sounds enchanting. I can't wait to see it. Oh, I thought you were bringing David Bulloch with you.

MABEL: So we did. He's parking somewhere.

SHEILA: Oh, I see. (*To Clarissa.*) You and your Davids! I was very nearly angry with you after breakfast.

MABEL: Nothing to what I was.

CLARISSA: Mummy, when? You weren't angry. You were . . .

MABEL: Darling, why not run along and talk to Jane?

SHEILA: Yes, what a good idea! You'll find her in her room. It's just beyond the bathroom on the left. Tell her to hurry up, from me! (*Rising and pushing Clarissa out of door.*)

> *Clarissa goes. Sheila crosses to drinks cupboard and gets out a bottle of gin. Takes it to drinks table in the window.*

MABEL: Really, that child – she must be quite half-witted, making such a terrible mistake. I couldn't be more sorry, Sheila, but I never dreamed the horrid little creature had that dreadful bounder's number.

SHEILA: How did she get hold of it?

MABEL: My dear, she says she asked him for it last night at the dance.

SHEILA: How very forward of her.

MABEL: That's exactly what I said. And she said that it wasn't any worse than asking for an autograph. What happened, Sheila? Did you ring him up?

SHEILA: Of course I did, my dear. Well, actually I thought that he was David Bulloch, and I asked him if he'd dine tonight.

MABEL: My dear, did he accept?

SHEILA: Yes, like a shot.

MABEL: Of course he did. He's hardly had a single invitation since poor Brenda Barrington. He only went last night because old Mary Bickersteth's his aunt by marriage. Darling – but it's too exciting. When's he coming?

SHEILA: He's not coming, thank the Lord. The moment I found out from you I put him off.

MABEL: You rang him up again? My dear, how too embarrassing.

SHEILA: I tried to, but he was out. I sent a telegram.

MABEL: My dear, how lucky that you rang me back.

SHEILA: Well, David Bulloch luckily got on to Jane.

MABEL: Oh, did he, why?

SHEILA: He wanted her to dine with him.

MABEL (*coldly*): Oh, really.

SHEILA (*affecting not to notice this*): So of course it wasn't him that I'd been talking to.

MABEL: Poor Jane! What an escape she's had.

SHEILA: Tell me about him, Mabel. Have you got a hanky, darling? (*To dry her hands which have got wet on the shaker.*) He sounds simply fascinating.

MABEL: Well, his mother's an Italian.

SHEILA: My dear, that's always dangerous.

MABEL: But don't I know it! Everybody seems to think that being married to a foreigner's a sort of compromise between a mistress and a wife, when in reality it couldn't be more homely usually I must admit, because the mistress angle's being taken care of on the side. At least, that's how Clarissa's father managed till I caught him out, and he was Scotch. Where was I, Sheila?

SHEILA: I don't know.

MABEL: Oh yes. David Hoylake-Johnston's mother. She was a Portofino, or a Positano – I forget – but you know how they call themselves a lot of things if they're anything at all out there. My dear, it must have been a come-down to be just plain Mrs Hoylake-Johnston after having lots of seaside holiday resorts strung through one's name like beads. But still she married him – he was a Consul in Milan, or something of that sort – and they had a son. Ah well, we've got to face it, Sheila, he's a menace. Not one single debutante is safe. Not one. Well, look at Brenda Barrington. My dear, I never told you all the story, did I? Well then, Nellie – you know, Nellie Barrington, she had a cocktail party for poor Brenda when the Season started, just before you came to London – and of all the people in the world, her husband brought him back.

SHEILA: Brought who back?

MABEL: The menace – the son. He praised up Brenda's dog, so Nellie said – a hideous old mongrel with bad breath and filthy habits. And then, at Cissy Orville's party that night at the River Room, he danced a waltz with Brenda, my dear, cheek-to-cheek, right from the start. Well, naturally, Nellie watched them like a hawk, right through the waltz, and then a foxtrot – then a sort of boogie-woogie thing with madly irritating music. Then she simply had to go off to the Ladies for a minute – –

SHEILA: Brenda, dear, or Nellie?

MABEL: Nellie, darling – leaving Colonel Barrington on guard. When she came back he'd gone off to the bar, and they'd gone as well. And just as she was going to rush downstairs and try to catch them, well, of course, they *had* to play 'The Queen' – and Nellie couldn't move. She stood there, simply rooted to the spot. My dear, she told me at the Derby that she never would have thought it possible that any piece of music could have lasted quite so long. And the most maddening thing of all, she said, was Colonel Barrington, who stood there like a poker with a sanctimonious expression on his face – when any sentry in his regiment who'd done what he'd done would have been court-martialled on the spot.

SHEILA: What happened?

MABEL: Well . . .

SHEILA: Oh . . . where?

MABEL: They never found that out. But does it matter? Probably his flat. He lives in bachelor chambers, as they call them, which is always a temptation in itself. But everyone knows what happened the week-end he stayed down with the Barringtons.

SHEILA: I don't. What did?

MABEL: My dear, Colonel Barrington found Brenda in *flagrante de . . . de . . .* oh well.

Phone starts ringing.

You know what I mean: in David Hoylake-Johnston's room at half-past one at night.

SHEILA (*at telephone*): You really are too naughty, Jimmy! Mabel and Clarissa are both here, and simply furious. I don't care how much they're over-playing, darling. Darling, it may be money for jam, but why not tell your partner to stop. I've no patience with those silly old men in Black's. Well, silly young men, then. (*Mabel crosses to drinks table with bag and leaves it on chair.*) Six hearts. He'd better get it. And you can tell him from me that I think he's very selfish. What do you mean – I can tell him myself? When? Tonight? At dinner? What are you talking about, Jimmy? Who are you playing bridge with? David Hoylake-Johnston! Jimmy, you're not to bring – ! He's hung up! (*She replaces the telephone.*) He can't have got my telegram. He's coming, Mabel.

MABEL: So I gathered, darling.

SHEILA: I must ring again and say he's got to stop him. (*She starts dialling feverishly.*) What can I say, Mabel?

MABEL: Really, it's a repetition of what happened at the Barringtons'. I told you – didn't I? – how Colonel Barrington brought him back to poor dear Nellie's flat.

SHEILA: Yes, yes, you did.

MABEL: I just can't wait to see what happens when he gets here.

SHEILA: He won't get here if I have anything to do with it.

MABEL: I wonder if he'll talk to Jane about her dog?

SHEILA (*at telephone*): Hullo – Black's? I want to speak to Mr Broadbent. Yes, it is. Mabel, what can I say?

MABEL: Say Jane's got distemper.

SHEILA: Stop it, Mabel. (*At telephone.*) Yes? Oh dear. (*To Mabel.*) He's left. (*At telephone.*) Was he alone? Another gentleman. I see. Good-bye! (*She hangs up.*) He's coming, Mabel.

MABEL: With another gentleman!

SHEILA: Oh Mabel, I'll hit you.

MABEL: Sorry, darling.

SHEILA: Mabel, what am I to do?

MABEL: If I were you, I'd have a drink.

SHEILA (*going over to the drink table*): They mustn't be alone one single second. Not one single second!

MABEL: I'd like one too, if you don't mind.

SHEILA: It's just like Jimmy, making friends with such an awful man! He hasn't got an ounce of judgement. Not a solitary ounce!

MABEL: Darling, be fair. He's only playing bridge with him. He didn't ask him out to dinner. I imagine David Hoylake-Johnston's very good at bridge – he sounds the type who knows exactly what he wants to make.

SHEILA: A cherry, Mabel?

MABEL: Thank you, darling.

Mrs Edgar enters.

MRS EDGAR: Mr Bulloch, madam.

MABEL: David, there you are. You know each other, don't you?

BULLOCH: No.

MABEL: Oh no, of course, you only knew his mother.

SHEILA: How do you do, David? I do hope you found somewhere nice to park.

BULLOCH: Yes, miles away, though. Almost back outside your flat, Lady Crosswaite.

MABEL: Oh dear, poor you! Perhaps we should have come in a taxi.

BULLOCH: I thought of that. But if we had we would have had to take one back again to get the car.

SHEILA: Really, how fascinating! Would you like a cocktail?

BULLOCH: I'd love one. Thanks.

SHEILA: A cherry?

BULLOCH: I'd love one.

SHEILA: Well then, there you are. (*Gives him hers.*)

BULLOCH: Oh, lovely, thanks! (*Pause.*) Are you going to Wimbledon this year?

SHEILA: No, I don't think so.

MABEL: Are you, David?

BULLOCH: No. (*Pause.*) I went last year, though.

MABEL: So did I.

BULLOCH: I turned right over Chelsea Bridge. It took me straight there on the Brighton Road. Perhaps you went that way?

MABEL: I don't think so. We went by train.

SHEILA (*pause*): I am so sorry about all that nonsense on the telephone this morning.

BULLOCH: Not a bit!

SHEILA: I do hope that the sergeant-major wasn't too annoyed.

BULLOCH: No, he was all right, really.

SHEILA: Well, he must have been. He gave you time to telephone Clarissa.

BULLOCH: Yes, rather. (*He looks nervously at Mabel.*)

MABEL: It's too sweet of you to take Clarissa out tonight!

BULLOCH: Oh, not a bit.

MABEL: Who are you dining with?

BULLOCH: Well, no one, actually.

MABEL: I thought Clarissa said it was a party.

BULLOCH: Oh, we're going on to Rhoda Gregson's dance, but we're not dining anywhere. I mean, not in a party.

MABEL: *Tête à tête.* I wonder if I ought to let you? What do you think, Sheila?

SHEILA: I'm quite sure you'll let them, darling.

Enter Clarissa.

CLARISSA: Jane's not nearly ready yet. Oh, hullo, David!

BULLOCH: Hullo.

SHEILA: Well, I think I'll go and finish dressing. You see you entertain yourselves. Now, Mabel, will you see to the drinks?

MABEL: But I'll come with you, darling.

SHEILA: Oh, don't bother.

MABEL: It's no bother. (*Going out with a self-satisfied smile and toasting Clarissa behind Bulloch's back, closing door behind her.*)

After Mabel and Sheila have gone, there is a pause of some duration, during which Bulloch is shy about Clarissa's adoring gaze.

BULLOCH: You doing Goodwood this year?

CLARISSA: Yes, I think so.

BULLOCH: Going down from London?

CLARISSA: Yes, are you?

BULLOCH: No, I'll be with friends in Hampshire. Down near Petersfield. I don't suppose you know them.

CLARISSA: Don't I?

BULLOCH: Shouldn't think so. They're called Swayne.

CLARISSA: S-w-a-i-?

BULLOCH: No. Y.

CLARISSA: I don't think I know anyone called Swayne.

BULLOCH: Oh, then you wouldn't know them.

CLARISSA: No.

BULLOCH: It's quite a good idea to go by Harting.

CLARISSA: Is it?

BULLOCH: Yes, it saves the main road traffic on the Midhurst Road. You come in from the west, past a big place, called . . . I can't remember what it's called.

CLARISSA: It doesn't matter, David.

BULLOCH: But if you come down from London, you'll be coming from the north.

CLARISSA: Yes, I suppose I will.

BULLOCH: So Harting wouldn't be much use to you.

CLARISSA: No, I suppose it wouldn't.

   Long pause.

BULLOCH: Still, it might be useful one day if you find yourself in Hampshire during Goodwood Week.

CLARISSA: Yes, thanks.

BULLOCH: Oh, not a bit!

   Another interminable pause, during which Clarissa fixes him again.

CLARISSA: David, are you in love with Jane?

BULLOCH: Who? Me?

CLARISSA: Yes.

BULLOCH: I dunno.

CLARISSA: I do. You are. It happened last night at the dance.

BULLOCH: Oh, did it?

CLARISSA: Yes, I felt it.

BULLOCH: You did?

CLARISSA: Yes, you sort of went away from me.

BULLOCH: Oh, did I? Sorry!

CLARISSA: That's all right. Do your knees knock together when you see her?

BULLOCH: Yes, they do a bit.

CLARISSA: And does your tongue get dry?

BULLOCH: Yes, it does rather.

CLARISSA: Well, that's it.

BULLOCH: How do you know?

CLARISSA: That doesn't matter at the moment. David, it's no good, you know.

BULLOCH: How do you know?

W.D.H.–BB

CLARISSA: It's obvious. She just can't stand the sight of you. It's sticking out a mile. Why don't you give it up?

BULLOCH: Why should I?

CLARISSA: Well, for one thing it's so boring for your friends. Like going round with someone who's forgotten something.

BULLOCH: Sorry.

CLARISSA: I don't mind.

BULLOCH: Oh, don't you?

CLARISSA: No. It's your affair. Not mine. If you're going to go all broody, why should it hurt me?

BULLOCH: I don't know really. I just thought it did.

CLARISSA: You mean you think that I'm in love with you?

BULLOCH: Well, I did rather – actually.

CLARISSA: Oh, did you? Well, I'm not.

BULLOCH: Oh, sorry. (*Pause.*) I know what the place was called. The big place after Harting. It's West Dean.

CLARISSA (*almost in tears*): Oh, thanks.

Enter Jane in her evening dress.

JANE (*coldly*): Oh, hullo, David.

BULLOCH (*rising*): Hullo, Jane.

JANE: Where's Mummy?

CLARISSA: Dressing.

Enter Mabel.

MABEL: Darling Jane, how simply sweet you look! (*Bulloch crosses to radiogram and looks at records.*) Who is it you remind me of? I know! Did you go to the Old Vic last winter? Well, I'll tell you. You look just like Juliet the evening she met what's his name.

Sheila enters and turns on lights, then moves over to the tray and shakes the shaker violently.

SHEILA: Another cocktail, Mabel!

MABEL: Thank you, darling. (*She turns back to Jane.*) Every time I see that play I want to cry, don't I, Clarissa?

CLARISSA: How should I know, Mummy?

MABEL: Darling child, of course I cry. (*Sitting.*) It wrings my heart to see that girl, so young and innocent and fresh to start with –

SHEILA: Mabel – –

MABEL : – only to be utterly destroyed by love. Yes, darling?

SHEILA : Cherry? (*Crosses to sofa with drink.*)

MABEL : Thank you, darling. Good luck, darling.

SHEILA : Now, Clarissa, what will you have?

CLARISSA : Could I have a cocktail, please?

SHEILA : Of course. (*She returns to the tray.*)

JANE : Oh, can I have one, Mummy?

SHEILA : No.

JANE : Why not?

SHEILA : Because I say not.

JANE : Mummy, honestly – –

SHEILA : Be quiet! I've more important things to think about. That young man evidently didn't get my telegram.

JANE : Oh, didn't he?

SHEILA : No. There you are, Clarissa. (*She hands her a cocktail.*)

JANE : Does that mean he's coming?

SHEILA : Yes. Your father's just been playing bridge with him in Black's.

JANE : So Daddy knows him?

SHEILA : Evidently.

JANE : Then he must be nice.

SHEILA : He isn't nice – so get that in your head.

JANE : But Daddy's friends are always nice.

SHEILA : They may be nice to Daddy, darling, but that doesn't mean that they're always nice to everybody else. He's a – he's – Mabel, what's the word I want?

MABEL : Well really, darling, are you sure you want it?

SHEILA : I know! A philanderer.

CLARISSA : I thought that that was someone who collected stamps.

SHEILA : What's Rhoda Gregson going to say?

JANE : She told us to bring anyone we liked.

SHEILA : But, darling, we don't like him. No one does.

MABEL : Except poor Brenda Barrington.

JANE : Mummy, he's not the man who – ?

SHEILA : Jane, be quiet.

JANE : I say!

SHEILA (*to Mabel*) : If we were in a party, like you were last night, it wouldn't be so bad.

MABEL: But you aren't, darling, are you?

SHEILA (*seeing David looking at drinks*): Oh, David, would you like another drink?

BULLOCH: I'd love one.

SHEILA: Cocktail? (*Crossing to drinks.*)

BULLOCH: Yes, I'd love one.

SHEILA: Good. (*Works on it for him.*)

MABEL: Where are you two dining, David?

BULLOCH: Oh, Quag's actually.

SHEILA: We're going there – –

BULLOCH: Oh, good!

SHEILA: I've had a simply wonderful idea. (*Crosses to Bulloch with his drink.*) Why don't we all join up and dine together?

BULLOCH: What, with me?

JANE: I'm sure that David doesn't want to, Mummy.

SHEILA: Oh, Jane darling, don't be silly. Of course he does. With Jimmy. It'll be such fun. Now say you will.

BULLOCH: I'd love to.

SHEILA (*triumphant*): Well, that's settled then. I'll get on to them now and say we'll be – how many – one, two, three, four, seven – you'll come, Mabel, won't you?

MABEL: No really, darling.

SHEILA: Nonsense, darling, but of course you will. I simply won't allow you to go home and read the 'Evening Standard' over a welsh rarebit. Now Jane, what's Quaglino's number?

JANE: How should I know, Mummy?

SHEILA: Never mind. I'm sure it's somewhere under 'Q'.

She goes to the telephone book and picks it up. There is a pause.

BULLOCH (*to Jane*): Are you going to Ascot this year, Jane?

Sheila starts dialling.

JANE: No.

CLARISSA: I am.

BULLOCH: Yes, so am I. From London?

CLARISSA: No, from Staines. We're staying there. Do you know Staines at all?

BULLOCH: Yes, rather. It's a bottleneck.

During the first lines of the following dialogue, Sheila signs to Bulloch to hand round some food, which he does.

SHEILA (*at telephone*): Hullo! Is that Quaglino's? Oh, good evening! This is Mrs Broadbent speaking. Mrs Jimmy Broadbent. I've a table in my husband's name for eight-thirty. That's right – for four. And Mr David Bulloch has one booked for two – at – –

BULLOCH: Eight-thirty.

SHEILA: Yes eight-thirty, too. Now could you put us all together at a table for – no, seven, yes, I know – but someone else is coming too. So even if we both agree that four and two makes six, another one makes seven. Thank you – now then, can you manage that? No, surely – not in some tiny corner? How much earlier? Yes, that'll be all right. Yes, yes, I promise. (*She rings off.*) That's all right, so long as we're there by eight.

JANE: It's ten to now.

SHEILA: Well, that's all right. I and your father will just have to follow on in a taxi. I'm so glad that it's all worked out all right. What fun it's going to be!

Sheila smiles at Mabel, who does not return it. The door opens, and Jimmy's voice is heard.

JIMMY (*off*): You go right on in, old boy, and face the music. I'll run along and change.

David Hoylake-Johnston comes in.

SHEILA: Good evening, Mr Hoylake-Johnston! It's so nice of you to come. I'm Jimmy's wife. How do you do? Now let me introduce you – Mabel Crosswaite.

DAVID: How do you do? (*They shake hands.*)

SHEILA: And Clarissa – Mabel's girl. You know each other, don't you?

DAVID: Yes, we met last night.

SHEILA: And this is Jane, my daughter.

DAVID: How do you do?

As he puts out his hand to Jane, Sheila catches it and takes him on to Bulloch.

SHEILA: And then, David Bulloch.

DAVID ⎱ (*together*) : ⎧ Hullo, David.
BULLOCH ⎰   ⎩ Hullo, David.

SHEILA: So you know each other?

DAVID: Yes, we met one week-end, staying in the country.

BULLOCH: At the Barringtons, actually.

SHEILA: Oh really, with the Barringtons! (*Crossing to drinks table.*) Now, Mr Hoylake-Johnston, I'm quite sure you'd like a drink.

DAVID (*following Sheila*): Please call me David.

SHEILA: But I hardly know you!

DAVID: You've already made me feel at home.

SHEILA: Oh, really? Did you win your bridge?

DAVID: Oh, yes, indeed.

MABEL: I'm sure you're very good.

DAVID: Oh no, your husband is the expert.

SHEILA: Have you known him long?

DAVID: No. I was standing by the bar, and Jimmy came and asked me to make up a four.

SHEILA: What a coincidence!

DAVID: Yes, wasn't it? Just like you on the telephone this morning.

MABEL: I declare it must be fate!

> *Sheila goes over to get another drink. David looks round, and decides to talk to Jane.*

DAVID: Well, have you had a busy day?

JANE: Not very, I'm afraid.

DAVID: How very honest. Usually the answer is, 'My dear, I'm utterly exhausted. Hair till lunch – and feet till two'.

> *Clarissa laughs. David smiles charmingly at Mabel, who again does not return it.*

Now let me guess exactly what you did. You took your dog in the Park!

> *Sheila jiggles with the shaker.*

JANE: I haven't got a dog. At least I haven't got one here. I've got lots in the country, though. Do you like dogs?

DAVID: I'm sure I shall like all of yours.

JANE: My spaniel's just had puppies.

DAVID: Really? How exciting.

JANE: They're half fox-terrier. She met him in the village. I was in the chemist's, buying toothpaste.

SHEILA (*giving David the drink*): Darling! (*She gets between David and Jane, nearly pushing him over.*) Oh, I beg your pardon. I'm quite sure Mr Hoylake-Johnston doesn't want to hear about your dogs.

DAVID: Oh, but I do!

SHEILA: It's very nice of you to say so, but I'm sure you don't. After your time out in Malaya, I'm afraid we must seem too parochial for words.

DAVID: What nonsense!

SHEILA: Do you know, I'm really quite ashamed of asking you to come tonight to go to a deb dance with these young people.

> *Sheila gesticulates with the hand containing the cocktail shaker, nearly knocking Jane's head. Bulloch misunderstands her.*

BULLOCH: Yes, I'd love a drop more. (*Rises and crosses to Sheila with glass.*)

DAVID: But I'm looking forward to it quite tremendously.

JANE: Do you like dancing?

DAVID: Yes, I love it.

MABEL: I expect you're very good at it.

DAVID: Well, actually, I had some lessons when I was in Singapore. I made a habit of it when I came back from the jungle. I got mad about it after watching native dances in the little villages.

SHEILA: Oh really! But how interesting.

JANE: What sort of dancing do they do out there?

DAVID: Oh, very primitive, but beautiful. The loveliest of all's a sort of wedding dance. You know, when a chief's daughter's getting married. It goes on for hours and hours. The whole tribe joins in first of all until they get exhausted. Then the numbers gradually get less and less, until the bride and bridegroom are left dancing on their own. It's wonderful to watch them, with the moonlight shining through the rubber-trees, their bodies swaying to the rhythm, and the movements getting more and more interpretive.

> *Sheila's hand involuntarily clutches Mabel.*

And then the music rising to a climax and then suddenly it sort of shudders into silence and he picks her up and kisses her and carries her away into his tent.

JANE: Go on.

SHEILA: But Mr Hoylake-Johnston's finished, darling. Jane, Jane. Run and get your coat, Jane; go and get your coat.

Exit Jane.

(*To David.*) I'm sorry we're rushing off the moment you've got here, but we're all dining together at Quaglino's, and they said they couldn't fit us in much after eight. Now cars: who's got a car?

DAVID: I have.

BULLOCH: I have. Mine's only a two-seater, I'm afraid.

DAVID: So's mine. And open.

SHEILA: Oh.

MABEL: I'm sure Jane would love that, Sheila. Open cars are so exhilarating.

SHEILA: I'm afraid I can't allow that, with her sinus.

MABEL: Has Jane got a sinus?

SHEILA: Yes, poor child. I know. If Mr Hoylake-Johnston took Clarissa — —

MABEL (*cutting in*): Darling, if Jane's really got a sinus, she must go to Clarissa's doctor. He's too marvellous. He says if she keeps out of draughts she may not need the operation.

SHEILA: Really, but you've never mentioned it before.

MABEL: Darling, I simply can't abide health talk . . . (*She smiles at David.*) being so rudely fit myself.

SHEILA: Well, as you're so healthy, we'll send you in the open car. How's that?

DAVID: Delighted.

MABEL: Thank you so much, darling. (*She is beaten, but she has one more shot. To Clarissa.*) Well, Clarissa, you'll go with David then?

CLARISSA: Yes, Mummy.

SHEILA: That's right. And I'm sure that you can squeeze in Jane as well.

BULLOCH (*delighted*): Yes, rather!

SHEILA (*smiling at the furious Mabel*): Then that's perfect. And then me and Jimmy'll come in a taxi. (*To Mabel.*) Hurry, darling, or we'll lose the table.

Bulloch helps Mabel to put on coat.

MABEL: Now where's my bag?

DAVID: Is this it? (*Picking it up from chair.*)

MABEL: Yes. Good-bye, darling, look after yourself. Well, Sheila, if I get pneumonia, I'll sue you with both lungs.

Mabel and David go. Jane comes in with her coat.

JANE: Where's he gone?

SHEILA: Only Quaglino's, darling.

JANE: With Aunt Mabel?

SHEILA: Yes, he's giving her a lift.

JANE: Why her?

SHEILA: Well, why not, darling? David's very kindly taking you two.

Jane looks furious and Clarissa looks delighted.

(*To Bulloch.*) Now then, David, are you ready with your load?

BULLOCH: Yes, rather!

CLARISSA (*rising*): Oh, dear!

SHEILA: What's the matter?

CLARISSA: I think I've split something! Jane, you haven't got a pin?

JANE: Yes, hundreds, in my room.

SHEILA: Oh, I'll come and help you.

Clarissa goes out followed by Sheila.

Jane, ring up for a taxi, darling, while you're waiting. I must go and hurry up your father. (*She goes out.*)

Jane goes to the telephone and starts dialling. David Bulloch seizes her.

JANE: David, go away. (*At telephone.*) Oh, could we have a taxi please at fourteen Victor Court? (*She hangs up.*)

BULLOCH: I love you, Jane!

Sheila comes in.

SHEILA: Where's my glass? (*Her face lights up as she sees the scene.*) Oh darlings – I'm so sorry! Never mind! (*She nips out again, down the passage.*)

BULLOCH: Jane, let me kiss you!
JANE: No.
BULLOCH: I must.
JANE: I won't!

>*He seizes her and she struggles violently back in a sinister silence. During this, Jimmy, in his shirt-sleeves, comes in, goes across, pours out a cocktail, and starts back with it to his room without taking any notice of the scene.*
>
>*As he is going, Jane slaps David Bulloch's face. The struggle stops, and Jane sees Jimmy.*

Oh, this is David Bulloch, Daddy.

JIMMY: Oh, good evening! Hope you're getting all you want. (*He goes out, leaving them together.*)

CURTAIN

ACT TWO

SCENE 1

The time is early morning. The flat is in darkness, but the passage light is on.
Sheila throws open the sitting-room door, and switches on the light, but before she does that she shouts in the passage.

SHEILA: Jane, darling, are you in? (*Coming into the sitting-room.*) Jimmy, look in her room.

JIMMY (*off*): All right.

> *Sheila switches on the light and comes into the sitting-room with a worried look on her face. She goes to the kitchen door and opens it.*

SHEILA: Jane! Jane!

> *Jimmy comes in.*

JIMMY: She's not in.

SHEILA: Jimmy, what are we to do?

JIMMY (*crossing towards the kitchen door*): What can we do? Wait and see.

SHEILA: Oh, Jimmy, you are useless!

JIMMY: Have a drink?

SHEILA: I wonder if we ought to?

JIMMY: Why the devil not?

SHEILA: Well – Jane – –

JIMMY: It won't make any difference to Jane how much we drink. It's what she drinks that matters. (*Exit into kitchen, switching on light.*)

SHEILA: No! I hadn't thought of that. You don't think he'll make her drunk?

JIMMY (*off*): Depends how much he gives her.

SHEILA: Oh, how can you be so callous, Jimmy?

JIMMY (*off*): Well, you asked me, darling. (*Noise of champagne cork.*)

SHEILA: How much drink would make her – make her – –

JIMMY (*off*): Make her drunk?

SHEILA : Well, yes.

JIMMY (*off*) : Depends how strong her head is.

SHEILA : Oh, thank goodness it isn't bad. Do you remember when she had some cherry brandy at the Point-to-Point, and backed two winners afterwards?

JIMMY (*in kitchen doorway*) : Oh, well, that's hopeful.

SHEILA : It's not funny, Jimmy.

JIMMY : No – I know it isn't. Here, hold that. (*Gives her a glass. As he pours:*) But still, it's no use letting your imagination run away with you. (*Having poured his own out.*) To absent friends. To Jane. Good luck to her!

SHEILA : To Jane . . . (*Sits on sofa.*) Oh . . . (*Bursts into tears.*)

JIMMY : Don't cry, darling. What's the matter now?

SHEILA : I feel so awful, Jimmy. And it's all my fault: I asked that dreadful bounder here, and if I hadn't, David Bulloch would have asked Jane out tonight. Oh, dear . . .

JIMMY : She's well out of that, if you ask me! I thought he looked well over half way round the bend.

SHEILA : His father's got a lovely place in Warwickshire.

JIMMY. What, Bulloch hall? Who gave you all this gossip?

SHEILA : It's all in the Peerage.

JIMMY : I was going to say I didn't think you'd got it out of David Bulloch. Hardly heard him utter once tonight except to tell some wretched girl the way to Pontefract. Is Mabel interested in David Bulloch for Clarissa?

SHEILA : Well, of course. Don't be silly. She was terrified at dinner he was getting interested in Jane.

JIMMY : Oh – was she?

SHEILA : Darling, don't men ever notice anything?

JIMMY : Yes, some things.

SHEILA : I think David Bulloch's very fond of Jane, in fact I'm sure he is. But how was I to know he was, when I invited David Hoylake-Johnston? He'd only seen her once. Oh dear – I've ruined Jane for life. What shall I do?

JIMMY (*rises, picks up champagne bottle from sofa table*) : Fill up your glass, old girl. (*He fills both the glasses.*) If horses went to dances, they'd be in clover. They sleep standing up.

SHEILA : Am I supposed to laugh at that?

JIMMY (*turns on light*): It's optional, my dear. How old Harold Gregson ever married Rhoda beats me.

SHEILA: She owns half Yorkshire.

JIMMY: Even so I'd sooner settle for the other half. Harold was saying the grouse have got disease this year.

SHEILA: Poor things.

JIMMY: Comes from not shooting them, he says.

SHEILA: Well, obviously they won't get it if you shoot them.

JIMMY: No. It's due to overcrowding.

SHEILA: Oh!

JIMMY If Rhoda Gregson's friends were grouse, the death rate would be pretty high. I thought she looked a bit like Groucho Marx tonight, except that her moustache was darker. Which was the Gregson girl?

SHEILA: In green, fair-haired.

JIMMY: Not that pretty creature? Isn't nature wonderful? As far as I remember, she was totally clean shaven.

SHEILA: Well, she's only seventeen.

JIMMY: Well, let's hope that she takes after Harold.

SHEILA (*whose mind has not been on the conversation at all*): If Dickie and Louisa hadn't come and talked to me, I would have seen them go. They must have disappeared like that. Louisa said, 'Sheila, I'm simply dying to see Jane. I hear she's too divine for words, and Dickie's mad to dance with her'. And I said, 'That's her with the dark young man' – and pointed at her and she wasn't there. She must have gone while I was talking to Louisa.

JIMMY: Yes, most careless of you, darling.

SHEILA: Me. What about you!

JIMMY: What about me? I watched that girl from half-past ten to half-past one, when you took over.

SHEILA: That's not very long.

JIMMY: Not very long! I'll have you know that sentries only do two hours. Like a cigarette?

SHEILA: Yes, please. (*Jimmy hands her a cigarette from box, also lighter.*) I'm sorry, Jimmy. What's the time?

JIMMY: Three.

SHEILA: Jimmy, how long does it take a native dancer to get hotted up?

JIMMY: I wouldn't know. Depends what time of day it is, I shouldn't wonder.

SHEILA: I don't mean that kind of hotting up.

JIMMY: No. I don't either. And on who he's dancing with. Why? Was it in a crossword?

SHEILA: No. I only wondered. Jimmy, do you think he's taken her back to his tent?

JIMMY: His what?

SHEILA: I mean his flat.

JIMMY: Quite possibly.

SHEILA: You don't!

JIMMY: It has been done.

SHEILA: Oh, Jimmy, we'll have to ring him up.

JIMMY: Why not?

SHEILA: What can we say?

JIMMY: Well, ask to speak to Jane.

SHEILA: Oh, what a good idea! (*Goes to telephone.*) What's the number?

JIMMY: I don't know.

SHEILA: I don't know either, Jimmy.

JIMMY: Who does know?

SHEILA: Jane wrote it on the table-cloth this morning.

JIMMY: Well, then – where's the table-cloth?

SHEILA: It all depends what day it is.

JIMMY: It's Thursday now.

SHEILA: That means that it was Wednesday this morning.

JIMMY: It's this morning now.

SHEILA: Oh, don't be so confusing, Jimmy. All I want to know is, was it Wednesday when we had breakfast yesterday?

JIMMY: Yes, very probably.

SHEILA: Then it's gone.

JIMMY: What has?

SHEILA: The table-cloth! The laundry goes on Wednesday.

JIMMY: Bad luck.

SHEILA: It must be fate. Oh, poor poor Jane!

JIMMY: Where did Jane get the number in the first place?

SHEILA: I got it.

JIMMY: Where from?

SHEILA: From Mabel.

JIMMY: Mabel!

SHEILA: Yes, she gave it to me by mistake for David Bulloch's.

JIMMY: Did she now?

SHEILA: I've got to have that number, Jimmy! Every minute counts!

JIMMY: Ring Mabel, then.

SHEILA: She won't be back.

JIMMY: She will. She never went.

SHEILA: Well, she'll be asleep.

JIMMY: The telephone'll wake her.

SHEILA: Poor, poor Mabel!

JIMMY: Which do you prefer, poor, poor Mabel or poor, poor Jane?

SHEILA: I daren't, Jimmy.

JIMMY: Why not?

SHEILA: She's the biggest gossip ever born.

JIMMY: We've got to risk it.

SHEILA: Risk it – it's a certainty.

JIMMY: Well, gossip's better than the other thing – –

SHEILA: Jimmy! You can't think that of your own daughter.

JIMMY: Yours as well!

SHEILA: What do you mean by that?

JIMMY: Nothing. Have some more champagne. (*He refills her glass.*)

SHEILA: How selfish we are, Jimmy, drinking when Jane's – –

JIMMY: Nonsense, it'll do you good!

SHEILA (*drinks. In doorway*): He is good-looking, isn't he?

JIMMY: Who?

SHEILA: David Hoylake-Johnston.

JIMMY: I suppose so, if you like that type of man.

SHEILA: Well, naturally I do. He's every woman's type. (*Coming back into the room.*) Tall, lean and handsome. Dark, broad-shouldered – what more could one want?

JIMMY: Nothing, I hope.

SHEILA: Don't, Jimmy!

JIMMY: Ring up Mabel. Go on! If you don't, I will!

SHEILA: Oh, no Jimmy, you mustn't. It'd sound much too important, if you did. I know – I'll ask her round for drinks tomorrow. (*Starts dialling.*)

JIMMY: What, at three a.m.?

SHEILA: No, seven.

JIMMY: Darling, it's three now. Hardly the moment to start sending invitations out.

SHEILA: Give me that glass . . . (*Jimmy gets Sheila's glass from sofa table and hands it to her. She dials. Nothing happens.*)

JIMMY: Give it a chance. I'll bet she snores like hell!

SHEILA (*at telephone*): Oh, hullo, Mabel darling! This is Sheila. Sheila! Sheila Broadbent. Did I wake you? I'm so sorry. Very early, yes. I'm sorry to be such a bore – but could you give me David Hoylake-Johnston's number? Yes, I know you did. But I've mislaid it – it's gone to the wash. It doesn't matter, darling. But I haven't got it. No, it's only Jane left her bag in his car – and Jimmy's so afraid it may be stolen in the night. Thanks so much, darling! (*To Jimmy.*) Looking in Clarissa's book. (*To telephone.*) Mayfair 6384. You are an angel, darling! Isn't she? Oh, Jane's been in for hours! We brought her back quite early. She was very tired, poor darling. Well, good night, Mabel darling – sorry to have woken you. (*She hangs up.*) I knew it – she's suspicious!

JIMMY: How do you know?

SHEILA: She wasn't angry, and that means she was interested. Now what's the number?

JIMMY (*writing it down on the back of a book of matches*): 6384 Mayfair.

SHEILA (*dialling*): And Clarissa's not in yet. She must be out with David Bulloch. They're probably engaged by now. No answer.

JIMMY: Let it ring a bit – he's probably asleep.

SHEILA: Jimmy! (*She sits and lets the phone ring.*) Oh, Jimmy, how are we to know if he's deliberately not answering?

JIMMY: We're not.

SHEILA (*holding it*): I can see him now, holding her away from the telephone – her strained, frightened little eyes, looking beseechingly up into his. His tense body waiting for the telephone to stop ringing.

JIMMY: Well – let it go on ringing.

SHEILA: Why – what difference will that make?

JIMMY: Well, anybody who's in the least bit sensitive – –

Sheila continues to hold it.

SHEILA: Oh, Jimmy, what are we to do?

JIMMY: I'm all for bed – –

SHEILA: How can you?

JIMMY: Well, what else do you suggest we do?

SHEILA: We've got to find them. If we find them – we might save the day.

JIMMY: Like Blücher.

SHEILA: Blücher?

JIMMY: Blücher saved the day at Waterloo.

SHEILA: Well, there you are – –

JIMMY: But I expect he had a map reference.

SHEILA (*replacing the receiver*): I'm going to put it back. She might be trying to ring us. Ought we to ring the police?

JIMMY: What for?

SHEILA: To tell them Jane's not in.

JIMMY: I doubt if they'd be interested.

SHEILA: How can you be so heartless. Don't you see, we'll have to pack her off abroad, like Brenda Barrington.

JIMMY: You don't mind jumping to conclusions, do you?

SHEILA: Well, with that young bounder. If only we knew where she was.

JIMMY: What does it matter where?

SHEILA: Who's jumping to conclusions now?

JIMMY: I'm damned if I'm not catching it from you.

SHEILA: Oh, Jimmy, I can't bear it!

JIMMY: What's the matter now?

SHEILA: Poor darling Jane! If only we were back to April – just before we came to London – when she had no thought of anything but playing croquet with her Daddy – and then now – –!

JIMMY: You know, you women beat me altogether. Just look at you! You think of nothing but this blasted London season all the winter. You rehearse it at Hunt Balls and so on and so forth. Then, when you get to the opening night, so to speak, you can't take it.

SHEILA: I don't know what you're talking about!

JIMMY: Of course you do. It's all your own fault – you and all the other mothers like you, behaving like a lot of refined White Slave traffickers. You bring a perfectly sweet and charming girl up from the country – a girl that even the Vicar's daughters have been proud to call their friend – –

W.D.H.–CC

SHEILA: Why bring them up?

JIMMY: Because they typify the decent life that Jane's led up to now.

SHEILA: That's what you think. I'll have you know a lot of people say that Bella isn't all that she's cracked up to be since the Hunt Ball.

JIMMY: I daresay not. Her mother didn't plan it, though, like you did. It was just an accident. I mean to say – no one could possibly have known that that dreadful fellow in the hired red coat had got her in the potting shed. I mean to say her mother didn't put her there and then ring up the fellow – –

SHEILA: Jimmy, don't!

JIMMY: I'm sorry, but we may as well face facts. In Bella's case it was an accident. And like all accidents, exciting and deplorable. But in our case it's different. Far less exciting and far more deplorable, because it's planned. We bring Jane up to London, throw her on the town with fifteen hundred pounds' worth of advertisement, dress her up in silks and satins, have her hair washed at five pounds a time, and then sit back and wait. And all for what? You don't have to tell me. I know well enough. To catch the eye of the young men. Can you deny that, Sheila? Can you possibly deny that that's the object of the exercise?

SHEILA: Well, naturally, we all want Jane to look her best.

JIMMY: With what object in view?

SHEILA: Well, don't you want your daughter looking nice?

JIMMY: Not if it leads to this.

SHEILA: This was an accident.

JIMMY: An accident indeed! We sit all through the summer waiting for a victim, like a fellow waiting for a tiger with a goat tied to a stake. When the tiger doesn't come, what do we do? Only ring up the biggest man-eater in London and invite him round to have a meal. Then, when he carries the goat off somewhere in the bush, you say it was an accident. The whole thing's fundamentally immoral!

SHEILA: Have you finished?

JIMMY: No. You just can't take it, that's what's wrong with you. You're like a woman on a race-course. You put everything you've got on some damned horse, and if it wins the sun comes out. But if it loses, you're in the car park long before the jockeys have weighed in. If you can't take it, then you shouldn't bet. In other words, you shouldn't put your daughter in the Marriage Stakes, however big the prizes are, in case she falls.

The telephone rings.

SHEILA (*at telephone*): Hullo, Jane darling. (*She checks suddenly.*) Oh, Mabel. Yes, so silly of me. I forgot she was in for a moment. Oh, how sweet of you to worry, darling. Yes. I did. And he promised to look in his car although he was in bed. Too sweet of him. What, darling? Oh, have they? Did they have a good time? Zizzi's. Oh, how lovely. Good night, darling. I must stop or Jimmy'll wake up. (*She hangs up.*) David Bulloch brought Clarissa back and they told Mabel Jane and David Hoylake-Johnston were at Zizzi's.

JIMMY: What on earth is Zizzi's?

SHEILA: Don't be silly, you remember, darling. We took Jane there on her birthday.

JIMMY: Not that damned cellar – with those fellows blowing trumpets down one's ear at point-blank range. Too primitive for words.

SHEILA (*gives phone book to Jimmy*): Don't, Jimmy, don't. Here. Look the number up.

JIMMY: Well, anyway, a night-club's better than a flat.

SHEILA: Oh, how I hope so.

JIMMY: Well, of course it is. I mean to say, two sardines can't get up to much inside their tin.

SHEILA: I lied to Mabel and she knew that I was lying. She'll have it all round London in the morning. It'll ruin Jane.

JIMMY: She can't talk.

SHEILA: Can't she?

JIMMY: She let David Bulloch take Clarissa.

SHEILA: That's quite different. He's a gentleman.

JIMMY: Oh, is he? Yes, I see. Here we are, Zizzi's. Gerrard 2446.

Sheila goes over to dial.

It beats me how that place keeps open. I thought dancing to a tom-tom and a penny-whistle was confined to cannibals. Come to think of it, perhaps it still is.

SHEILA (*at telephone*): Hullo. Oh, is that Zizzi's? Oh, it is. And is that Mr Zizzi speaking? You're Bert? I see, and who is Bert? Bert Brown? I see. Good evening, Mr Brown. I was just wondering if I

W.D.H.–CC*

could speak to my daughter. How do you know she ain't? Oh, I see. I'm so sorry to have troubled you. Good night – er – good morning. (*She hangs up.*)

JIMMY: Had Bert passed out?

SHEILA: No. He was the night watchman. They're closed. Oh, Jimmy, what'll happen if she brings him back here for a drink?

JIMMY: I'm not a prophet, darling.

SHEILA: She'll see that we've been waiting up for her.

JIMMY: Well, so we have.

SHEILA: She mustn't, Jimmy. Psychologically it's wrong to let her see that we are worried. Even if she isn't interested in David Hoylake-Johnston, if we look as if we'd be against it if she was, she will be.

JIMMY (*repeating – bewildered*): If she was, she will be – –

SHEILA: What I mean is that we've got to wait up – but she mustn't know we are – –

JIMMY: What – up the chimney?

SHEILA: Don't be silly, Jimmy – in the kitchen. Then we'll hear if we're wanted.

JIMMY: But we won't be wanted. If it's all above board, then we won't be wanted. If it isn't, we won't be wanted either.

SHEILA: Yes, we will – if he assaults her. (*Runs to the door.*)

JIMMY: Where are you going now?

SHEILA: I was seeing if our door's shut. Now, you go into the kitchen.

JIMMY: Into the kitchen? (*Rising.*)

SHEILA: Darling – and see if you can hear me!

JIMMY: I can hear you from here.

SHEILA: Darling, do try and understand. We're hiding in the kitchen, and we've got to hear what's going on – so run along.

JIMMY: Yes, rather!

Jimmy goes into the kitchen, leaving Sheila in the room.

SHEILA: Jimmy!

JIMMY (*coming back*): What's the matter?

SHEILA: Shut the door.

JIMMY: I thought that we'd hear better with it open.

SHEILA: Jimmy, shut that door!

JIMMY: Yes, right, my dear!

He again goes into the kitchen and shuts the door, leaving Sheila alone once more. She takes off evening wrap and puts it on chair.

SHEILA (*turning away from kitchen door*): Don't! Don't! How dare you! Take your hands off me, you beast . . .

JIMMY (*rushing in*): What's the matter? What's the matter, darling?

SHEILA (*to Jimmy*): Did you hear me?

JIMMY: Yes, of course I did!

SHEILA: Well, that's all right – the moment that we hear her key, we'll turn the lights out here and nip in there – you understand?

JIMMY: Yes, darling – but what happens if she doesn't kick up a shindy?

SHEILA (*crossing towards him*): Don't be silly, but of course she would.

JIMMY: He might have gagged her with a handkerchief.

SHEILA: What, in the street?

JIMMY: No, here.

SHEILA: Well – we'd hear that all right.

JIMMY: I doubt it. Handkerchiefs don't make much noise.

SHEILA: Oh, Jimmy, he'd say things as he tied it on.

JIMMY: Perhaps, but only in an undertone.

SHEILA: How do you know?

JIMMY: Well, naturally his passions are aroused – –

SHEILA: Then he'd make a noise.

JIMMY: No – not that kind of passion.

SHEILA: Well, you make some passion noises, and I'll see if I can hear you. (*She goes towards the kitchen and turns at the door.*) Isn't this tremendous fun! (*She nips happily into the kitchen and shuts the door.*)

JIMMY (*alone, shouting*): You ready, darling?

SHEILA (*coming back*): But I thought you said he wouldn't make a noise.

JIMMY: Go back. I haven't started yet.

> *Sheila goes back.*

(*Alone again.*) Ha, ha! My pretty dove! I've got you now. Ha, ha!

SHEILA (*coming back*): What are you laughing at?

JIMMY (*furiously*): Go back! That's just the way they do it.

SHEILA: Sorry! (*She goes back again, shutting door.*)

JIMMY (*alone, playing his part with relish*): Ha! I love you! Don't you understand? You devil – you divinity . . . you *woman!* Can't you see I love your innocent and frightened eyes! I love – –

> *Enter Jane.*

JANE: Daddy, I think it's high time you were in bed. Where's Mummy?

JIMMY: In the kitchen.

> *Jane goes to the kitchen door, opens it, and Sheila falls into the room.*

SHEILA: Jane! Hullo, darling! We were just going to bed.

JANE: Oh, good.

SHEILA: Darling, where have you been?

JIMMY: To Rhoda Gregson's dance.

SHEILA: Be quiet, Jimmy. I'm asking Jane. Jane, darling? Where have you been?

JANE (*removes gloves and stole, puts them on a chair*): Out with David, Mummy.

SHEILA: David Hoylake-Johnston?

JANE: Yes.

SHEILA: Where to?

JANE: Oh, almost everywhere.

JIMMY: Hang on to 'almost', Sheila.

SHEILA: Jimmy, please be quiet. (*To Jane.*) What do you mean by 'almost everywhere'?

JANE: Oh, I don't know, Mummy. You ask him, Mummy. He'll know.

SHEILA: How can I ask him if he isn't here?

JANE: He is. He's coming up. He's gone back for my bag – I left it in the car.

JIMMY: That's one in the eye for Mabel.

SHEILA: He'll wake up Mrs Edgar.

JANE: No, he won't. He's got my key.

SHEILA: Why is he coming up?

JANE: Because I asked him to.

SHEILA: What for?

JANE: To have a drink.

SHEILA: A drink! Darling! At four o'clock?

JANE: Well, what else could I offer him?

JIMMY: Yes – what indeed?

SHEILA: Jimmy, why don't you go to bed?

JIMMY: Why don't we all? I mean, you and I.

Enter David Hoylake-Johnston.

DAVID: May I come in?

SHEILA (*all sweetness and light*): Good evening, Mr Hoylake-Johnston. How sweet of you to bring Jane home!

DAVID: That was the least that I could do. (*To Jimmy.*) Hello!

JIMMY: Hullo! Have you had fun?

DAVID: Yes, rather! I've been showing Jane the hot-spots.

SHEILA: Oh, how kind of you.

JANE: We danced and danced and danced.

SHEILA: Oh, really, darling. How exciting!

JANE: Yes, it was.

DAVID: I'm sorry that I didn't ask you if you minded Jane and me departing, but we couldn't see you anywhere.

SHEILA: Oh, that's all right! We quite forgot about you – didn't we, Jimmy?

JIMMY: Yes, we forgot all about you! I'm off to bed. Jane, you know where the drinks are.

JANE: Thank you, Daddy.

JIMMY: David'll know which is which. Come along, darling. I'd like a nap before the office, if you wouldn't mind. (*Exit Jimmy.*)

SHEILA: All right. Good night, then, Mr Hoylake-Johnston.

DAVID: Good night – and thank you for a most delightful evening!

SHEILA: Not at all! (*Kissing Jane.*) Now darling, don't stay up too late. (*Exit.*)

Jane goes and shuts the door, which Sheila has left hopefully open.

DAVID: I hope your mother's not too angry with me – –

JANE: Don't mind Mummy – have a drink?

DAVID: Yes, please.

JANE: What can I offer? Knowing Daddy, I should say there's everything but water!

DAVID: I'd love some water.

JANE: Would you really?

David nods.

I'll have to get it from the kitchen. (*She goes halfway to the door and turns.*) Would you like a rich tea biscuit?

DAVID: Yes, I'd love one.

JANE: Oh, good. So would I!

> *Jane turns and opens the door into the kitchen and Sheila comes through it again.*

Mummy, what are you doing?

SHEILA: I was looking for my ear-rings, darling.

JANE: Which ones?

SHEILA: The diamonds.

JANE: But you weren't wearing them.

SHEILA: Oh, wasn't I? Then it must be the gold ones . . .

DAVID: Can I help you, Mrs Broadbent?

SHEILA: No, no – please don't bother! I'm quite happy looking for them!

> *Jane has gone into the kitchen. Sheila and David look about the room.*

DAVID (*finding the ear-rings behind ashtray, under drinks cupboard*): Gold, you said?

SHEILA: I think so.

DAVID: Would these be them?

SHEILA: No, I don't think so. But – yes! How too extraordinary! I must have left them there this . . . How too kind of you. I couldn't be more grateful.

JANE (*coming out of the kitchen*): David, here's your water.

SHEILA: Oh, Jane darling, Mr Hoylake-Johnston won't want water.

DAVID: Oh, but I do.

SHEILA: Don't you drink, then?

DAVID: Very seldom.

SHEILA: Won't you have a cigarette?

DAVID: No, thank you – I don't smoke.

SHEILA: Indeed?

JANE: Oh, David, did I leave the tap on? Would you be an angel?

> *David goes into the kitchen.*

Mummy, go to bed. You're vulgar – you're so obvious.

SHEILA: But darling, he's – –
JANE: He's not. He's sweet.
SHEILA: You don't know him.
JANE: I do.
DAVID (*coming back*): It wasn't on.
JANE: Oh, good! I'll get the biscuits. (*She goes out.*)

> *Jimmy comes in.*

JIMMY: Sheila, come along, for heaven's sake!
SHEILA: I'm coming, darling. I've been seeing Mr Hoylake-
Johnston has got everything he wants.

> *Jimmy takes Sheila by the arm.*

Good night!

> *They go out. Jane comes back with a plate of biscuits and a glass of milk.*

JANE: Has Mummy gone?
DAVID: Yes. I hope she doesn't mind me doing this?
JANE: Oh, no! – we've lots of biscuits. (*Puts biscuits down on coffee table. Drinks.*)

> *David laughs.*

Weren't you surprised when Mummy rang you up this morning?
DAVID: Yes – I was a bit.
JANE: I can't think why you came.
DAVID: Oh, just for fun.
JANE: And have you had it?
DAVID: Well, I'm having it.
JANE: Oh, good! (*She drinks again.*)
DAVID: Are you?
JANE: Yes.
DAVID: Did you like the night-club?
JANE: Which one?
DAVID: All, or any of them?
JANE: Yes – I like this better, though.
DAVID: Yes, so do I.
JANE: Because we're alone – just you and I.
DAVID: And Mother, off and on!

JANE: Not now. She's gone to bed. (*Drinks again.*) I've only been to one once before, on my birthday.

DAVID: A night-club?

JANE: No – but you have, often, haven't you?

DAVID: Yes.

JANE: Thousands?

DAVID: Oh no – I hope not!

JANE: Hundreds, then?

DAVID: Perhaps.

JANE: With lots of girls?

DAVID: Oh, no – just one.

JANE: With one girl lots of times – or lots of girls just once?

DAVID: Well, anyway – not one girl lots of times.

JANE: Did you take Brenda Barrington out to a night-club ever?

DAVID: Yes.

JANE: How many times?

DAVID: I really can't remember – once or twice.

JANE: Another water? I'd like another milk.

DAVID: All right.

> *Jane gets up, taking both glasses, and goes to the kitchen. She opens the door, and there is Jimmy.*

JANE: Daddy! What are you doing?

JIMMY: Hullo, Jane! I'm filling up your mother's bottle.

JANE: I'll do it. Go and talk to David. (*Exit.*)

> *Jimmy comes in.*

JIMMY: Hullo, David!

DAVID: Hullo.

JIMMY: Don't get up. You getting all you want to drink?

DAVID: Yes – Jane's just getting me another glass.

JIMMY: What of?

DAVID: Of water.

JIMMY: Water! Do you really drink the stuff?

DAVID: Yes, frequently.

JIMMY: Have you got something wrong with you?

DAVID: No – not that I'm aware of.

JIMMY: Good. How's Jane for a dancing partner?

DAVID: Very good.

JIMMY: And her conversation?

DAVID: Sweet.

JIMMY: Oh, good! Has she been sweet to you?

DAVID: Yes, rather.

JIMMY: Good. I hope that you've been sweet to her – –

DAVID: I hope so, too.

JIMMY: You shouldn't have gone off like that, alone. Her mother nearly had a fit. She thought – well, you know what she thought.

DAVID: I can imagine it.

JIMMY: I bet you can't imagine it as vividly as she can!

Jane comes in.

JANE: It's boiling, Daddy. Here you are. (*Gives him the bottle.*)

JIMMY: Thanks.

JANE: Run along – or Mummy'll be screaming for you!

JIMMY: Yes, that's right. Well, good night – don't get up! (*He goes.*)

Jane gives David his water, then sits on sofa. There is a long pause while they drink.

DAVID: Well, I suppose I ought to go.

JANE: There's no need to. I'm not the least bit sleepy yet. Are you?

DAVID: No – not a bit.

JANE: That can't be very comfortable. Why don't you sit on this? It's lovely!

David sits on the sofa.

DAVID: All right.

JANE: I sleep here all day long.

DAVID: Oh, do you?

JANE: Yes – except when Mummy's dragging me round exhibitions, and dress shows and things.

DAVID: Does she do that?

JANE: Yes – nearly every day. She's educating me.

DAVID: Oh yes – I see.

JANE (*pause*): What would you like to do now?

DAVID: What would you?

JANE: I don't know. Yes, I do. I'd like to kiss you.

DAVID: Why?

JANE: Because I like you.

DAVID: Oh, do you kiss everybody that you like?

JANE: I don't like anybody, except you. There couldn't be a better reason, could there?

DAVID: No, I suppose not.

JANE: Well, can I?

DAVID: Well, yes, if you want to.

JANE: I do want to. Turn your face round. (*She kisses David.*) Did I do it right?

DAVID: Very nicely.

JANE: Not so bad, considering it was the first time?

DAVID: Not so bad at all.

JANE: You weren't very good, though, were you?

DAVID: Wasn't I? I'm sorry.

JANE: No – you didn't seem to have your heart in it. Perhaps you didn't – when we started, anyhow.

DAVID: Not when we started – no.

JANE: But you were getting better when we finished. Would you like to try again?

DAVID: Yes, please. (*He does.*)

JANE: Oh, David – is that how you kissed – –

> *Jimmy comes in.*

JIMMY: Jane, darling, your mother thinks . . . Oh, don't get up. (*To Jane.*) Your mother thinks you ought to go to bed.

JANE: Oh, she's a nuisance!

JIMMY: Yes, I know.

DAVID: I'd better go. Good night, Jane. Good night, Jimmy.

JIMMY: Good night, David.

> *David goes out and the flat door shuts.*

(*Pause.*) Well, I'll toddle back to bed. Night, Jane.

JANE: Night, Daddy.

> *Jimmy goes off down the passage. We hear his door shut.*
> *Jane goes and collects stole and gloves. Turns out lights by kitchen door. Crosses to window, turning out fire as she passes it. Opens curtains and looks out. Moves back as David enters.*

JANE (*whispering*) : David, darling!
DAVID (*whispering, too*) : Your key!
JANE : Oh!

> *David hands over the key.*

DAVID : Well, good night!
JANE : Good night, David – –

> *They are about to fall into each other's arms.*

JIMMY (*off in passage*) : Yes, it is on all right, darling, I'll turn it out.

> *David and Jane spring apart. Jimmy comes in, without seeing them, and absent-mindedly flicks off the light; then he goes back to his room. They smile and embrace again.*

CURTAIN

SCENE 2

Breakfast time, the same day. There is a bouquet of flowers lying on the back of the sofa.

David Bulloch is pacing up and down. He is in full Guards uniform with a bearskin in one hand and a sword in the other. He sits on sofa as the telephone rings. After looking at it for some time, he goes to telephone. Finding that he's unable to lift receiver because of sword, he puts sword down .

BULLOCH (*at telephone*) : Hullo ? I dunno. I'll have a look. (*He looks at the dial number.*) Yes, it is. No, I'm not. Well, David Bulloch. Who ? Oh, hullo, David. Well, I'm looking for my cigarette-case, actually. I left it here last night. So I came round to get it. No, I haven't actually. But I'm still hoping. No, she's not. I mean, she's still in bed. They all are, actually. At least, there's no one having breakfast yet. What ? I say, steady on, old chap. I can't do that. I can't just barge in in my uniform. Well, we're rehearsing trooping the colour. No, sorry, David, it's not done. I'll take a message, if you like. All right, then you'd better ring again. (*He puts down the telephone and resumes his seat on sofa.*)

Jimmy enters, partly dressed. David Bulloch stands up awkwardly.

Good morning, sir.

JIMMY (*looking round and shuddering*): Great Heavens, has war broken out?

BULLOCH: No, we're rehearsing for the trooping the colour.

JIMMY: Oh, good show.

BULLOCH: At ten.

JIMMY: Good. Have some breakfast?

BULLOCH: No, thanks. I've had mine.

JIMMY: Oh, good. Would you like to read the 'Express' while I have mine?

BULLOCH: No, thanks. Could I see Jane, sir?

JIMMY: I don't think that she's awake yet.

BULLOCH: Oh dear, and I'm on parade at ten.

JIMMY: Yes, so you said.

A pause.

BULLOCH: Sir, may I marry Jane, sir?

JIMMY: May you what?

BULLOCH: Sir, marry Jane, sir.

JIMMY: You'd better ask my wife. She deals with all that side. She'll be in in a minute.

BULLOCH: Oh, good. Thank you, sir.

Jimmy stands watching Bulloch as he walks away. Another pause.

JIMMY: Why don't you put that bird's nest down somewhere?

BULLOCH: Oh, right, sir. Thank you, sir. (*He puts down the bearskin.*)

JIMMY: Feel better?

BULLOCH: Yes, thank you, sir. (*Pause.*) I haven't asked Jane yet.

JIMMY: Oh, haven't you? Well, that's important.

BULLOCH: Yes, I know it is. I tried to last night, but she wouldn't listen. Then she disappeared.

JIMMY: Indeed?

BULLOCH: That's why I rushed round here this morning.

JIMMY: Quite.

BULLOCH: I only hope it's not too late.

JIMMY: Too late? She's only seventeen.

BULLOCH: No – I mean David Hoylake-Johnston. He's – –

Enter Sheila.

JIMMY: Ah, Sheila, here you are. Here's David.

BULLOCH: Oh, good morning, Mrs Broadbent.

SHEILA (*delighted*): David, what an early call! And what a pretty suit! I do hope Jimmy's given you some breakfast.

JIMMY: David hasn't come for breakfast. He wants to marry Jane.

SHEILA (*to Bulloch*): David, are you and Jane engaged?

BULLOCH: Well, no – I haven't asked her yet.

SHEILA: I'll go and get her.

JIMMY: Don't you ask her, Sheila. Leave all that to David.

SHEILA: Really, Jimmy, I'm not utterly half-witted! (*Going out shouting.*) Jane! It's David . . .

JIMMY: You were saying about David Hoylake-Johnston?

BULLOCH: Yes, sir. I was going to say that he's a cad.

JIMMY: Oh, were you?

BULLOCH: Yes, well you know about Brenda Barrington and him?

JIMMY: Not officially, no.

BULLOCH: Good Lord. I thought that everybody knew about the week-end when Colonel Barrington found Brenda in his room.

JIMMY: In whose room?

BULLOCH: David Hoylake-Johnston's. In the middle of the night.

JIMMY: Indeed. What were they doing there?

BULLOCH: Well, what do you expect? He gave her brandy.

JIMMY: Brandy – really?

BULLOCH: And nuts.

JIMMY: Nuts. Good Lord!

BULLOCH: Then, what with all the brandy and the nuts, it was a piece of cake.

JIMMY: What was?

BULLOCH: Well, surely you can guess.

JIMMY: You must forgive me if I got confused with all these different foodstuffs. Do you mean that when the nuts were finished, and the brandy, Brenda, so to speak, was finished, too?

BULLOCH: That's right.

JIMMY: How do you know all this?

BULLOCH: Well, I was staying there.

JIMMY: Oh, were you? Were you really?

Sheila comes in followed by a tidier Jane.

SHEILA: Here's Jane.

BULLOCH: Oh, hullo, Jane!

JANE: It's you! Oh, Lord!

SHEILA: Jane, don't be rude!

JANE: Why are you dressed like that?

BULLOCH: Because I'm on parade at ten.

JANE: Oh, good.

BULLOCH (*takes flowers from sofa*): I've brought you these.

JANE: What for?

BULLOCH: To give to you, of course.

JANE: Oh. Sugar please, Daddy.

SHEILA: Darling, David's come to see you and he's in a hurry and it's rather special really.

JANE: What is?

SHEILA: David's visit. David will enlighten you.

JANE: Oh, don't slop, Mummy.

SHEILA: Well, it's high time that I went and dressed. Jimmy, it's getting late – you ought to go and shave.

JIMMY: I have. Oh, right. Yes, rather. Anybody like 'The Times'? No?

SHEILA: No one wants it, Jimmy. Take it with you. Go on, dear. You always have for twenty years.

> *He goes and – after a smile, nauseating to Jane – Sheila goes too. Jane helps herself to egg from trolley, taking coffee pot and milk jug back with her.*

BULLOCH (*grabs Jane from behind*): Jane, darling – –

JANE: Go away. Your hands are cold. (*Bulloch steps back.*) What do you think you're doing here at this hour in the morning?

BULLOCH: I came specially to see you.

JANE: Why on earth?

BULLOCH: Because I want to marry you.

JANE: Oh, don't be goofy!

BULLOCH: But I do.

JANE: Whatever for?

BULLOCH: Because I love you.

JANE: Oh, since when?

BULLOCH: Two nights ago – –

JANE: You've got a funny way of showing it.

BULLOCH: What do you mean?

JANE: Attacking me last night, when I was telephoning.

BULLOCH: You aren't telephoning now.

JANE: I'm eating scrambled eggs. That's just as bad.

BULLOCH: Does that mean I can kiss you, when you've finished?

JANE: No, it doesn't.

BULLOCH: Please, Jane. I'm in love with you.

JANE: You've said that once.

BULLOCH: Well, then – –

JANE: Well, then – I'm not in love with you.

BULLOCH: Then who are you in love with?

JANE: Nobody.

BULLOCH: You're lying. You're in love with David Hoylake-Johnston.

JANE: Don't be silly.

BULLOCH: Well, who then?

JANE: With nobody, I said.

BULLOCH: I don't believe you. I'm in love with someone all the time.

JANE: Then you're over-sexed.

BULLOCH: Well, I can't help it if I am.

JANE: I'm sorry – I can't either.

BULLOCH: But you've got to – –

JANE: David, go away.

BULLOCH: I won't. I've got to kiss you. I'll go mad if I don't, Jane. I will. I've felt so awful ever since I've wanted to. I think I've got a temperature.

JANE: Well then, you shouldn't go on parade. Shall I ask Mummy for her clinical thermometer?

BULLOCH: No, please don't. Please, Jane, I do love you.

JANE: David! That's three times.

BULLOCH: I can't help that. Come here, Jane – Jane.

JANE: How can you in the morning, David? David – leave go –

David, I'll call Mummy if you don't. I'll scream if you don't let me go.

BULLOCH: Well, call her then. I just don't care.

JANE: Mummy – Mummy – Mummy!

Sheila rushes in.

SHEILA: Yes, darling? Here I am.

JANE (*running to her*): Oh, Mummy.

SHEILA (*misunderstanding the calling*): There, there, darling. David – (*To David.*) dearest boy.

JANE: Oh, Mummy, don't be silly. It's not on.

SHEILA: What isn't on? But, darling, I thought David asked you – –

JANE: So he did – –

SHEILA: And you said no?

JANE: That's right.

SHEILA: But, darling, why?

BULLOCH (*interrupting*): I say, I really ought to go.

SHEILA: Must you really? Oh, David, I'm so sorry.

BULLOCH: Good-bye, Mrs Broadbent. Good-bye, Jane.

JANE: Good-bye.

BULLOCH (*picking up bearskin*): I hope we'll meet again. (*He turns to go.*)

SHEILA: Of course you will. Tonight, at Susan Shelly's dance!

BULLOCH: Oh, good.

SHEILA: You wouldn't dine with us?

JANE: Oh, Mummy – honestly —

SHEILA: But we've got no one else.

JANE: If David comes then I won't go.

SHEILA: How can you be so petty, Jane?

JANE: I mean it.

SHEILA: I'm so sorry, David.

BULLOCH: That's all right. Good-bye, Mrs Broadbent.

Feeling something missing, he looks round and Sheila sees his sword and hands it to him. He goes.

SHEILA: Why must you be so utterly unreasonable? We've got nobody to dine tonight.

JANE: I'd rather that than Goofy.

SHEILA: You're selfish, that's what's wrong with you. You never seem to think of all the work I have to do to get a dinner-partner for you.

JANE: Please don't bother, Mummy, I can get my own.

SHEILA: Who? David Hoylake-Johnston, I suppose!

JANE: Why not?

SHEILA: Because he's undesirable.

JANE: He's not.

Enter Jimmy.

JIMMY: I heard a lot of shouting. Anybody hurt?

JANE: No, Goofy's gone, that's all.

JIMMY: Oh, good.

SHEILA: What do you mean, 'oh good'?

JIMMY: Well, good for us and good for Jane.

SHEILA: It isn't good for Jane.

JANE: Oh, Mummy, be your age. I couldn't love him less.

SHEILA: Love. You're talking like a school-girl. Love, indeed! What do you know of love?

JANE: A lot more than you think.

SHEILA: What do you mean?

JANE: Exactly what I say.

JIMMY (*reading 'The Times'*): Hullo, the Duke of Positano's dead.

SHEILA: Who cares?

JIMMY: The Duchess, probably. Oh no, she's dead as well.

SHEILA: Jimmy, please stop reading that newspaper.

JIMMY: I'm sorry, but it's very interesting. It says he's been succeeded, through the female line, by – –

SHEILA: Oh, for heaven's sake stop going on about the Duke of Positano.

JIMMY: Sorry, darling, but I thought you'd be interested.

SHEILA: I couldn't be less interested.

JIMMY: In that case I'll stop reading. What's the matter?

JANE: Nothing, Daddy. I'm in love, that's all.

JIMMY: Bad luck.

JANE: It's not bad luck. I love him terribly.

JIMMY: Who?

JANE: David.

JIMMY: David. But I thought you'd given him the push.

JANE: No. David Hoylake-Johnston.

JIMMY: Oh.

SHEILA: It's no use sitting there and saying 'oh'.

JIMMY: Oh, isn't it?

SHEILA: How can you be so babyish? To get infatuated with a man like that.

JANE: It's not infatuation, Mummy. That's what David Bulloch's got for me. But mine for David Hoylake-Johnston's love.

SHEILA: I never heard such nonsense. You'll be saying next that he's in love with you.

JANE: I think he is.

SHEILA: How can you be so silly? Give me just one reason why he should be.

JANE: I could give you many more than that but I'd rather keep them to myself. (*She has a beatific smile on her face.*)

SHEILA (*suspicious*): Were you at Zizzi's all the time last night – from when you left the dance until you came back here?

JANE: Yes, Mummy.

SHEILA: You went nowhere else at all?

JANE: No, Mummy, we were dancing almost non-stop. Why should we go somewhere else?

SHEILA: Your father thought he might have taken you back to his flat.

JIMMY: I – –

JANE: Daddy, but whatever for?

JIMMY: You'd better ask your mother, Jane.

JANE: Mummy, whatever for? I mean to say, what's his flat got that this one hasn't got?

SHEILA: I've never seen it, I'm happy to say, so I couldn't tell you.

JANE: Well, I'm sure it isn't half as comfortable.

SHEILA: Jimmy, can't you say something to her?

JIMMY: What? Yes, rather. Oh yes, by the way, you left the light on.

JANE: When?

JIMMY: Last night.

JANE: Where?

JIMMY: In here.

JANE: I'm sorry, Daddy.

JIMMY: That's all right. I came along and turned it out.

JANE: I know.

JIMMY: How do you know?

JANE: Well, it's not on now.

JIMMY: Now, say you're sorry to your mother.

JANE: But I'm not. I won't be blamed for something that I'm not to blame for. Mummy introduced me to him, after all.

JIMMY: That's fair enough.

SHEILA (*rounding on Jimmy*): So it's my fault?

JIMMY: I never said so, darling.

SHEILA: You implied it, though.

JIMMY: Well, if it isn't yours initially, whose is it?

SHEILA: Yours!

JIMMY: Mine? I like that. Now how on earth could it be mine?

SHEILA: It's in your family.

JIMMY: What is?

SHEILA: That sort of thing.

JIMMY: What sort of thing?

SHEILA: She's bred for it.

JIMMY: Don't talk about me as if I were a horse.

> *Jane, seeing that the storm is diverted from her own head for the moment, carries on unconcernedly with her breakfast.*

SHEILA: Of course, I never should have married you, with all that rotten Broadbent blood.

JIMMY: My blood's all right.

SHEILA: How can you say that, Jimmy? What about your sister Rose?

JIMMY: Be careful, Sheila. I'm extremely fond of Rose.

SHEILA: Of course, men always are.

JIMMY: Oh, Sheila, shut up, will you?

SHEILA: And then your Uncle Richard. Look at him!

JIMMY: How can I look at him, he's dead!

SHEILA: What about cousin Alec – living in Algiers, pretending that he paints.

JIMMY: Your family's above suspicion, I suppose?

SHEILA: It's not as bad as yours, I'm happy to say.

W.D.H.–DD

JIMMY: Oh, isn't it? You're not forgetting brother Harold, are you? Asked to leave his regiment.

SHEILA: That's not fair. You know quite well he asked to leave.

JIMMY: He didn't have to ask 'em twice, though, did he?

SHEILA: Now, Jimmy, how could Harold help it if the silly little woman fell in love with him?

JIMMY: Quite easily – according to Arbelle.

SHEILA: Arbelle – she doesn't understand him. How he ever married her's beyond me.

JIMMY: Yes, it was unlike him, wasn't it? Except that he was broke!

SHEILA: Are you implying Harold married Arbelle for her money, Jimmy?

JIMMY: Well, she couldn't very well have married him for his.

SHEILA: What do you mean by that?

JIMMY: Nothing, darling. Your father told me he'd paid up for Harold seven times.

SHEILA: Father exaggerates. You must know that by now.

JIMMY: Well, you've got that in common, anyway.

SHEILA: What do you mean by 'anyway'?

JIMMY: Oh, nothing.

SHEILA: Jimmy.

JIMMY: Darling, I just meant you weren't very like your father. I'm not sorry. I prefer you as you are.

Sheila kicks his ankle and runs out of the room.

She kicked me!

JANE: How simply fascinating knowing what I got born into after all these years.

The telephone rings. Jimmy goes to it.

JIMMY (*at telephone*): Hullo – yes. Yes, it is. Hold on. I'll get her. Jane, for you.

JANE: Who is it, Daddy?

JIMMY: David.

JANE: David which?

JIMMY: You'd better ask him: he should know.

JANE: Hullo? Who is it? David? Oh, David, it's you! Hullo! Yes. Very well. And how are you? Oh, good! But I'm not dressed yet. David, you are awful. All right. But you mustn't mind if I'm still having breakfast. What? Oh, David, don't be silly! (*She giggles and hangs up.*) That was David, Daddy.

JIMMY: Thanks for taking me into your confidence.

JANE: He's coming round.

JIMMY: Not David Bulloch, I presume?

JANE: No fear. Do you like David Hoylake-Johnston, Daddy?

JIMMY: Yes, your mother doesn't, though. I hope she won't be rude to him this morning. She's rather overwrought.

JANE: I expect it's just a hang-over.

JIMMY: It's more than that. It's David Hoylake-Johnston's reputation.

JANE: Daddy, honestly – to have this hate against poor David just because he slipped up once – –

JIMMY: Was it once?

JANE: Well, it was once, wasn't it?

JIMMY: Yes, so one hopes.

JANE: You'd think that Mummy didn't know a thing! You ought to educate her, Daddy.

JIMMY: In what way?

JANE: Well, every young man does that sort of thing provided that he gets the opportunity.

JIMMY: Indeed?

JANE: Or didn't they do things like that in your day?

JIMMY: Are you speaking generally, or are you asking me a question?

JANE: Daddy, who was the first woman you made love to?

JIMMY: Sylvia O'Brien.

JANE: Daddy, who was she?

JIMMY: The Vicar's daughter in our village.

JANE: Was she beautiful?

JIMMY: No – striking is the word.

JANE: And did you kiss her?

JIMMY: Certainly.

JANE: Where?

JIMMY: In the usual place – somewhere around the mouth.

JANE: No, Daddy – don't be silly! I mean whereabouts? The garden or – the river? You know what I mean?

JIMMY: I kissed her in the graveyard after evensong.

JANE: Oh, Daddy, what a rip you were! How old were you?

JIMMY: Thirteen – and she was nine.

JANE: What happened to her?

JIMMY: She went home to tea.

JANE: No, afterwards, I mean?

JIMMY: She joined the A.T.S. when she grew up. I met her in the war, in Worthing.

JANE: Did you kiss her then?

JIMMY: No! Just inspected her.

JANE: Daddy, what do you mean?

JIMMY: Exactly what I say. I met her on parade. She had a ladder in her stocking.

JANE: Did you tell her?

JIMMY: No. I think she knew.

JANE: But when did you make love to someone properly?

JIMMY: Oh, some years later.

JANE: What was her name?

JIMMY: Solange.

JANE: Solange!

JIMMY: She was French.

JANE: And where did you make love to Solange, Daddy?

JIMMY: At a house in Paris.

JANE: Her own home?

JIMMY: No – not exactly – she was working there.

JANE: You mean she was a maid?

JIMMY: No, not exactly.

JANE: Well, what was she doing there?

JIMMY: Oh, this and that.

JANE: Oh, Daddy, aren't you wicked? You're just as bad as David! And then you met Mummy?

JIMMY: Yes.

JANE: And did you kiss her?

JIMMY: Ultimately.

JANE: And that's why I'm here. Oh, isn't life extraordinary?

JIMMY: Yes, I suppose so when you look at it like that.

JANE: Oh, Daddy, I do love you. What I'd do without you, I don't know.

JIMMY: Me?

JANE: Yes. Because you are on my side, aren't you, Daddy?

JIMMY: I've not said so.

JANE: No, I know. But then you can't — because you can't go against Mummy and convention. I can understand all that.

JIMMY: That's most broadminded of you.

JANE: Not a bit. It's elementary. I know you've got to bluff it out with Mummy to the end. But, actually, let's face it, from the moment you met that French girl you'd had it as a moralist.

Mrs Edgar enters.

MRS EDGAR: Mr Hoylake-Johnston, sir.

Enter David. Jane rises to meet him.

JIMMY: Good morning, David.

DAVID: Hullo, Jimmy. Hullo, Jane. I've brought you these. (*He holds out a bouquet of flowers.*)

JANE: Oh, darling David, they're simply lovely. (*She falls into his arms.*)

JIMMY: Well, I suppose I'd better go and have another shave?

Jimmy goes out.

JANE: Oh, David darling, it seems ages since you went away.

DAVID: It's only three hours actually.

JANE: I know, but doesn't it seem years?

DAVID: Er yes . . . Jane, what was David Bulloch doing here?

JANE: Who told you he was here?

DAVID: I rang up earlier. He answered.

JANE: Oh.

DAVID: He said he came to get his cigarette case.

JANE: Oh.

DAVID: I don't believe it, though. What did he want?

JANE: Oh, nothing much. Just me.

DAVID: You. Do you mean that he proposed to you?

JANE: That's right.

DAVID: Good heavens! What infernal cheek. Jane . . . I've got something to tell you, darling.

JANE: That's all right, my darling. I already know, and I don't mind.

DAVID: Oh, so you've seen 'The Times'?

JANE: It isn't in the paper, is it?

DAVID: Yes, this morning.

JANE: Do you mean she's suing you?

DAVID: What are you talking about?

JANE: Brenda Barrington, of course.

DAVID: Oh, don't be silly.

JANE: Well, what is it?

DAVID: My great-uncle's died.

JANE: Oh, poor, poor you. I'm sure you loved him terribly.

DAVID: I never met him actually. He was Italian. My mother's uncle. He was very rich. And I'm his heir. It's through the female line. So I'm not David Hoylake-Johnston any more.

JANE: Who are you then?

DAVID: The Duke of Positano. Do you mind?

JANE: No. Ought I to?

DAVID: It means I'd have to live there half the time.

JANE: Oh, darling.

DAVID: Have you ever been to Italy?

JANE: Yes. Florence, once, with Daddy.

DAVID: Well, that's where I'll live. I've got a sort of palace there.

JANE: What do you mean, 'a sort of palace'?

DAVID: Well, it is a palace, actually. It's much too big to live in.

JANE: Oh.

DAVID: But there's a villa on Capri.

JANE: Oh, David darling, what a lot of housekeeping.

DAVID: Oh, darling, I can't tell you how relieved I am you've taken it so well.

They embrace.

Jane, darling – –

JANE: Yes?

DAVID: You wouldn't – –?

Sheila comes in and finds them in each other's arms. They break as David sees her.

Oh, good morning, Mrs Broadbent.

SHEILA: Jane.

JANE: Yes, Mummy.

SHEILA: What on earth is Mr Hoylake-Johnston doing?

JANE: Giving me some flowers.

SHEILA: Jane, leave the room. At once. At once, I said.

JANE: But, Mummy, David's come to see me.

DAVID: Go on, Jane. I'll wait.

Jane kisses David again and, picking up the flowers, she goes out.

SHEILA: Now, Mr Hoylake-Johnston, please explain yourself. What are you doing here?

DAVID: I came to give Jane some flowers. And I was hoping you'd let me take her out to Susan Shelley's dance tonight.

SHEILA: I'm sorry, Mr Hoylake-Johnston, Jane's already going out.

DAVID: Oh, but I thought she said last night – –

SHEILA: What Jane said last night is not important. What's important is what I am saying now. Will you be kind enough to leave this flat?

DAVID: But I told Jane I'd wait.

SHEILA: Please, Mr Hoylake-Johnston.

DAVID: I'm sorry, Mrs Broadbent, but I said I'd wait.

SHEILA: I see. In that case, I'm afraid I'll have to ask my husband to remove you. (*Opens door and calls off stage.*) Jimmy. Jimmy!

JIMMY (*off*): Hullo, darling.

SHEILA (*calling*): Would you come here a minute, please?

JIMMY (*off*): Right, darling.

SHEILA (*comes back into room*). He won't be a minute.

DAVID: Oh, thank you.

There is a long pause.

SHEILA (*goes back to doorway and calls*): Jimmy!

JIMMY (*off*): Coming, darling.

There is another pause, then the sound of water flushing. Sheila still stands waiting. Jimmy comes in.

Hullo, darling. What's the matter?

SHEILA: Everything. I came in here and found Jane in this young man's arms.

JIMMY: I say!

SHEILA: And now he has refused point-blank to leave the flat.

JIMMY: Oh.

SHEILA: Will you please remove him, Jimmy?

JIMMY (*looking nervously at David*): Better chuck him out, eh?

SHEILA: Well, then, come along.

JIMMY: You'd better go, my dear. It may not be too nice to watch.

SHEILA: Take care of yourself.

JIMMY: Yes, darling.

> *Sheila goes off, he looks after her bravely. Turning to Hoylake-Johnston and, by mistake, moving towards him.*

Well, I'm sorry.

DAVID (*aggressively*): You'll be sorrier if you start anything.

JIMMY (*deprecatingly*): No, no, I mean I'm sorry about your great-uncle. How old was he?

DAVID: Ninety-five.

JIMMY: Oh, asking for it, wasn't he?

SHEILA (*off, shouting*): Jimmy, are you all right?

JIMMY (*shouting*): Yes, darling. (*To David.*) We'd better make a show. (*Both at door, with door open slightly, speaking loudly.*) Now look here, young fellow— —

DAVID (*loudly*): Yes, I'm looking, Broadbent— —

JIMMY (*loudly*): If you aren't out of here in two minutes, I'll chuck you out.

DAVID (*loudly*): Right, have a try.

JIMMY: That gives us two minutes. (*David sits on sofa.*) Now then, are you in love with Jane?

DAVID: Yes?

JIMMY: Want to marry her?

DAVID: Of course.

JIMMY: So much for the future, pretty rosy-looking, if it wasn't for the past. But what about that lost week-end when brandy flowed like water and poor Brenda Barrington's morale was cracking with the nuts?

DAVID: Who on earth told you that?

JIMMY: Never mind who told me. Not a very pretty story, is it?

DAVID: Not a very true one either.

JIMMY: Isn't it? I'm not surprised. Now if it'd been champagne and caviare.

DAVID: Oh, it was brandy, actually. I had some in my suitcase.

JIMMY: Was your suitcase full of nuts as well?

DAVID: No. They were Colonel Barrington's.

JIMMY: What?

Pause.

DAVID: I can see I'll have to tell you.

JIMMY: Yes, I think you'd better.

DAVID: Well then, David Bulloch and I stayed a week-end with the Barringtons in May. Well, after we'd gone to bed on Sunday night, I had a damn good book.

JIMMY: What was it? I've not read a damn good book for years.

DAVID: 'The Wilder Shores of Love'.

JIMMY: I must remember that.

DAVID: Well, I was reading happily just after one, when Brenda Barrington came rushing in and said that David Bulloch had attacked her in her room.

JIMMY: Why did she come to you?

DAVID: Because I was next door, and she was frightened. Well, she started crying, so I got the brandy out. Well, it worked wonders. She stopped crying. And then suddenly she said that she was hungry and would I go down and get her something from the kitchen. Well, I couldn't find the lights, and so I groped around for a bit, then I suddenly hit my knuckles on a plate of nuts that we'd had at dinner, and I took them up. Well, when I got back to my room the flask was lying empty on the floor, and Brenda Barrington was lying on the bed.

JIMMY: Not empty!

DAVID: No. Well, I suppose I must have made a noise . . .

JIMMY: Lie down.

DAVID: I beg your pardon?

JIMMY: Lie down. I think I hear Sheila. (*David lies behind the coffee table with his head on it. Jimmy crosses to door.*) Not yet, darling. You wouldn't like it. (*Shuts door and returns to sofa.*) Carry on.

DAVID: Well, as I was saying, I must have made a noise downstairs, because the next thing that I knew was Colonel Barrington was standing in the doorway in a dreadful yellow dressing-gown accusing me of playing fast and loose with Brenda.

JIMMY: I say. Then what happened?

DAVID: Nothing. He just pointed at my suitcase and said 'pack'.

JIMMY: What did you do?

DAVID: I packed and drove straight back to London. Then next morning Brenda rang me up and said that she was being taken off to Switzerland by her mother in the afternoon. And that she hadn't told her father about David Bulloch because that'd make it look as if she made a habit of it and anyway he might have made her marry him, whereas she knew he wouldn't make her marry me.

JIMMY: So you accepted being thought a cad?

DAVID: Well, what else could I do? The evidence was circumstantial.

JIMMY: I should say it was.

DAVID: That's all, except that David Bulloch naturally seized his chance and spread the story round to Mabel Crosswaite and of course I'd had it then.

JIMMY: Of course. And do you realize that Mabel knows about your escapade last night, which means that Jane'll get a reputation just like Brenda Barrington?

DAVID: We're getting married, so it doesn't matter.

JIMMY: Are you?

DAVID: Yes, with your permission.

JIMMY: My permission. You can have that any time you like. Then I can cancel that damn dance, and save myself a thousand quid.

DAVID: Well then?

JIMMY: But I don't sign the permits round here. My wife does that. And as things stand at present you two haven't got a hope of getting married, unless you are prepared to tell her what you've just told me.

DAVID: Would she believe it?

JIMMY: Of course not. In her eyes, the Bulloch boy can do no wrong.

DAVID: Then what am I to do?

JIMMY: There's only one thing for it. You'll have to give up seeing Jane.

DAVID: I can't.

JIMMY: Then what do you suggest?

DAVID: I wish I knew.

JIMMY: Of course, she doesn't know that you're the Duke of Positano.

DAVID: Would that bring her round?

JIMMY: It might.

DAVID: You mean that she's a – –

JIMMY: Aren't we all?

DAVID: Let's tell her then.

JIMMY: No. We can't face her with it, just like that. Her prestige is at stake. We've got to let her do it on her own, somehow. Leave it all to me. Where are you going now?

DAVID: I wouldn't know.

JIMMY: Well, go to Black's. And get there at the double and keep near the telephone.

SHEILA: Jimmy, are you all right?

JIMMY: Yes, darling.

> *After a mock struggle, during which Jimmy drops an ashtray on the floor, they shake hands and David goes out. Jimmy throws the sofa cushions on the floor. Sheila comes in.*

SHEILA: Jimmy, are you all right?

JIMMY: Yes, darling.

SHEILA: Jimmy, I admire you so.

JIMMY: Oh, it was nothing.

> *The telephone rings and Sheila goes to it.*

SHEILA: Hullo. Yes? Oh, hullo, Mabel. What's that? Did he really? Red carnations. How too lovely. And he's taking her to Susan Shelley's dance. How lovely for her. Who's Jane going with? (*Lying.*) Oh, a great friend. You'll see tonight. Well, good-bye, Mabel – I must rush. (*She hangs up.*) Oh, Jimmy, David Bulloch's taking out Clarissa.

JIMMY: Two nights running – well, I never! Mabel'll soon be getting his telephone number by heart.

SHEILA: Oh, Jimmy, it's been all my fault. If I'd let things be, Jane might have married him.

JIMMY: She's well out of that, if you ask me.

SHEILA: But that lovely place in Warwickshire.

JIMMY: It isn't lovely. It's riddled with dry rot.

SHEILA: You mean it's crumbling?

JIMMY: Yes, nearly derelict.

SHEILA: Oh, Jimmy, you're so sweet to me. You mean I haven't spoilt her life?

JIMMY: Not yet.

SHEILA: But don't you see, when Mabel spreads the story round about last night, she'll lose her reputation.

JIMMY: Very probably.

SHEILA: And that means no more invitations.

JIMMY: Nonsense, she'll get plenty when the word gets round.

SHEILA: What word?

JIMMY: That she's worth taking out.

SHEILA: Jimmy!

JIMMY: Darling, you asked me yesterday what the young men wanted. Now you know. Well, what's the orders for tonight?

SHEILA (*profoundly depressed*): Oh, drinks at seven. Then dinner for Susan Shelley's dance. I've no one to dine – I must have someone tonight.

JIMMY: What, after all that we've been through?

SHEILA: Yes, even after that.

JIMMY: You're game, I'll give you that.

SHEILA: Well, who am I to get?

Jane rushes in.

JANE: Where's David?

SHEILA: Mr Hoylake-Johnston's gone.

JANE: Gone! But he said he'd wait.

SHEILA: We didn't let him wait. Your father put him out. We both decided that he's undesirable and that you mustn't see him any more.

JANE: You haven't, have you, Daddy? It's all Mummy, isn't it?

SHEILA: Now, listen to me, Jane. Consider yourself lucky that I'm not like Mrs Barrington. Consider yourself lucky that your father and I haven't packed you off home by the ten-fifteen. We haven't though. We've both decided that you've been a victim of infatuation, and of inexperience, and that therefore it's our duty to stand by you. In fact, when you rushed in here just now and rudely interrupted us, we happened to be on the point of fixing up a dinner-party for you tonight.

Jane bursts into tears. Jimmy goes out to get his hat and umbrella.

I'm sorry, darling, but I am your mother and I do know what's best for you, honestly I do. I know I asked him in the first place, but that wasn't my fault – it was Mabel's. She deliberately gave me the wrong number as she wanted David Bulloch for Clarissa. Do stop crying, darling. Where's your handkerchief?

JANE: Haven't got one.

SHEILA: Well, have mine, darling. (*She wipes Jane's eyes.*) There, dry your eyes. Darling, please believe me. He's really not a very nice young man. Good-looking and attractive, yes – but he's not very nice. And you'll forget him in a day or two. I know you will. Now, dry your eyes again and help me think of someone for tonight. We'll put our heads together and get someone really nice.

> *Jimmy comes in again.*

Now, Jimmy, have you thought of anybody?

JIMMY: Why not try the Duke of Positano?

SHEILA: Who on earth's the Duke of Positano?

JIMMY: His great-uncle's died, according to my paper, and they've given his address as Black's. He's twenty-six, they say.

SHEILA: Oh, Jimmy, do you know him?

JIMMY: Might have played bridge with him, I shouldn't wonder, but apart from that – –

SHEILA (*excitedly*): Jimmy, will he be at Black's now?

JIMMY (*surreptitiously looking at his watch.*): With a bit of luck.

SHEILA: Please ring him for me, Jimmy.

JIMMY: No, no. I'm in a hurry. It'd come much better from you.

SHEILA: Well, what's the number?

JIMMY: Whitehall 8688.

SHEILA (*while dialling*): That's right, darling. You're being very brave. We only want you to be happy, darling. Don't we, Jimmy?

JIMMY: Yes.

SHEILA (*at telephone*): Hullo, is that Black's? Oh, is the Duke of Positano in, by any chance? It's Mrs Broadbent speaking. Please. (*To the others.*) He's just come in.

> *Jimmy winks at Jane, and goes out.*

(*At telephone.*) Hullo, is that the Duke of Positano? Oh, good morning. Isn't it a lovely day? My name is Sheila Broadbent. I don't think you know me, but my husband's Jimmy Broadbent, who's a member of your Club. I'm quite sure that you've met him playing bridge or something. Well, it's the most awful cheek of me to ask you, but I wondered if you'd come and dine tonight for Susan Shelley's dance. Oh, just my husband and myself and Jane – our daughter – she's come out this year. You will come? (*To Jane.*) My dear, he sounds heavenly. (*At telephone.*) Oh, how charming. Well, then, sevenish for seven-thirty, fourteen Victor Court, the Sloane Square end of Eaton Square. At seven-thirty. Well, till then.

> *During the last few lines of the conversation the Curtain slowly falls.*